An Equal Share of Freedom

Jacob Rader Marcus Series on the American Jewish Experience

The Jacob Rader Marcus Series on the American Jewish Experience is a joint project of the University of Cincinnati and the Jacob Rader Marcus Center of the American Jewish Archives (AJA). Adding to the over 10 million objects in the AJA collection, this new series examines the impact religious and secular American Jews have made in history, politics, and culture from the colonial era to the present. Together with the AJA's vast collection of primary source materials and the open-access *American Jewish Archives Journal*, this new series seeks to enhance the field of history through the inclusion of diverse voices and the publication of original monographs, edited collections, and new anthologies. With a focus on the impact of Jews in the American setting from the colonial era to the present, the series seeks to showcase new work on the history, politics, and culture of American Jewry, including Jewish life in America's heartland, namely the Mississippi River basin, which aligns with the regional studies list of the University of Cincinnati Press. Coedited by Dr. Mark A. Raider (University of Cincinnati) and Dr. Gary Phillip Zola (Hebrew Union College-Jewish Institute of Religion), the series is guided by an international series advisory board.

AN EQUAL SHARE OF FREEDOM

AMERICAN JEWS, ZIONISM, AND WORLD WAR I

EDITED BY
MARK A. RAIDER, ZOHAR SEGEV, AND GARY PHILLIP ZOLA

FOREWORD BY JEHUDA REINHARZ
AFTERWORD BY SUSANNAH HESCHEL

University of CINCINNATI | PRESS

About the University of Cincinnati Press

The University of Cincinnati Press is committed to publishing rigorous, peer reviewed, leading scholarship accessibly to stimulate dialogue between the academy, public intellectuals and lay practitioners. The press endeavors to erase disciplinary boundaries in order to cast fresh light on common problems in our global community. Building on the university's longstanding tradition of social responsibility to the citizens of Cincinnati, state of Ohio, and the world, the press publishes books on topics which expose and resolve disparities at every level of society and have local, national, and global impact.

The University of Cincinnati Press, Cincinnati 45221

ucincinnatipress.uc.edu

Library of Congress Cataloging-in-Publication Data

Names: Raider, Mark A., editor. | Segev, Zohar, editor. | Zola, Gary Phillip, editor.
Title: An equal share of freedom : American Jews, Zionism, and World War I / edited by Mark A. Raider, Zohar Segev, and Gary Phillip Zola.
Other titles: American Jews, Zionism, and World War I
Description: Cincinnati : University of Cincinnati Press, [2024] | Series: Jacob Rader Marcus series on the American Jewish experience ; 1 | "The [origin] of this volume can be traced to a 2018 international conference held in Cincinnati, Ohio titled 'Re-Thinking the Balfour Declaration of 1917: Zionism, American Jews, and World War I in Historical Perspective' "—CIP galley. | Includes bibliographical references and index. | Summary: "Essays illustrating the American Jewish experience during World War I. An Equal Share of Freedom sheds new light on several important and interrelated dimensions of American, Jewish, and world history in the World War I era. Paying close attention to the Balfour Declaration as a hub around which to explore the period's unfolding and turbulent social, cultural, and political developments, this collection of essays covers a diverse range of topics including Jewish doughboys, Zionist women authors, and political elites such as Golda Meir and Woodrow Wilson. The volume demonstrates the complex nature of Jewish ethnonational consciousness in the American setting and the impact of Zionism on US wartime and postwar activity. The essays in this volume overturn timeworn assumptions that have long shaped the fields of American history and modern

Jewish history. Taken as a whole, they demonstrate the war's profound impact on American Jewish life and the transformation of American Jewry's relationship with wider American society. These essays also illustrate the centrality of Zionism to the American Jewish experience and the extent to which American Jewry's national consciousness and the future direction of the Zionist project were forged in the crucible of the Great War. An Equal Share of Freedom is the first volume in the Jacob Rader Marcus Series on the American Jewish Experience. The series highlights the myriad possibilities for expanding and deepening scholarly understanding of American Jews and the shared history of American society and the Jewish people in the twentieth century, starting with a look at World War I"— Provided by publisher.

Identifiers: LCCN 2024013183 (print) | LCCN 2024013184 (ebook) | ISBN 9798885500036 (hardback) | ISBN 9798885500043 (pdf) | ISBN 9798885500050 (epub)

Subjects: LCSH: Jews—United States—History—20th century. | World War, 1914–1918—Jews—United States. | Zionism—United States—History—20th century. | Balfour Declaration. | Zionists—Political activity—United States. | Jews—United States—Politics and government—20th century. | United States—Ethnic relations—History—20th century. | United States—Politics and government—1901-1953. | BISAC: HISTORY / General | HISTORY / Jewish

Classification: LCC E184.353 .E68 2024 (print) | LCC E184.353 (ebook) | DDC 940.3089/924073—dc23/eng/20240613

LC record available at https://lccn.loc.gov/2024013183

LC ebook record available at https://lccn.loc.gov/2024013184

ISBN 979-8-88550-003-6 (hardback)

ISBN 979-8-88550-004-3 (e-book, PDF)

ISBN 979-8-88550-005-0 (e-book, EPUB)

Designed and produced for UC Press by Alisa Strauss and Julie Rushing
Cover design by Alisa Strauss and Julie Rushing

Typeset in Trajan Pro and Palatino

Editorial and production interns, Jared Brancatelli and Haley Zaker

Printed in the United States of America

First Printing

CONTENTS

Acknowledgments

The gestation of this volume can be traced to a 2018 international conference held in Cincinnati, Ohio titled "Re-Thinking the Balfour Declaration of 1917: Zionism, American Jews, and World War I in Historical Perspective." Cosponsored by the Jacob Rader Marcus Center of the American Jewish Archives and the University of Cincinnati's History Department and the Center for Studies in Jewish Education and Culture, with support from the Charles Phelps Taft Research Center, the conference was a milestone event. Occasioned by the centenary of the British government's proclamation of the Balfour Declaration and the end of World War I, the gathering focused squarely on American Jewry's wartime circumstances, engagement with the fledgling Zionist movement, and relationship to the war-torn Jewish communities of Europe and Palestine.

Now, as the volume goes to press, it is striking to consider the coincident timing of the book's publication opposite the hundredth anniversary year of the death of Woodrow Wilson

(1856–1924), who championed the "war to end all wars," and in our own day the resurgence of antisemitism across the globe and the tragic outbreak of the Russia-Ukraine and Israel-Hamas wars. That the world's "longest hatred" and the dynamic regions of eastern Europe and Israel-Palestine remain hinges of the geopolitical landscape is a stark reminder of the many ways the twenty-first century is beholden to its predecessor.

As historians, we seek to throw light on the complex relationship of the past to the present. Our work, however, is not conducted in isolation and we owe a considerable debt to the many friends and colleagues who have participated in our journey. In addition to our esteemed co-contributors, we are grateful to the other 2018 conference participants whose expertise helped to shape and sharpen our deliberations: Yaarah Bar-On, Steven Conn, Elizabeth B. Frierson, Michael A. Meyer, Stephen Porter, and Haim O. Rechnitzer.

Behind the scenes, the book project spawned by the conference profited from the guidance of three scholars who generously served as peer reviewers. Their important insights, suggestions, and recommendations honed the manuscript overall. We also benefited from the aid of several colleagues, archivists, and librarians who responded with good cheer to numerous research queries, permissions requests, and much more. Here at last we are able to publicly acknowledge their critical assistance and support: Herbert Block, Jessica Cloer, Rachel Farkas, Ashley Hutchison, Sigrun Haude, Sean P. Keating, Dorian Keefe, Eisha Neely, Maura O'Connor, Christopher Phillips, Christopher J. Prom, Hagar Raved, Jenny E. Robb, the late Al Simandl, Patrick J. Stevens, David Stradling, Willard Sunderland, Tom Teper, and Elaine L. Westbrooks.

Special thanks are due to Elizabeth Scarpelli, editor of the University of Cincinnati Press, who embraced the project from the outset and provided sage guidance. Editorial, design, and production manager Pamela Wissman and editorial assistants Sophie Ballah, Jared Brancatelli, and Haley Zaker were unflagging in their efforts. We also wish to express our appreciation to

Dr. Alisa Strauss (1968–2024) for her creative design work on the volume as well as sadness at her untimely passing. We are deeply grateful to our colleagues at the American Jewish Archives. Lisa B. Frankel and Dana Herman were, as always, helpful at every turn. Mary K. Brunson, Steve Collins, Jacob Heisler, Elisa Ho, Ady Manory, and Joe Weber provided critical archival and technical assistance.

We are delighted to note this is the inaugural volume of the Jacob Rader Marcus Series on the American Jewish Experience cosponsored by the University of Cincinnati Press and The Jacob Rader Marcus Center of the American Jewish Archives. We express our profound appreciation to the American Jewish Archives for funding the new series. We, the co-editors, Mark A. Raider and Gary Phillip Zola, also wish to thank our fellow founding members of the editorial advisory board Cheryl Greenberg, Jenna Weissman Joselit, and Eli Lederhendler for their selfless investment in promoting the scholarly study of American Jewish history. This volume's publication was also supported by a generous grant from the Sir Isaac Wolfson Chair in Jewish Religious Thought and Heritage, University of Haifa.

Last but not least, it is a special pleasure to thank our families, especially Naama Brenner, Miriam B. Raider-Roth, and Stefi Zola, for their steadfast encouragement.

M.A.R. and G.P.Z.
Cincinnati, Ohio

Z.S.
Haifa, Israel

Editor's Note

This volume reflects the course of historical events that shaped the history of American Jewry, Zionism, and Palestine during the tumultuous era of World War I. While not intended as a comprehensive treatment, it is designed to complement scholarly works that examine American history and modern Jewish history generally as well as studies that focus on the history of World War I.

Each chapter is relatively self-contained and seeks to plug a gap in the historical literature on American Jews, Zionism, and World War I. Interspersed throughout the book are eighteen hitherto unpublished and rarely seen images, several of which help to preface and complement the chapters—photographs, political cartoons, sketches, posters, and paintings—that highlight the vast and rich reservoir of primary sources available to enhance the study of the historical record. A timeline following the chapters situates American Jewish history in the overlapping contexts of American and global history, with an emphasis on developments related to Zionism and Palestine. It is hoped that the mix of essays and other materials will create multiple points of entry into the subject matter and enhance the volume's utility in college classes.

The volume utilizes specific locutions pertinent to Jewish and Zionist history because of their cultural and historic value. In various essays one will note the use of terms such as Mandatory Palestine, the *Yishuv* (pre-state Israeli society), and so on. In many instances, common English spellings have been retained and/or inserted for the sake of ease and readability (e.g., Jaffa, Safed). In general, we have deployed a simplified orthography and transliteration of Hebrew and Yiddish terms to give English-speaking readers as clear and consistent a phonetic equivalent as possible without introducing complex diacritical marks and special linguistic values.[1] Exceptions in this regard are terms and names for which a common usage is highly familiar (e.g., kibbutz, Passover seder). Square brackets within quotations indicate additions intended to clarify the meaning of the original text. A glossary is also included to assist readers unfamiliar with Hebrew and Yiddish terms and cultural-historical terminology used frequently in the chapters.

In sum, the volume presents a road map of the history of the Jews in the United States in relation to the rise of Jewish nationalism, the outbreak of World War I, and the war's unfolding impact on Europe, Palestine, and the modern world. We hope that the essays and materials gathered here will be of interest to a broad range of students, researchers, and interested lay readers and help to stimulate new research on American Jews, Zionism, and the Great War.

Endnote

1 The exception to this is chapter 4, in which Philip Hollander, a Hebrew literature scholar, adopts a more exacting style of transliteration.

Moses Jacob Ezekiel, *Rabbi Isaac M. Wise Memorial Window*, 1909

Source: Moses Jacob Ezekiel, Design for Memorial Window in Philadelphia's Keneseth Israel Congregation (1909), Moses Jacob Ezekiel Collection, MS4, Box 2, Folder 5, Jacob Rader Marcus Center of the American Jewish Archives, Cincinnati, OH.

The celebrated American Jewish artist Moses Jacob Ezekiel (1844–1917), born to a Richmond, Virginia family of Sephardic origin, fought with the Confederate army during the Civil War and later relocated to Europe, where he studied at the Prussian Academy of Arts and then settled in Rome. Ezekiel became known internationally for his classical sculptures depicting religious themes, American liberty, and European and American historical figures. In addition to iconic sculptures like the statue of Thomas Jefferson at the University of Virginia (1901), he is identified with the so-called "Lost Cause" of the South at the turn of the nineteenth and twentieth centuries, and created the Virginia Military Institute's statue of Confederate General Thomas J. "Stonewall" Jackson (1912) and the "New South" memorial to Confederate soldiers at Arlington National Cemetery (1914).[1] In 1911, Reform Congregation Keneseth Israel (Philadelphia, Pennsylvania) dedicated Ezekiel's stained glass memorial window (pictured here) honoring Rabbi Isaac M. Wise (1819–1900), the architect of Reform Judaism in the United States. Ezekiel had become well acquainted with Wise when he lived in Cincinnati, Ohio, and he also sculpted a bust of the famous rabbi. At the top of the arched window is inscribed *vayehi or* (Hebrew for "let there be light") from Genesis 1:3, used by Wise as the motto of the *American Israelite,* a newspaper he founded in 1854. Beneath a shower of sunlight, a virile heroic figure holds aloft a sword and banner on which "Maccabee" is illuminated in Hebrew. Rising to a commanding height against a verdant landscape and a fortress city, the figure symbolizes the dual biblical themes of election and freedom. In the lower left corner, a crowned female figure, partially clothed, bows her head solemnly, hands clasped before a barren vine and stump, symbolizing ancient Israel's affliction. In the lower right corner, a handsome youth, wearing a colorful tunic and head covering, kneels and attentively studies a scroll, while palms burst with vitality at his feet and above him, representing enlightenment and a hopeful future. Below the image is a panel that reads: "The wise shall shine as the brightness of the firmament; they that turn many to righteousness as the stars forever and ever" (Daniel 12:3). The window is an intriguing expression of American Jewry's sense of belonging and optimism at the dawn of the new century.

— M.A.R

Endnote

1 Owing to recent controversy surrounding Jim Crow-era monuments that valorize the myth of the Lost Cause, Ezekiel's statue of Stonewall Jackson was relocated from the Virginia Military Institute campus to Virginia's New Market Battlefield State Historical Park.

FOREWORD

JEHUDA REINHARZ

Despite longstanding interest in the history of the Jews and Zionism during World War I, only a handful of scholarly studies probe the myriad ways the war impacted the course of modern Jewish history. The present volume, *An Equal Share of Freedom: American Jews, Zionism, and World War I,* is the first concerted effort in a generation to plug this gap with respect to the American Jewish experience.

American Jews, as this collection of essays demonstrates, were deeply affected and influenced by the war in Europe. Of course, by 1914 no other single country in the world was home to as large a Jewish population as the United States. Over three million strong, American Jewry was exceeded only by the aggregate numbers of its Old World progenitor, whose centuries-old eastern and western European Jewish communities stood at over nine million. The most populous urban Jewish communities in Europe—located in Warsaw, Lodz, Budapest, Vienna, Berlin, and Odessa—were dwarfed by New York's Jewish community of 1.35 million. However, shifting demographics accounted only in part for the dramatic changes in the relationship of American and European Jews. As the *American Jewish Year Book*, a chronicle of American and global Jewish affairs, reported in 1917:

> At the outbreak of the present international struggle, more than nine and half million of the 13,000,000 Jews in the world, or 73 percent, inhabited belligerent countries, over three and one-half million residing in the territory of the three Polands, the scene of the most sanguinary fighting. When the war opened, there were a million and half Jews in Russian Poland and two million in Galicia, while Servia [sic] had more than 30,000. As to Turkey in general and Palestine in particular, though they were not the scenes of military operations during the first months of the war, it is important to note that there were 250,000 Jews in the Ottoman Empire of whom 78,000 lived in the Holy Land. With each nation involved in the struggle straining its every effort and applying its entire resources toward military success, there was thus only one source to which the non-combatant Jewish populations could look for the amelioration of their unfortunate lot and the alleviation of their suffering, namely, the great, prosperous community in America; and the Jews of the United States learned quickly that their coreligionists overseas were instinctively turning their beseeching eyes to peaceful America.[1]

Between 1914 and 1917, American Jews from all walks of life became increasingly enmeshed socially and politically in the war's orbit. In part, this can be explained on the basis of long-established patterns of kinship including the traditional notion of *klal yisrael* (Jewish solidarity). Indeed, even before the United States entered the conflict in April 1917, a small band of mostly Yiddish-speaking Jewish immigrants to the *goldene medine* (golden land), animated by shared cultural ties, personal relationships, and religious values, joined the British military's Thirty-Ninth and Fortieth Battalions of Royal Fusiliers (also known as the Jewish Legion). Thereafter, over 225,000 American Jews, constituting approximately 4.5 percent of all Americans in uniform, inspired by President Woodrow Wilson's declaration that "the world must be made safe for democracy" by "the champions of the rights of mankind,"[2] served in the US armed forces, including some 9,000 commissioned officers, many of whom attained high rank. Robert S. Marx, a decorated war hero wounded in the Meuse-Argonne offensive, well-known Cincinnati judge, and founder of the Disabled Veterans of America, would later deride Henry Ford, the American inventor and antisemitic fabulist whose *Dearborn Independent* contended "the Jew is disloyal to our government" and "a traitor to the American flag," by describing "the Jewish part in the World War" as "an answer written in deeds and not in words... given by more than a quarter of a million American Jews who served with honor and credit from the humblest private in the ranks all the way up to Brigadier General [Charles Henry] Lauchheimer[3] in the Marine Corp and from the humblest sailor on the seas all the way up to the Rear Admiral [Joseph] Strauss[4] who commanded America's so-called Suicide Fleet in the North Sea."[5]

To be sure, as noted in this volume, the war also served as a catalyst with respect to American Jewry's internal dynamics and evolving communal agenda. The seemingly disparate strands of the American Jewish landscape—native-born American Jews and recent Yiddish-speaking immigrants, Jews of central and eastern European ancestry, religious and secular Jews, workers, white collar professionals, and entrepreneurs, radical activists, political moderates, and conservative elites—united around the cause of helping their brethren in war-torn Europe and Palestine. The net result was the creation of an intricate network of communal vehicles and philanthropic instruments as well as an evolving mutual bond of Jewishness and Americanness, a synthesis otherwise in strikingly short supply among rival factions and groups comprising the American Jewish spectrum in the early twentieth century.

Nor can the distinctive perch of American Jewry in 1917 be overstressed. Not only did American Jews occupy a unique position as the major diasporic community in the west unscathed physically by the war, but it was also swiftly emerging as an ethnic political bloc of key importance in American life. Marshaling the community's growing cultural-political clout and sense of confidence, American Jewish activists, groups, and leaders championed (at first separately and ultimately as a unified body) an unprecedented strategy vis-à-vis the wartime crisis in Europe and Palestine. The decimated Jewish communities of the eastern war zone and the embattled *Yishuv* in Ottoman Palestine became the twin foci of American Jewry's economic and political attention. To this end, American Jewish leaders and organizations mobilized a loose coalition of forces that coalesced around a countrywide communal campaign of immense scale. Possessed of modest but appreciable resources, disparate American Jewish groups and agencies responded to the humanitarian crisis and distress of their brethren overseas with alacrity and generosity. By the end of 1916, American Jews generated some $6 million in funds for Jewish war relief efforts and in 1917 alone the community raised over $10 million. These sums, mustered by a diverse array of grassroots activists, communal organizations, and elite patrons, were deployed to care for destitute and brutalized Jews throughout war-torn Europe and provided aid and assistance to hundreds of thousands of refugees.

The nexus of the war and other international developments, including the eruption of the Russian Revolution and the stunning announcement by Great Britain of the Balfour Declaration, played a critical role in the rise of a new American Jewish confidence. The new spirit that animated American Jewry found expression in an ongoing commitment to securing Jewish relief, minority rights, and citizenship in postwar Europe as well as the mobilization of large numbers of adherents to the Zionist cause. In fact, by the war's end, American Jewry, meeting twice in a national democratically elected plenary known as the American Jewish Congress, adopted a new communal platform in which Zionism played a central role. The future of the Jewish national project in Palestine remained far from certain. Yet a sea change in modern Jewish politics had occurred. American Jews, acting with a unified voice, now committed ideationally and structurally to the realization of an autonomous Jewish commonwealth under British auspices.

American Jewish historiography is replete with innovative studies of religion, immigration, politics, women, gender, and other significant themes. Interestingly, however, American Jewry's historic transformation during World War I, including the pivotal role played by Zionism in this regard, has been largely neglected by scholars. Seeking to plug this gap, the essays in this volume offer a broad-ranging and multifaceted assessment of what happened to American Jews during World War I, the roles they assumed individually and collectively in prosecuting the war, and the impact Zionism had on the shaping of American Jewish attitudes to postwar reconstruction. Introducing fresh perspectives and revising outdated assumptions, *An Equal Share of Freedom* is a timely and welcome contribution that opens the door to new scholarly research on American Jews, Zionism, and World War I.

ENDNOTES

1 "Jewish War Relief Work," *American Jewish Year Book*, vol. 19 (Philadelphia: Jewish Publication Society of America, 1917), 194.

2 President Woodrow Wilson's Declaration of War Message to Congress, April 2, 1917; Records of the United States Senate; Record Group 46; National Archives; https://www.archives.gov/milestone-documents/address-to-congress-declaration-of-war-against-germany.

3 Charles Henry Lauchheimer (1859–1920), a graduate of the US Naval Academy and Columbia University Law School in 1881 and 1884, respectively, rose through US naval ranks from midshipman, to brigadier general, to adjutant and inspector of the US Marine Corps.

4 Joseph Strauss (1861–1948), the first Jewish admiral in the US Navy, participated in the USS *Lancaster*'s blockade of Cuba during the Spanish-American War and in World War I as a commander responsible for laying the North Sea Mine Barrage. In 1921, he was elevated to the rank of admiral and placed in command of the Asiatic Fleet. He invented several systems for mounting guns on ships and submarines.

5 Robert S. Marx, "Memorial Day Address" (1927), Robert S. Marx Papers, 1904–1974, MSS-903, Folder: "Miscellaneous Speeches," Cincinnati History Library and Archives, Cincinnati, OH.

Jewish Welfare Board Hut, US Army & Navy, Iowa State Fair, c. 1918–1919

Source: "Jewish Welfare Board Headquarters, US Army & Navy, Iowa State Fair, Des Moines, Iowa" (c. 1918–19), Jewish Welfare Board Photos, PC-2077, Jacob Rader Marcus Center of the American Jewish Archives, Cincinnati, OH.

Approximately 225,000 American Jews enlisted in the US military forces during World War I. With the support of Secretary of War Newton D. Baker (1871–1937), twenty-two American Jewish organizations established the National Jewish Welfare Board (JWB) in 1917. Under the chairmanship of Colonel Harry Cutler (1875–1920), a successful manufacturer and Rhode Island communal leader, the JWB emerged as a robust framework for supporting Jewish soldiers, sailors, marines, and chaplains serving in the US military. During the war, the JWB organized a variety of initiatives on behalf of the US military at home and overseas. In addition to providing Jewish recruits with distinctive spiritual, educational, and recreational support, including the provision of kosher food and worship and holiday services, the organization indirectly sought to neutralize ambivalence and hostility to Jews in American society. Writing in the *American Israelite*, one observer noted the JWB aimed "to help Jewish boys to adjust themselves to understand and sympathize with their gentile brothers-in-arms and to be in turn understood by them."[1] In August 1919, tens of thousands of Iowans celebrated the end of World War I at the Iowa State "Victory" Fair. In addition to US military parades and exhibits of weapons and tanks, fairgoers marveled at a reenactment of the Battle of Chateau Thierry in France that turned the tide of the war against Germany in 1918. Among the varied display booths, fairgoers were greeted by a Jewish Welfare Board welcome tent (pictured here). In this photo, a young JWB representative mans a military tent adorned with American flags. The large sign, "Headquarters Jewish Welfare Board U.S. Army and Navy," underscores the JWB's message of the intertwining of American and Jewish life. The placards positioned at either side of the tent's entrance showcase the JWB's services: "Religious Work at Camp" (Friday Evening Service, Sabbath Service, Daily Service), "Educational Work" (French Classes, American History & Civics), "Social & Recreational Activities" (Literary Clubs, Discussion Groups, Entertainments, Concerts), "Personal Service" (Hospital Visitations, Legal Advice, General Personal service), "Work in Town" (Entertainments, Home Hospitality, Patriotic Celebrations, Supplies for Soldiers, Comfort Kits), and "Club Rooms" (Reading, Writing, Billiards).

— M.A.R

ENDNOTE

1 "War Chest Uniting People," *American Israelite* (November 14, 1918), 4.

INTRODUCTION

OVER THERE, OVER HERE: AMERICAN JEWS AND THE CRISIS OF WORLD WAR I

MARK A. RAIDER

Reporting on the American Jewish Congress, a national plenary of American Jewry meeting in Philadelphia in December 1918, the *Washington Times* noted the gathering's determination "to send representatives to the peace conference at Versailles to seek for the Jews an equal share of freedom and opportunity in the new settlement of world conditions."[1] Though the *Times* hinted at the gravity of the forthcoming deliberations, it did not explicitly indicate that the Paris Peace Conference was set to consider the disposition of the Middle East in the New World order, the possibility of a British protectorate in Palestine, and the future status of the *Yishuv* (pre-state Israeli society). The matter-of-fact article concerning American Jewry's envoys appeared on page six alongside a smattering of other news items including Norway's "Break with Bolsheviki," "KY Mob Lynches Negro Ex-Soldier," "French Prepare for After-War Tourists," the "Child Labor Problem in Europe," and a challenge to the "constitutionality of the Espionage Act."[2] Hemmed in by advertisements for "tailored to measure trousers," cold syrup, bank loans, and wristwatches, and a comic strip penned by the well-known syndicated artist Clare A. Briggs—*Movie of a Man and a Busted Shoelace*—news of the American Jewish delegation's departure no doubt appeared to the casual reader as yet another data point in a fast-paced world punctuated by postwar upheaval, domestic violence, shifting political winds, and the daily grind of commerce.

In reality, of course, a lively public discussion had percolated for nearly a year concerning Great Britain's issuance in November 1917 of the Balfour Declaration. The unprecedented declaration, just sixty-eight words long, proclaimed in carefully crafted and studiously ambiguous language the British government's sanction of the Zionist project:

> His Majesty's Government view with favor the establishment in Palestine of a National Home for the Jewish people, and will use their best endeavors to facilitate the achievement of this object, it being clearly understood that nothing shall be done which may prejudice the civil and religious rights of the existing non-Jewish communities in Palestine or the rights and political status enjoyed by Jews in any other country.[3]

The Balfour Declaration, as time would tell, marked a pivotal shift in modern Jewish politics and opened a new pathway in the campaign for Jewish statehood. In September 1918, President Woodrow Wilson took a significant stride in this direction when he countermanded the US government's neutral stance concerning the crumbling Ottoman empire's Middle East territories and endorsed the British statement. In a public greeting to American Jews on the eve of the Jewish New Year, he stated:

> . . . I welcome an opportunity to express the satisfaction I have felt in the progress of the Zionist movement in the United States and in the Allied

> countries since the declaration by Mr. Balfour on behalf of the British Government, of Great Britain's approval of the establishment in Palestine of a national home for the Jewish people, and his promise that the British Government would use its best endeavors to facilitate the achievement of that object, with the understanding that nothing would be done to prejudice the civil and religious rights of non-Jewish people in Palestine or the rights and political status enjoyed by Jews in other countries.[4]

Shortly thereafter, Wilson invited American Jewish leaders to accompany him to the Paris Peace Conference. The president's invitation signaled American Jewry's debut on the world stage and heralded the reorientation of US foreign policy.

It is commonplace to observe that the Balfour Declaration remains a matter of lively scholarly and public debate. Yet there is no gainsaying the enduring importance and impact of the British statement on the course of world and Middle East history. In the public arena, Zionism's supporters and detractors have long sparred over the declaration's origins, meaning, and impact on global affairs. In 1949, the Hungarian-born Jewish writer and journalist Arthur Koestler famously characterized it as "one of the most improbable political documents of all time" in which "one nation solemnly promised to a second nation the country of a third."[5] Half a century later, the scholar Jonathan Schneer, echoing Koestler's sentiment, described the declaration as "the highly contingent product of a tortuous process characterized as much by deceit and chance as by vision and diplomacy."[6] The historian and political analyst Martin Kramer alternatively asserts the declaration was "not only" dependent upon "the tacit or explicit agreement of the Allied powers, but that agreement had been secured by the Zionists themselves..."[7] The devil and the angels are, of course, in the details. As the historian Mark Tessler judiciously notes, the declaration was a product of the broader context of "intense [European] rivalry for influence in the Middle East;" meanwhile, the British government believed its "general bargaining position would be enhanced by an opening to the Jews" and that American Jews in particular could help "to rally the United States to the Allied war effort."[8]

Among modern Jewish historians, the declaration is typically described as "Zionism's greatest diplomatic achievement."[9] It marks a transformation in the movement's status, according to the historian Anita Shapira, "from one national liberation movement among many pressing foreign ministries around the globe for a hearing… to a movement recognized by the Great Powers and in international law."[10] Indeed, the Zionist Organization of the pre-state era, no less responsive to the shifting geopolitical winds of the global arena than other national minorities, recognized the outbreak of World War I created a singular and potentially historic opportunity. With Chaim Weizmann and later David Ben-Gurion at the helm, the scholar Michael Brenner points out, a pragmatic center-left coalition of Zionist groups seized upon the declaration as a catalyst to "the practical advancement of the Zionist cause" believing, at least until World War II, that "far-reaching [Jewish] autonomy under British or international rule seemed a more realistic option than full independence."[11]

Against this complex backdrop, the present anthology offers fresh analyses and new findings concerning American Jewry's engagement with domestic and global affairs and the Zionist movement during the World War I era. The genesis of the volume can be traced to a scholarly conference held in Cincinnati, Ohio, titled "Re-Thinking the Balfour Declaration of 1917: Zionism, American Jews, and World War I in Historical Perspective." Sponsored by the Jacob Rader Marcus Center of the American Jewish Archives, the University of Cincinnati's Department of History and the Center for Studies in Jewish Education and Culture, and the Charles Phelps Taft Research Center, the conference introduced new and innovative scholarship on this important but notably understudied topic. Unlike the involvement of American Jews in the American Civil War, World War II, and the Vietnam War—each of which has in recent decades yielded a sizable quotient of scholarly literature—the history of American Jews and World War I suffers from a relative paucity of interest. Indeed, of the recent scholarly publications and academic symposia (including some occasioned by the centenary of World War I)—to name just a few key works, Albert I. Slomowitz's *The Fighting Rabbis: Jewish Military Chaplains and American History* (1999), Derek S. Penslar's *Jews and the Military* (2013), Marsha L. Rozenblitt and Jonathan Karp's *World War I and the Jews: Conflict and Transformation in Europe, the Middle East, and America* (2017),[12] Edward Madigan and Gideon Reuveni's *The Jewish Experience of the First World War* (2019),[13] and Jaclyn Granick's *International Jewish Humanitarianism in the Age of the Great War* (2021)—the Cincinnati conference stands out among these pathfinding efforts as "overdue recognition of World War I as a major field in modern Jewish history" for squarely focusing on the American Jewish setting, American Jewish responses to the wartime crisis, and American Jewry's engagement with postwar developments.[14] In a word, amid the growing corpus of scholarship on Jews and World War I, *An Equal Share of Freedom: American Jews, Zionism, and World War I* plugs a gap in the literature and stakes a claim for the critical importance of American Jewry's social, cultural, and political engagement in the wartime international and domestic contexts and developments that transformed the twentieth century. A multifaceted exploration of American society, American Jewry, and the trajectory of Zionism, this volume throws new light on the overlapping themes of presidential power, American society's wartime mobilization, American Jewish leadership, Jewish-Christian relations, ethnic-cultural identity, Jewish and non-Jewish responses to Zionism, Hebraism in America, philanthropic and relief activity, and case studies of individuals who demonstrate the impact in real time of the exigent conditions of World War I.

I.

Modern Jewish historians have long noted the distinctive nature of the American Jewish experience. Unlike European Jewry and the Jews of the Islamic world, the post-emancipationist American Jewish setting has been historically characterized by a decentralized framework of religious and lay authority figures and affinity groups, all of which compete in the marketplace of ideas to shape and direct an elusive overarching communal agenda. Since before the Civil War, nominal leadership of American Jewish affairs rested in the hands of a small group of influential Reform rabbis and wealthy Jewish entrepreneurs and lawyers of central European ancestry. Initially, the Board of Delegates of American Israelites, established in 1859 as the first Jewish civil rights organization in the United States, and then the American Jewish Committee (AJC), created in 1906 in response to waves of pogroms in eastern Europe, sought to represent and safeguard American Jewry's interests. For the most part, the AJC leaders used a mix of elite connections and backroom channels to address political and diplomatic concerns facing Jewish communities at home and abroad. They deployed their significant personal wealth to help create, fund, and sustain an array of initiatives and projects aimed at supporting Jewish immigrants, including relocation agencies, settlement houses, health care services, vocational training activity, and educational and cultural institutions, as well as providing substantial overseas relief for Jewish communities in distress.

As the twentieth century dawned, American Jewry proved to be anything but an isolated diaspora outpost. The centuries-old Jewish problem "forced its way into the consciousness of the American Jew" and stoked intra-communal American Jewish tensions.[15] Developments abroad, notably pogroms in Russia and Rumania, the Dreyfus affair (1898), the Mendel Beilis affair (1913), and the devastation during World War I of Jewish communities in the eastern European war zone had a "shattering impact" on American Jews from all walks of life.[16]

No less threatening, the scholar Leonard Dinnerstein observes, were homegrown displays of antisemitism—centered on theological allegations of the Jews as "Christ-killers," fantasies that "in all the leading banking institutes of the world the Jews hold the reins," and scaremongering about "the Jewish invasion of America"—which caused widespread alarm, fear, and anxiety.[17] The spectrum of anti-Jewish hostility ranged from genteel animus—e.g., the refusal by the Grand Union Hotel in Saratoga Springs, New York to open its doors in 1877 to the prominent banker Joseph Seligman; celebrated author Henry James's widely noted lamentation in 1896 about "the little Jews [who] wagged their big noses" at an English resort;[18] and the eugenicist Madison Grant's warning in *The Passing of the Great Race* (1916) of America's mongrelization by "very inferior" Jewish "alien hordes"[19]—to overt forms of discrimination and violence, e.g., the Dillingham and Burnett Immigration Bills in 1911–12 sought to bar "those who can only read or write in Hebrew or Yiddish;"[20] the sham trial and lynching in 1915 of Leo Frank, a New York Jew who relocated to Atlanta, Georgia, falsely accused of raping and murdering a Christian girl; and American higher education's quota systems on Jews owing to their "undesirable" traits and "clannishness."[21] That such manifestations of bigotry, nativism, and malice were but a few steps removed from the degradation and terrorization of American Black people and atrocities inflicted on other vulnerable minorities in this period was not lost on American Jews.[22]

To defend "American Israel" and meet "with full confidence the currents" of the new century, communal leaders sought to shape, sustain, and mobilize the highly variegated and decentralized Jewish landscape that unfolded coast to coast.[23] In 1914, the statistician Joseph Jacobs reported the nation's Jewish population stood at 2,933,374 and within a year would "reach the three million mark, or in other words... one out of every thirty Americans, and in the urban districts, one out every sixteen."[24] Distinguishing between "native-native," "native-foreign," and "foreign-born" Jews, Jacobs determined American Jewry included over two million Yiddish speakers and roughly 250,000 other immigrants who spoke "German, English, French, and even Ladino, or Judeo-Spanish."[25] The total "native-born" population of 1,300,000, he explained, although "already American Jews in every sense of the word," was "being added to at the rate of close on to 75,000 per year" including "about three-quarters the amount added by immigration."[26] "It will be some time," he surmised, "before the numbers of native-born American Jews will equal those of the foreign-born."[27] This meteoric growth and development, noted Herman Bernstein, editor of the *American Jewish Year Book,* with marked understatement, "will doubtless attract much attention."[28] Indeed, the sprawling American Jewish scene, a voluntary patchwork of synagogues, mutual aid societies, hospitals, schools, settlement houses, banks, recreation centers, and other vehicles, many of which were supported by a plethora of religious bodies, advocacy groups, trade unions, fraternal orders, women's societies, charitable enterprises, education associations, and political parties, prompted considerable external interest. "Mixed and sometimes confused" discussions among non-Jews about the so-called melting pot and the problem of Jewish clannishness, the American social and literary critic Irving Howe has observed, centered on "clear presuppositions as to who would melt whom."[29] As for the Jews themselves, the historical record attests to Howe's assessment that "if only they were allowed to compete on equal terms in the worlds of business, education, and culture, they would thrive well enough."[30]

The nearly 2.5 million eastern European Jewish immigrants who arrived on American shores in the decades that spanned the nineteenth and twentieth centuries benefited from the protection and largesse of American Jewry's affluent and influential establishment.[31] But the Yiddish-speaking masses also brought with them a strong national consciousness, first-hand experience with anti-Jewish hostility, and a pent-up desire for communal autonomy that spawned a plethora of social, cultural, and political institutions, groups, and vehicles, including a vibrant Yiddish press. The latter, lamented the distinguished Reform rabbi Judah L. Magnes, inflamed intra-communal tensions by setting "'uptown' against 'downtown,' the German over against the Russian."[32] This comment was a little unfair but not entirely untrue. The Yiddish press, like the Jewish immigrant community as a whole, benefited from the patronage and protection of American Jewry's patricians even as it amplified dissenting voices that balked at the establishment's model of "self-appointed leadership" and top-down hierarchical social control.[33]

Writing in 1915, Israel Friedlaender, a Polish-born, German-and-French-educated Jewish public intellectual and professor of Semitics and Bible at the Jewish Theological Seminary, described the American setting and the cultural clash between the *yahudim* (American Jewry's elite patricians) and the *yidn* (the Yiddish-speaking rank-and-file) in the following terms:

> America has, in less than one generation, become the second largest center of the Jewish Diaspora, and bids fair to become the first, instead of the second, within another generation. No other country in the world offers, even approximately, such a favorable combination of opportunities for the development of Diaspora Judaism, as does America: economic possibilities, vast sparsely populated territories, freedom of action, liberty of conscience, equality of citizenship, appreciation of the fundamentals of Judaism, variety of population, excluding a rigidly nationalistic state policy, and other similar factors. It is no wonder, therefore, that in no other country did Reform Judaism [brought from central Europe], as the incarnation of Diaspora Judaism, attain such luxurious growth as it did in America. It discarded more radically than in Europe, the national elements still clinging to Judaism, and it solemnly proclaimed that

Judaism was wholly and exclusively a religious faith, and that America was the Zion and Washington the Jerusalem of American Israel.

On the other hand, the emigrants from Russia brought the antithesis on the scene. They quickly perceived the decomposing effect of American life upon Jewish doctrine and practice, and they became convinced more firmly than ever that Diaspora Judaism was a failure, and that the only antidote was Palestine and nothing but Palestine. The nationalists among them beheld in the very same factors in which the German Jews saw the possibilities of Diaspora Judaism the chances for organizing Jewry on purely nationalistic lines. Nowhere else, except perhaps in Russia, can be found a greater amount of Palestinian sentiment, as well as a larger manifestation of a one-sided nationalism, than is to be met with in this country.

This conflict of ideas became extraordinarily aggravated by numerous influences of a personal character. The division between the so-called German Jews and the so-called Russian Jews was not limited to a difference in theory. It was equally nourished by far-reaching differences in economic and social position and in the entire range of mental development. The German Jews were the natives; the Russian Jews were the newcomers. The German Jews were the rich; the Russian Jews were the poor. The German Jews were the dispensers of charity; the Russian Jews were the receivers of it. The German Jews were the employers; the Russian Jews were the employees. The German Jews were deliberate, reserved, practical, sticklers for formalities, with a marked ability for organization; the Russian Jews were quick-tempered,

> emotional, theorizing, haters of formalities, with a decided bent toward individualism. An enormous amount of explosives had been accumulating between the two sections which if lit by a spark might have wrecked the edifice of American Israel while yet in the process of construction.[34]

In addition to Friedlaender, several key communal leaders sought to bridge the cultural divide separating the *yahudim* and the *yidn* by appealing to a broad sense of Jewish peoplehood that pervaded the American Jewish social, religious, and political spectrum. Stephen S. Wise, Julian W. Mack, and Magnes, among American Jewry's uptown celebrities, and Joseph Barondess, Chaim Zhitlowsky, Zvi Hirsch Masliansky, and Shmarya Levin, among its downtown icons, played significant roles in this regard. Magnes's "fiery" oratorical style and ability to give a "rouser," for example, including his articulation of a worldview "quickened by Zionism" and sensibility "in turn deepened by Judaism," drew large audiences who came "specifically to hear him speak."[35] In 1915, he helped raise "more than $1 million" in contributions of "cash, jewels, checks, and pledges" at a mass meeting that "packed Carnegie Hall to the doors" with an appeal that emphasized the plight of Jewish war victims in the eastern war zone, the collective responsibility of American Jews, and the struggle for Jewish national rights abroad.[36] "What will you do, my brothers and my sisters," he declaimed, "...in this hour of calamity ...in this crisis that has come upon you and upon me and upon the Jewish people?"

> Three million Jews in this blessed land... enjoying liberty, prosperity, fatness, everything that they need, more than they can use... A million and a quarter [dollars] we want from you right away... We can send this money off right away, tonight, tomorrow... this comparatively insignificant sum from the Jews – the prosperous Jews

> of New York and America... Are there any Jews here tonight who will take the rings from their fingers, and the jewels from their ears, and the money from their pockets and give it to us now? ...while those beyond the seas in Russia, in Galicia, in German Poland, in Siberia, throughout the Ottoman empire, and in the cradle of our race, in Palestine, are waiting for our answer?[37]

In the battle for hearts and minds in the Jewish public arena, a panorama of competing secular, religious, cultural, and political forces came to the fore. On the eve of World War I, an array of seventy-one national Jewish organizations, hundreds of local Jewish organizations, and 117 periodicals in English, Yiddish, and German as well as Hebrew and Ladino in all forty-eight states of the union provided the connective tissue of the American Jewish experience.[38] A rich "ethno-national diaspora" stretched from coast to coast comprised of diverse regional and national "elements [that] became inextricably intertwined and suffused" and which, albeit predisposed to varying ideas about authority and autonomy, constituted a marketplace of ideas teeming with competing and complementary strategies for American Jewish solidarity.[39] Surveying this dynamic landscape, historians Ezra Mendelsohn and Matthew Frye Jacobson have each called attention to a new American Jewish sensibility that arose in the early twentieth century, a synthesis of "elements of acculturationism and integrationism" stamped by a "basically platonic" form of Zionism.[40] Consistent with a "recognizable American pattern" among ethno-national groups of European ancestry, American Zionism, in parallel with the Irish Clan na Gael and Polish National Alliance, proved to be a "primary instrument for emigrant action" and defined "the range of political possibilities which emigrants of the period thought both practical and possible."[41] In a related vein, as Lucy S. Dawidowicz observes, the political behavior of "immigrant Jews demonstrated they were not nearly so class-conscious as they sounded."[42] That is to say, despite the lexicon of eastern European Jewish radicals, the post-emancipationist environment of the New World—in contrast to the pre-emancipationist yoke of tsarist Russia's *ancien regime*—provided the scope and inducement for a creed of "liberal-humanitarian utopianism, rational and this-worldly" and an emphasis on "*tachles* [Yiddish for brass tacks], the purposeful striving for improvement."[43]

II.

The new American Jewish ethos, buffeted by intracommunal stresses and wartime exigencies, prompted calls for an American Jewish Congress. The notion of a democratically elected national plenary embodying the interests of the whole of American Israel, it was rightly assumed, threatened the dominance in American Jewish affairs of the AJC and the cosmopolitan leaders of the Jewish labor movement. A loose coalition of pronationalist urban immigrant and middle-class forces had the potential to wrest control of organized American Jewry and elevate Zionism as a hallowed communal ideal. The Brandeis group, a talented coterie of lawyers, rabbis, and scholars led by Louis D. Brandeis, a celebrated figure in Progressive-era politics and close adviser to President Woodrow Wilson, met this challenge with tenacity and aplomb. Stephen S. Wise, second only to Brandeis in the American Zionist orbit, argued the Brandeis group should aim to win over the "great mass of neutrals [in American Jewry] with regard to Zionism... instead of vainly trying to convert our opponents..."[44] "It is better," Wise explained, "to isolate the empoisoned spots and devote ourselves to constructive dealing with the wholesome elements of the community throughout the nation."[45] As veterans of Wilson's successful 1912 presidential election campaign, the Brandeis group was alert to the hold of American ideals on the Jewish community's collective imagination, particularly the keen sense of marginalization and disenfranchisement experienced by Jewish immigrants, women, Zionists, socialists, and others. The passion for universal suffrage, democracy, and minority rights, Brandeis and his lieutenants reasoned, animated the Jewish public square. They wagered even those whose Jewish national consciousness did not include Zionism could still be coaxed toward a broader sense of *klal yisroel politik* (Jewish political solidarity).

Breaking the mold hitherto typical of American Jewish political behavior, the Brandeis group launched a massive countrywide "American-style campaign" on behalf of the congress.[46] Brandeis, Wise, Julian W. Mack, and other members of Brandeis's inner circle carefully engineered an activist public relations strategy that made visible the support of distinguished nonpartisan American Jews, many of whom were elected and appointed US officials. For example, assistant US treasurer Charles B. Strecker, appearing with Brandeis and Shmarya Levin before a crowd of "more than 5000 persons" at Boston's Symphony Hall stated, "We have, as it were… taken advantage of our fortunate neutrality and have assumed the responsibility for all those tasks and obligations, which were heretofore borne by our European brethren."[47] "Indeed, we have gone farther," Strecker explained, "for we are assuming not only the obligations that existed, but in addition we are striving so that the sequence to this world chaos shall be the opportunity for that resplendent vision – world equality for the Jewish people."[48] Likewise, Henry Moskowitz, president of New York's Municipal Civil Service Commission, declared American Jewish "unity" to be "a solemn obligation" necessary to "alleviate the distress of Jewish war victims."[49] "How much more sacred is the duty of the American Hebrews," Moskowitz opined, "to help secure for their persecuted brethren in foreign countries those civil and political rights which they have long enjoyed as American citizens?"[50] Sounding a Brandeisian note, he called the proposed congress "an American method" and insisted it had "its sanction in the New England town meeting, the cradle of American liberty," its analogy in "the national political convention, a distinctly American institution," and its "firm support in every American who believes in the sovereignty of the popular will be expressed through accredited representatives..."[51] He also refuted the opponents of popular self-governance, who preferred the "delicate nuances" of "secret diplomacy" to "the noisy methods of a congress," flatly declaring he was "not afraid of the intelligence and judgment" of a "congress of Jews."[52] Nor would he countenance the notion the congress was "un-American because it accentuates a hyphenated distinction."[53]

> Is it un-American for Jews to gather for the purpose of extending American rights? Were Irish Americans afraid to voice in assemblies their sympathy and to give aid to their kin in their struggle for home rule in Ireland? Did American citizens criticize them for their assertive love of liberty? On the contrary, they won their abounded respect...[54]

In sum, Moskowitz argued, the congress opponents' "attitude of timidity" was "characteristic of the 'Golus' [exile]." "It is a spirit which the masses of our people," he declared, "nurtured by American ideals and institutions of freedom resent" and it is "essentially groveling and undignified..."[55]

If the idea of the American Jewish Congress represented a milestone in Jewish political consciousness, it also offered a striking contrast to the predicament of other American minorities. People of color and recent immigrants from southern and eastern Europe and Asia, beleaguered on the domestic front by Jim Crow, xenophobic hostility, and the Red Scare, suffered from a mix of disenfranchisement, marginalization, and victimization at all levels of society. American Jewry, by contrast, found itself, paradoxically, in a privileged *and* an embattled position. Cognizant of the "broader pattern" of American racism—African Americans, Asian immigrants, and Mexican immigrants were targets of state-sponsored repression—Jewish leaders recognized their community's double-bind as a largely white non-Christian minority in Protestant America.[56] On the one hand, they savored the New World's philosemitism and the American republic's idealistic embrace of the values of individual liberty and church-state separation. "Some of us who were not born in the atmosphere of freedom and equality which is guaranteed by the stars and stripes," asserted the Chicago lawyer Jacob. G. Grossberg, originally from Kovno (Kaunas), Lithuania, "have a keen appreciation of what it means to have equality before the law and the equal protection of the laws" unlike "in darkest Russia" and "in darkest Romania" where for "two thousand years one-half of the Jewish race," denied "equal protection of the laws," has been "bending and struggling to survive."[57] In sum, as the historian Michael S. Neiberg observes, American Jews, "aware as they were that the United States had saved them from pogroms and the horrors of the Eastern front," were apt "as much if not more than any of the hyphenated groups" to profess "their loyalty first and foremost to the land of their adoption."[58] On the other hand, the amalgam that yielded an unprecedented legal status for Jews in the United States, described by the historian Salo W. Baron as "for all practical purposes nearly equal to that of other inhabitants," fell short of full acceptance in the public square.[59] Though primed to pass into American society, Jews remained susceptible to the misperception of being "too foreign" and "too Jewish" and preoccupied by the challenge of putting "an end to the thraldom of the Jews."[60]

Upheaval on multiple fronts prompted a mix of alarm, concern, hope, and romantic idealism among American Jews. In an era riven by racism, nativism, and inequity on the domestic scene and fraught with social and political tensions, rival claims to American Jewish communal authority burst into the open and spawned the American Jewish Congress movement. Meanwhile, with the eruption of the Great War, the chaos of global conflict plunged the vulnerable east European Jewish population into destitute misery and threatened the fragile stability of the nascent *Yishuv*. American Jews responded to the unprecedented nature and magnitude of these challenges with new strategies for intracommunal organization and cooperation. The network of synagogues and communal vehicles dominated by elite Jewish entrepreneurs, lawyers, and rabbis of central European ancestry provided a first line of defense in response to the crises threatening Jewish communities overseas. Meanwhile, American Jewry's vast and ardent Yiddish-speaking rank-and-file created a host of new communal vehicles and relief frameworks. The groundswell of American Jewish fundraising activity and political activism resulted in the formation of the American Jewish Relief Committee, the Central Relief Committee, and the People's Relief Committee, which subsequently united under the aegis of the Joint Distribution Committee.

III.

The critical year during the war was 1917. The overthrow of Russian tsarism, the idealistic motivation of the United States' entry into the war, and the British conquest of Palestine (the battles of Gaza, Beer Sheva, Jerusalem, and Jaffa occurred between October and December), punctuated by the Balfour Declaration's recognition of Palestine as the "national home" of the Jewish people, stirred a fever of enthusiasm. As a consequence, Zionism acquired influence in American Jewish circles it had not previously enjoyed. The organized movement dated from 1897, and there had been proto-Zionist groups as early as 1882, but the anemic American movement, led by acculturated businessmen, scholars, and Hebraic intelligentsia of modest means, was extremely limited in its size and effectiveness. The coming of war, the neutrality of the United States, the looming probability of the Ottoman empire's dissolution, and the uncertain fate of Palestine's new Jewish society-in-the-making infused American Zionism with a high sense of purpose and renewed energy.

Louis D. Brandeis, who joined the Zionist political fray in 1914 and immediately assumed active leadership of the Federation of American Zionists (FAZ), imbued Zionism in America with instant credibility. Brandeis's singular "persona and mystique," the historian Jonathan D. Sarna observes, brought unparalleled stature, national visibility, and energy to American Zionism.[61] Supplanting the movement's old guard—who, in the words of a Zionist leader in Fort Worth, Texas, "by no means agreed as to their [own] program"[62]—Brandeis swiftly imposed organizational discipline. He recast American Zionism as a national enterprise with taproots in "the Jewish spirit," which he referred to as "our great inheritance," and top roots in "America's fundamental law [which] seeks to make real the brotherhood of man."[63] Brandeis's perspective also mirrored the Progressive era's social tenor and political trends. On a conceptual level, his recalibration of Zionism as a form of "transactional morality" equipped a diverse array of individuals, including the sizable Yiddish-speaking constituency, with "a basis for civic engagement" and a vision of becoming "productive democratic citizens."[64] Meanwhile, at the ground level, American Zionism's "organizational advances," fueled by "general processes" shaping the American Jewish scene, dovetailed with the "eclecticism" of American forms of "ad hoc populism from which it was only one step to an ad hoc nationalism."[65]

The Brandeis group adapted Zionism to the American Jewish outlook by stressing Palestine as a refuge for oppressed Jews and a place where an ideal society would be built. It unapologetically avoided interpreting all lands except Palestine as exile (*galut*). The *Yishuv*, as the philosopher Horace M. Kallen asserted, was to be "a center of reference" and "spiritual capital" to which American Jews "could turn for inspiration."[66] In this way, the Zionist idea appealed to a broad array of American Jews as a Jewish counterpart of Woodrow Wilson's vision of a New World order and the "self-determination of nations."[67] Brandeis himself proved to be an especially eloquent spokesman for American Zionism and an exemplar of the rise of the new American Jewish consciousness. In a public address before the Eastern Council of Reform Rabbis, a New York City-based group founded by Wise as a challenge to the Cincinnati-based Reform establishment, Brandeis addressed the question of divided loyalties:

> Let no American imagine that Zionism is inconsistent with patriotism. Multiple loyalties are objectionable only if they are inconsistent. A man is a better citizen of the United States for being also a loyal citizen of his state, and of his city; for being loyal to his family, and to his profession or trade; for being loyal to his college or lodge. Every Irish American who contributed towards advancing home rule [in the Irish Free State] was a better man and a better American for the sacrifice he made. Every American Jew who aids in advancing the Jewish settlement in Palestine, though he feels that neither he nor his descendants will ever live there, will likewise be a better man and a better American for doing so.[68]

By the summer of 1914, the World Zionist Organization (WZO), headquartered in Europe, was crippled by the outbreak of World War I. Against the backdrop of pressure "on both sides of the Atlantic to shift the leadership of the world body to the United States," the FAZ, renamed the Provisional Executive Committee for General Zionist Affairs (PEC), held an extraordinary conference in September to "discuss taking over the work of the Zionist Central Bureau" in Berlin and "the necessity for united action on the part of American Jewry in the matter of extending relief to Jewish sufferers from the war, and in the event of peace negotiations."[69] In fact, although the WZO formally moved its central office from Berlin to Copenhagen where it remained "officially neutral" and "had the ear both of the Central Powers and the Entente," it was evident that America was to play a leading role in preserving, sustaining, and directing the movement's affairs for the duration of the war.[70] To this end, the conference appointed an executive committee made up of representatives of all Zionist groups, with Brandeis as its chairman. American Zionism's newly sanctioned role vis-à-vis the WZO elevated the PEC's stature in American Jewish affairs and added gravitas to its pronouncements and activity concerning wartime relief and postwar reconstruction. Guided by Brandeis's ambitious organizational vision, the PEC embarked on a countrywide campaign and rallied American Jews to the Zionist cause under the banner of "Men! Money! Discipline!" Within a year, the American movement grew from 12,000 to 20,000 dues-paying members; in the same period, the organization's fundraising coffers climbed from $12,000 to over $170,000 (roughly equivalent to $4,325,000 today).[71]

The Great War, as Rozenblitt and Karp point out, was "a global conflagration involving Jews from several continents and from many different countries" in which there was "no typical 'Jewish' experience."[72] In comparison to European Jews and Ottoman Jews, the experience of "the much larger contingent of American Jews" was characterized by the United States' late entry into and the "sheer brevity" of its involvement in the war, including the participation of roughly a quarter of a million American Jewish servicemen and women.[73]

Even before the United States became a combatant, the war's escalation prompted calls by the Russian Zionist leader Zeev Jabotinsky for the creation of a Jewish Legion, a British-sponsored military auxiliary force, that would recruit American Jews. The concept gained traction in Jewish immigrant circles owing to the publicity and recruitment efforts of David Ben-Gurion, Yitzhak Ben-Zvi, and Pinhas Rutenberg, Zionist leaders expelled by the Turkish regime from Palestine owing to their Russian ancestry. Ben-Gurion, Ben-Zvi, and Rutenberg, each of whom spent extended time in the United States as exiles during the war, played pivotal roles organizing the American regiments of the 39th and 40th Battalions of Royal Fusiliers. The Jewish Legion's task was defined in Wilsonian terms as making the world safe for democracy and in Zionist terms as establishing a Jewish foothold in the Land of Israel. Although the unit's contribution to the total Allied war effort was minimal, it had great symbolic value for American Jews who relished the image of a Jewish military force that combated the stereotype of immigrant Jews as rootless, cowardly, and defenseless.[74]

It was also at this juncture that the engine of British colonial expansion, the exigent circumstances of World War I, and the superlative talents of Chaim Weizmann drove forward the Balfour Declaration—the first public endorsement by a world superpower of the Zionist cause and Jewish national aspirations in Palestine. Indeed, as Israel Zangwill, the revered Anglo-Jewish writer and public intellectual, observed even after the United States joined the Allied war effort: "...Notwithstanding the dominant moral and military weight of America, the center of gravity of the world situation with all of its possibilities" still lay in Britain.[75] What might be described as the rear-guard action of American Zionism—a persistent behind-the-scenes effort that kept channels of communication open between London and Washington—was sparked by Weizmann's request for Brandeis to personally intercede with Wilson and win the president's support for the new British pro-Zionist policy. Brandeis's perch as a close personal adviser to Wilson and the country's best-known American Jewish leader gave added weight to his resonant Progressive-era conception of Jewish national aspirations. Privately, Brandeis was extremely discrete and strategic in his efforts to advise Wilson on matters pertaining to wartime policy including the Zionist cause. In public, prior to his appointment in June 1916 to the US Supreme Court, he championed the campaign to convene the American Jewish Congress.

The American Jewish Congress movement succeeded in orchestrating a countrywide Jewish election in June 1917 in which roughly 335,000 ballots were cast.[76] By this time, the "capitalist-socialist bloc" (a loose coalition of anti-Jewish nationalist forces that cohered around the leadership of the American Jewish Committee and the Jewish labor movement) had compromised, and soon thereafter the Balfour Declaration, endorsed by the United States, appeared to settle the Palestine question.[77] That a turning point had presumably been reached in American and world Jewish affairs was forcefully articulated by a variety of American Zionist leaders, including Stephen S. Wise:

It has come to pass—the day long wished for in all its momentous and farthest-reaching consequences to Israel and the world. The British government, true to a policy of two hundred years of sympathy with and friendship for the Jew, leads the way in indicating to its allies and to the world that the day has come for the establishment in Palestine of a national home for the Jewish people and that it will use its best endeavors to facilitate the achievement of this object.

However important may be Mr. Balfour's declaration on behalf of Great Britain, nothing more than the first step has been taken. We have done no more than pass out of the realm of hope into the field of possibility. This is the hour that will test the soul of the Jew. They who have shared the dream of their people must now serve as they have never served before, and they who, up to this time, have held aloof will find the fullest opportunity for high and devoted service. This is the prime duty of the hour. May not we who have borne the burden of the day in expressing our joy and gratitude call to mind the wisdom and statesmanship of our leaders, who alike in England and America have made possible the coming of the great day—Justice Brandeis, loved and honored leader of Zionists in our own land, and Dr. Chaim Weizmann of England, who has carried the infinitely difficult and delicate negotiations with the British government to the point of glorious triumph? The privilege it has been of all my associates and myself of the Provisional Committee and allied Zionist organizations to hold up the hands of our leaders. The greatest and heaviest of tasks yet lies before us. We summon every

> Jew in America to the post of service and honor—
> under the Zionist flag.[78]

When in December 1918, the American Jewish Congress finally convened—following the British conquest of Palestine and the armistice with Germany—367 delegates from eighty-seven cities gathered for several days of impassioned public debates and stormy plenary negotiations. Mack, Wise, and other leading Zionists, with the support of the eastern European Jewish immigrant community, capitalized on the event to fundamentally alter the terms of the public debate concerning American Jewry's political priorities. A sparkling array of talented left-wing Zionist and pro-Zionist leaders (Chaim Zhitlowsky, Nachman Syrkin, Meyer London, Joseph Barondess, Baruch Zuckerman, and others) underscored the commitment of the rank-and-file to democratic principles and three cardinal issues: minority rights, postwar Jewish reconstruction, and "the development of Palestine into a Jewish commonwealth"—all issues championed by the Brandeis group.[79] The net result was a broad-based platform and a new mandate for organized American Jewry. In the event, the American Jewish Congress appointed Mack and Louis Marshall, both distinguished jurists and venerable communal leaders, as co-chairs of the delegation to join Wilson at the Paris Peace Conference. Well-equipped by dint of their professional stature and political capital, Mack and Marshall brought ample legal and diplomatic skill to the delegation which "symbolized unity" in American Jewish life.[80] They bridged the divide between American Jewry's old and new guard, personified the balance of forces apparent at the Congress, and served as a moderating influence on the delegation's other distinguished figures who represented "nearly all elements in the American Jewish community."[81]

IV.

An Equal Share of Freedom throws new light on several important overlapping and interconnected dimensions of American,

Jewish, and world history in the World War I era. Paying close attention to the Balfour Declaration as a hub around which to explore the period's unfolding and turbulent social, cultural, and political developments, the volume demonstrates the complex nature of Jewish ethno-national consciousness in the American setting and the impact of Zionism on US wartime and post- war activity.

In chapter 1, Daniel J. Tichenor argues that Woodrow Wilson, like other Progressive-era thinkers and activists, entered the White House devoted to reforming the principles and structures of American constitutional government, which he considered too outmoded to meet the demands of disquieting social and economic changes. Building on the example of Theodore Roosevelt, he sought to fulfill a Progressive reform agenda through strong, executive-centered government that rested upon vigorous leadership and recast the presidency in both domestic and foreign affairs. Yet the impact of his presidency ultimately reflected contending strands of American Progressivism, juxtaposing ideals of social justice and democratization with new forms of repression in the name of white supremacy and national security. Tichenor's study maps the contours of Wilson's presidency and helps to contextualize the dynamic response of America's ethnic and racial minorities, including American Jews, to the changing landscape of the home front during World War I.

In chapter 2, Christopher M. Sterba contextualizes the Balfour Declaration as but one in a series of earth-shaking events that transformed American Jewish attitudes toward the United States' participation in the Great War. Focusing on the wartime responses and actions of New York's eastern European Jews as a case study, he explains why Gotham's Jewish immigrants, who above all wished for tsarist Russia's defeat, eventually came to strongly support the American war effort. The shift in this regard reflected the deepening engagement of immigrants with the public life of their adopted country and raises important questions about transnational identity and historical contingency.

In chapter 3, Jessica Cooperman analyzes American Jewry's response to the implications of the Balfour Declaration, particularly the Jewish Welfare Board's (JWB) concern over how the declaration and the Zionist project might be framed and discussed in the United States. In the months following the declaration's proclamation, the JWB, including its chairman Colonel Harry Cutler, found itself in a delicate position as it sought to represent Judaism and advocate for Jewish soldiers and sailors in the American military, while simultaneously working to prove American Jews' patriotism and dedication to their country.

In chapter 4, Philip Hollander investigates the impact of dedicated eastern European Hebraists who arrived in the United States in the first decade of the twentieth century. In small clubs in various New York neighborhoods and in major cities throughout the Northeast and Midwest, Hebraist groups functioned like fraternal organizations or *landsmanshaftn* (mutual aid societies) and assisted their members in striking root in America. Among the American institutions established by Hebraists were the seminal Hebrew literary journal *Hatoren* (The Mast), the Histadrut Haivrit Beamerikah (Organization of Hebrew in America), and a network of Hebrew schools and Hebrew training colleges. While they never renounced the Land of Israel's significance for Zionism or Hebraism, the Hebraists saw Hebrew culture as a way for American Jews to cultivate their particularity and lead richer American lives.

In chapter 5, I consider Zionism's impact in the American Jewish setting and reassess the relationship between Woodrow Wilson and the so-called Brandeis group, a cohort of American Jewish leaders grouped around Louis D. Brandeis, the famous "People's Attorney" and first Jew to be appointed to the US Supreme Court. Anxious to harmonize the Zionist political agenda and the Wilson administration's wartime strategy, I contend the Brandeis group mobilized a national campaign for the American Jewish Congress and rallied American Jews in support of Zionism—with the aim of sustaining Wilson's support for the Zionist cause and winning the president's endorsement of the Balfour Declaration. Despite the collapse of Wilson's postwar efforts, the US Congress endorsed the Balfour Declaration in the joint Lodge-Fish Resolution, which was signed into law by President Warren G. Harding and in turn codified America's new postwar Palestine policy.

In chapter 6, Gary Phillip Zola conducts a close reading of the wartime diary of Jacob Rader Marcus. Although hundreds of soldier diaries have survived from the Great War, Marcus's diary is arguably sui generis. It is the only known record by a highly educated, strongly identified American Jewish doughboy. By examining Marcus's daily entries into his journal, almost all of which were made in "real time," we become historical witnesses to the many ways that military service and, more generally, the war itself influenced Marcus's inchoate convictions concerning the future of Jewish life in America, the intractability of antisemitism, the debate on Zionism, and the allure of the secular over the sacred.

In chapter 7, Sarah Imhoff examines the Zionist activist Jessie Sampter's thought as a political-theological story—a narrative about how someone could simultaneously espouse internationalism, nationalism, and pacifism. In a richly textured case study, Imhoff argues that Sampter's worldview was not wholly unique and in fact her synthesis of internationalism and Jewish nationalism was quite typical of many American Jews. In short, Sampter's embodied life and political life were profoundly characterized by apparent dissonance—and yet, she was committed to living with seemingly incongruous tensions.

In chapter 8, Pnina Lahav scrutinizes the case of Golda Meir in relation to the Balfour Declaration. When the declaration was issued, Lahav explains, Golda was nineteen years old and living with her parents in Milwaukee, Wisconsin. Within three decades, as one of the leaders of the *Yishuv,* she led the struggle to create a Jewish state. At that stage, she was quite involved in the implementation, or lack thereof, of the Balfour Declaration. This chapter is divided into two parts. In the first part, Lahav investigates history "from the bottom up": What did ordinary American Jews, Golda included, think of the declaration when it was made? In the second part, she explores history "from the top down": What did Golda, as a leader of the ruling Mapai party (Workers Party of the Land of Israel), think and do to challenge the British interpretation of the Balfour Declaration and promote the Labor Zionist vision of an independent Jewish state?

In chapter 9, Zohar Segev shows how American Zionist support was essential to the ability of Chaim Weizmann and the Zionist movement to build the Jewish national home in the wake of the Balfour Declaration. Yet the leadership of the American Zionist movement from the 1920s through the partition of Palestine in 1947, Segev argues, was not content with simply providing economic and political support. Rather, Louis D. Brandeis, Abba Hillel Silver, and other key figures sought to use their transnational influence and power to shape the development and structure of the Zionist movement, its policies, and the future of the Jewish national home. In this way, Brandeis, Silver, and other key figures, all of whom cherished American social, cultural, and political norms and principles, imbued American Zionism and the Zionist movement's program of Jewish state-building with a distinctive American Jewish sensibility.

In the afterword to the volume, Susannah Heschel examines recent trends in the historiography of Zionism and Balfour Declaration and probes the complex history of the declaration's impact on modern Jewish identity and politics, Jewish-Arab relations, and geopolitical developments involving Israel, Palestine, and the Muslim world. Heschel's insightful and generative assessment expands the range of possibilities for thinking about the declaration's lasting significance, its role in shaping the complex and fraught relations of Jews and Arabs before and since the establishment of the State of Israel, and the possibility of finding a path forward in which the Balfour Declaration's "positive contributions" may constructively inform "Israelis and Palestinians seeking peace."[82]

Last, it is worth noting that the images interspersed throughout the volume—accompanied by headnotes and primary sources that contextualize their historical and cultural significance—constitute a sort of overarching visual essay that parallels and highlights many of the key themes, events, and developments explored in the chapters.

In sum, *An Equal Share of Freedom* seeks to overturn timeworn assumptions that have long shaped the fields of American history and modern Jewish history. It makes the case for the centrality of World War I in the context of American Jewish history. Taken as a whole, it demonstrates the war's profound impact on American Jewish life and the transformation of American Jewry's relationship to wider American society. It underscores the impact of Zionism on the American Jewish experience and the extent to which American Jewry's national consciousness and the future direction of the Zionist project were forged in the crucible of the Great War. To be sure, the scholarship presented here does not claim to portray American Jewry's wartime history in its totality. It is our hope, however, that the volume highlights some of the myriad and fruitful possibilities for expanding and deepening our understanding of American Jews during World War I and the shared history of American society and the Jewish people in the twentieth century.

ENDNOTES

1 "Jewish Congress to Name Envoys,"*Washington Times* (December 17, 1918), 6.

2 *Ibid.*

3 Quoted in Chaim Weizmann, *Trial and Error: The Autobiography of Chaim Weizmann* (New York: Harper and Brothers, 1949), 208.

4 "Letter (Endorsing Zionist Movement)" of Woodrow Wilson to Stephen S. Wise (September 1, 1918), in *Supplement to the Messages and Papers of the Presidents, Covering the Second Term of Woodrow Wilson, March 4, 1917 to March 4, 1921* (Washington, DC: Bureau of National Literature, 1921), 8575.

5 Arthur Koestler, *Promise and Fulfillment* (London: Macmillan, 1949), 4.

6 Jonathan Schneer, *The Balfour Declaration: The Origins of the Arab-Israeli Conflict* (New York: Random House, 2012), 369.

7 Martin Kramer, "The Forgotten Truth About the Balfour Declaration," *Mosaic* (June 5, 2017), 21, https://scholar.harvard.edu/files/martinkramer/files/forgotten_truth_balfour_declaration.pdf.

8 Mark Tessler, *A History of the Israeli-Palestinian Conflict* (Bloomington: Indiana University Press, 1994), 149–150.

9 Ezra Mendelsohn, *On Modern Jewish Politics* (New York: Oxford University Press, 1993), 83.

10 Anita Shapira, *Land and Power: The Zionist Resort to Force, 1881–1948* (New York: Oxford University Press, 1992), 84.

11 Michael Brenner, *In Search of Israel: The History of an Idea* (Princeton, NJ: Princeton University Press, 2018), 12, 99.

12 On American Jews and World War I, see Carole Fink, "Jewish Diplomacy and the Politics of War and Peace," chap. 3; Jessica Cooperman, "Unintentional Pluralists: Military Policy, Jewish Servicemen, and the Development of Tri-Faith America during World War I," chap. 12; Gennady Estraikh, "American Yiddish Socialists at the Wartime Crossroads: Patriotism and Nationalism versus Proletarian Internationalism," chap. 13; and M. M. Silver, "Louis Marshall during World War I: Change and Continuity in Jewish Culture and Politics," chap. 14, in *World War I and the Jews: Conflict and Transformation in Europe, the Middle East, and America*, eds. Marsha L. Rozenblit and Jonathan Karp (New York: Berghann, 2017).

13 See Sarah Panter, "Between Inclusion and Exclusion: The Experiences of Jewish Soldiers in Europe and the USA, 1914–1918," in *The Jewish Experience of the First World War*, eds. Edward Madigan and Gideon Reuveni (London: Palgrave Macmillan, 2019), 159–82.

14 Jonathan Karp and Marsha L. Rozenblit, "Introduction: On the Significance of World War I and the Jews," in *World War I and the Jews: Conflict and Transformation in Europe, the Middle East, and America*, eds. Marsha L. Rozenblit and Jonathan Karp (New York: Berghann, 2017), 5–6.

15 Jonathan Frankel, *Prophecy and Politics: Socialism, Nationalism, and the Russian Jews, 1862–1917* (Cambridge: Cambridge University Press, 1984), 453.

16 *Ibid.*, 473.

17 Quoted in Leonard Dinnerstein, *Antisemitism in America* (New York: Oxford University Press, 1994), 37, 46, 61.

18 Henry James, *Embarrassments* (London: William Heinemann, 1896), 69.

19 Madison Grant, "The Racial Transformation of America," *North American Review* 219, no. 820 (March 1924), 352.

20 "House Passes Burnett Bill," *New York Times* (December 19, 1912), 1.

21 Quoted in Harold S. Wechsler, "The Rationale for Restriction: Ethnicity and College Admission in America, 1910–1980," *American Quarterly* 36, no. 5 (Winter 1984), 650–51.

22 John Higham, *Strangers in the Land: Patterns of American Nativism, 1860–1925*, revised ed. (New Brunswick, NJ: Rutgers University Press, 2002), 277–85.

23 Abram S. Isaacs, "The Jews of the United States," *American Jewish Year Book* 1 (1899), 14.

24 Joseph Jacobs, "B. Jewish Population of the United States," *American Jewish Year Book* 17 (1914), vi.

25 *Ibid.*, 348–50.

26 *Ibid.*, 358.

27 *Ibid.*

28 Herman Bernstein, "Preface," *American Jewish Year Book* 17 (1914), vi.

29 Irving Howe, *World of Our Fathers: The Journey of the East European Jews to America and the Life They Found and Made* (New York: Simon and Schuster, 1976), 411.

30 *Ibid.*

31 See "Table V. Jewish Migrations, 1881–1930" and "Table VI. Jewish and General Immigration to the United States from 1899 to 1944" in *The Jew in the Modern World: A Documentary History*, eds. Paul Mendes-Flohr and Jehuda Reinharz, third ed. (New York, Oxford University Press, 2011), 883.

32 Judah L. Magnes, "Memorandum: A Yiddish Morning Daily" (c. January 1913) in *Dissenter in Zion: From the Writings of Judah L. Magnes*, ed. Arthur A. Goren (Cambridge: Harvard University Press, 1982), 132.

33 Quoted in "Chicago Convention Calls for American Jewish Congress on February 22," *Sentinel* 21, no. 4 (January 28, 1916), 9.

34 Israel Friedlaender, "The Division Between German and Russian Jews" (1915), in *The Jew in the Modern World: A Documentary History*, eds. Paul Mendes-Flohr and Jehuda Reinharz, third ed. (New York, Oxford University Press, 2011), 545–46.

35 Moses Rischin, "Introduction" to *Like All the Nations? The Life and Legacy of Judah L. Magnes*, eds. William M. Brinner and Moses Rischin (Albany, NY: State University of New York Press, 1987), 7; Daniel P. Kotzin, *Judah L. Magnes: An American Jewish Nonconformist* (Syracuse, NY: Syracuse University Press, 2010), 74, 95, 128.

36 "Million Dollars Raised for War Victims," *American Jewish World* 2, no. 17 (December 31, 1915), 323.

37 Quoted in *ibid.*, 323–25.

38 See the following entries in *American Jewish Year Book* 17 (1914): (a) "Jewish National Organizations of the United States," 276–311, (b) "New Jewish Local Organizations in the United States," 312–27, and (c) "Jewish Periodicals Appearing in the United States," 328–34.

39 Gabriel Sheffer, *Diaspora Politics: At Home Abroad* (Cambridge: Cambridge University Press, 2003), 9, 40.

40 Ezra Mendelsohn, *On Modern Jewish Politics* (New York: Oxford University Press, 1993), 132.

41 Mendelsohn, *On Modern Jewish Politics*, 132; Matthew Frye Jacobson, *Special Sorrows: The Diasporic Imagination of Irish, Polish, and Jewish Immigrants in the United States*, reprint (Berkeley: University of California Press, 2002), 53.

42 Lucy S. Dawidowicz, *The Jewish Presence: Essays on Identity and History* (New York: Holt, Rinehart and Winston, 1977), 121.

43 *Ibid.*, 121–22.

44 Stephen S. Wise to Maximilian H. Heller, February 6, 1915, Box 6, Folder 8, Maximilian H. Heller Papers (MS-33), Jacob Rader Marcus Center of the American Jewish Archives, Cincinnati, OH (hereafter: "AJA").

45 *Ibid.*

46 Morris Frommer, "The American Jewish Congress: A History, 1914–1950 (PhD diss., Ohio State University, 1978), 60–61, 103; Frankel, *Prophecy and Politics*, 516–19.

47 Quoted in "Zionist Leaders Make Appeals at Big Gatherings in Boston and About $7000 is Contributed for the Cause," *B'nai B'rith Messenger* 18, no. 33 (October 9, 1914), 9.

48 *Ibid.*49 Quoted in "A Million Jews Favor a Congress," *Sentinel* 20, no. 4 (October 22, 1915), 2.

50 Quoted in *ibid.*

51 Quoted in *ibid.*

52 Quoted in *ibid.*, 2, 3.

53 Quoted in *ibid.*, 3.

54 Quoted in *ibid.*

55 Quoted in *ibid.*

56 Karen Brodkin, "How Did Jews Become White Folks?" in *Off White: Readings on Power, Privilege, and Resistance*, eds. Michelle Fine, Lois Weis, Linda Powell Pruitt, and April Burns, second ed. (New York: Routledge, 2004), 17.

57 Quoted in "Chicago Convention Calls for American Jewish Congress on February 22," *Sentinel* 21, no. 4 (January 28, 1916), 2.

58 Michael S. Neiberg, *The Path to War: How the First World War Created Modern America* (New York: Oxford University Press, 2016), 198.

59 Salo W. Baron, "The Emancipation Movement and American Jewry" in Salo W. Baron, *Steeled by Adversity: Essays and Addresses on American Jewish Life*, ed. Jeannette Meisel Baron (Philadelphia: Jewish Publication Society, 1971), 96.

60 Quoted in (a) Kirsten Fermaglich, 'Too Long, Too Foreign... Too Jewish': Jews, Name Changing, and Family Mobility in New York City, 1917–1942," *Journal of American Ethnic History* 34, no. 3 (Spring 2015), 50; (b) quoted in "Chicago Convention Calls for American Jewish Congress on February 22," *Sentinel* 21, no. 4 (January 28, 1916), 3.

61 Jonathan D. Sarna, "'The Greatest Jew in the World since Jesus Christ': The Jewish Legacy of Louis D. Brandeis," *American Jewish History* 81, nos. 3–4 (Spring-Summer 1994), 354.

62 "Texas News," *Jewish Herald* 4, no. 15 (December 28, 1911), 2.

63 *The Jew in the Modern World*, eds. Mendes-Flohr and Reinharz, 556.

64 Paul Stob, "Louis D. Brandeis and the Rhetoric of Transactional Morality," *Rhetoric and Public Affairs* 14, no. 2 (2011), 279.

65 Evyatar Friesel, "Brandeis' Role in American Zionism Historically Reconsidered," *American Jewish History* 69, no. 1 (September 1979), 36; Frankel, *Prophecy and Politics*, 454, 461–62.

66 Quoted in Daniel Greene, "A Chosen People in a Pluralist Nation: Horace Kallen and the Jewish-American Experience," *Religion and American Culture* 16, no. 2 (Summer 2006), 171.

67 Wise also advocated appealing to the British government to grant "home rule to the Irish people." See Wise's letter to Woodrow Wilson (April 11, 1917) in *The Papers of Woodrow Wilson*, ed. Arthur S. Link, vol. 42 (Princeton, NJ: Princeton University Press, 1983), 41–42, 44–45.

68 Louis D. Brandeis, "Zionism is Consistent with American Patriotism," in *The Jew in the Modern World: A Documentary History*, eds. Paul Mendes-Flohr and Jehuda Reinharz, third ed. (New York, Oxford University Press, 2011), 555.

69 Melvin I. Urofsky, *Louis D. Brandeis: A Life* (New York: Pantheon Books, 2009), 426; "Federation of American Zionists," *B'nai B'rith Messenger* 18, no. 29 (September 11, 1914), 8–9.

70 Marsha Rozenblit, "The European Jewish World 1914–1919: What Changed?" in *World War I and the Jews: Conflict and Transformation in Europe, the Middle East, and America*, eds. Marsha L. Rozenblit and Jonathan Karp (New York: Berghahn, 2017), 40.

71 *American Jewish Year Book* (1915), 292; Urofsky, *Louis D. Brandeis*, 418–23. By 1919, the FAZ, renamed the Zionist Organization of America (ZOA), boasted over 176,000 members, a national executive made up of many of American Jewry's most distinguished and wealthy communal leaders, and a robust countrywide fundraising apparatus. See *American Jewish Year Book* 22 (1920), 319.

72 Karp and Rozenblit, "Introduction," 4–5.

73 *Ibid.*

74 The Jewish Legion assumed an importance in the public sphere disproportionate to its actual wartime role. Both the 38th and 39th Battalions were stationed in Palestine near Jericho. On September 22, 1918, the Jewish Legion routed the Turks from a strategic ford of the Jordan River, north of the lake of Galilee, and helped to open the way to Damascus for the Australian and New Zealand cavalry. After the war's conclusion, a group of 280 American legionnaires provided the nucleus for the establishment of Avihayil, a *moshav ovdim* (workers' cooperative) near the oceanside town of Netanya. The former legionnaires comprised a significant quotient of the 600 American Jews who settled in Palestine during the 1919–23 postwar wave of Zionist immigration.

75 Telegram from Israel Zangwill to Henry Hurwitz (October 16, 1917), Jacob H. Schiff papers (Intercollegiate Menorah Association folder), 453/1, AJA.

76 Silver, "Louis Marshall during World War I," 314.

77 Quoted in Jonathan Frankel, "The Jewish Socialists and the American Jewish Congress Movement," *YIVO Annual of Jewish Social Science* 16 (New York: YIVO Institute for Jewish Research, 1976), 286.

78 "It Has Come to Pass—Eloquent Utterance of Foremost Jewish Orator in America Over the Great Prospect for Establishment of Jewish States in Palestine Made Possible by British Declaration and Endorsement of Allies," *Charlevoix County Herald*, August 2, 1918, 6.

79 Quoted in Harry Barnard, *The Forging of an American Jew: The Life and Times of Julian W. Mack* (New York: Herzl Press, 1974), 241; Frankel, *Prophecy and Politics*, 541–46.

80 Gerald Sorin, *A Time for Building: The Third Migration, 1880–1920* (Baltimore: Johns Hopkins University Press, 1992), 213.

81 *Ibid.*

82 Susannah Heschel, Afterword, "The Balfour Declaration in Historical and Political Perspective," 418.

William Charles Morris, *Can He Produce the Harmony?* February 1919

Source: William Charles Morris, "Can He Produce the Harmony?" *Brooklyn Citizen* (February 1919), The Ohio State University, Billy Ireland Cartoon Library and Museum, Columbus, OH.

In January 1918, President Woodrow Wilson announced his Fourteen Points plan for European peace. Intended to promote democracy in Europe and the world, it sought to solve the problems that led to World War I and called for arms reductions, free trade, open diplomacy, and the creation of the League of Nations, a new international organization to settle disputes without war. Other points called for national sovereignty for peoples in east central Europe as well as guarantees of civic and religious freedoms for local religious minorities, including the Jews. Within this context, a vigorous public discussion also emerged concerning the postwar future of the Middle East and the wartime Balfour Declaration's commitment to a Jewish national home in Palestine.

In response to Wilson's Fourteen Points, the graphic artist Charles William Morris (1874–1940) published "Can He Produce the Harmony?" in the *Brooklyn Citizen*, a newspaper edited by Andrew McLean (1880–1922), the influential Scottish immigrant journalist and Democratic Party political activist. In the editorial cartoon, Morris depicts a blissfully unaware Wilson, baton in hand as musical notes waft through the air, conducting a cacophonous "All Nations" orchestra in the "World Peace Symphony." The orchestra's musicians, sheet music, and instruments are variously identified as "Jugoslavs" (sic), Belgium, Japan, Poland, Russia, France, Spain, Sweden, Italy, England, Greece, Holland, Portugal, Norway, and (in a racialized stereotype) China.

— M.A.R

CHAPTER 1

WOODROW WILSON, PROGRESSIVISM, AND THE GREAT WAR: CONFLICTED LEADERSHIP IN A NEW CENTURY

DANIEL J. TICHENOR

Embodying many of the rival strands of early twentieth-century Progressivism, the presidency of Woodrow Wilson was ambitious, transformative, and ultimately suffused by contradictions between democratic and illiberal agendas.[1] Few of Wilson's predecessors were more determined to make the presidency a leading instrument of the popular will, and few were as successful in advancing major domestic policy reforms long favored by the public. Among the stark disparities that characterized Wilson's politics, a divergent attitude to American Jews and African Americans stands out as especially striking. In an era of overt antisemitism, Wilson sustained many visible and close relationships with prominent American Jews including the lawyers Louis D. Brandeis (whom he later appointed to the US Supreme Court), Henry Morgenthau (his appointee as US ambassador to Turkey), and Samuel Untermeyer, the financiers Bernard Baruch (his appointee as chairman of the War Industries Board) and Jacob H. Schiff, the philanthropist Nathan Straus, and Rabbi Stephen S. Wise. He also enjoyed the acclaim of an American Jewish public that celebrated his philosemitism, support for abrogating the Russo-American Treaty of 1832 owing to the tsarist regime's refusal to honor the US passports of American Jews, and liberal views on eastern and southern European immigration (he consistently opposed anti-immigrant restrictionist measures). By contrast, Wilson's myopic view of African Americans as "an ignorant and inferior race,"[2] a product of his racist upbringing in the Deep South, fueled his anti-Black delusion that "no matter how much we may deplore" the institutionalization of Jim Crow "things do not happen rapidly in the world, and prejudices are slow to be uprooted."[3] Segregation, he concluded, stemmed from "the genuine desire to serve the convenience and agreeable feelings of everybody concerned."4 In sum, although the Wilson administration expressed support for issues of paramount concern to American Jews and opened its doors to American Jewish leaders, it steadfastly opposed African American civil rights, not only tolerating, but at times openly promoting, racial discrimination.[5]

On the world stage, Wilson gradually developed a wartime foreign policy that made the conflict with Germany a crusade for freedom and democracy around the globe. Wartime footing, however, convinced Wilson and his subordinates that unwavering order and patriotism were essential on the home front; dissenters, pacifists, German Americans, media critics, socialists, and others faced harsh repression.[6] By 1919, Wilson saw himself as especially well-suited to build a lasting peace among nations on the basis of international cooperation, democratization, liberty, sovereignty, and self-determination. In the end, his vision for postwar reconstruction would be defeated most decisively by the US Senate, which rejected both Wilson's independent course in foreign policy and his signature diplomatic achievement, the League of Nations. Amid major social, economic, and international dislocations, the Wilson administration envisioned a modern presidency that projected new kinds of popular, legislative, and world leadership. In its form and substance, however, Wilson's presidency exhibited important tensions and conflicts in both times of peace and war.[7]

Wilson was an unlikely American president. In a Democratic party torn between the fiery populism of William Jennings Bryan and northern party machines like Tammany Hall, Wilson was nominated in 1912 as a late compromise choice on the forty-sixth ballot of a deadlocked national convention. He had a scant two years of elected political experience as New Jersey's governor, having numbered among a wave of newly elected progressive Democrats who gained office in 1910. Wilson's victory in the general election owed significantly to the division of Republican votes between incumbent President William Howard Taft and the historic Progressive Party candidacy of Theodore Roosevelt; Wilson won 42 percent of the vote, while Taft and Roosevelt split 50.5 percent (the Socialist candidate, Eugene V. Debs, garnered 6 percent). It was a campaign that featured markedly different ideas about how the United States should respond to major dislocations in the social, economic, and global orders.[8]

At the same convention that nominated Wilson, the Democratic party adopted a platform that expressed deep suspicion of executive power, calling for presidents to serve a single term. Yet Wilson had no intention to diminish the power of the White House. Indeed, he entered office in 1913 deeply impressed by the possibilities of Theodore Roosevelt's reinvention of the American presidency as an "energetic steward" of the people.[9] This scholar-politician was committed to making the executive office into a vehicle of democratic activism and policy innovation, with a focus on meeting the challenges of a new twentieth- century world.

For Progressive era reformers like Wilson, the goal was to rededicate the presidency to direct popular leadership and to place the White House at the center of growing federal government commitments. The audacious hope—or conceit—of Progressives was to make Lincoln's extraordinary leadership during the Civil War and the religiosity of abolitionists that the battle against slavery spurred into enduring features of American politics. Thus, members of Congress were no longer understood as more authentic representatives of the people, but rather as obstreperous actors who were compromised by the partial interests of their states and districts, powerful business lobbies, and by the arcane, antimajoritarian rules of the legislative branch. The recrudescence of localized party organizations that preempted the moral struggles of the Civil War and Reconstruction also came under fire as "boss-ruled" and irrevocably corrupt, leading to reforms that weakened parties as checks on presidential power. By contrast, many Progressive reformers saw the modern presidency that emerged in the early twentieth century as a dynamic force that might give institutional form to a national democracy. "America is coming out of the leading strings of parties and is beginning to transact the great business of humanity," Wilson proclaimed.[10]

During a first term focused on modernizing what Wilson considered an outmoded constitutional system, his administration sought to make governing institutions more responsive to popular majorities through a dramatic set of progressive policy reforms that combined "new freedom" (authored by Louis D. Brandeis) and "new nationalism" (associated with Herbert Croly and Roosevelt) principles. In particular, his presidency embraced two key elements of Roosevelt's new nationalism: interpreting and shaping mass public opinion and deploying national administrative power. Wilson recalibrated TR's approach by joining direct appeals to the public with a new form of partisanship where the president, rather than Congress, would "stand at the intersection of party organization and national popular opinion"—where he might "harness each to great national effect."[11] Poaching from the Progressives' platform, he reversed the emblematic stand of his own party on business regulation and pressed for the creation of a Federal Trade Commission with broad discretion in moving against unfair practices. Similarly, Wilson persuaded the Democratic Congress to accept a Federal Reserve Act that established a board to oversee the national banking and currency system. In each case, Wilson overcame the Democratic Party's traditional antipathy to national administrative power, suggesting that with the advance of progressive democracy, party leaders in Congress were induced to sacrifice programmatic principles to maintain the White House.[12]

Wilson's institutional and policy innovations drew the attention of groups and movements fighting for democratic inclusion. Ethnic and immigrant groups found a defender in Wilson during his first term, as he repeatedly vetoed nativist legislation designed to impose draconian restrictions on southern and eastern European immigration. Yet Americans subjected to racial subjugation discovered that Wilson's conceptions of liberal democratic reform were fused with deeply entrenched commitments to white supremacy. Wilson, a native of Virginia elected to the White House in large part because of white Southern support, allowed his administration to actively promote racial segregation in the national government's departments and agencies. Moreover, Wilson bowed to pressure from southern Democrats in his patronage appointments: he appointed only two African Americans during his first term, while he dismissed many Black incumbents and put pressure on others to resign.[13] During a dramatic confrontation with African American leaders at the White House on November 12, 1914, that made the front page of the *New York Times,* Wilson again argued "the policy of segregation had been enforced for the comfort and best interests of both races in order to overcome friction." The president also told his visitors the practice would continue, assuring them that segregation would nurture "the independent development… of the Negro race."[14]

Wilson's racist personnel policies, his seeming indifference to, if not endorsement of D. W. Griffith's landmark film *The Birth of a Nation* (1915), and his deafening silence in the face of growing mob violence against African Americans ensured the National Association for the Advancement of Colored People's (NAACP) commitment to public protest and other forms of direct action "commanded the loyalty of the majority of educated Blacks."[15] During the 1916 election, W.E.B. Du Bois "called a plague" on any major presidential candidate because "the Negro must expect from him, as chief executive, the neglect, indifference and misunderstanding" of lynching, disenfranchisement, and segregation.[16] Yet civil rights activists, mobilizing in opposition to lynching, did not feel they could give up on the White House; they still believed, as Megan Ming Francis argues, that "the road to racial equality went through the executive branch."[17] Tellingly, Alice Paul and women suffragettes drew the same conclusion as they sought to harness the power and authority of the modern presidency to advance their cause, pressing Wilson with confrontational protests from his first inauguration through World War I.[18] Hence, the NAACP, which spearheaded the campaign against mob violence, "realized that in order for its program of political protest to succeed," their organizations "would have to continue to work to change Wilson's attitude on racial issues."[19]

Shortly after Wilson began his second term, riots in East Saint Louis were among the worst outbreaks of urban violence the United States experienced in peacetime. During the summer of 1917, urban and racial tensions resulting from Black migration out of the South exploded into a brutal race war, with hundreds of African Americans shot or lynched by angry white mobs. Marcus Garvey, a Jamaican-born champion of Black nationalism, condemned the riot as "one of the bloodiest outrages against mankind," a "wholesale massacre of our people."[20] The victims were murdered "for no other reason than they are Black people seeking an industrial chance in a country that they have labored for three hundred years to make great."[21] It was time, Garvey told his Harlem audience, "to lift one's voice against the savagery of a people who claim to be the dispensers of democracy."[22] Just as the women's movement had used the exigencies of war to pressure Wilson into supporting women's suffrage, so civil rights leaders hoped to take advantage of the president's preoccupation with a unified war effort to support their campaign against white mob violence.[23] Wilson's idealistic progressive principles did not include the protection of civil rights or liberties; to the contrary, his view that the war was a moral crusade actually inspired intolerance toward those who disagreed. Indeed, the struggle between the Wilson administration and wartime dissenters, pacifists, and free speech advocates fueled the creation of a new movement that culminated with formation of the American Civil Liberties Union (ACLU).[24]

The First World War deeply divided Progressive reformers who fought against racial injustice. The prominent social justice reformer Jane Addams joined with other anti-imperialists in resisting US involvement in the war. She and other war opponents, including the well-known American Jewish figure Lillian D. Wald, who served as president of the American Union Against Militarism, protested that the nation should use its "vast neutral power to extend democracy throughout the world."[25] Addams was a revered cofounder of the NAACP, but her antiwar position put her at odds with Du Bois, who calculated that an international conflict framed between democracy and autocracy was "full of social possibilities."[26] As his July 1918 *Crisis* editorial "Close Ranks" read, "Let us, while the war lasts, forget our special grievances and close our ranks shoulder to shoulder with our white fellow citizens and the allied nations that are fighting for democracy."[27]

Du Bois was hardly alone in being moved by the possibilities raised by Wilson's vision of internationalism, "self-ruling people," and the "self-determination of nations" as core aims of the US involvement in the "Great War."[28] The "Brandeis group," as Mark A. Raider's chapter in this volume highlights, likewise seized upon these ideals and opportunities to enmesh American and Zionist wartime goals. Wilson eloquently appealed to the nation to abandon traditional positions of neutrality in European conflicts to advance a more just and democratic world order. "It is a fearful thing to lead this great peaceful people into war, into the most terrible and disastrous of all wars," Wilson declared. "But, the right is more precious than peace, and we shall fight for... a universal division of right by such a concert of free peoples as shall bring peace and safety to all nations and make the world itself at last free."[29] Significantly, Wilson's vision of expansive freedom and democracy abroad was coupled with draconian social controls and repression of civil liberties at home.

When we look back at the World War I today, the immediate dangers posed by the conflict to the nation's safety seem modest compared to those of the Civil War, World War II, or 9/11 and the war on terror. But to many Americans of the early twentieth century, the war's threats to domestic security were significant. They were especially alarmed by the prospects of espionage and sedition on the home front, fears that were heightened by presumed disloyalty among the nation's large foreign-born population. Wilson, credited by executive scholars with consolidating the popular rhetorical presidency, used his "bully pulpit" in a manner that stoked these anxieties.[30] Although Congress delegated extraordinary powers to the executive branch during the war, Wilson also led the pressure campaign to win significant delegatory statutes, implemented them with zeal, labored to keep them intact well after the hostilities of war ceased, and undertook a variety of independent actions that further limited civil liberties. Let us focus our attention on a few telling examples of how Wilson influenced and dealt with the security-liberty balance.

Wilson's wartime rhetoric fueled nativist and anti-German sentiment in the United States, as well as both popular and official intolerance of any overt expression of antiwar beliefs. After the sinking of the *Lusitania* in July 1915, Wilson warned the public that significant portions of the country's foreign-born population, both naturalized citizens and newly arrived immigrants, imperiled national security. "The gravest threats against our national peace and safety have been uttered within our borders," he declared. "There are citizens of the United States, I blush to admit, born under other flags but welcomed by our generous naturalization laws to the full freedom and opportunity of America, who have poured the poison of disloyalty into the very arteries of our national life."[31]

On the same day that Wilson's War Resolution passed Congress (April 6, 1917), Wilson issued an executive order imposing regulations for controlling noncitizens of German ancestry living in the country. The regulations included an extensive list of restrictions on the movement, employment, property, and activities of these so-called enemy aliens. These enemy aliens were required to register and provide fingerprints to the federal government, and they were subject to summary arrests by federal officials. During the course of the war, more than 6,300 noncitizens of German descent were arrested and more than 2,300 were confined to internment camps.[32] Wilson issued a secret executive order the next day that empowered federal bureaucratic heads to remove any employee considered a loyalty risk "by reason of his conduct, sympathies, or utterances, or because of other reasons growing out of the war."[33] Publicly, Wilson warned German Americans and legal permanent residents that if they demonstrated an ounce of disloyalty, "it will be dealt with with a firm hand of stern repression."[34]

Wilson also demanded legislation in 1917 authorizing his administration to limit press and speech freedoms. "From the very outset of the present war," Wilson averred, Germany "has filled our unsuspecting communities and even our offices of government with spies and set criminal intrigues everywhere afoot against our national unity."[35] Congress responded to Wilson's urging with passage of the Espionage Act of 1917, which made it a crime for anyone to convey information that might hurt the operations or success of the US armed forces or promote the success of its enemies. Section 3 of the law stipulated sentences of up to twenty years in prison for those who "shall willfully cause or attempt to cause insubordination, disloyalty, mutiny, or refusal of duty in the military or naval forces of the United States, or shall willfully obstruct the recruitment or enlistment service of the United States."[36] One year after the law was enacted, Eugene V. Debs, the Socialist Party presidential candidate, was arrested and sentenced to ten years in prison for making a speech that "obstructed recruiting."[37] Two thousand others were prosecuted under the Espionage Act, including roughly 150 leaders of the Industrial Workers of the World (IWW). Additional delegatory statutes gave Wilson an unprecedented hold over the nation's economic life, as well as its communication and transportation systems.

Wilson's postmaster general, Albert Burleson, was vested with vast authority to suppress critical opinion during World War I. Under the Espionage Act, the postmaster general was empowered to declare any magazine, newspaper, circular, pamphlet, letter, or other material that violated the statute to be barred from the mails. On October 12, 1917, Wilson issued an executive order creating a Board of Censorship headed by Burleson to scrutinize all correspondence and communications leaving the country. The order strengthened Burleson's authority to scrutinize private letters and other materials using the postal system.[38] Strikingly, Attorney General Thomas Gregory wrote a detailed memo to Wilson raising serious doubts as to whether the censorship powers granted to the postmaster general were constitutional. As Gregory saw it, Burleson's new authority could not be constitutionally justified because it gave an executive official "far reaching inhibitory effect upon the right of free public discussion."[39] Wilson dismissed Gregory's concerns, reaffirming Burleson's broad censorship powers "upon evidence satisfactory to him."[40] Burleson maintained draconian control over domestic and international mails, including stringent restrictions on dozens of periodicals that either lost their mailing privileges or were compelled to print nothing about World War I for its duration. When prominent figures such as Herbert Croly or Upton Sinclair privately complained to Wilson about Burleson's iron rule over the mails, he staunchly defended his postmaster as using censorship powers as the president intended to curb disloyal speech.[41]

During World War I, some notable voluntary associations opposed the war and championed civil liberties, including various German American, peace, and socialist organizations. Significantly, vocal socialist and antiwar voices were either imprisoned or deported. The German American Alliance was actively suppressed out of existence by the government. Yet the broadest grassroots mobilizations of the period favored restrictions on the liberties of German Americans and political radicals assumed to be disloyal. In response to public pressure, for example, the California Board of Education banned the teaching of German in public schools and fired teachers with German accents. Local libraries removed German books from the shelves, and public burnings of German literature was commonplace. The speaking of German and the playing of German-composed music in public were prohibited in some states. Backed with Justice Department funding, more than 250,000 citizens joined an organization called the American Protective League (APL) to help ensure 100 percent loyalty. Badge-wearing volunteers of the APL spied on neighbors, opened mail, eavesdropped on conversations, and harassed persons of German descent. This group was only the largest of many citizen groups that helped limit individual and group freedoms.[42] Wartime anxieties sometimes boiled over into brutal mob violence. One wartime dissenter, Richard Brazier, described the American people as absorbed in "an unprecedented height of frenzy" that fueled vigilante activities from lynching to tarring and feathering. "A law-ridden nation we are," he wrote, "yet at the same time a most lawless one."[43] These challenges to democratic freedoms spawned the creation of a National Civil Liberties Bureau in 1917 by prominent social reformers led by a St. Louis settlement worker, Roger Baldwin. The organization later became the ACLU and enjoyed prominent support from Jane Addams, Clarence Darrow, John Dewey, and Felix Frankfurter. But its limited impact during World War I is exemplified by Baldwin's arrest and conviction during the conflict.

At the urging of the administration, the Sedition Act of 1918 extended the Espionage Act to make it illegal to speak out against the government. "Dangerous enemies within our confines," Wilson officials warned, exploited "the lack of laws relating to disloyal utterances."[44] The law added eight new criminal offenses to the Espionage Act including "uttering, printing, writing, or publishing any disloyal, profane, scurrilous, or abusive language" directed toward the US government.[45] Enforcement of the Espionage and Sedition Acts was shaped by district attorneys and judges scattered across the country who implemented the new laws almost invariably with severity. Attorney General Gregory privately worried both before and after passage of the laws about how popular anxieties and local prejudices might lead to overzealous prosecutions.[46] Oliver Wendell Holmes soberly concluded that the federal judiciary proved "hysterical" in its treatment of charges brought under the Espionage and Sedition Acts.[47] Likewise, the Justice Department investigators quietly noted that both judges and juries, eager to demonstrate their support for the war effort, were often too quick to convict suspects under these laws and regularly imposed overly harsh sentences.[48] Over 1,200 Americans were rounded up and imprisoned during the war.

As World War I drew to a close, the editors at *The Nation* unleashed a blistering attack on Burleson for draconian and capricious enforcement of his fleeting censorship authority. Yet they reserved their fiercest criticism for Wilson, who, in their estimation, sat silently by as unconscionable abuses of power took place on his watch. As "every tenet of democracy was violated," they noted, there was "scarcely a protest from the great democrat in the White House."[49] Not only did Wilson permit abuses of power in the name of national security, but he played a key role in nurturing the hysterical climate that made legislation like the Espionage and Sedition Acts possible. Perhaps most revealing of all, Wilson ordered administration officials to continue to target and prosecute hundreds of cases under the Espionage and Sedition Acts well after the armistice of November 11, 1918. As late as May 1920, Wilson vetoed a bill that would have terminated the Espionage and Sedition laws, and thereby restored many of the civil liberties and constitutional checks and balances that were in place before the United States entered the Great War. The President was unwilling to surrender the vast set of prerogative powers that his administration accumulated in the name of national security.

Wilson was equally determined to set an independent and high-minded course for postwar American foreign policy, with little interest in the views of influential members of Congress or others who might disagree with his ambitious blueprints for lasting peace under a new world order. He entered office with little expectation that international relations would be a preeminent concern during his presidency. "It would an irony of fate if my administration had to deal chiefly with foreign affairs," Wilson noted during his first term.[50] Yet once his second term became consumed with fighting in a calamitous "total war" and negotiating its aftermath, Wilson was committed to making US foreign policy transcend the selfish economic and strategic goals that characterized Roosevelt's *realpolitik* approach to international engagement. After a calamitous total war, Wilson outlined a postwar vision of foreign relations rooted in "Fourteen Points" that he hoped would usher in a "new diplomacy" based on moral principles.[51]

Among Wilson's Fourteen Points was a vision of open covenants between nations rather than the labyrinth of secret treaties and agreements that helped lead the way to World War I. His most famous proposal was a new League of Nations, an international organization comprised of all democratic nation-states that would have power to arbitrate and resolve future disputes between countries. Wilson also called for a general disarmament in the postwar era, beginning with the Germans and Austrians, but followed by the victorious nations. Wilson's blueprints included plans for universal freedom of the seas, free trade on a global basis, and even fair treatment for revolutionary Russia. Wilson's plans to revolutionize international relations also included the dismantlement of colonial holdings of the world's major imperial powers, replaced by gradual self-determination and democratization across the globe. These designs for ending imperialism notably included a call for immediate independence in all European sections of the Ottoman and Austro-Hungarian empires.

In December 1918, Wilson set off for Paris on behalf of the United States to join other victorious Allied Powers (Britain, France, and Italy)—collectively, they were known as "The Big Four"—to remake the world. He led an American peace delegation that numbered close to two hundred, becoming the first US president to travel to Europe while in office. As he visited France, Britain, and Italy, Wilson was greeted by large, cheering crowds who heard him make direct appeals for popular European support for the Fourteen Points. Yet the Allied leaders—Britain's David Lloyd George, France's Georges Clemenceau, and Italy's Vittorio Orlando—were unmoved by Wilson's call for a merciful and lasting "peace without victory."[52] Instead, they pressed aggressively for German territorial occupation, complete disarmament, and significant reparations. During secret negotiations, Wilson made little headway on his major proposals with the three other major diplomatic players at the Paris meeting. The Treaty of Versailles ultimately imposed harsh punishments on the defeated Central Powers. The peace treaty was especially punitive and costly to Germany, which lost territory and was forced to pay heavy reparations. The Austro-Hungarian empire was split into smaller central European nations. It was in this context that the Big Four reflected on the fate of a defeated Ottoman empire, including the political future of Palestine. Consistent with so many other notable ambiguities, if not contradictions, in his record, Wilson not only endorsed the Balfour Declaration but also pressed at the 1919 Paris peace conference for an inquiry into the political views of ordinary people in Arab lands of the former Ottoman empire.[53]

Wilson's disappointments at the Paris negotiation table were matched by his frustrations with formidable US Senate opposition at home. When he returned to Washington, the president was convinced that he alone possessed the institutional prerogatives to dictate American foreign policy. Just as wartime footing led Wilson to abandon his avowed commitments to civil liberties and democratic norms in favor of "100 percent Americanism" and executive command of the home front, he also claimed independent authority over international relations with little regard for the constitutional separation of powers, or more aptly, the framers' prescription for "separate institutions sharing powers."[54] In the end, this authoritarian streak doomed senate ratification of the Versailles Treaty and Wilson's League of Nations. Most Democrats backed Wilson and the treaty. But the US Senate was controlled by Republicans, who fiercely opposed the treaty either because they feared the League would compromise US power and independence or because they were deeply isolationist. In hopes of rallying popular support against Republican opposition, Wilson launched a desperate and ill-fated whistle-stop speaking tour in twenty-nine cities spanning ten thousand miles. The campaign-style tour failed, and the treaty went down to defeat.

Like other Progressive-era thinkers and activists, Woodrow Wilson entered the White House devoted to reforming the principles and structures of American constitutional government, which he considered too outmoded to meet the demands of disquieting social and economic changes. Building on the example of Theodore Roosevelt, he sought to fulfill a progressive reform agenda through strong, executive-centered government that rested upon vigorous leadership and recast the presidency in both domestic and foreign affairs. Yet the impact of his presidency ultimately reflected contending strands of American progressivism, juxtaposing ideals of social justice and democratization with new forms of repression in the name of white supremacy and national security. By 1919, Wilson assumed he had both special moral authority and political prerogatives to build a lasting peace among nations on the basis of a revolutionary "new diplomacy" of international cooperation, liberty, sovereignty, and self-determination. He discovered that neither the prime ministers of France, Italy, and Great Britain nor a strong Republican majority in the US Senate shared his vision of postwar international relations, and certainly none of these actors were willing to bow to his claims of special authority. The Wilson administration envisioned a modern presidency that projected an ambitious model of popular, legislative, and world leadership, but it was most decisively defined by profound contradictions between its democratic and illiberal agendas.

ENDNOTES

1 Daniel Rodgers, "In Search of Progressivism," *Reviews in American History* (December 1982), 113–32; Sidney Milkis and Jerome Mileur, eds., *Progressivism and the New Democracy* (Amherst: University of Massachusetts Press, 1999).

2 Quoted in Ronald J. Pestritto, *Woodrow Wilson and the Roots of Modern Liberalism* (Lanham, MD: Rowman and Littlefield, 2005), 45.

3 Woodrow Wilson to the Colored Delegation, at the White House Offices, November 6, 1913, WW18149, Woodrow Wilson Papers, Library of Congress, Washington, DC, http://presidentwilson.org/items/show/29819.

4 *Ibid.*

5 Megan Ming Francis, *Civil Rights and the Making of the Modern American State* (New York: Cambridge University Press, 2014); Desmond King, *Separate and Unequal* (New York: Oxford University Press, 2007).

6 Geoffrey Stone, *War and Liberty—An American Dilemma: 1790 to the Present* (New York: W. W. Norton, 2007).

7 Arthur Link, *Woodrow Wilson* (New York: Wiley-Blackwell, 1979); Peri Arnold, *Remaking the Presidency* (Lawrence: University Press of Kansas, 2009).

8 W. Barksdale Maynard, *Woodrow Wilson* (New Haven, CT: Yale University Press, 2008); Brett Flehinger, *The 1912 Election and the Power of Progressivism* (New York: Bedford/St. Martin's, 2002).

9 Doris Kearns Goodwin, *The Bully Pulpit* (New York: Simon and Schuster, 2013); Sidney Milkis, *Theodore Roosevelt, the Progressive Movement, and the Transformation of American Politics* (Lawrence: University Press of Kansas, 2009).

10 Woodrow Wilson, "A Campaign Address in Burlington, New Jersey" in *The Papers of Woodrow Wilson*, ed. Arthur Link, vol. 25 (Princeton, NJ: Princeton University Press, 1992), 490–91, 492.

11 Scott James, "The Evolution of the Presidency" in *The Executive Branch*, ed. Joel Aberbach and Mark Peterson (New York: Oxford University Press, 2005), 19.

12 Scott James, *Presidents, Parties, and the State: A Party System Perspective on Democratic Regulatory Choice, 1884–1936* (New York: Cambridge University Press, 2000).

13 Richard B. Sherman, *The Republican Party and Black America from McKinley to Hoover* (Charlottesville: University Press of Virginia, 1973), 113–44.

14 Sidney Milkis and Daniel Tichenor, *Rivalry and Reform* (Chicago, IL: University of Chicago Press, 2019), 102.

15 *Ibid.*, 102–8.

16 August Meier, "The Negro and the Democratic Party: 1875–1915," *Phylon* 17 (June 1956): 173–91; Sherman, *The Republican Party and Black America from McKinley to Hoover*, 121–22; David Levering Lewis, *W.E.B. Du Bois: Biography of a Race, 1868–1919* (New York: Henry Holt and Company, 1993), 522.

17 Francis, *Civil Rights and the Making of the Modern American State*, 70.

18 Daniel J. Tichenor, "Presidents, Social Movements, and Contentious Change," *Presidential Studies Quarterly* (March 1999), 14–25.

19 Francis, *Civil Rights and the Making of the Modern American State*, 70–71.

20 "Speech by Marcus Garvey, July 8, 1917," in *The Marcus Garvey and Universal Negro Improvement Association Papers*, ed. Robert Hill, vol. 1 (Berkeley: University of California Press, 1983), 142.

21 *Ibid.*

22 *Ibid.*, see also Herbert Shapiro, *White Violence and Black Response: From Reconstruction to Montgomery* (Amherst: University of Massachusetts Press, 1988).

23 Tichenor, "Presidents, Social Movements, and Contentious Change."

24 Geoffrey Stone, "Mr. Wilson's First Amendment," in John Milton Cooper, *Reconsidering Woodrow Wilson* (Baltimore: Johns Hopkins University Press, 2008), 213; Robert Cottrell, *Robert Nash Baldwin and the American Civil Liberties Union* (New York: Columbia University Press, 2001).

25 Quoted in Milkis and Tichenor, *Rivalry and Reform*, 108–9.

26 Lewis, *W.E.B. Du Bois*, 556.

27 *Ibid.*

28 Carl Hodge and Cathal Nolan, *U.S. Presidents and Foreign Policy* (Santa Barbara, CA: ABC-CLIO, 2007), 396–98.

29 *Ibid.*, 396.

30 Jeffrey Tulis, *The Rhetorical Presidency* (Princeton, NJ: Princeton University Press, 1988). Other scholars identify much earlier origins of popular rhetorical leadership by our chief executives, including Melvin Laracey, *Presidents and the People* (College Station, TX: Texas A&M Press, 2002) and *Speaking to the People: The Rhetorical Presidency in Historical Perspective*, ed. Richard Ellis (Amherst: University of Massachusetts Press, 1998).

31 President Woodrow Wilson's Annual Message of December 7, 1915, *Congressional Record*, 64th Congress, 1st Session, 95–100.

32 *Annual Report of the Attorney General, 1917* (Washington, DC: Government Printing Office, 1917), 57–59; David Cole, *Enemy Aliens* (New York: New Press, 2003).

33 Paul Van Riper, *History of the United States Civil Service* (Evanston, IN: Row, Peterson, 1958), 266.

34 *Congressional Record*, 65th Congress, Special Session, April 2, 1917, 104.

35 *Ibid.*

36 18 US Code, Section 2388.

37 Glenn Longacre, "Free Speech on Trial," *Prologue* (Winter 2017–2018), 4; Eugene V. Debs, "The Canton, Ohio Speech, June 16, 1918," *Call* (June 1918), 1.

38 John R. Mock, *Censorship 1917* (Princeton, NJ: Princeton University Press, 1941), 110–30.

39 Daniel J. Tichenor, "Historical Set Points and the Development of US Presidential Emergency Power," *Perspectives on Politics* (September 2013), 777–78.

40 *Ibid.*

41 *Woodrow Wilson: Life and Letters*, ed. Ray Stannard Baker, vol. 7 (New York: Scribner's Sons, 1946), 313, 318–19.

42 Tichenor, "Historical Set Points and the Development of US Presidential Emergency Power," 779–80; and Daniel J. Tichenor, "Same Old Song," *Nation*, August 28, 2006.

43 Richard Brazier, Retrospective Notes, Roger Baldwin Papers, Mudd Library, Princeton University, Box 4, Folder 24.

44 Daniel J. Tichenor, "Democracy Wartime's Deficits: The Prerogative Presidency and Liberal Democracy in America," in *Imperfect Democracies: The Democratic Deficit in Canada and the United States*, eds. Patti Tamara Lenard and Richard Simeon, (Vancouver, BC: University of British Columbia Press, 2012), 206.

45 *Ibid.*

46 Harry N. Scheiber, *The Wilson Administration and Civil Liberties, 1917–1921* (Ithaca, NY: Cornell University Press, 1960), 22–23.

47 *Ibid.*

48 *Ibid.*, 43.

49 *Nation*, vol. 108 (May 3, 1919), 674.

50 H.W. Brands, "Woodrow Wilson and the Irony of Fate," *Diplomatic History* 28 (September 2004), 503–12.

51 Tichenor, "Historical Set Points and the Development of US Presidential Emergency Power."

52 Brands, "Woodrow Wilson and the Irony of Fate," 503–12.

53 Frank W. Brecher, "Woodrow Wilson and the Origins of the Arab-Israeli Conflict," *American Jewish Archives Journal* 39 (April 1987): 23–47.

54 Gary Gerstle, *American Crucible* (Princeton, NJ: Princeton University Press, 2017), 43–44; Richard Neustadt, *Presidential Power and the Modern Presidency* (New York: Free Press, 1991), 3.

Sidney H. Riesenberg, *Civilians*, 1918

Source: Jewish Welfare Board, "Fundraising Poster for United War Work Campaign" (1918), SC-17250, FF: C5/D7, Jacob Rader Marcus Center of the American Jewish Archives, Cincinnati, OH.

Illustrated posters played a central role in generating mass American support for the US military campaign during World War I. Characterized by bold graphics and patriotic imagery, wartime posters served as inspiring and concise propaganda vehicles that resonated with Americans from all walks of life. Adorned with well-known symbols such as Columbia, Uncle Sam, the Statue of Liberty, and the American flag, the posters included pithy banner headlines that exhorted viewers to actively support the war effort. For example, "Wake up, America! Civilization Calls Every Man, Woman, and Child!" implores a slumbering Columbia, clothed in red, white, star-spangled blue, to bestir herself. In another instance, a paternal and kindly Uncle Sam solemnly explains to two ruddy-cheeked middle-class children, "Boys and Girls! You can help your Uncle Sam Win the War—Save your Quarters, Buy War Savings Stamps."

The artist and illustrator Sidney H. Riesenberg's (1885–1971) "Over the Top for You," depicting a doughboy climbing out of a battlefield trench and clutching a billowing American flag, became one of the period's most iconic images. Riesenberg, considered "one of the greatest illustrators of the World War I era," deployed a distinctive American Impressionist style in his work.[1] In the poster Riesenberg produced for the Jewish Welfare Board (reprinted here), the theme of soldiers taking risks for the safety and welfare of Americans at home again takes center stage. In front of a crouching group of embattled soldiers, a valiant doughboy stands erect, gun slung over his shoulder, eyes and mouth open, his left hand stretched forward to halt the viewer. "Civilians," he cries, "When we go through this, we need all the help and comfort you can give." A blue star of David in a circle, a symbol frequently used in Jewish Welfare Board public relations materials, is prominently featured below the banner headline, just above the doughboy's right hand and the heads of his comrades. At the doughboy's feet, the poster is anchored by the Jewish Welfare Board's name, printed in bold letters, together with an indication of the "United War Work Campaign," a national fundraising effort to raise $170 million cosponsored by the American Library Association, the Jewish Welfare Board, the Knights of Columbus, the Salvation Army, the War Camp Community Service, and the Young Men's Christian Association and Young Women's Christian Association.

— M.A.R

Endnote

1 Karal Ann Marling, *Old Glory: Unfurling History* (Piermont, NH: Bunker Hill Publishers, 2004), 45.

CHAPTER 2

WARTIME MOBILIZATION AND POLITICAL CONSCIOUSNESS: THE CASE OF THE EAST EUROPEAN JEWISH IMMIGRANTS OF NEW YORK

CHRISTOPHER M. STERBA

Abraham Cahan, like millions of other democratic socialists around the world in the first year of the Great War, found it difficult to maintain his neutrality and pacifism. By 1915, his commitment to international class solidarity faltered. "All civilized people [must] sympathize with Germany," he wrote in the *Forverts* (Forward).[1] "Every victory she attains over Russia is a source of joy."[2] Three years later, after the United States had entered the conflict, Cahan's paper expressed a very different view in supporting the Allies. "It is no longer a capitalist war, neither is it imperialistic or nationalistic. It is a war for humanity."[3]

Cahan's evolving position reflected not only a struggle with ideological principles, but also the fact that he was an immigrant. An American citizen living in New York City, and the publisher of the largest Yiddish newspaper in the world, Cahan understood the war much like his hundreds of thousands of readers: in a vivid transnational context, where each earth-shaking event in Europe and the Middle East had direct consequences and often compelled immediate action in the immigrants' new home in New York.

This essay will describe how New York's eastern European Jews came to actively support the American war effort, not as a result of government repression or manipulation, but because of the population's continuing ties to Europe and their own aspirations and claims to settlement in the United States. As will be seen, the Balfour Declaration, the Treaty of Brest-Litovsk, and a series of home front events, including the American military draft, refugee relief efforts, and the Socialist candidacy of Morris Hillquit for New York mayor, were especially critical in influencing Jewish attitudes toward the war.

As the scale and significance of these events suggest, the home front experience was an important moment for New York's eastern European Jews. The war pulled the city's most recent Jewish residents into public life more than ever before and redefined the world map, providing new and reinvigorated sources of cultural pride. Given the immense population's varying national origins, religious attitudes, and political ideologies, its transformation into a prowar bulwark inevitably took time and was contingent on a series of dramatic events and pressures. Out of this turbulent experience emerged a new voice in politics, one that combined an innovative and articulate desire for social justice with an activist role in foreign affairs. Participation in the American war effort provided the sense of security and entitlement necessary to make these demands in the electoral arena. Whatever their initial positions on the war, they now viewed the United States as their permanent home. For the vast majority of New York Jews, the last year of the conflict made that relationship all the more important.

I.

From the outbreak of the war in 1914 until American intervention, eastern European Jewish immigrants understandably focused their attention more on events on the eastern front, on the fighting in and near the Russian Pale, than on the crisis facing France and Belgium. This initially put them at odds with the pro-Allied direction in which the United States was moving. Between 1914 and early 1917 the vast majority of New York's 1.5 million Jews wished above all else to see Germany crush the Russian tsar and his army.

This was not so much a desire for German triumph as for Russian defeat. As Joseph Rappaport explains in his careful study of the wartime Yiddish press, "the pro-Germanism of America's immigrant Jews was an inevitable consequence of their Russophobia."[4] The possibility of a tsarist government energized by nationalist fervor and military victory, and the even grimmer prospect of Russian conquest of new territories inhabited by Jews were sources of tremendous anxiety.

Shocking contemporary reports from eastern Europe, meanwhile, blended with the immigrants' historical memories of forced removal and pogroms in Russia, as the Jewish Pale of Settlement quickly became the setting of a no man's land that extended for hundreds of miles. The scorched earth policy of the retreating Russian troops increased the area's devastation. Viewing the Jewish population as potentially hostile, the tsar's army forcibly sent 600,000 Jews eastward, their property and livelihoods lost overnight. The refugees soon faced starvation and epidemics of cholera and typhoid.[5]

When the tremendous hardships of the Russian war effort finally forced Nicholas II to abdicate on March 15, 1917, New York's Jews celebrated with rallies and wild street demonstrations. The regime's collapse caused many American Jews to reconsider their positions on the war. The Allied powers were now all democracies or constitutional monarchies, fighting the autocratic empires of Germany, Austro-Hungary, and Turkey. When the United States entered the war in early April, much of American Jewry, with the crucial exception of the Jewish left, had already swung its support to the much-admired French republic, a Britain that would soon declare its approval of a Jewish homeland in Palestine, and a fledging Russian government that needed aid and protection to ensure its survival.

A series of events in New York during the summer and fall of 1917 accelerated this sea change in Jewish sympathies. With each experience, Gotham Jews deepened both their inclusion in American public life and distanced themselves from the worlds they had left behind, whether they actively opposed or supported the American war effort, or simply acted on humanitarian impulses to help save kin and refugees in the war zones of eastern Europe.

When the Wilson administration launched the United States' first-ever nationwide draft in June 1917, New York Jews in fact provided two of the most important sources of opposition. The No Conscription League led by Emma Goldman and the People's Council for Democracy and Peace, led by a coalition of Jewish progressives, socialists, and union leaders, agitated strongly for neutrality. They found a receptive audience among "downtown" working-class immigrant Jews that spring, as the Selective Service Act raised ugly memories of conscription in tsarist Russia, a major reason why many Jews had emigrated to the United States. It is well known that Emma Goldman was arrested and eventually deported for defying the new draft law. The People's Council, however, along with Abraham Cahan, the city's Socialist party, and the Jewish-led unions, urged young men to follow the Selective Service guidelines.[6] For the remainder of the war, tens of thousands of New York Jews registered for the draft, were inducted into the army, or claimed their right to exemption from the draft. Hundreds also served on neighborhood draft boards. In the end, many immigrants who became soldiers (and obtained US citizenship as a result) expressed pride in their service and a sense of duty to their adopted country. In interviews and questionnaires after the war, Jewish veterans adamantly distinguished the American draft from Russian conscription.[7]

Downtown's Socialist Party and trade unions, however, were at the same time eyeing a very different opportunity to demonstrate their opposition to the war. In August 1917, it looked as though the Latvian-born Morris Hillquit, a Socialist candidate who was running on an openly antiwar platform, might win the mayoralty race.[8] The possibility of "making New York City safe for socialism" fueled activity in heavily Jewish neighborhoods that the party had always written off, and involved a far greater number of volunteers. Immigrant union members, women, and even school children contributed to the most participatory electoral season in the history of Jewish immigration to Gotham.[9] "These were indeed exciting times, unforgettable and delirious nights," recalled one Harlem candidate, whose district "was ablaze with hope of victory and great enthusiasm."[10]

Ironically, this surge in participation took place in the midst of one of the most destructive periods of political repression in American history. During the three months leading up to the November 1917 election, mobs lynched an Industrial Workers of the World (IWW) organizer in Montana and horsewhipped a People's Council activist in Ohio. In the late summer, Justice Department officers in Chicago raided the national headquarters of the IWW and the Socialist party. In New York, the Postmaster General's office threatened the mailing privileges of the Socialist *Call* and the *Forward,* and two Columbia University professors were fired for their pacifist activities. Across the country, dissent had become an offense punishable by federal mandate and brute force.

Nevertheless, New York's immigrant and second-generation east European Jews strongly supported a party that ran on a pacifist platform. "We are the party of peace," a Socialist candidate proclaimed at an East Side rally, "and we are the party that will work for peace, and there is no crime in saying that."[11] A large body of Gotham voters, most notably elements within the Irish, German, and African American populations who were disgusted with the American war effort and its alliances, also lent their support. This third-party protest vote gave Hillquit a chance in the mayoralty race. But the Jewish neighborhoods alone provided the Socialist majorities needed to elect the party's candidates to office. Inspired by the Russian Revolution and the Kerensky government's peace proposals, much of downtown Jewry had the feeling that anything was possible. With strong institutions to back up their convictions—the unions, radical Jewish press, Workmen's Circle branches, and Rand School among them—they had the ability to put up a good fight. Unlike the rest of the country, New York City had a remarkably open discussion of the war in English and many other languages, though dissent was most often articulated in Yiddish.

Three activities in particular show how the campaign brought immigrant Jewish union members, women, and students into the rough-and-tumble world of city politics. The first, street speaking, was the mainstay of any Socialist campaign, and was ubiquitous in Jewish neighborhoods that fall. Louis Waldman, a candidate for state assembly, described the immediacy that existed between speaker and audience before microphones and sterile auditoriums: "There was something intimate and inspiring about those street corner meetings.... We had the sky above us, and on clear nights the moon and stars."[12] Plainclothes policemen were also present, but there were no arrests of party speakers during the campaign, and in fact the surveillance boosted the candidates' reputations.[13]

A second set of campaign activities, more critical to the party's success, was the effort to make the election as clean as possible. Tammany Hall's entrenched system of corruption made Socialist vote counting difficult and often dangerous work. In the weeks leading up to the election, the party organized "an army of honest ballot soldiers" who went from tenement to tenement to validate persons registered to vote. Election observers were also needed to watch the voting process at the city's more than two thousand polling places, and the party held preparatory classes on the finer points of machine rule. The sense of moral authority that came with fighting corruption clearly contributed to the Hillquit campaign's enthusiasm and crusade-like appeal.[14]

The last experience drawing downtown Jewry into the political system that fall was the thrill of winning an electoral victory. "The East Side didn't sleep election night," reported a socialist paper.[15] In a spontaneous act of celebration, thousands of men and women marched from the party's campaign headquarters to the *Forward* building.[16] Hillquit did not win, but received fifteen times the number of votes that non-Jewish socialists had polled in previous races. Of the eighteen party members who were elected that fall, sixteen were Jews of east European descent.[17] Their triumph would be short-lived, as Tammany Hall quickly moved to counter the third-party threat in the next election. But the enthusiasm that greeted socialist victories in the Bronx, Brownsville, Williamsburg, and the East Side represented a declaration of ethnic political independence that could no longer be ignored.

And yet, within less than six months, New York's immigrant Jewish left would become strong supporters of the American war effort. The local scene did not produce this change of heart. The catalyst was a series of events taking place far away, in Petrograd and London, in Palestine and Ukraine, in the trenches along the Vesle River and deep in the Argonne Forest. In the last year of the Great War, from the end of the 1917 New York electoral season through the signing of the armistice, the world map changed dramatically, and Gotham's Jews felt this transformation deeply. The Bolshevik Revolution, the collapse of the German, Austro-Hungarian, and Ottoman empires, and the real possibility of a Jewish homeland in Palestine signified both a new stage of settlement for downtown Jews in New York and an equally important cutting of ties to the past.

A combined fund drive to aid refugees and American Jews now in the military set the tone for Jewish perceptions of the dramatic events of late 1917. Even before the United States entered the war, the major Jewish relief agencies had agreed to raise $10 million nationwide that year. As December approached, however, the various divisions of the Joint Distribution Committee were still $4 million short of their goal. A drive to raise the remaining amount in New York City was set for December 3 to 16. Though only a month had passed since the mayoralty election, organizers were optimistic that the city's diverse Jewish population would work together to save 3 million Jews living in desperate conditions. "We are no longer orthodox and reformed, conservative and radical," Rabbi Nathan Krauss urged, "but we find all Jews dropping their distinctions in the face of the common suffering, united by that ancient formula, I am a Jew."[18]

New York Jewry had been raising money for war sufferers in Europe and Palestine since the autumn of 1914. What made this new campaign special was not only the huge sum involved, but also the fact that it was being collected simultaneously with a $1 million appeal for the Jewish Welfare Board (JWB). Recently formed, the Board's mission was to provide religious and recreational services for the tens of thousands of Jews serving in the armed forces. Leaders of the Joint Distribution Committee and the JWB shared essentially the same pro-war attitude and decided that money for the two causes would be collected in common. Though both drives sought to assist fellow Jews, it was clear that the welfare board benefited tremendously from its link to refugee work. It is hard to imagine that the Lower East Side, so soon after the Socialists' electoral triumph, would have thrilled to a campaign that supported the war effort, however indirectly.[19]

Yet the pairing of the two campaigns provoked little opposition. "It is high time to stop debating about militarism and pacifism," one Zionist labor leader urged, "when the community is faced by the fact that thousands of Jewish boys in the camps have to resort to the YMCA for their spiritual comfort."[20] With this broad support, the two-week effort was a smashing success. At the Astor Hotel banquet kicking off the drive, Jacob H. Schiff donated $200,000 and goaded his rich dining companions into contributing a one-night total of more than a million. A few days later the *New York Herald* reported from the other side of the giving spectrum. "One woman yesterday brought an ordinary bed pillow—all she had to offer."[21] Children from the city's Talmud Torah schools donated their Hanukkah gift money, the stars of the Yiddish stage held benefit performances, and kosher butchers donated a percentage of their earnings. Meanwhile, future entertainment moguls William Fox, Adolph Zukor, and Marcus Loew formed a committee to solicit funds from the theater industry. Al Jolson told a mass meeting that "he remembered enough of his early life in Shrednik, near Kovno, to realize how much the money was needed" when he gave two thousand dollars.[22] These and countless other activities did not go unrecognized. President Wilson issued a public letter of praise, while the city papers provided daily coverage, complete with lists of contributors.[23]

Though familiar "our crowd" names such as Schiff and Guggenheim dominated the donor lists, Jewish labor raised $1.25 million, the largest single donation to the cause. Joseph Schlossberg of the Amalgamated Clothing Workers claimed that "no one can bring [the refugees and soldiers] help except we here, in this country.... It is now our turn to do our share."[24] Bombarded simultaneously by reports of starvation in Europe and pleas to comfort "the soul of the Jewish immigrant" in uniform, downtown labor's opposition to the war effort rapidly weakened.[25] Raising $5 million in a fortnight, the campaign was also dramatic proof to the immigrant population of its developing status in the New World. Gotham Jewry had great resources at its disposal and knew how to use them.[26]

Events in Petrograd did much to make this rapprochement on the war issue possible. Within days of the November 1917 election, news of Russia's second great revolution commanded the headlines of every New York Yiddish daily. More than any other single factor, the October Revolution in Russia stilled the downtown left's opposition to the war. Preserving the new revolutionary government from destruction became the main priority of many Jewish socialists, and overnight Germany became the chief threat and needed to be stopped. This change in policy was most visible among the radical wing of the socialist movement, which quickly abandoned its former pacifism.[27]

Less colorful but more complicated was the response of the majority of Jews in the Socialist Party and unions. The *Forward* and the other Yiddish papers on the left had been critics of the Bolsheviks before the revolution, favoring Kerensky's provisional government during the fall of 1917. The moderate Jewish left not only opposed the new regime on theoretical grounds (for moving too fast for underdeveloped Russia) but also feared its autocratic tendencies. Despite these concerns, downtown could not resist admiring the first workers' state in world history, or the Bolsheviks' principled demands for open diplomacy and a democratic peace. In January 1918, the Amalgamated Clothing Workers praised the new government for its "directness, frankness, and firmness" in working to bring an end to the war.[28]

While a range of opinions greeted the October Revolution, immigrant Jewry's response to the Treaty of Brest-Litovsk was unanimous. For most Brownsville and Williamsburg residents, the earth trembled far more during February and early March of 1918, when Bolshevik foreign minister Leon Trotsky broke off negotiations with the Central Powers and adopted a policy of "no war, no peace."[29] The decision to demobilize the Russian army proved disastrous, as German troops immediately swept into the Baltic provinces, Russian Poland, and Ukraine. Now compelled to sign an even more drastic treaty, the Bolsheviks ceded roughly 60 million Russians and one-third of the country's factories and arable land to foreign rule. Most important for downtown Jews, the occupied territory contained nearly all of the former Jewish Pale of Settlement. While most Americans understood the treaty in terms of a Bolshevik betrayal, immigrant Jewry saw the naked aggression of the Central Powers. So recently liberated from tsarist tyranny, their kin back home once again fell under the domain of an autocratic power. Attitudes now came full circle. A year before immigrant Jews supported Germany because of their hatred of the Russian tsar. Now they vigorously supported the United States out of hatred for the German kaiser.

For the second time in less than a year, immigrant Jewish concerns coincided with the initiatives of the Wilson administration. Wilson's Fourteen Points peace proposal of January 8, 1918, a calculated attempt to satisfy much of the democratic program of liberals and the left, finally provided Jewish leaders of the unions and Socialist Party with a statement of principles they could endorse, and the administration's Third Liberty Loan offered an ideal opportunity to demonstrate this support in action as well as words. On March 11, 1918, the United Hebrew Trades bought $1 million worth of bonds, followed by the Amalgamated Clothing Workers' purchase of half a million. "The United States of America, of which we all are good and loyal citizens," declared the press organ of the Ladies' Garment Workers' Union, "is waging a life-and-death struggle with a militarist power that tramples upon and outrages every free country upon which it can manage to lay its blood-and-iron claws."[30] The prowar tide rolled through the rest of the Jewish left's organizations and presses, which declared their support at May Day celebrations and conventions during the spring and summer. Bernard Marcus, the chairman of the East Side Liberty Loan and Red Cross Committees, cited just one reason for the tremendous jump in bond subscriptions in his district, from $500,000 for the first Liberty Loan drive to over $15,000,000 for the third. "No sooner was the ink dry on the treaty of Brest-Litovsk," he claimed, "than the East Side began to turn all allegiance, not only of the lip but of the heart, to the United States."[31] The immigrants' primary concern may have been with conditions in the Old World, but they were also making a statement about their relationship to their new home.

This was especially striking in the case of downtown's working-class leaders and institutions. Committing themselves to the American war effort, they abandoned a heritage of revolutionary mass movement politics made increasingly irrelevant by two decades of development in the United States. The success that the immigrant left enjoyed in Gotham clearly distanced them from their radical Bundist past in Russia. No longer harassed or outlawed, the trade unions and radical Yiddish press flourished in New York, and despite the Wilson administration's repressive tactics during the war, the Socialists reached their greatest strength, and the membership and influence of the downtown unions expanded dramatically.[32]

With constituencies that were several hundred thousand strong, local Socialist officeholders and the Jewish-led unions shared more in common with the British Labour Party than with Emma Goldman and the No Conscription League or the rest of the American Socialist Party for that matter. With representatives in the state and municipal legislatures and a voice in the various federal labor boards, leaders like Abraham Cahan and Sidney Hillman did not take to the barricades. Pauline Newman, an International Ladies' Garment Workers' Union organizer and socialist candidate, recalled years later that for her, the decision to support the war was difficult but ultimately pragmatic. "It wasn't just a feeling that you had against war—you had to think of the consequences if you stayed out. To say that we liked it, or were terribly enthusiastic about it, I would say no.... We wanted Germany not to win, and if we didn't want Germany to win, we had to do our share."[33] During the war, downtown's moderate left did not lose faith in gradualism and the power of the ballot. Leon Trotsky best expressed the differences between Gotham's Jewish left and their revolutionary comrades in Russia. Having lived briefly in New York, Trotsky claimed that Morris Hillquit's brand of socialism was most popular among "successful dentists."[34]

A veteran social worker on the East Side pointed out the full political meaning of these developments. Dr. Henry Moskowitz, writing less than a week before Brest-Litovsk, viewed the East Side as a "political barometer" for New York rather than a radical aberration.[35] He claimed that the ghetto thus far had experienced three different and coexisting stages of political development: the power and patronage of Tammany Hall, the idealism of the progressives, and the social welfare program of the Socialist Party. The future lay in the weaving together of these strands. "We are on the eve of a fundamental change in our municipal policies," Moskowitz wrote, pointing to the immigrant Jews' independence and keen sense of social justice as a crucial factor.[36] More concretely, he saw the benefits of a healthy rivalry between the socialist and the Tammany machine that was co-opting much of their program, and identified Al Smith and Robert Wagner as important leaders of a new urban politics. After the Red Scare and the left's struggle with Bolshevism in the immediate postwar years, progressives like Moskowitz and Wagner and Jewish social democrats like Louis Waldman and Sidney Hillman would be working for a middle way, somewhere between laissez-faire and the Comintern. In less than a generation after the Great War, these hopes would culminate in the New Deal and the Congress of Industrial Organizations (CIO).

II.

Events in the Middle East, meanwhile, coincided with the Bolsheviks' seizure of power in Russia, giving New York Jews still another major connection with the war. In his carefully worded letter, Britain's foreign minister J. Arthur Balfour, appeared to usher in a new epoch in Jewish history. The statement captured the imagination of Jews worldwide. In New York, the Orthodox and center-left Yiddish press hailed the declaration's intentions, while the *Forward* stood alone in opposition, calling the pledge a capitalist ploy. But when British troops captured Jerusalem on December 11, 1917, a sense of the declaration's tremendous historical significance pervaded all the Yiddish papers. Coinciding with Hanukkah and New York Jewry's $5 million fund drive for refugee relief, the victory demonstrated how Allied power could make the Balfour Declaration a reality.[37]

The issue of Palestine never generated the same level of anxiety or activity among Gotham's Jews as the horrors confronting Jews still living in the former Russian Pale. But the profound cultural resonance of Zionism helped swing support to the Allied cause. Regardless of how small the Zionist societies' memberships were, or how meager the circulation of their journals, Jewish nationalism served as a crucial lens for interpreting current concerns. The war, by exposing the vulnerability of east European Jewry more than ever, bridged the gap between culture and action, as relief efforts and hopes for security in the postwar future pointed increasingly to Palestine. With at most 15,000 adherents nationwide in 1914, American Zionist groups approached the 200,000 mark by the armistice. Most of these new members were of east European origin, and their support for the war and the Allies was never stronger.[38]

The dramatic growth in Zionism's popularity might seem surprising in the hyperpatriotic atmosphere of wartime America. But the movement in the United States brought into play contradictory impulses, enabling it not only to coexist with 100 percent Americanism but also to overcome two major opponents within the Jewish population, uptown Jewry and the left. During the war, acculturated American Jewish leaders such as Louis D. Brandeis, Stephen S. Wise, and Henrietta Szold advocated the homeland idea in terms of universal benefit rather than narrow political or religious self-interest, proposing a democratic and progressive society that would serve as a model for the entire world. This appeal was fully compatible with the crusading spirit of Woodrow Wilson's war aims. As important, American Zionists accepted their status as a diasporic population and considered Palestine as a refuge for persecuted Jews from Europe, not from the United States. With their European coreligionists living in ruins or on rations, American Jewry accepted fundraising and advocacy as its main contribution to the Zionist cause. This combination of universalist principles and limited participation set a precedent for American Jewish involvement in Palestine that would persist long after the Great War had ended.[39]

With Wilson's tacit approval of the Balfour Declaration, the American Jewish Committee's traditional anxiety over "dual loyalty" further diminished. On April 28, 1918, the organization cautiously endorsed the British pledge, stressing once again its conviction that the primary allegiance of American Jewry would be to the United States. The left, in contrast, responded more to grassroots sentiment than high-level diplomacy. For decades, downtown Socialists had condemned Zionism as a bourgeois diversion and a veil for British imperial interests. But conditions in Russia and the pressing need for protection of Jewish rights worldwide changed the minds of many union leaders and rank and file members. In late April, delegates from more than two hundred organizations met at the *Forward* building to form the Jewish Labor Conference for Palestine. "We are convinced," one of their resolutions proclaimed, "that Palestine can become a Jewish land only when Jewish labor will devote its strength and energy for Palestine and in Palestine."[40]

With these opponents either quieted or converted, the Zionist presence in New York was able to blossom. Despite the failure of Versailles and the schism that divided Zionists after the war, the goal of restoration was never again so strongly attacked as a dream, or so vilified as a dangerous call for self-segregation, as it had been before 1918. American Zionism was able to move out of the ethnic enclave and into the mainstream, working within the cultural and political institutions of the United States. Smaller organizations of women (Hadassah), youth (Young Judea and the Intercollegiate Zionist Association), and workers (the Poalei Zion party) launched campaigns to raise medicine, food, and money for Palestine. Public display of the Zionist flag was one of the clearest manifestations of the movement's growth in confidence as well as in numbers, and the symbol of the future state of Israel became a standard feature at meetings and rallies.[41]

The boldest example of local Zionist support was the campaign to recruit men for the Jewish Legion then preparing to fight in Palestine. Less than a year earlier, conservative leaders in both the pro- and anti-Zionist camps attacked the legion and its separatist message. But by the spring of 1918 former critics like the *American Jewish Chronicle* aggressively supported the idea. "The very fact that Jews as Jews are participating in the struggle for Palestine will not fail to impress the nations and will strengthen our position considerably in every respect."[42] This rhetoric mirrored the legion's own exaggerated sense of its importance. Since the United States was not at war with Turkey, only men who were exempt from the American draft could join, and then could only serve as British soldiers. Though of meager military value, the roughly five hundred volunteers from New York were a public relations triumph. Imitating the previous year's draft calls, Zionist clubs held send-off celebrations on the Lower East Side, drawing huge crowds. One member described the legionnaires' loyalties in the most acceptable manner possible. "These men prefer service in the ranks of the Jewish regiment not because they love America less," explained Gershon Agronsky, "but because they love Palestine too, they do not cherish American culture less, but they glory in their own history too. No true American requires a fuller explanation."[43] In April the legion received the approval of New York Mayor Mike Hylan, who reviewed a contingent of volunteers at city hall and presented them with the "the flag of David." With Tammany Hall's endorsement, the men began their long journey to the Palestinian front.[44]

It was not until August 31, 1918, the eve of the Jewish New Year, that Woodrow Wilson publicly endorsed the Balfour Declaration and the Zionist cause for the first time. The president followed the lead of Mayor Hylan, as well as the governments of Britain, France, and Italy, both of the wartime popes, and such diverse American groups as Protestant clergymen, and Irish and Polish Catholic nationalists. Whether truly sympathetic to a Jewish homeland or based purely on self-interest, these declarations of support boosted the movement's respectability and the optimism of Zionist supporters to unprecedented heights.

At about the same time Wilson finally gave his approval, Rabbi Leon Spitz witnessed a curious melding of American and pro-Zionist sentiments. Spitz was serving as a Jewish Welfare Board representative at Camp Upton in Yaphank, Long Island, where most of the New York City draftees were sent for military training. One day he was assisting new recruits as they stepped off their New York trains and marched past the camp's athletic field. A baseball game was taking place while a brass band played "Hatikvah" (The Hope), the Zionist hymn that later became the anthem of the state of Israel. "Can you imagine," the rabbi commented, "how those hundreds of Jewish rookies hailing from Pitkin Avenue and Herzl Street in good old Brownsville on their first day in camp felt?"[45] Spitz appreciated the psychological comfort of the moment, if not the cross-cultural irony: "The strains of 'Hatikvah' on the baseball diamond of Yaphank dissipated much of that void and heartache and loneliness that every new recruit experiences."[46] Baseball and the diaspora, *shtetl* (Yiddish for hamlet) migrants and the US army, John Phillip Souza and Theodor Herzl, the war brought these disparate elements together, and for the time being they were able to work together toward a common goal.

III.

When the armistice was declared, New York's Jewish neighborhoods, like the city as a whole, responded with a daylong celebration in the streets. Serenaded by sirens and church bells, New Yorkers built bonfires, blanketed the streets with confetti, and danced and marched in hundreds of spontaneous parades. Lewis Feuer, then a young boy living on the East Side, remembers how his heavily Jewish neighborhood did its full share of celebrating. "When the war ended, it evoked such a display of American patriotism as I have not since witnessed," he wrote six decades later.[47] "Our street, like many others, had a great block party. The kaiser in effigy was berated, while American flags and banners waved from lines strung from houses across the street. The children sang 'Over There' and 'My country, 'tis of thee'; the men in uniform were heroes."[48]

Feuer's recollection illustrates how Gotham's Jews had become receptive to the government's call to arms. Though the reversal of the left certainly accelerated the process, booming demand in the garment industry also made Jewish sections hum with prowar activity in the spring of 1918. Schoolchildren selling War Savings Stamps, neighborhoods raising service star flags, and women marching in Red Cross uniforms became as familiar activities in Williamsburg or Jewish Harlem as they were in any other large city district. Residents also encountered the federal government in a variety of new ways, from regulation of the needle trades to the setting of a fair price for *matzoh* for Passover.[49]

Perhaps most important was the deepened sense of commitment, and the mounting peer pressure within the community, which came with having local men overseas. Service flags flew from tenements as well as shops, schools, and synagogues. "I have a boy (at an army training camp)," was the reason a Kiev-born pushcart vendor gave for aiding a Thrift drive.[50] "He is helping the government and I would be ashamed of myself, if for one day I could not give up socks and suspenders for War Stamps."[51] During the armistice celebration, garment workers paraded behind a banner marked "We made the clothes by the boys who canned the Kaiser."[52] So strongly opposed to conscription a year earlier, the Jewish-led unions now boasted of its members in the service and vowed to protect their "returning heroes" from postwar unemployment and exploitation.[53]

Lewis Feuer's recollections also reveal the singular meaning of the armistice for New York Jewry. The songs the East Side children sang, the flags the people waved, and the soldiers that everyone cheered were American. Downtown's Jews brandished no evidence of their Russian or Romanian pasts, nor did they display symbols of future nations or homelands, of Poland or Palestine, the Baltics or the Balkans. However deeply New York Jewry might have felt about the suffering in eastern Europe or the prospect of creating a Jewish state in the Middle East, there was very little sentiment for their own return migration. The political and cultural aspirations downtown articulated during the Socialist campaign of 1917 and the final year of the war had become linked to life in the United States. New York's immigrant Jews proved their ability to assimilate on their own terms. Committing themselves to a role in the political arena and establishing a new cultural reference point in Palestine, Gotham

Jewry thought and acted within a very different framework after 1918. Events of local, national, and worldwide significance made this possible. Acting on humanitarian, ideological, and ethnocultural impulses, New York discovered enduring sources of unity in the maelstrom of the last year of the war.

ENDNOTES

1 Quoted in Joseph Rappaport, "Jewish Immigrants and World War I: A Study of Yiddish Press Attitudes" (PhD diss., Columbia University, 1951), 88.

2 *Ibid.*, 90.

3 *Ibid.*, 168.

4 Rappaport, "Jewish Immigrants and World War I," 78.

5 Beryl Segal, "A Jew in the Russian Army During the First World War," *Rhode Island Jewish History Notes* 7 (November 1975), 105–39; Salo W. Baron, *The Russian Jew Under Tsars and Soviets* (New York: Shocken Books, 1984), 156–67; Abraham G. Duker, *Jews in the World War: A Brief Historical Sketch* (New York: American Jewish Committee, 1939); American Jewish Committee, *The Jews in the Eastern War Zone* (New York: American Jewish Committee, 1916); and National Workmen's Committee, *The War and the Jews in Russia* (New York: National Workmen's Committee, 1916).

6 For a more extensive discussion of New York Jews and the World War I military draft, see Christopher M. Sterba, *Good Americans: Italian and Jewish Immigrants During the First World War* (New York: Oxford University Press, 2003), 53–81.

7 See especially the questionnaires of Solomon Novin, Michael Shalinsky, and Jack Kovar in the American Jewish Committee—Office of Jewish War Records Collection, American Jewish Historical Society, New York, NY; Henry Berry, *Make the Kaiser Dance* (New York: Doubleday, 1978), 322–23, 343; Maurice Samuel, *Little Did I Know: Recollections and Reflections* (New York: Alfred A. Knopf, 1963) 14–15; and *Memoirs of the Harvard Dead in the War Against Germany*, eds. Ralph Henry Lasser in M.A. DeWolfe Howe (Cambridge: Harvard University Press, 1922) 3:248–70.

8 On the election, see John F. McClymer, "Of 'Mornin' Glories' and 'Fine Old Oaks': John Purroy Mitchel, Al Smith, and Reform as an Expression of Irish American Aspiration," in *The New York Irish*, eds. Ronald H. Bayor and Timothy J. Meagher (Baltimore, MD: Johns Hopkins University Press, 1996), 374–94; and Kenneth S. Chern, "The Politics of Patriotism: War, Eth-

nicity, and the New York Mayoralty Campaign, 1917," *New York Historical Society Quarterly* 63 (1979), 290–313.

9 *New York Call*, September 8, 1917 and October 23, 1917. For studies that deal more specifically with Jewish aspects of the campaign, see Sterba, *Good Americans*, 138–45; Gil Rabak, "'For Peace, Not Socialism': The 1917 Mayoralty Campaign in New York City and Immigrant Jews in a Global Perspective," *American Jewish History* 101 (2017), 465–88; Irwin Yellowitz, "Morris Hillquit: American Socialism and Jewish Concerns," *American Jewish History* 68 (1978), 163–88; and Zosa Szajkowski, *Jews, Wars, and Communism* (New York: KTAV, 1972), 141–61.

10 August Claessens, *Didn't We Have Fun* (New York: Rand School Press, 1953), 89.

11 *New York Call*, September 20, 1917.

12 Louis Waldman, *Labor Lawyer* (New York: E.P. Dutton, 1944), 44.

13 Baruch C. Vladeck, *Memoirs*, Vladeck Papers (on microfilm) Section 2, General Material, c. 1907–1938, Box 7, Tamiment Library; Charles Leinenweber, "Socialists in the Streets: The New York City Socialist Party in Working-Class Neighborhoods, 1908–1918," *Science and Society* 41 (1977), 152–71; *New York Call*, September 17 and 18, 1917, October 3, 1917; and Louis Eisenstein, *A Stripe of Tammany's Tiger* (New York: R. Speller, 1966), 27.

14 Claessens, *Didn't We Have Fun*, 101; and Waldman, *Labor Lawyer*, 79–81; *New York Call*, September 26, 1917, October 22 and 23, 1917, and November 5 and 6, 1917.

15 *New York Call*, November 7, 1917.

16 *Ibid.*, November 7 and 8, 1917; and Vladeck, *Memoirs*, 98.

17 Bernard K. Johnpoll and Harvery Klehr, *Biographical Dictionary of the American Left* (Westport, CT: Greenwood Press, 1986), 69–71, 156–57, 244–46, 308–9, 364–65, 392–97, 400–402.

18 *New York Times*, December 3, 1917; *Jewish Communal Register of New York City, 1917–1918*, second ed. (New York: Kehillah (Jewish Community) of New York City, 1918) 1462–78; and *American Hebrew*, November 30, 1917 and December 7, 1917.

19 *American Jewish Chronicle*, November 2, 1917. There was some internal debate over the wisdom of the campaign among members of the Joint Distribution Committee. Albert Lasker, a JDC officer from Chicago, argued that "by dividing the moneys collected with the Welfare Board, I am afraid the showing will be so small for War Relief work as to spell the death of the movement." Albert Lasker to Jacob Billikopf, October 26, 1917, Folder 1, Box 452; and Jacob Schiff to Albert Lasker, October 29, 1917, Folder 6, Box

453, Jacob H. Schiff Papers, Jacob Rader Marcus Center of the American Jewish Archives, Cincinnati, OH (hereafter "AJA").

20 *American Jewish Chronicle*, November 16, 1917.

21 *New York Herald*, December 5, 1917.

22 *New York Times*, December 11, 1917.

23 *American Jewish Chronicle*, November 9 and 16, 1917, December 7, 1917; *Advance*, December 28, 1917; and correspondence of Jacob H. Schiff to William Sirovich, September 25, 1917; and William Sirovich to Jacob H. Schiff, September 19, 1917 and October 2, 1917, Folder 2, Box 452, Schiff Papers, AJA. For reporting on the dual campaign, see *New York Herald*, December 5, 8, and 9, 1917; *New York Call*, February 17, 1917; and *New York Times*, December 3, 5, 10, and 11, 1917.

24 *Advance*, December 14, 1917.

25 *Ibid.*

26 *Advance*, December 7–28, 1917, January 4, 1918, and March 1, 1918; *Ladies' Garment Worker*, January and February 1918.

27 Benjamin Gitlow, *I Confess: The Truth About American Communism* (New York: E.P. Dutton, 1940), 18, 20–21; *Advance*, October 26, 1917; *New York Journal American*, 1 (March 1918); and *New York Call*, March 2 and 27, 1918.

28 Rappaport, "Jewish Immigrants and World War I," 302–3, 323–24, 354–55; Harry Roskolenko, *The Time That Was Then: The Lower East Side, 1900–1914, An Intimate Chronicle* (New York: Dial Press, 1971), 85; and *Advance*, November 30, 1917 and January 18, 1918.

29 William Mulligan, *The Great War for Peace* (New Haven, CT: Yale University Press, 2014), 235–39; and Alexander Rabinowitch, *The Bolsheviks in Power: The First Year of Soviet Rule in Petrograd* (Bloomington: Indiana University Press, 2008), 131–80.

30 *American Jewish Chronicle*, October 19, 1917.

31 *New York Times*, August 4, 1918.

32 Eisenstein, *A Stripe of Tammany's Tiger*, 26; Steve Fraser, *Labor Will Rule: Sidney Hillman and the Rise of American Labor* (New York: Free Press, 1991), 114–78; and Melvyn Dubofsky, "Organized Labor in New York City and the First World War, 1914–1918," *New York History* (October 1961), 380–401.

33 Transcript of Newman interview by Barbara Wertheimer, "The Twentieth Century Trade Union Woman: Vehicle for Social Change Oral History Project" (Ann Arbor: University of Michigan, 1978), 51–52.

34 Melech Epstein, *Jewish Labor in USA*, (New York: Trade Union Sponsoring Committee, 1953), 2:71; *Advance*, November 30, 1917 and February 22, 1918; *New York Call*, March 14 and 29, 1918.

35 *The Outlook*, February 27, 1918.36 *Ibid.*

37 Charles Goldblatt, "The Impact of the Balfour Declaration in America," *American Jewish Historical Quarterly* 58 (1968), 480–83; Rappaport, "Jewish Immigrants and World War I," 326–34; *New York Times*, December 13, 1917; *New York Herald*, December 11, 1917; and *Maccabean*, January 1918.

38 *Jewish Communal Register*, 1340–409; Selig Adler, "The Palestine Question in the Wilson Era," *Jewish Social Studies* 10 (1948), 315; *New York Times*, October 31, 1918 and December 6, 1918; *New York Herald*, October 31, 1918; *American Jewish Weekly News*, October 25, 1918, November 1 and 8, 1918; and *Maccabaean*, July to December, 1918.

39 Allon Gal, "The Mission Motif in American Zionism," *American Jewish History* 76 (June 1986): 363–85 and "Independence and Universal Mission in Modern Jewish Nationalism: Comparative Analysis of European and American Zionism (1898–1948)," *Studies in Contemporary Jewry* 5 (1989), 242–74 (especially useful are the comments of Arthur Goren and Ezra Mendelsohn). See also Mark A. Raider, *The Emergence of American Zionism* (New York: New York University Press, 1998) and "Idealism, Liberalism, and Pragmatism: Stephen S. Wise, Nahum Goldmann and Abba Hillel Silver in United States," in *Nahum Goldmann: Statesman Without a State*, ed. Mark A. Raider (Albany: State University of New York Press, 2009); Michael Berkowitz, *Western Jewry and the Zionist Project, 1914–1933* (Cambridge: Cambridge University Press, 1997); Urofsky, *American Zionism*, 195–245; and Yonathan Shapiro, *Leadership of the American Zionist Organization, 1897–1930* (Urbana: University of Illinois Press, 1971), 99–134.

40 Moses Rischin, "The American Jewish Committee and Zionism, 1906–1922," *Herzl Year Book* 5 (1963), 65–81; *American Jewish Chronicle*, December 7, 1917, April 26, 1918, May 3, 1918; *New York Call*, May 19, 1918; and Joseph Rappaport, "Zionism as a Factor in Allied-Central Power Controversy (1914–1918)," in *Early History of Zionism in America*, ed. Isidore S. Meyer (New York: Arno Press, 1977), 311–25.

41 *Jewish Communal Register*, 1340–409; Adler, "The Palestine Question in the Wilson Era," 315; *New York Times*, October 31, 1918, December 6, 1918; *New York Herald*, October 31, 1918; *American Jewish Weekly News*, October 25, 1918, November 1, 8, 1918; and *Maccabaean*, July to December 1918.

42 *American Jewish Chronicle*, March 8, 1918.

43 *Ibid.*, April 12, 1918.

44 *Ibid.*, March 29, 1918; *American Hebrew*, April 6, 1917, March 1 and 8, 1918; *New York Herald*, October 31, 1918; *American Jewish Weekly News*, October 25, 1918, November 1 and 8, 1918; and *Maccabaean*, July to December 1918.

45 Leon Spitz, *The Memoirs of a Camp Rabbi* (New York: Bloch, 1927), 7.46 *Ibid.*

47 Lewis S. Feuer, "The Legend of the Socialist East Side," *Midstream* (February 1978), 25.

48 *New York Times*, November 12 and 13, 1918; Feuer, "Legend of the Socialist East Side," 25; Marie Jastrow, *Looking Back: The American Dream Through Immigrant Eyes* (New York: W.W. Norton, 1986), 165–66; and *American Hebrew*, November 15, 1918.

49 Abraham Okun to Louis Marshall, October 7, 1918, Louis Marshall Papers, AJA; B. Hoffman to Cyrus Miller, November 25, 1918, 178:6, Warburg Papers; *Yiddishes Tageblatt*, September 12, 1918; *American Hebrew*, February 15, 1918, March 15, 1918, and October 18, 1918; *American Jewish Weekly News*, May 17, 1918, July 5 and 12, 1918.

50 *Buffalo Jewish News*, May 31, 1918.

51 *Ibid.*

52 *New York Times*, November 12, 1918.

53 *Advance*, October 12, 1917; *Ladies' Garment Worker*, April, May, and June 1918; *New York Times*, February 18 and 27, 1918, November 12, 1918; and *New York Call*, March 1, 1918.

Passover Seder at Camp Sherman, Chillicothe, Ohio, 1919

Source: "Jewish Welfare Board Passover Seder, Chillicothe, Ohio" (1919), PC-698, Jacob Rader Marcus Center of the American Jewish Archives, Cincinnati, OH.

During World War I, the Jewish Welfare Board (JWB)[1] coordinated a variety of spiritual, educational, and recreational support for Jewish servicemen, including the provision of kosher food and worship and holiday services. In 1919, the JWB interceded with the US War Department and the American military to secure furloughs for enlisted men stationed in the United States who wished to celebrate the Passover holiday. The Chicago-based *Reform Advocate*, an English-language weekly founded and edited by Emil G. Hirsch (1851–1923), a prominent Reform rabbi and biblical scholar, published the following article a month before the holiday:

> Two-day furloughs will be granted to all officers and men of the Jewish faith in the army stationed in the United States during the Passover holydays [*sic*], it was made known today in a communication sent to Colonel Harry Cutler, chairman of the Jewish Welfare Board, by Adjutant General Ralph Morrison.
>
> Instructions have been sent to all commanding officers in the United States informing them that furloughs are to be granted from noon April 14 to midnight April 16 in order that Jewish men may attend services at their homes or in nearby towns.
>
> The official communication to Colonel Harry Cutler… from the office of the adjutant-general is as follows: "With reference to your request of January 8 for furloughs for all Jewish officers and men in the Army, you are advised that the following instructions have been sent to all commanding officers in the United States: The Secretary of War desires that furloughs be granted to members of the Jewish faith for Passover from noon April 14 to midnight April 16, 1919, provided this does not interfere with the public service."

> For the comfort of all soldiers who cannot go home for Passover, the Jewish Welfare Board will distribute matzoths [*sic*] in camp, hospital, and at all canteens. Seder services for men in uniform will be conducted at all Jewish Welfare Board centers, in cities throughout the country, and wherever a large number of Jewish men are to remain in camp, services will be conducted in the Jewish Welfare Hut.[2]

The photo reproduced here shows a group of enlistees and visitors celebrating the Passover holiday in Chillicothe, Ohio, the site of Camp Sherman, one of the country's largest training cantonments. At right, Sidney H. Riesenberg's JWB poster titled *Civilians* is visible (see see Sidney H. Riesenberg, *Civilians*, 1918 elsewhere in this volume).

— M.A.R

Endnotes

1 On the Jewish Welfare Board, see also the headnote to Sidney H. Riesenberg, *Civilians*, 1918.

2 Quoted from "Camp News of Our Boys, US Army and Navy," *Reform Advocate*, March 1, 1919, 82.

CHAPTER 3

THE JEWISH WELFARE BOARD AND THE CHALLENGES OF ZIONISM IN WARTIME AMERICA

JESSICA COOPERMAN

On December 2, 1917, Colonel Harry Cutler, chairman of the Jewish Welfare Board (JWB), received a telegram from the Jewish Ministers Association of America (JMAA) exclaiming that the "movement to establish a homeland in Palestine is facing a moment of great significance owing to recent declaration of the British government supporting Zionistic aims. . . ."[1] Cutler, the message continued, was invited to attend a conference featuring "the greatest statesmen and celebrities of the country" to discuss the Zionist movement and the Balfour Declaration that had been announced on November 2, just a month prior. The telegram closed with assurances the conference would also "express loyalty to our President in the name of all Jews and urge all to rally behind the American flag for the cause of democracy and the protection of small nations."[2] Cutler declined the invitation citing a previous engagement. In his response, he chided his would-be hosts, venturing "there is no need to urge our citizens of Jewish faith to express loyalty, for every Jew worthy of the name and true to his tradition, from the humblest to the most exalted... is eagerly demonstrating his real patriotism not merely by resolution but by service in every branch civil and military."[3]

This exchange between Cutler, who identified himself as supporter of the Zionist movement, and the JMAA, an Orthodox rabbinical organization which described itself as "unanimously resolved to work for the restoration of Palestine,"[4] reveals both American Jewish excitement over the implications of the Balfour Declaration, and concern over how the declaration and the Zionist project more broadly should be framed and discussed in the United States against the backdrop of the Great War. The JMAA was not alone in seeing the Balfour Declaration as an event significant enough to warrant attention from "statesmen and celebrities," but even they felt the need to offset celebrations like the one to which Cutler was invited with unequivocal declarations of patriotism and support for the American government—and they were wise to do so. Historians have noted that Jewish Americans were more often spared from accusations of "conflicting loyalties" during the war than other immigrant and ethnic groups, like Irish or German Americans, but proclamations of sympathy for foreign nationalist movements could still be dangerous business in wartime.[5]

During World War I, the Wilson administration vastly expanded the reach of the federal government and its ability to crack down on dissenters. President Wilson's presumed support of the Balfour Declaration, combined with appropriate statements about rallying to the flag, may have made the JMAA feel that their conference would not be perceived as a challenge to American wartime loyalties, but Cutler was chairman of a board charged with representing the interests of Jews serving in the American Expeditionary Forces; and the US military, in the middle of a war, was a difficult place in which to express complex, multilayered, and perhaps conflicting national loyalties.[6]

In the months following the Balfour Declaration, the JWB, together with its chairman, found itself in a delicate position as it sought to represent Judaism and advocate for Jewish soldiers and sailors in the American military, while simultaneously working to prove American Jews' patriotism and dedication to their country. Expressions of Zionist sympathy among some of the nearly 250,000 Jewish servicemen in the American armed forces created an uncomfortable situation for the JWB. In other settings Cutler might have greeted the Balfour Declaration and its implications for the establishment of a Jewish national home in Palestine with enthusiasm, but not while working to support the United States' war effort. When confronted with questions about Zionism in the American military, the JWB and Cutler found themselves unsure of what to say. Instead, they generally preferred not to talk about it.

The JWB was created specifically to represent the interests of Jews in the US military. It was established in April 1917 by a small group of influential men, likely organized by Cyrus Adler, acting president of the Jewish Theological Seminary of America. The group included Judges Julian W. Mack and Irving Lehman, the financiers Jacob H. Schiff, Mortimer Schiff, and Felix Warburg, and prominent New York attorney Louis Marshall among other well-established and well-connected community leaders, many associated with the American Jewish Committee.[7] They set out to create an organization that would serve as the Jewish representative to the US War Department's newly formed Commission on Training Camp Activities (CTCA), providing what became known as soldiers' welfare services.

President Wilson, Secretary of War Newton Baker, and General John Pershing, commander of the American Expeditionary Forces, all agreed the US military should not be merely a fighting force, but also a laboratory within which they could reform society by turning nearly 5 million men from almost every conceivable background and circumstance into morally upright, physically fit soldier-citizens committed to "100 percent Americanism."[8] The CTCA was a crucial component of this plan to "improve" the quality and character of American men during their military service. Under the leadership of its chairman, Raymond Fosdick, the CTCA worked in American military camps and bases to promote uplifting educational and recreations programs that would keep soldiers and sailors inspired, occupied, and out of trouble, while instilling in them a somewhat vaguely defined sense of American values and ideals.

As the country prepared for war it became clear that the CTCA would require civilian partners to adequately staff these programs and provide desired services to the rapidly growing number of men conscripted into the military. The first agency that the government turned to for help was the evangelizing Protestant Young Men's Christian Association (YMCA), which eagerly accepted the commission and the opportunity to provide recreation and moral guidance to young men in the military. The influence of the YMCA meant the American values conveyed by this government program were enmeshed with deeply embedded assumptions about Protestant normativity. Concerned about protecting the religious loyalties and wellbeing of "their" boys from the ministrations of the YMCA, the JWB, and Catholic Knights of Columbus rushed to offer their services as well[9]

As the war effort got underway, however, it was far from certain the War Department would be receptive to the idea of taking on Jewish or Catholic partners to its soldiers' welfare programs. Both Secretary Baker and CTCA chairman Fosdick had argued the YMCA, as a nondenominational Protestant organization, represented a "non-sectarian" approach to caring for the moral and physical wellbeing of the men. When Cutler and his board began their quest for official recognition from the War Department, they were informed that this would be impossible because adding a Jewish agency would introduce an undesirable element of sectarian division within the soldier's welfare program and among the men.[10]

The JWB pushed back against these assumptions, arguing Jewish soldiers could not truly develop their character as Americans without the guiding moral influence of a Jewish soldiers' welfare agency which would welcome all soldiers, but also, in Adler's words, "make adequate provision especially for the needs of soldiers and sailors of the Jewish faith, whose particular requirements could be fulfilled only by an understanding Jewish organization."[11] Judaism, the JWB argued, was a necessary source of the sort of moral and patriotic American values Wilson, Baker, and Pershing wanted to instill in the country's young men; and the only one that could truly speak to the needs of Jewish men in the American military.

By the time Cutler received the telegram from the JMAA inviting him to a conference celebrating the Balfour Declaration, the JWB had only just managed to receive its long-desired appointment to serve as the only Jewish agency authorized by the War Department to participate in the government's vast social and civic experiment. Cutler and his colleagues at the JWB had spent all the eight months since the United States entered the war lobbying for this position, and they were extremely conscious of the terms under which the commission had been secured.

To make its case to the War Department, the JWB had argued that Judaism was a religious tradition inherently compatible with and supportive of American ideals. It argued against any form of Jewish segregation or separation in the military, and insisted American Jews saw the United States as their true homeland. As Cutler explained in a speech given at Independence Hall in Philadelphia, American Jews "come to this hallowed spot with a feeling as though [they] were going to the holy resting place of our great forefathers Abraham, Isaac, and Jacob."[12]

American democracy, they argued, provided the ideal environment in which Judaism could flourish. As JWB executive director Chester Teller proclaimed to his audience at the annual meeting of the Jewish Publication Society of America in 1918, "worship of God, 'each man according to his own conscience,'" was "the basic principle of the Democracy."[13] "Thank God," Teller continued, "we understand now better than ever before what American means. The President has made that clear for all time. 'Self-determination of peoples' is his undying phrase—not only self-government, but free self-realization for every man. In giving full expression to our best selves as Jews, we are not only better Jews—we become better Americans."[14]

For some American Jews, formulations of Jewish identity like the one Teller advanced on behalf of the JWB were perfectly in keeping with the goals and ideals of the Zionist movement. Justice Louis D. Brandeis was certainly the best-known advocate of this line of thinking, arguing that support for Zionism was part of the "moral mission of American Jews."[15] Brandeis and his supporters claimed that by supporting Zionism, and contributing materially to the movement's success, American Jews could alleviate the suffering of their coreligionists in Europe, while building the sense of communal responsibility that would make them better American citizens.[16] Likewise, Julian W. Mack, a JWB executive committee member, who was also part of the justice's inner circle (the so-called "Brandeis group") echoed Brandeis arguing there was "absolutely no incompatibility between Zionism and Americanism."[17]

> A true man ought to be and is no less a dutiful son because he becomes a faithful husband, or later an affectionate father; for him there is no incompatibility between the three relations. Indeed, on the contrary, just because the loyalty of affection is not single and exclusive, each branch of it should be strengthened by the strengthening of every other branch. The more devoted a man is as a husband, the better he should be as a son and a father.[18]

Zionism, Mack, like Brandeis, reasoned, was one of these loyalties of affection that could only help to strengthen the others, and he pointed to the sentence in the Balfour Declaration stating that "nothing shall be done which may prejudice the rights and political status enjoyed by Jews in any other country,"[19] as absolute proof that an American Jew could—and should—offer spiritual and material support for the Zionist project even while one's "political allegiance to the United States must and will remain single and undivided."[20]

According to these American Zionists, there was room within the relationship between American democracy and religious freedom for patriotic Jewish Americans to express their support for both Balfour and Zionism. President Wilson's claim that the United States was fighting for the rights of small nations, and his eventual support for the goals of the Balfour Declaration, created space for American Zionists to advocate for a Jewish national home in Palestine without feeling they were acting against American war aims. For a Jewish organization working through the War Department within the military, however, the stakes of asserting support for Zionism were far higher than they were for prominent citizens like Brandeis and Mack.

The Wilson administration, for all its advocacy of global democracy, also instituted harsh policies policing the behavior and loyalties of its citizens.[21] Jews as a group did not face the same sort of scrutiny directed at pacifists, socialists, or German Americans, but communal leaders remained alert to accusations that Jews were not fully supportive of the American war effort. These anxieties were heightened by the German origins of some of the country's most influential Jewish leaders, including JWB executive board member, Jacob H. Schiff. Like many American Jews, Schiff initially favored the German cause (or at least preferred American neutrality) to US support for England and France, both of which allied with the despised and antisemitic Russian tsarist regime.[22] The JWB, including board members like Schiff, wanted to ensure American Jews were seen as supportive of their country's war effort. The revolution in Russia and its subsequent withdrawal from the war certainly made it easier for American Jews to join the fight on the side of Britain, but they took care to stress the importance of public displays of Jewish patriotism. "From no where [*sic*]," Cutler warned, "must there be a challenge that the American Jew is lukewarm in his patriotism or does not concern himself with his country... The record that we ... make during the progress of the war," he pre-dicted, "is going to be either to our credit or our shame as an element of American citizens."[23]

Fear of arousing suspicions of Jewish disloyalty offered one incentive for the JWB and its chairman to avoid expressing a public opinion on either Zionism or the Balfour Declaration. Dissent within the JWB, however, offered another compelling motive. The JWB was comprised of representatives from all the major Jewish congregational and rabbinic organizations, the Young Men's Hebrew Association, and the Jewish Publication Society, as well as prominent community leaders affiliated with the American Jewish Committee, which was decidedly not pro-Zionist in its orientation. The Federation of American Zionists and its spokesmen, including Brandeis and Rabbi Stephen S. Wise, were not invited to join. Mack may have been willing to advocate for the compatibility of Zionism and Americanism, but other influential JWB members, including Adler, Marshall, and Jacob and Mortimer Schiff (respectively, father and son), were far from convinced that Zionism and American patriotism were appropriate companions.

The Schiffs were particularly concerned about the negative implications of expressions of Zionist support within the American military. When asked by pro-Zionist economist Elisha Friedman in July 1917 to lend his influential voice to those calling for the restoration of the Jewish homeland, Jacob H. Schiff said no. He argued that while he was not anti-Zionist, he felt increasingly convinced that Jewish nationalism was, in his words, incompatible with "true and sincerely loyalty to America."[24] To add weight to his claim, the elder Schiff told Friedman he had reliable evidence "that a great majority of the Russian-American Jews, who cling so tenaciously to Jewish nationalism have... no intention to wholeheartedly submit to the conscription laws."[25]

Schiff's reservations about Zionism preceded the war, but the suggestion that American Jews might evade the country's draft in the name of Jewish nationalism placed it beyond the pale. As historian Derek Penslar argues, military service was often an effective means by which Jewish men could assert their masculinity and their worth as citizens of the modern nation state. But refusal to serve or demonstrations of half-hearted loyalty could do the opposite, and the government was unyielding in its condemnation and prosecution of "shirkers" and draft resisters.[26] Schiff and other JWB leaders were very anxious to see Jewish men, particularly the newly arrived eastern European immigrants among them, live up to the ideals of virtuous male citizenship that military service offered and the War Department sought to inculcate in its soldiers through the CTCA's programs. They felt convinced that military service in the United States' massive war effort would provide an unparalleled opportunity to prove what Jewish citizens could offer their county and to demonstrate Jewish men were just as fundamentally American as their fellow citizens.

To Schiff, therefore, the biggest concern after the possibility Jewish immigrants would not respond to the draft at all, was that despite the assurances the JWB had given to the War Department about the essential Americanness of Judaism, expressions of Jewish identity would lead men to segregate themselves from other soldiers and sailors, demonstrating Jewish difference from rather than sameness with other Americans. Mortimer Schiff, in accord with his father's position, wrote repeatedly to Cutler emphasizing that the JWB "must at all hazards endeavor to prevent segregation and getting where the Jewish soldier and sailor will be considered a separate quantity."[27] "I think," the younger Schiff stressed, "it would for obvious reasons be a grave mistake if ... Jewish soldiers and sailors were segregated from their comrades, and would likely lead to prejudice and other consequences which would be very much deplored."[28]

To the Schiffs and their allies, Zionism represented a threat to American patriotism, not a complement to it. Despite the insistence by Zionists that there was no conflict in supporting Jewish settlement in Palestine and the American war effort, the Schiffs, Adler, and Marshall perceived too much of a risk in the attempt to do both at once. "In the present crisis," Schiff wrote to philosopher and Zionist supporter Horace M. Kallen, "good

Zionists must show, first, that the weal of the country, of which they happen to be citizens, must be their main concern."[29] After the end of hostilities, perhaps, different conversations might be possible, but not in the middle of a war and not when the ability to prove the loyalty and value of American Jewish servicemen was at stake.

Cutler and Teller found themselves having to tack delicately between the opinions of JWB members like Mack and the wealthy and powerful Schiffs. The most prudent course of action seemed to be to say as little as possible on the subject. Thus, the JWB tended to emphasize the religious components of its work and to downplay anything that smacked too strongly of Jewish nationalism. "Throughout," Cutler reported at the end of the war, "it has been the aim of the Jewish Welfare Board to conserve the religious beliefs of the sailors and marines of the Jewish faith."[30] From the "very beginning," an institutional report claimed:

> The Jewish Welfare Board has realized that one of its primary functions is the maintenance of the spiritual contact that the men made during their civil life, and in all of our religious activities we are guided by the principle that we are to conserve every religious belief represented among the Jewish men in the camp.... there are generally the biblical discussions and Jewish forum meeting which give an opportunity to the men not only for intellectual development but for the retention and for the strengthening of the influences of Jewish spiritual life.[31]

Even when discussing the more social aspects of its work with soldiers, the JWB report continued, care was taken to avoid specific mention of national identity, Zionism, or anything else that distinguished Jewish men from their non-Jewish brothers-in-arms:

> Though it is difficult to conceive of anything distinctively Jewish in entertainment and in a recreational program, yet the Jewish Welfare Board has been able to give to its entertainments, the fine feeling of brotherhood and Jewish social life that the soldiers have been accustomed to in their family reunions and in their club meeting. The men in camp look forward to these nights when they can gather informally, and spontaneously give expression in folk singing to all that is dear to them in Jewish social life.[32]

Family reunions, expressions of brotherhood, club meetings, and folk songs were deemed appropriate to the American Jewish identity that the JWB wished to shape among soldiers, and to project to the War Department and the military. These commitments, like the "loyalties of affection" described by Mack, aligned with the conceptions of religion sustained by the War Department and the Protestant YMCA. In a word, the JWB promoted a sense of Jewishness defined in terms of religious and spiritual practices, or social and cultural habits, rather than national loyalties. It was not an explicitly anti-Zionist position, but neither was it pro-Zionist. It was a Jewish identity that emphasized Americanism and loyalty to the flag, while presenting Jewishness as an unthreatening complement to those larger commitments. As Teller told an audience of Jewish communal workers in 1918: "Has not an organization like this, created in an emergency, representing the American Government, organized Jewry, the plain Jewish people and the local communities of America, a unique opportunity? And shall not we Jews avail ourselves of it by rising now as never before, to a truly national consciousness of our community?"[33] The national community he referred to was the United States.

Cutler, in his speeches, sometimes celebrated the "spirit of the Maccabees," which would lead even "a little shoemaker or tailor"[34] to take up arms, but he took care not to focus on where the Maccabees had lived or for what they fought. Instead the JWB emphasized American Jewish soldiers' unwavering commitment to the United States and the country's war aims. Even matters as seemingly minor as office stationery were scrutinized for appropriate patriotism, so that when Teller inadvertently approved an order for letterhead with the American flag positioned at the bottom and a Star of David at the top, Cutler asked him to the recall the offending design and make sure it did not find its way into the hands of unsuspecting servicemen, fearing what he described as the "moral effect" such a slip might have on both letter writers and recipients.

Silence on questions about Zionism was a strategy that minimized the possibility of conflict among JWB executives and constituent members. It was, moreover, a way of accentuating claims that Judaism led men to unswerving and unshakable loyalty to the United States, without emphasizing the ways it might also connect them to Jews in other countries or to the rights of other nations. Silence from the JWB, however, did not guarantee silence from the soldiers themselves. At least some of the Jewish men serving in the American military saw Zionism as a significant part of their Jewish identity. Trying to keep them quiet about it was a task that caused significant headaches for the welfare board ostensibly there to serve them.

One matter that caused consternation at JWB headquarters was the display of Zionist flags and materials in Jewish Welfare Board buildings on US military bases. In May 1918, Jacob de Haas writing on behalf of the Provisional Executive Committee for Zionist Affairs, led by Brandeis, wrote to Cutler stating: "It has been reported to me that someone in the Welfare Board has been objecting to Zionist propaganda in the camps ... What is there to this?"[35] Cutler replied carefully: "...The problem which you raise is not limited only to Zionist propaganda. There is a large question of principle involved, namely in how far it is legitimate in the American Army to engage in propaganda for any cause whatsoever, other than a directly military or patriotic cause...." The JWB, he assured de Haas, has permitted "lectures and talks on any Jewish theme.... But the Board cannot see its way clear to allow Zionistic propaganda ... in the camps."[36] To bolster his argument, Cutler cited military orders stating: "Field Representatives [of the JWB] are instructed neither to encourage nor give official sanction to the organization of any group of men in uniform in which membership is restricted to Jews only.... I believe that this should make our position clear, a position which is necessitated by the elementary demands of a true democracy and by the traditions of the United States Army."[37]

De Haas, however, was not satisfied. A few weeks later, he wrote to executive director Chester Teller, citing Cutler's letter, and pressing the JWB to adopt an explicitly pro-Zionist stand. Teller echoed Cutler's position, but softened it somewhat, backing away from his claims about the demands of democracy and stressing the need to remain neutral on this controversial and potentially divisive issue. "The attitude of this Board with respect to Zionism is a strictly neutral one. As a body representing all Jews, you can well see how any other position on our part would be quite untenable.... We cannot permit the Welfare Board to be used as a medium for propaganda of any kind. We are, in short, not anti-Zionist, but anti-propaganda."[38]

De Haas appears to have thereafter dropped the issue of distributing Zionist propaganda in the camps, but efforts to press the JWB to take a pro-Zionist stand were far from over. In July, Louis Lipsky of the Federation of American Zionists wrote angrily to Cutler. It had come to his attention the JWB representative in Norfolk, VA, Moses (Moe) Levy, had ordered the Zionist flag taken down, stating "he did not recognize any flag but the American flag and that there was no such thing as a Jewish flag." The Zionists of Norfolk, Lipsky reported, were indignant, and demanded to know what the JWB thought of the Mr. Levy's actions.[39]

Cutler again attempted to settle the matter by referring to military regulations, stating "on several occasions, officers of the

War Department have indicated to me the impropriety of showing any anything but the national colors in the army or navy posts in this country." He stressed he had spoken to Mack about this issue and that "Mr. Mack was emphatic in his statement that no flag should be exhibited in the camps other than the American flag."[40]

An undated letter from the JWB to Moe Levy likewise addressed the issue of raising a Zionist flag, this time at a JWB center in town rather than at any of the nearby army or navy bases. In this context, the JWB relented concerning the policy of flying only the American flag but still took care to distance itself from overtly pro-Zionist sentiment.

> The attitude of this Board with respect [to] Zionism is strictly neutral. Nevertheless, the conclusion has been universally reached that, whereas the blue and white flag formerly was symbolic of the emblem of the Zionist… It is no longer necessary to be Zionist to recognize the traditional value and significance of the blue and white flag, nor do we make propaganda for Zionism, when we yield to the request for men in uniform for the display of this emblem which may be so dear to them. The Board tries to reflect in its program every desirable element of Jewry, and it tries to conserve in the Jewish soldier every quality that makes him a more patriotic American and a better Jew.[41]

This response regarding the flying of the Zionist flag on JWB properties outside of military camps reflects careful crafting, and while this copy is unsigned, it resembles Teller and Cutler's other attempts to tack between competing demands. It allowed the "indignant" Zionists of Norfolk to fly their blue and white flag, but makes clear that one need not recognize the flag as a Zionist symbol. It reflected Mack's framing of the complementary nature of Zionism and Americanism, but demonstrates the JWB's effort to remain entirely neutral on the issue. Neutrality was, of course, a hard path to walk during the war. It did not entirely satisfy Zionism's advocates or opponents in the JWB or the military camps, but it was perhaps the best option available as the JWB worked to please its many constituencies, while enacting policies in line with the wishes of the US War Department.

Finding ways for local Zionist organizations to fly their flags at JWB buildings without recognizing them as Zionist symbols was a creative way of not voicing an opinion, but it did not silence the debate. Zionist soldiers in the camps were also a challenge for the JWB. In October 1918, de Haas forwarded Cutler a letter from a soldier named Alex Kantor, whom de Haas claimed, cast a negative light on the JWB. In the letter, Kantor asserted he was working hard at "spreading the seed of Zionism at [Camp] Wadsworth [in Spartanburg, SC]" after "smothering the soldiers with it [at his previous post] in Savannah," but he was frustrated in his efforts to promote "Zionistic propaganda" by the local JWB representative. De Haas demanded an explanation of the JWB's policies. Cutler replied that while he celebrated Kantor's sincere enthusiasm for the cause, he thought the young man lacked prudency and tact. "I am frank to say," Cutler wrote, this letter "does not cast a side light on the Welfare Board.... It casts a direct light rather... [on] one man who is unacquainted with the difficulties, with which the Jewish Welfare Board has had to deal... in order to keep the loyalty of the Jewish people in this country, unsullied as far as possible."[42]

Keeping the reputation of American Jews "unsullied by Zionism," or any ism other than Americanism or Judaism, which it promoted as a faith inherently connected to Americanism, was a key component of the JWB's mission in the US military. While some JWB members, and even Cutler himself, sympathized with the movement, they feared the backlash it could create among non-Jewish soldiers and against the image of Judaism they sought to promote. Foreign flags and political propaganda ran the risk of sowing division and damaging the image of Jews as good American citizens. What symbolism, after all, might underscore Jewish segregation from other American servicemen more than the desire to rally behind a foreign flag in a time of war? Young men like Kantor may have possessed enthusiasm but not, in Cutler's opinion, the sort of political prudency necessary for keeping Jews welcome in America.

It was surely with a similar sense of concern and dread that Schiff received a missive from Abram Elkus, the US ambassador to Turkey—marked "Strictly Private and Confidential"—on the eve of America's entry into the war. In the letter, Elkus expressed his displeasure with the recent publication of Alexander Aaronsohn's book *With the Turks in Palestine* (1916).[43] While Aaronsohn used the book as a chance to criticize the Turks and praise the Americans, Elkus could not celebrate its message. Instead, he lamented the rashness of Aaronsohn's decision to "write about things which had better never have been written or talked about," including the names of officials who had helped Aaronsohn escape the Turkish army and leave Palestine with false documents.[44] Schiff responded sympathetically, agreeing to the "great unwisdom of such publications" and the dangers of Jewish overzealousness in such fragile times.[45] "We are trying hard here to instill some spirit of unity in the many Jewish factions that now exist," Schiff responded, but noted "the Zionists are most difficult to handle, for really they are constantly playing their own kind of politics…"[46] He expressed hope that "even the Zionists now understand we must pull together…"[47]

The JWB Schiff helped to create strove to act prudently and to keep the name of American Jews "unsullied" by any accusation that might put their loyalties at risk. Not surprisingly, the JWB leadership was alarmed to learn the Middlesex Regiment of the British military had opened offices in Boston and New York to actively recruit soldiers to serve in a Jewish battalion, under the British flag, in Palestine. In March 1918, Teller wrote to Cutler to say he had received a letter from one Isaac Fishman who reported "Dr. Shohan who has in charge the recruiting of a Jewish battalion for the Palestinian front under the British flag, has sent in a request to the Mass. [*sic*] branch for permission to maintain their headquarters at the Hospitality House."[48] Teller asked how to reply. Somewhat surprisingly, especially given his reluctance to see the JWB implicated in any form of Zionist "propaganda," Cutler responded, "I can see no objection to granting this permission provided no act is committed either through accident or design, which may compromise our Massachusetts branch and thereby reflect on the National Board."[49] Teller conveyed the JWB's position to Fishman, but more emphatically spelled out the limits placed on the battalion's activities in a JWB building: "[W] e can see no objections to granting this permission, provided it is definitely understood that the Massachusetts Hospitality House gives space for the administration of the work, without assuming responsibility whatsoever for its polices or management."[50] Even more importantly, Teller reminded Fishman, the JWB would strictly adhere to US government's policy regarding recruitment. "The regulations," he noted, "require that only friendly aliens—no American citizens—can be accepted as recruits for the Jewish battalion," and he warned that should some delinquent manage to enlist in the British forces under false circumstance, it would not reflect well on American Jews.[51]

A few weeks later, Fishman wrote to ask for additional assistance. With no lack of presumption, he wrote to tell Teller: "You are no doubt aware of the fact that a successful effort is being made in this city [Boston] to organize a Jewish battalion to serve under the British flag in Palestine... We feel that this work is war work and hence within the domain of your activities. The committee feels that the hospitality extended to the Jewish recruits should be part of the hospitality work contributed by you."[52]

A few days later Mack wrote to Cutler to reinforce this request, asking whether the JWB could provide assistance to men who had enlisted in the Jewish battalion while they awaited transport. As they were not American citizens but were now Allied soldiers, Mack suggested the JWB should undertake to provide them with religious and social services, just as British

Jews might do for American soldiers as they passed through British ports. "It would seem eminently proper for the Jews of America to extend at least some measure of hospitality to the Jews belonging to the forces of our Allies who are temporarily with us."[53] After all, he claimed, we are "practically amalgamating" our forces with the British Army.[54] "There can be no question," Mack continued, "that American Jewish hospitality extended to Jews of our allied forces will be most gratefully appreciated by the recruiting officers of those forces in this country, will tend to allay the feeling which, as you know, has heretofore been strong among them and is still unfortunately strong in the higher political circles of Great Britain and France, that the American Jews were pro-German and that so many of the them are still only half-heartedly for the Allied cause."[55]

Cutler initially refused both Mack and Fishman's requests. Despite Mack's suggestion that supporting Jewish recruits into the British military would make American Jews appear more supportive of the United States and its allies, Cutler worried about the appearance of diverting JWB resources away from the American military. But then Cutler changed his mind. He wrote to both Mack and Schiff saying he had been persuaded the JWB had an obligation to offer hospitality to these men. Cutler argued "the fair name of American Jewry demand[s] that we should extend proper hospitality to our brothers enlisting in the forces of our ally, Great Britain, while they are sojourners in our midst.... In all this, believe me, I have conscientiously taken an impartial view, giving primary consideration, as my duty requires, to the interests of our Board and the mission with which we are charged, divorcing it entirely from my concern in and for the Zionistic cause."[56]

In this response, Cutler again tried to separate Zionism from the issue at hand, framing aid to these soldiers as a form of assistance to fellow Jews and to Great Britain, without asserting investment in the "Zionistic cause" per se. The fact that the men in question were only "sojourners" and not citizens was central to this accommodation. When a postwar reference to these

Jewish Legionnaires appeared in JWB board meeting minutes and referred to them as American Jews, the phrase was crossed out and "aliens formally residing in America" was written into the margins.

The JWB had a hard job serving as a government appointed representative of Jews and Judaism to the US military. It had to balance the desires of Jewish soldiers against the demands of a country at war, and the requirements of the US War Department against the diverse opinions of the Jewish public, including those represented among its members. The neutral stance it tried to maintain vis-à-vis Zionism is a reminder of both the contentiousness of the cause among American Jews, and the fact that for the JWB pro- or anti-Zionist declarations did not merely reflect personal convictions but also the specific contexts of the wartime American state.

Military service promised to be a context in which Jewish men could demonstrate their valor and value as American citizens, and in which the JWB could assert Judaism to be an American religion, worthy of equal representation in military and government policy because of the many ways it reinforced American ideals. Zionists pointed to the United States' commitment to the rights of small nations as evidence of the ways Zionism furthered the goals of American democracy; those skeptical of Zionism disagreed. For men like Cutler and the JWB representatives working within the military it seemed better to remain quiet. As Teller put it, the JWB should engage in "no activity involving controversial matters whatsoever" and maintain "a degree of aloofness toward every question dividing Jew from Jew" or Jews from other Americans.[57]

Silence in fact remained JWB policy even after the war had ended. In 1919, the JWB hosted a Passover seder for American servicemen still in Europe and invited Jewish delegates to the Paris Peace Conference to attend the meal. After reviewing a copy of the *haggadah* the JWB had prepared for the occasion, Rabbi William Rosenau, a JWB board member and past president of the Central Conference of American Rabbis, wrote to

Teller noting the Zionist anthem *Hativkah* (Hebrew for "The Hope") was included in the service. "It is distinctly 'Zionistic' and the Jewish Welfare Board is not presumed to make propaganda for any one party in Jewry... I hope that 'Hattikvah' [*sic*] will be eliminated from the... service."[58] Teller's response was polite, but almost despairing as he related incident after incident in which the JWB tried to adhere to its own policy of neutrality while facing down criticism from all sides:

> One day, we have a complaint from Zionists that we are not Zionistic enough; the next day, their opponents protest that we are far too Zionistic. One day the Reform wing complains, the next day the Orthodox. Surely in a matter so vital, those of us within the organization should at least be one. With such agreement achieved, we shall be able to steer serene, confident that we have taken a middle tack free from the dangers of one direction or the other.[59]

Teller's dream of steering a middle path through the Passover seder faced just as much resistance as the JWB's earlier efforts at navigating the thorny issues of flags, agitators, and recruitment strategies. Rosenau responded angrily and with more than a slight edge of sarcasm, "I do not know to what extent the old Haggadah is known among my colleagues on the Board. Suffice it to say that it does not include Hattikvah [*sic*]... the Hattikvah has no place in the book just because the Hattikvah is Zionistic, when the book in question is to be made the ritual of the Seder in which Jewish boys of every possible shade of religious conviction are expected to participate." Rosenau closed the letter by stressing he expected the executive committee to take up his demand for the removal of the anthem at its next meeting, at which time he "should like to see the matter settled forever."[60]

The seder that followed this exchange of letters undoubtedly left Rosenau only partially appeased. Zionists present, however, were left equally unsatisfied. A description of the JWB seder, published in French by an N. Frank and translated for JWB officers back in New York, expressed pleasure at finding a "real discovery; they sing with the tune of the Hattikwa [*sic*], the psalm (126) 'When God brought the prisoner from Sion [*sic*] it seemed to us we were dreaming'.... the words go beautifully with the melody."[61] Frank praised the beauty and warmth of the moment, but noted angrily that "our old Hagada [sic] finishes by a phrase which expresses the wish of all the Jewish people and which is said everywhere on such a day.... This phrase which came from the hearts of our ancestors, we never pronounce it without tears in our eyes: *Leschana habbaha birouschlaim*" [*sic*] (Hebrew for "Next year in Jerusalem").[62] At the JWB seder in Paris, however, the latter phrase was inadvertently omitted.

ENDNOTES

1 Telegram to Col. Harry Cutler, December 2, 1917, I-180, Box 336, Folder: Palestine 1918, American Jewish Historical Society, New York, NY (hereafter: "AJHS").

2 *Ibid.*

3 Telegram from Harry Cutler to Dr. de Sola Pool, December, 3, 1917, I-180, Box 336, Folder: Pool, Dr. David de Sola, 1917–1918, AJHS.

4 *Jewish Communal Register of New York City, 1917–1918*, second ed. (New York: Kehillah (Jewish Community) of New York City, 1918), 1189.

5 See for example, Matthew Frye Jacobson, *Special Sorrows: The Diasporic Imagination of Irish, Polish, and Jewish Immigrants in the United States* (Cambridge, MA: Harvard University Press, 1995), 222–23.

6 See Christopher Sterba, *Good Americans: Italian and Jewish Immigrants During the First World War* (New York: Oxford University Press, 2003), 153–74 and Nancy Gentile Ford, *Americans All!: Foreign-born Soldiers in World War I* (College Station, TX: Texas A&M Press, 2001), 16–44.

7 See Cyrus Adler "An Account of the Origin of the Jewish Welfare Board," in *I Have Considered the Days* (Philadelphia: Jewish Publication Society of America, 1941), 219; and Oscar Janowsky, "The Origins of the National Jewish Welfare Board," chap. 1 in *The JWB Survey* (New York: Dial Press, 1948).

8 On the CTCA see Nancy Bristow, *Making Men Moral: Social Engineering During the Great War* (New York: New York University Press, 1996).

9 On work of the Jewish Welfare Board and the impact of the Jewish soldier's welfare program, see Jessica Cooperman, *Making Judaism Safe for America: World War I and the Origins of Religious Pluralism* (New York: New York University Press, 2018).

10 *Ibid.*, 67

11 Jewish Welfare Board, Final Report of War Emergency Activities (New York), 13.

12 Harry Cutler, Address at Independence Hall, Philadelphia, PA, December 18, 1918, I-180, Box 333, Folder, "History 1918–1919" #1 of 3, AJHS.

13 Address of Chester Teller, March 24, 1918, I-180, Box 337, Folder: "Reports 1917–1918," 1.

14 *Ibid.*

15 Mark A. Raider, *The Emergence of American Zionism* (New York: New York University Press, 1998), 25–28.

16 See Naomi W. Cohen, *The Americanization of Zionism* (Hanover, NH: Brandeis University Press, 2003), 23–25.

17 Julian W. Mack, "Zionism and the Palestine Restoration Fund," 1, I-180, Box 334, Folder: Mack, Hon. Julian, 1917–1918, AJHS.

18 *Ibid.*, 3

19 *Ibid.*

20 *Ibid.*

21 For a discussion of policies intended to discipline public behavior, see Christopher Capozzola, *Uncle Sam Wants You: World War I and the Making of the Modern American Citizen* (New York: Oxford University Press, 2008), 117–43.

22 See Naomi W. Cohen, *Jacob H. Schiff: A Study in Jewish Leadership* (Hanover, NH, Brandeis University Press, 1999). On Jewish responses to the war, see Sterba, *Good Americans*, 53–81 and Joseph Rappaport, *Hands Across the Sea: Jewish Immigrants and World War I* (Lanham, MD: Hamilton Books, 2005), 35–46.

23 Col. Harry Cutler, Address to the JWB Training School, I-180, Box 333, Folder: "History 1918–1929," AJHS.

24 Letter from Schiff to Friedman, July 6, 1917, I-180, Box 343, Folder: "Zionists," AJHS.

25 *Ibid.*

26 See Capozzola, *Uncle Sam Wants You*, 55–82.

27 Mortimer Schiff to Harry Cutler, October 22, 1917, MS 456: Schiff, Jacob, H. Papers 1917, Box 453/I-L, folder 10: "Jewish Welfare Board," Jacob Rader Marcus Center of the American Jewish Archives, Cincinnati, OH (hereafter: "AJA").

28 Mortimer Schiff to Harry Cutler, October 9, 1917, MS 456: Schiff, Jacob, H. Papers 1917, Box 453/I-L, folder 10: "Jewish Welfare Board," AJA.

29 Letter from Jacob Schiff to Horace Kallen, July 25, 1917, MS 456, Box 453, folder 13: "Horace Kallen," AJA.

30 Colonel Harry Cutler, "Report of the Jewish Welfare Board Activities in the US Navy and Marine Corps, Jan. 1st, 1919-Dec. 31st, 1919," I-337, Subgroup I, Series C, Subseries 3, Box 163, Folder: Rabbi Lee Levinger, WWI 1919–1920 (#1 of 6), AJHS.

31 Untitled document, no author listed, I-337, Subgroup I, Series C, Subseries 3, Box 163, Folder: WWI, 1919–1920 (#5 of 6), AJHS.

32 I-337, Subgroup I, Series C, Subseries 3, Box 163, Folder: WWI, 1919–1920 (#5 of 6), AJHS.

33 Chester Teller, "The Jewish Welfare Board: Its Work and Its Opportunity," Prepared for the National Conference of Jewish Charities, Kansas City, MO, May 12–15, 1918, I-337, Subgroup I, Series C, Subseries 3, Box 163, Folder: WWI, 1917–1941 (#3 of 3), AJHS.

34 Col. Harry Cutler, Address to the JWB Training School, I-180, Box 333, Folder: "History 1918–1929," AJHS.

35 Jacob De Haas to Col. Harry Cutler, May 14, 1918, I-180, Box 330, Folder "De Haas, Jacob, 1917–1918," AJHS.

36 The author appears to be Cutler, as this is a direct response to De Haas's letters to Cutler, although this copy of the letter is unsigned, June 12, 1918, I-180, Box, 336, Folder: "Pool, Dr. David de Sola," AJHS.

37 *Ibid.*

38 De Haas's letter of June 14 is cited in Teller's reply. Chester Teller to Jacob de Haas, June 19, 1918, I-180, Box 330, Folder: "De Haas, Jacob, 1917–1918," AJHS.

39 Letter from Louis Lipsky to Harry Cutler, July 19, 1918, I-180, Box 334, Folder: "Louis Lipsky," AJHS.

40 Harry Cutler to Louis Lipsky, July 22, 1918, I-180, Box 334, Folder: "Louis Lipsky," AJHS.

41 Copy of letter from JWB to Moe Levy, Norfolk, VA, I-337, Subgroup I, Series C, Subseries 3, Box 163, Folder: WWI, 1919–1920 (#4 of 6), AJHS.

42 Letter from Cutler to De Haas, October 22, 1918, I-180, Box 330, Folder: "De Haas, Jacob, 1917–1918," AJHS.

43 Alexander Aaronsohn, *With the Turks in Palestine* (New York: Houghton Mifflin Company, 1916), https://archive.org/details/cu31924027811458.

44 Letter from Elkus to Schiff, January 12, 1917, MS 456, Jacob Schiff Papers, Box 452, Folder 10: Elkus, Abram I, AJA.

45 Letter from Schiff to Elkus, February 17, 1917, MS 456, Jacob Schiff Papers, Box 452, Folder 10: Elkus, Abram I, AJA.

46 *Ibid.*

47 *Ibid.*

48 Letter from Chester Teller to Col Harry Cutler, March 18, 1918, I-180, Box 341, Folder: Chester Teller, 1917–1918, AJHS.

49 Letter from Harry Cutler to Chester Teller, March 19, 1918, I-180, Box 341, Folder: Chester Teller, 1917–1918, AJHS.

50 Letter from Chester Teller to Mr. Isaac Fishman, March 20, 1918, I-180, Box 336, Folder: Palestine 1918, AJHS.

51 *Ibid.*

52 Isaac Fishman to Chester Teller, April 2, 1918, I-180, Box 333, Folder: Jewish Legion in Palestine 1918, AJHS.

53 Letter from Julian Mack to Col. Harry Cutler, April 11, 1918, I-180, Box 334, Mack, Hon. Julian 1917–1918, AJHS.

54 *Ibid.*

55 *Ibid.*

56 Letter from Col. Harry Cutler to Julian Mack, April 12, 1918, I-180, Box 334, Mack, Hon. Julian 1917–1918, AJHS.

57 Letter from Teller to Rosenau, March 5, 1919, I-180, Box 341, Folder, "Chester Teller, 1918–1919," AJHS.

58 Letter from Rosenau to Teller, March 1, 1919, I-180, Box 341, Folder, "Chester Teller, 1918–1919," AJHS.

59 Letter from Teller to Rosenau, March 5, 1919, I-180, Box 341, Folder: "Chester Teller, 1918–1919," AJHS.

60 Letter from Rosenau to Teller March 11, 1919, I-180, Box 341, Folder: "Chester Teller, 1918–1919," AJHS.

61 "The Jewish Welfare Board's Seder," I-180, Box 333, Folder, "History 1918–1920 (#2 of 3), 2, AJHS.

62 *Ibid.*, 3.

National Hebrew School for Girls and *Beit Sifreinu*, cover, 1918

Source: *Anu ovrim*, cover art of *Beit Sifreinu* (1918). Pupils march from National School for Girls in New York City to a Hebrew University on the Mount of Olives. David and Fela Shapell Digitization Project, Jewish Historical Press, National Library of Israel and Tel Aviv University, courtesy of the Hebrew Union College Library.

"It was in the years before and during World War I," the scholar Alan Mintz explains, "that the Hebrew scene in America came alive."[1] Indeed, the *Jewish Communal Register of New York City*, a monumental two-volume work published in 1918 which lists virtually every Jewish organization in New York City of the time, amply documents the developments in this regard. Surveying the rise of Hebraism and Hebrew language instruction in the United States in this period, Reuben Brainin (1862–1939), a well-known Russian Jewish immigrant writer and literary critic, observed "the knowledge of Hebrew in this country is not limited any one class or group of Jews":[2]

> You will find it among the native Jews, as well as among the wealthy, as well as among the poor. True, the preponderating number of Hebraists is to be found among the Orthodox Jews and among the nationalists... But Jews who know Hebrew may also be found among our extreme radicals and socialists of all brands and, in passing, it may be said that although these last are generally neither religious nor nationalistic, they are very much alive to all the spiritual and communal problems of our people...
>
> Till about ten years ago America was a most unfavorable spot for the fostering of the Hebraic spirit. There were here many Jews who knew Hebrew. There was even a considerable number reading Hebrew books. But they were scattered. Hardly any effort was made to organize them and for many years there was no center around which Hebraists of this country could rally...
>
> The last ten years, however, saw a profound change in the Hebraic movement. Many modern Hebrew schools sprang up. The number of capable Hebrew teachers kept on increasing. These young pioneers blazed the trail... The two

Hebrew weeklies (*Hatoren* and *Haibri*) have been appearing now for two years, consecutively—a rather unusual record of longevity for Hebrew periodicals in America—and are gaining firmer ground from day to day...

The Bureau of Jewish Education,[3] which was founded by the Kehillah,[4] has centered around it many of the best Hebraists. Through the publication of textbooks, a training school for teachers, a juvenile Hebrew monthly of very fine caliber, in short, through diligent, systematic, organized work, it has vastly contributed to the spreading of the Hebrew language and literature among our younger boys and girls.

In recent years a Palestinian contingent of Hebraists arrived in this country. These young men and women, numbering about five to six hundred, speak Hebrew almost exclusively and they display unusual zeal for everything that pertains to Hebraic culture and the revival of Hebrew. They are, no doubt, a very powerful leaven to the Hebrew movement in this country. Another important factor is the National Hebrew School for Girls (Madison Street, New York). This school has about five hundred pupils and during the eight years of its existence has contributed greatly to diffusing the knowledge of Hebrew among our girls.

...All of this is symptomatic of the rising Hebraic spirit in this country. It is a fact that the number of devotees to the living Hebrew word is continually growing and American Jewry is beginning to evince a desire to go back for its inspiration to its old spiritual sources.[5]

The cover art of the National Hebrew School for Girls publication, *Beit Sifreinu* (Our Schoolhouse), includes the headline *"Gilyon hanukat habayit"* (Dedication Ceremony Program). Given that the school was founded in 1905 and the publication references a 1918 housewarming event—it is also priced at twenty-five cents (noted at the bottom)—it may be part of a fundraising effort. Visible beneath the scroll (containing the words *beit sifreinu*) are the faces of four girls emerging from the blossoms of a flowering vine. The girls at either side grasp the scroll with outstretched hands and their modern hairstyles include hair bows. The girls at the center are depicted in profile nodding towards a book that anchors the illustration. Just below the girls a line reads *"Kovetz yotzeh leor al yadei talmidot Beit Hasefer Haleumi"* (roughly, a collection produced by the female students of the National Hebrew School), followed by the publication information (New York and the date according to the Hebrew calendar). In the lower half of the page, a throng of pupils marches across a stone bridge—beneath clouds reminiscent of the pillars of cloud and fire noted in chapter 13 of the Book of Exodus which lead the Israelites out of Egyptian captivity—linking the National Hebrew School for Girls in the foreground to a distant shore inscribed with the words "Mount of Olives," a mountain ridge east of and adjacent to Jerusalem's Old City. The buildings in the background, which resemble the architecture typical of Palestine's ancient fortress cities, are flanked by a flag with a star of David and the words "Hebrew University" (the spelling of university is not modern Hebrew) and palm trees. Interestingly, the America-Holy Land interrelationship depicted here is not anchored by a male iconography—typically, Hebraist and Zionist literature of the period is adorned with cherubs and patriarchs, boys and men pouring over sacred texts, and brawny male pioneers tilling the land—but rather by a distinctly protofeminist portrayal of girls and young women whose modernizing agency is on full display and who appear to be pivotal to the nation-building future of the Jewish people.

— M.A.R

Endnotes

1 Alan Mintz, "Introduction," in *Hebrew in America: Perspectives and Prospects* (Detroit: Wayne State University Press, 1993), 15.

2 Quoted from Reuben Brainin, "The Hebraic Movement in America and the Histadruth Ibrith in New York," *Jewish Communal Register of New York City, 1917–1918*, second ed. (New York: Kehillah (Jewish Community) of New York City, 1918), 1215.

3 Founded in 1909 as a branch of the New York Kehillah (see note 4), the Bureau of Jewish Education (BJE) was the first central Jewish educational agency in North America. Until his retirement in 1941, the BJE was directed by Samson Benderly (1876–1944), a Palestinian Jewish immigrant to the United States and noted Hebraist educator. Under Benderly's guidance, the BJE helped to professionalize the field of Jewish education and ran model Jewish schools in the 1910s.

4 The New York Kehillah, a nonsectarian effort to create an all-inclusive citywide Jewish communal structure, lasted from 1908 to 1922.

5 Brainin, "The Hebraic Movement in America and the Histadruth Ibrith in New York, 1215–18.

CHAPTER 4

The Big Tent's Collapse: The Balfour Declaration and Emergent Cleavages in American Hebraism

PHILIP HOLLANDER

In the months prior to the Balfour Declaration's promulgation, one finds the American Hebrew community's diverse interests reflected in the variegated material published in the American Hebrew weekly *ha-Toren* (The Mast).[1] Coeditors Yitzhak Dov Berkowitz and Shemaryahu Levin cultivated this variety and also lent their prestige to the journal.[2] A prominent Hebrew writer who made a name for himself in Europe before immigrating to America, Berkowitz published original and translated fiction in *ha-Toren*. In fact, his Hebrew translations from the *oeuvre* of his father-in-law Sholem Aleichem attracted readers desperate to get their hands on every text by the popular Yiddish master. Meanwhile, Levin, a former Russia Duma deputy, World Zionist Organization central committee member and a popular Zionist orator in the United States, who had become coeditor earlier in the year, gave the journal political heft. Levin employed his Hebrew rhetorical skills in the paper's editorial section *Parshat ha-shavua* (Portion of the Week) to address issues of contemporary import. One also found original and translated literary works by emerging American Hebrew talents, literary criticism, scholarly articles on diverse topics in Hebrew and Judaic Studies, autobiographies and memoirs, discussions of Jewish education, and examination of Jewish and world politics. Additionally, each issue featured digests containing material culled from newspapers published in the United States and abroad in various languages and other sources. They provided updates about world and Jewish affairs; there was even a Zionist movement digest. Finally, each issue concluded with updates about recent events in the American Hebrew community, invitations to upcoming Hebraist events, advertisements for goods and services, and help wanted ads.

Ha-Toren's service as a big tent accommodating the needs and views of a diverse group of Hebraists living on American shores would gradually cease following the Balfour Declaration's announcement. Individuals with different conceptions of Jewish nationalism found their writings coalescing on the journal's pages, because the Great War had created conditions that precluded Hebrew culture's development and flourish elsewhere. Most Hebraists shared the millennial dream of a Jewish return to Zion. Yet, prior to the Balfour Declaration's dissemination, this goal seemed unrealizable. Consequently, few Hebraists had fully considered how much they were willing to sacrifice for its realization and how their devotion to Hebrew culture related to Zionist settlement in Palestine. Should one prioritize acquisition of Hebrew linguistic proficiency, preservation of Hebrew cultural treasures, and creation of modern Hebrew culture with contemporary relevance, or should free time, financial resources, and even one's life be sacrificed to ensure a Jewish state's creation? The pages of *ha-Toren* attest to the fact that after issuance of the Balfour Declaration a small contingent of Hebraists who considered language, nation, and land to be the Jewish national project's foundations abandoned the United States for Palestine and Europe, where they felt better able to advance the Jewish national project. Most American Hebraists, who continued to maintain diverse views about land's relationship to Jewish nationalism, however, chose to remain in the United States. They prioritized Hebrew cultural revival and education of American Jewish children and youth in its spirit. During the interwar period, these American Hebraists developed a distinctive Hebrew national outlook that ran counter to the Palestinocentrism dominant in Zionist circles, even within the United States, and advanced a Hebrew national vision less at odds with the diasporic past and the Jewish religious tradition than the one developing in Palestine.[3]

Prominent Hebraists Engage an American Hebrew Future

The Great War disrupted Jewish life in the emergent Palestinian Jewish center and the east European Jewish heartland.[4] The threat of physical violence, starvation, and disease and sometimes even forcible expulsion brought many prominent Hebraists with extensive literary and journalistic experience to the United States.[5] Having fled Palestine, Eliezer Ben-Yehuda spent much of the war in the New York Public Library, where, thanks to American Jewish patronage, he dedicated himself to composition of his seminal Hebrew dictionary.[6] The "father of modern Hebrew" also contributed to *ha-Toren*, publishing installments of his memoir *ha-Halom ve-shivro* (The Dream and its Interpretation) and op-ed pieces on events of the day. Following their expulsion from Palestine in 1915, David Ben-Gurion, Israel's first prime minister, and his sidekick Yitzhak Ben-Zvi, Israel's second president, journeyed to New York. Both men continued their work on behalf of the Poalei Zion party. In addition, they wrote *Yizkor,* a volume touting Palestinian Jewish pioneers' exploits and the gallantry of Jewish watchmen who died protecting Jewish property, and *Eretz Yisroel*, a volume orienting Jews to the physical Land of Israel, its history and culture. Both Yiddish volumes, Hebrew-language excerpts of which were published in *ha-Toren*, sold well. They enriched the two men and helped gain them increased notoriety.[7]

Shemaryahu Levin, who had been on an extended speaking tour in the United States when the war broke out, numbered among the prominent European Hebraists who found refuge in the United States. Expelled from Germany as Russian nationals, Berkowitz and religious Zionist leader Rabbi Meir Berlin (Bar-Ilan) also travelled to the United States from Europe.

Like Hebraists who arrived in the United States prior to the war, the recently arrived were uncertain about what would happen in its aftermath.[8] Could the east European Jewish cultural center be resurrected? Would enough Zionist infrastructure remain intact in Palestine to enable the construction of a better Jewish future there? Clear answers to these questions did not exist. Veteran Hebraists confronted the possibility that the United States constituted the only viable location for Hebrew national culture's development. Berlin explicitly made this point: "We hope that our newspaper, *ha-'Ivri* (The Hebrew), will exist, grow, and develop in this land, the land of the present of our nation's remnant."[9] Consequently, veteran Palestinian and European Hebraists numbered among those establishing *ha-Histradrut ha-'Ivrit be-Amerikah* (the Hebrew Organization of America) in 1916, pushing to democratize the American Jewish community and better advance Hebrew and Zionist interests, and looking to introduce Hebrew education into the public school system, something that had up until that point been a key institution in the Americanization of immigrant Jewish youth, to promote Hebrew and Jewish national interests.[10] Many within the Jewish community, as well as many outside it, pushed back against these efforts. Nonetheless, uncertain about any other path, Hebraists engaged with the possibilities of America.

The Temporarily Obscured Founders of the American Hebrew Center

While Berlin reestablished a European Hebrew paper in the United States, Berkowitz and Levin had not brought *ha-Toren* or Hebrew culture to America. In fact, Hebrew usage among non-

Jews and Jews dates back to the colonial times, Furthermore, the first American Hebrew periodical *ha-Tzofeh ba-Aretz ha-Hadashah* [The Watchman in the New Land] was published in 1871, and the American Hebrew organization *Shochare Sefat Ever* [Hebrew Advocates] was founded in 1880. Yet, when a new type of Jewish immigrant began arriving in the United States in the early twentieth century, the conditions necessary for the establishment of a journal like *ha-Toren* and for the maturation of the American Hebrew center were finally met.[11]

Prior to the war, an average of nearly one hundred thousand east European Jews immigrated to the United States every year.[12] Among them were young men and teenagers possessing a sense that production and consumption of Hebrew letters united them with other producers and consumers belonging to a borderless Hebrew literary republic. When the number of these individuals achieved critical mass, it led to the United States' emergence as a full-fledged Hebrew cultural center.[13] As scholar Alan Mintz explains, "for the younger Hebraists [...] Hebrew served as the very existential medium through which the anguish and excitement of the nation's rebirth were taking place. [...] Hebrew, in its catholic embrace, was the ground itself of the new national reality, the essence of the revolution."[14] While these young men and teenagers were younger than established Hebraists like Levin and Ben-Yehuda, lacked the strong European Hebrew pedigrees of Berkowitz and Berlin, and did not have the Palestinian Hebrew journalistic experience of Ben-Gurion and Ben-Zvi, they shared their commitment to a Hebrew literary republic.[15] They set out building its American infrastructure soon after their arrival in the United States and created cultural institutions that effectively integrated wartime refugees. *Ha-Toren*'s initial editors, Shimon Ginzburg, Abraham Goldberg, Shalom Ber Maximon, Daniel Persky, and Benjamin Silkiner numbered among these young men and teenagers.

These young men and teenagers brought a sense of membership in a Hebrew literary republic, akin to Benedict Anderson's imagined community, with them from eastern Europe.[16] This perception had gained legs there when political upheaval, enlightenment, industrialization, urbanization, immigration, and social change, whose effects became increasingly felt, reduced extant Jewish communal structures' effectiveness and fractured individual Jews' sense of self in the 1880s.[17] The male scions of the traditional east European Jewish middle class, who had received a classical Jewish education and attained Hebrew literacy, now turned to Hebrew literature broadly understood to process their experience and find the aesthetic sustenance necessary to go on facing it. Thus, "a truly national reading public numbering in the hundreds of thousands" emerged.[18]

This vibrant public sphere profoundly affected east European Hebraists who immigrated to America. They grew up in a Jewish world that supported Hebrew dailies, specialized literary almanacs, literary journals, and book series. Furthermore, they witnessed Jews looking for direction analyzing these materials in a way once reserved for Talmudic passages. Hebrew libraries were founded to enable widespread access to these texts and they served as locations where members of the Hebrew literary republic could rub shoulders. Similarly, proto-Zionist and Zionist groups were established that discussed these materials, as well as issues of the day, in Hebrew and offered Hebrew lessons to those who wanted to join their community. In so doing, Hebrew activists came together as a modernizing Jewish community working to create a culture synthesizing traditional Jewish cultural elements with the best of the modern secular world.

As the lives of *ha-Toren*'s first editors attest, early twentieth century American Hebraists participated in the east European Hebrew public sphere as consumers of modern Hebrew culture and made preliminary steps to contribute to its development and dissemination prior to immigrating to America. Goldberg and Persky actively participated in the Hebrew public sphere from a young age. Like many Hebraists, Goldberg left the *yeshivah* world after exposure to modern Hebrew literature introduced him to a whole new way of looking at the world. When he travelled to Berdichev at the age of sixteen to pursue secular studies, he got involved in the activities of the Zionist organization "Bnei Tzion" (Sons of Zion). He participated in their Hebrew discussions; when he began teaching Hebrew language in their evening school, he helped spread their cultural message.[19] Similarly, as he became increasingly devoted to the Hebrew language, Persky shirked off traditional piety. Not only did he study it and its literature intensely, but he also participated in numerous Hebrew organizations like "Dovre Ivrit," (Hebrew Speakers), "Tzion u-sefatah" (Zion and its Language), and "Sefatenu" (Our Language), taught Hebrew language on a voluntary and professional basis in his teens in Minsk, and published his first articles in the Warsaw Hebrew newspaper *ha-Tzofeh* (The Spectator) in 1903.[20]

Silkiner and Ginzburg were even more involved in Hebrew literary affairs prior to their emigration. Both made their way to Odessa, a leading turn-of-the-century east European Jewish cultural center that competed with Warsaw for Hebrew cultural ascendency. A tight knit circle of prominent Hebrew writers made their home there, including Asher Ginsburg (Ahad ha-Am), Hayyim Nachman Bialik, and Sholem Yankev Abramovits (Mendele Moykher Sforim). Silkiner chose to continue his studies in Odessa and soak in the ambience. During this period, he published his first poem in the Vilna Hebrew paper *ha-Zeman* (The Times). Through his service as Abramovits's secretary between 1909 and 1912, Shimon Ginzburg interacted even more intimately with Hebrew literature's leading lights. This interaction led to his publication of Hebrew poetry in *ha-Shiloah* (The Shiloam) beginning in 1910.[21] Founded by Ahad ha-Am in 1896, *ha-Shiloah* was the leading Hebrew literary journal of the time and publication in its pages marked one's arrival on the Hebrew literary scene.[22]

Like Goldberg, Maximon's exposure to modern Hebrew literature played a role in his loss of faith and his decision to abandon *yeshivah* study. Subsequently, he earned his livelihood as a Hebrew teacher, submitted Hebrew fiction for publication and participated in Zionist organizations. Following his emigration from the Russian empire in 1902, his involvement in literary matters grew. In London, where he lived until he immigrated to the United States in 1913, he helped found the *Dovre 'Ivrit* club. Soon Maximon and other club members, under the leadership of Yosef Haim Brenner, an emergent Hebrew literary star, founded the seminal journal *ha-Me'orer* (The Alarm; 1906–1907). *Ha-Me'orer* filled a void created by the temporary cessation of Hebrew publishing in the Russian empire following the 1905 Russian Revolution. Through his contribution to the journal's daily function and distribution, Maximon played a pivotal role in sustaining the Hebrew republic of letters. During his time in London, Maximon also published his first article in *ha-Shiloah*.[23]

Maximon's involvement with *ha-Me'orer* and the publication of his work in *ha-Shiloah* demonstrate that while a sense of Hebrew literary community first struck root in eastern Europe, it was not confined by borders and proved highly portable. Nothing precluded its spread to England, America, Palestine, and beyond. Thus, when young Jewish men who had participated in the east European Hebrew public sphere faced isolation and the difficult process of acclimating to life in United States, they did not join *landsmanshaftn* or fraternal orders popular among their immigrant and native-born American Jewish contemporaries.[24] Looking to recreate the type of community they had enjoyed in eastern Europe, Hebraically literate men and even some Hebraically literate women joined together in the early twentieth century to form small organizations that united them around their shared commitment to Hebrew culture. Thus, one finds such groups meeting on East Broadway and Henry Street, in Brownsville and Brooklyn, in Chicago and Milwaukee, and at various points throughout the United States and Canada.[25]

To ground their relations with other members of their specific organization, develop their connections with members of other American Hebrew organizations, and proactively participate in the transnational Hebrew literary world, prominent members of these scattered organizations sought to publish literature reflective of their distinctive American experiences. Initially, they turned to veteran Hebraists familiar with the publishing business to aid them in their endeavors. Reuven Brainin had edited the Viennese Hebrew journal *me-Mizrah ume-ma'arav* (From East and West; 1895–1898) and volumes of the prominent Warsaw Hebrew literary almanac *Luah Ahi'asaf* (The Ahi'asaf Calendar; 1893–1904). When he arrived in America in 1908, young Hebraists turned to him for help. As he recounts, these young Hebraists "who gained their knowledge of our language and their love for it in the lands of the East" and whose "poetic spirit first shined in the land of freedom and God's wide open spaces" wanted to "pay off their national debt" through "resurrection of our language and our literature."[26] These Hebraists' desire to show that "American Jewry does not just want to receive with an outstretched hand and a lowered head. It wants to give, inspire, and provide" found voice in the poetry collection *Senunit* (Swallow; 1910) and the short-lived weekly *ha-Deror* (The Sparrow; 1911) edited by Brainin.[27]

Shortly after *ha-Deror* ceased publication, members of the various Hebrew organizations who had recently banded together to form the umbrella organization *Ahi'ever* (Hebrew Brotherhood) hatched a plan to create an American Hebrew journal that could sustain itself over the long term. Rather than rushing a journal to press and relying on subscriptions alone, organizers sold individual shares in the Hatoren Publishing Association for five dollars.[28] After raising close to five hundred dollars in capital, they started publishing *ha-Toren* in June 1913.

Many young immigrant Hebraists were putting themselves through college and lacked financial resources. Nonetheless, they viewed "a sustained journal of good quality" as an "internal criterion of success" and viewed it as their duty to contribute to the kickstarter-like campaign to ensure the long-term financial stability of a top-tier Hebrew journal.[29] As Alan Mintz explains:

> Since the days of the Berlin Haskalah and *Hame'asef* through to Ahad Ha-am's *Hashiloah* in Odessa and

> Aronowitz's *Hapo'el hatsa'ir* in Eretz Yisrael, the most visible expression of the new Hebrew literature had been the periodical, whether miscellany or monthly. If New York was to achieve the status of a center for Hebrew culture—not Odessa perhaps, but who could tell? —then its arrival, or the prospects for the same, could only be marked by the appearance of a worthy journal.[30]

Between 1913 and 1925, 320 issues of *ha-Toren* appeared and its circulation peaked at more than 13,000. By skimping and buying shares in Hatoren Publishing Company, young early twentieth-century American Hebraists launched a flagship journal that ensured the American Hebrew center's maturation. The longevity and cultural contribution of *ha-Do'ar* (The Mail; 1921–2005), the Hebrew Organization of America's newspaper, has obscured *ha-Toren*'s contribution, but it built the cultural foundation upon which its successor developed and flourished. In the wake of the Balfour Declaration, the young Hebraists behind the founding of *ha-Toren* emerged from the shadows of their more prominent Palestinian and European contemporaries and put their distinct stamp on American Hebrew culture.

THE BALFOUR DECLARATION AS THE "BEGINNING OF REDEMPTION'S GROWTH"

The American Hebrew community ecstatically greeted the Balfour Declaration, and *ge'ulah*, the Hebrew word for redemption, became ubiquitous on the pages of *ha-Toren*. Shemaryahu Levin's first editorial on the topic was entitled "ha-Besorah ha-rishonah le-ge'ulah," (The First Gospel of Redemption).[31] The next month, one reads of American Zionists leaders' establishment of the Ge'ulah Fund to raise one million dollars for political organization, recapitalization of the Anglo-Palestine bank, and two expeditions to Palestine, one medical and the other to help the governance institutions of the *Yishuv* get back on their feet.[32]

Numerous congratulatory advertisements welcomed the newborn Ge'ulah Volitzsky into the world.[33] Likewise, many of those sending out Rosh Hashanah greetings to their fellow Hebraists made use of the word *ge'ulah* in September 1918.[34] For example, the board of the Hebrew organization "Ahi'ever" wishes "its members and all Hebrews wherever they might be found a year of *ge'ulah* for our land, *ge'ulah* for our nation, and *ge'ulah* for our language." Similarly, Israel Efros's poem "Mit'orerot tikvot noshanot" (Old Hopes Awaken), published in *ha-Toren* in December 1917, bundles distinct redemptions together as the Balfour Declaration's inevitable consequence.[35]

Born in 1891 in Ostrog, Poland, Efros immigrated to the United States in 1905. A few years later, he received rabbinic ordination from Rabbi Isaac Elhanan *yeshivah*—something that reflected the extent of his earlier religious training. Within a decade, he added ordination from the Jewish Theological Seminary and a doctorate in medieval Jewish philosophy from Columbia University to his list of credentials. Subsequently, he headed off to Baltimore to administer its *Talmud Torah*; he later founded the Baltimore Hebrew College, a Hebrew teachers' training college. [36] Eventually he moved to Buffalo to teach Jewish philosophy at the University of Buffalo and New York City to teach at Hunter College. During this latter period, he developed into a top-tier American Hebrew poet; he emerged as a prominent representative of the immigrant generation that brought the idea of a transcontinental Hebrew literary community to America and employed it to integrate into American life.

Rather than prefiguring the concise lyrical style that later earned Efros poetic renown, "Old Hopes Awaken" engages the effusive style dominant in Hebrew poetry from the east European pogroms of 1881–1882 to the First Zionist Congress in 1897. In contrast with early twentieth-century Hebrew poetry that typically features a lyrical speaker giving intricate expression to an expansive interior world as full and unfathomable as the natural world, "Old Hopes Awaken" showcases a prophetic speaker, evocative of the ones featured in Hibbat Tzion period emulations of biblical prophecies of consolation, whose fate is inextricably linked to his people's fate. In this way, Efros strove to provide his readers with the confidence and strength to act in momentous times.

Through extensive catalogs of Jewish suffering and frequent evocation of the Land of Israel in its former glory or current desolation, Hibbat Tzion period poems modelled on biblical prophecies of consolation draw Jewish readers together as a downtrodden national collective and proceed towards optimistic endings that voice the renewed kingdom foretold in biblical prophecy and promise a better Jewish future in the Land of Israel.[37]

Naphtali Herz Imber's "ha-Tikvah" (The Hope) and Bialik's "'El ha-tzippor" (To the Bird; 1892) constitute two prominent examples of Hibbat Tzion poetry familiar to Hebrew readers that display a marked similarity to "Old Hopes Awaken." After being edited down and assuming an abbreviated form, "The Hope" became Israel's national anthem; as Bialik's first published poem, "'El ha-tzippor" was placed on Israel's Hebrew literature curriculum as an example of the type of diasporic Jewish yearning for Zion that propelled Zionism's emergence.

"To the Bird" employs the springtime arrival of a migratory bird on the speaker's windowsill to frame his reflections about winter-like diasporic Jewish suffering and the possibility of a spring-like Jewish rebirth in the Land of Israel's fecund landscape.[38] "Old Hopes Awaken" also employs the theme of spring's arrival, as well as new day and resurrection themes to create a narrative frame: "Old hopes rise and forgotten dreams awaken,/ invigorated boughs loaded with resurrective dew shake in the distance,/ ringing news and fog-encased hints hover/ in the pale trembling [horizon] lines shifting as the night comes to an end,/ no eye sees a sun, yet the heart feels its proximity/ in another moment it will appear with its glory and splendor on the Eastern mountains."[39] While the eye cannot yet discern the changes afoot and provide empirical evidence of them, the rhetoric of bodily resurrection, spring, and a new day convey the heart's belief that momentous news (*besorah*) will soon arrive.

Despite the opening paragraph's foreshadowing of coming redemption, subsequent paragraphs catalog the tribulations the Jewish people faced in the Land of Israel and in the diaspora. While Jews have long maintained their nobility and honor, they have reached a breaking point. The increasing divergence between the heart's belief in the possibility of Jewish life's positive transformation and empirical observation of contemporary reality leads the speaker, as well as his readers, to question whether the speaker's heart betrays him. The world war has unleashed widespread destruction. Those with a living God, a nation, and a land might see a future, but the speaker forecasts destruction for all. Rather than acting, he gazes upon the growing conflagration and despairingly recalls the Jerusalem Temple ablaze.

When the poem concludes, however, irrefutable evidence comes to light that confirms the arrival of the previously forecast new day. At his most despairing moment, the speaker's heart and eye finally align. Just as the Hebrew Bible's narration of the Jewish people's exodus from Egypt and their subsequent redemption began at night and continued into a new day, the redemption of contemporary Jews has begun in the night-like darkness of the Great War and will continue into the future. The speaker recognizes this due to an outstretched arm's appearance: *"mi-Ba'ad timrot-shalhevet netuyah li zero'a"* (from amid billowing flames an arm was outstretched to me).[40] Yet, in contrast with Exodus 6:6 or Psalms 136:12, where an outstretched arm (*zero'a netuyah*) metaphorically conveys God's use of his power for the Jewish people's benefit, the British government's outstretched arm initiates redemption. It appears "with a scroll in its hand, the scroll of [the speaker's] liberation and redemption," and the speaker soon hears "the freedom tune of the nations."[41] Subsequently, the speaker recognizes how the flames or rays of the new day's sun will create a forge where he will be able to place his soul on an anvil, beat down on it with his mighty hammer, and refashion it to voice his nation's freedom song. Indeed, the speaker's forging and his brethren's implied forging of new free souls will require that they endure pain, but the speaker asserts that the ends will justify their trial. It will enable contemporary Jews to establish the earthly and heavenly Jerusalems (*malkhut-'olam u-malkhut-shamayyim mi-me'al*) that their ancestors dreamt about.[42]

PRIORITIZING A HEAVENLY JERUSALEM

The pages of *ha-Toren* detail the serious crises facing the Jewish people in eastern Europe and Palestine and the need for substantial amounts of money and ongoing commitment to respond effectively to them. Yet, if the American Hebrew movement was to build a firm foundation that would guarantee Hebrew and Jewish cultures' survival in America and cultivate a philanthropic spirit among American Jews that would galvanize them to contribute to European Jewish relief and reconstruction and state-building in Palestine, money needed to be earmarked for these purposes and support needed to be given to those willing to dedicate their time to their accomplishment.

In fact, these objectives effectively aligned with the broader vision of spiritual or cultural Zionism as envisioned by its founder Ahad ha-Am.[43] Shimon Ginsburg and Benjamin Silkiner interacted with Ahad ha-Am in Odessa and Shalom Maximon developed a strong tie to him during his sojourn in London, but, even if American Hebraists had never met Ahad ha-Am, they were shaped by his writings. In fact, Alan Mintz asserts that Ahad Ha-Am's influence pervades the whole American Hebrew project.[44] Thus, even though most American Hebraists shared Ahad ha-Am's hope that the Land of Israel would develop into the Jewish people's spiritual center (*merkaz ruhani*), they prioritized the struggle against Jewish assimilation; they viewed the creation of a vibrant contemporary Hebrew culture as the best way to bind Jews to their heritage.

In eastern Europe, as proto-Zionists (proponents of the *Hovevei Tzion* movement) and Zionists struggled against entrenched traditionalists for the hearts and minds of the Jewish street, they looked to take control of local communal organizations and synagogues. Yet, when they encountered powerful resistance, they shifted their attention to Jewish education. There were two intertwined stages to their plan. First, they developed *hadarim metukanim* (improved *heders*, or Jewish primary schools) to educate children in accordance with a cultural Zionist perspective. Subsequently, they planned to branch out to create Zionist-infused *talmud torahs*. While *heders* and *talmud torahs* were both primary school level Jewish schools whose graduates could pursue further education in *yeshivot*, parents paid *heder* tuition for their children and communities generally paid *talmud torah* expenses to educate children of less affluent parents who could not afford to educate their children privately. In the modern period, the educational scope of *talmud torahs* expanded. In many cases, Jewish education beyond the primary school level was offered to children who would not pursue *yeshivah* study. Thus, by taking control of these Jewish educational institutions, spiritual Zionists looked to bloodlessly impose their vision on Jewish life.

Spiritual Zionist objectives led to the institution of *'Ivrit be-'Ivrit* (Hebrew in Hebrew) as a central instructional methodology in *hadarim metukanim*. In contrast with the traditional east European *heder*, where the teacher employed Yiddish as a language of instruction and students learned the Hebrew Bible by memorization of each Hebrew word and its Yiddish translation, a *heder metukan* employed an immersion technique to enable instruction of all subjects in Hebrew.[45] Consequently, *heder metukan* instructors sharpened their Hebrew skills on a daily basis and many students acquired a meaningful facility in Hebrew language that enabled their participation in Hebrew's national revival.

Spiritual Zionism's development and spread in America paralleled and sometimes even preceded its European development and spread. Thus, while historian Ehud Luz points to a *heder metukan* that opened in Pinsk in 1895 and served as a model for additional *hadarim metukanim* throughout eastern Europe, Zvi Hirsh Neumann established the Shaare Zion school in Brooklyn in 1893.[46] It employed the *'Ivrit be-'Ivrit* methodology to educate students in a Zionist spirit. Consequently, even before large numbers of Hebraists arrived in the United States in the early twentieth century, spiritual Zionists employed Hebrew to spread their ideology.

While Samson Benderly, the founder of New York's Bureau of Jewish Education, and his disciples have rightfully been credited for developing American Jewish education, many important innovations in American Jewish education, like the *'Ivrit be-'Ivrit* method, originated with American Hebraists like Neumann and were spread by them.[47] In 1905, a conference of Hebrew-speaking clubs resolved to introduce the *'Ivrit be-'Ivrit* methodology into more schools; soon thereafter, Ephraim Kaplan put this resolution into practice when he established the National Hebrew School in Brooklyn.[48] In the next decade, similar schools employing this method would open in Detroit, Chicago, Buffalo, Cleveland, Indianapolis, Minneapolis, and Pittsburgh. Through their staffing of these and similar schools throughout the United States, American Hebraists were on the front lines in efforts to conquer young Jewish hearts and minds.

In many cases, Hebraists who received their Jewish education in Europe went off to teach in cities lacking any coherent Jewish educational program and they played a critical role in providing these cities with a firm Jewish educational foundation. In fact, when reading through advertisements that ran in *ha-Toren* in 1917 and 1918, one sees the paper matching qualified Hebrew teachers and administrators with Jewish communities looking for talented individuals to man their schools. Thus, one finds ads for positions in locations throughout the United States, including the states of Connecticut, Illinois, Indiana, Iowa, Kentucky, Louisiana, Maryland, Massachusetts, Minnesota, Missouri, Nebraska, New York, Ohio, Rhode Island, Tennessee, Virginia, and Wisconsin.

As the now dominant use of the term Hebrew school, rather than the more traditional term *talmud torah* or the earlier American term Sunday School, indicates, American Hebraists successfully promoted their agenda in American Jewish education and impacted it strongly. As a 1911 editorial in the *Jewish Advocate* newspaper remarked, "To the zealots for Hebrew as a living tongue must be given credit for the evolution of a Jewish system of education."[49] For them, this constituted the path towards a secularized version of the heavenly Jerusalem, or *"malkhut-shamayyim mi-me'al,"* that Efros envisioned.

While spiritual Zionism struggled against entrenched traditionalists for dominance of the communal agenda in eastern Europe, the Jewish establishment aided Hebraists promoting spiritual Zionism in their takeover of American Jewish education. In the late nineteenth century, American Jewish leaders had been concerned about both eastern European Jews' reticence to Americanize and their slow acculturation. Yet the massive early-twentieth-century expansion in Jewish immigration to the United States and the associated challenges that it posed led them to worry about overly rapid Jewish assimilation. Consequently, they underwrote key institutions, like the Teachers Institute of the Jewish Theological Seminary (TI), founded in 1909, and New York's Bureau of Jewish Education, founded in 1910, to stem the tide.[50] Soon American Jewish leaders would establish Jewish education bureaus in many other American metropolitan centers with significant Jewish populations. These bureaus of Jewish education then strove to centralize Jewish education in schools following professionally designed curriculums and staffed by qualified teachers, many of whom were trained at TI and other Jewish teachers training schools that opened in additional Jewish urban centers. Both these Jewish education bureaus and these teachers training colleges became Hebraist strongholds. In a word, "zealots for Hebrew as a living tongue" staffed Jewish education bureaus; founded, organized, and staffed Hebrew teachers training colleges; administered and taught in K-12 Jewish schools.

Even in the wake of the Balfour Declaration, the bulk of American Hebraists considered development of a secularized American version of a heavenly Jerusalem a more easily realizable and significant endeavor than efforts to build a Jewish state in Palestine, especially one that rejected traditional elements of Jewish culture they sought to preserve. While American Hebraists only prepared a small cadre of individuals to fully take part in their Hebraist vision and contribute to its ongoing development, their achievement of important Zionist goals should not be disregarded. They inculcated a commitment to Jewish peoplehood that transcended national boundaries and a sense that American Jews needed to materially support Jews throughout the world, especially in the Land of Israel, to generations of American Jews whose supplementary education they oversaw.

Regardless of the feelings of impending redemption that brought thousands of American Jews to the form of Zionism championed by Louis D. Brandeis and helped fill the coffers of the Ge'ulah Fund, the bulk of American Hebraists endeavored to stay the course. They worked to advance the spiritual mission of the Jewish nation on American soil and tamped down their desire for earthly redemption in the Land of Israel. Consequently, as Zionist fundraising prioritized Palestinian Zionist development after the Balfour Declaration was proclaimed, American Hebraists made an impassioned call to keep a portion of these funds at home for cultural purposes. This struggle over the direction of Zionist fundraising and the place of spiritual Zionism within the Zionist movement found poignant expression in concerted efforts to meet a $10,000 capital campaign goal so the National Hebrew School (*Bet sefer le'umi*) for girls in Manhattan could move from its 183 Madison Street location to a new building at 206 East Broadway.

When it was founded in 1910, this unique girls' school stood out favorably from its surroundings. While the community survey of Jewish education in New York City composed that year detailed the failure of the city's Jewish institutions to meet even basic educational standards, the aforementioned school operated at a high level from its inception.[51] The youth and inexperience of its founder Hayyim Abraham Friedland made this success particularly surprising.[52] Friedland only arrived in the United

States in 1907, after years of intensive *yeshivah* study in his native Lithuania, and he founded the supplementary school after a few additional years of study at the Isaac Elhanan Yeshivah. Friedland eschewed rote memorization and harsh discipline, and he engaged his students through the study of Hebrew language and literature, the Hebrew Bible, and Jewish history. Furthermore, he recognized that for his educational efforts to succeed he needed to immerse his students in a pleasurable Hebrew language environment outside of regular instructional hours. Consequently, he developed a wide range of extracurricular activities for his students to pursue, including literature, drama, a newspaper, singing, dancing, drawing, and Zionism.[53] Additionally, he composed Hebrew short stories using a reduced vocabulary (which was also stressed during regular instruction) to promote Hebrew reading among his students during their free time at home.[54]

Despite the school's status as a pilgrimage site for American Hebrew educators looking to emulate its innovative approach and its enrollment of five hundred students, many of whom went on to become talented and dedicated Hebrew educators, short news items and advertisements in *ha-Toren* failed to persuade American Jews, even dedicated Hebraists, to aid the school in quickly achieving its financial goal.[55] Consequently, one finds a group of prominent Hebraists, including Joseph Barondess, Reuven Brainin, Joseph Eron, Zvi Hirsch Masliansky, and former *ha-Toren* editor Shmuel Melamed publishing an open letter to American Hebraists in *ha-Toren*:

> We now turn to Hebrew readers and lovers of Hebrew, both within New York and outside it, with this request: You need to make up the difference. One *shekel* that comes from a Hebrew source, from a man who truly understands this school's value and the character of its work, is more valuable and beloved than a hundred *shekels* from an alternate source. There is another reason that Hebrew support is so important now: This

> support will protect the school's soul and guard it from evil spirits likely to follow the money. Therefore, grant our request and remember that it is not just for your school's body but also for its soul.[56]

This letter did not fall on deaf ears. One finds a list of fifteen donors published in *ha-Toren* the next month. Contributions of a dollar or two point to efforts by Hebraists of even limited financial means to do their part.[57] In May 1918, *ha-Toren* announced a week-long celebration in June to mark the new school building's dedication and its position as the Lower East Side's central Hebraic institution. The celebration was set to feature parties, balls, and receptions directed towards different Hebrew, Zionist, and Jewish constituencies.[58]

Prioritizing an Earthly Jerusalem—Rhetoric and Reality

While the 206 East Broadway building's dedication should be read as a victory for American Jewry, especially for the young women who received an empowering Jewish education there, the 183 Madison Street building's long-term disrepair and American Jewry's failure to appreciate the importance of what these students achieved and what this accomplishment demanded of its teachers, point to its lack of identification with cultural Zionist goals and its devaluation of those who dedicated their lives to realizing them in the United States. As the aforementioned open letter declaimed, Manhattan's Hebrew National School looked to create a "healthy and normal" Hebrew environment to endow Jewish children with a vibrant Hebrew spirit.[59] Yet, the American Jewish community, as well as many Palestinocentric Zionists, did not prize this goal, especially for young women whose education they considered secondary to that of men. Consequently, the school was housed in a building that "was old and dilapidated, a dark and tiny ruin without light and without air;" the classrooms were "narrow and inadequate" and the furniture "damaged and broken."[60] The students crowded four to a bench and they shivered from the cold in the winter.

Even in this horrendous environment, the school succeeded and "raised a generation of female Hebrew readers" devoted to "sacred elements of the nation, as well as its hopes and aspirations."[61] In the absence of adequate resources, spiritual Zionist observers believed the reasons behind the school's success were self-evident. The school's "leaders and administrators devoted their lives (*masru et nafsham*) to maintaining it, [and] its teachers dedicated the best of their abilities and their dreams to it."[62]

Rather than accepting Jewish martyrological rhetoric's employment to convey the dedication and self-sacrifice of Friedland and his staff (the latter Hebrew phrase literally means "to deliver one's soul"), most American Jewish men and many Palestinocentric Zionists viewed these educational efforts as secondary. Men who taught girls Hebrew language were neither akin to those who gave up their lives in sanctification of God's name nor those who sacrificed their lives on the behalf of a homeland, Jewish or American.

Most American Jewish men were looking for a Zionist identity that would supplement their American identity and leave them feeling on par with their non-Jewish contemporaries, and efforts to build an earthly Jerusalem, either directly or indirectly, aligned more effectively with what non-spiritual Zionist men sought to achieve.[63] Indeed, most European and Palestinian Hebraists who had found sanctuary in the United States during the war ceased to give further thought to the American Jewish future following the Balfour Declaration's proclamation. Instead, they prioritized what they saw as necessary for an earthly Jerusalem's construction. Therefore, one finds prominent members of this group employing the rhetoric of self-sacrifice deployed by spiritual Zionists to promote a Zionist masculinity grounded in a readiness to die to ensure a Palestinian Jewish state's creation.

At a large assembly sponsored by the Poalei Zion party and held at New York's Cooper Union on November 30, 1917, Yitzhak Ben-Zvi and David Ben-Gurion relied heavily on martyrological rhetoric. Ben-Zvi turned to the audience and declared that "if we do not dampen it with our sweat and water it with our blood and the marrow of our bones, the declaration will not suffice for the Land of Israel's acquisition."[64] Audience members should not be intimidated by this demand, he argued, because "the first pioneers, who sacrificed their souls and their whole beings on the altar of our nation and our land (*she-hikrivu et nafsham u-me'odam al mizbeah 'artzenu ve-'amenu*), will always stand before us as a living example of how to work to bring about our redemption."[65] Subsequently, Ben-Gurion "spoke in the name of the martyrs and the heroes, the Palestinian guardsmen and workers, who delivered their souls (*she-masru et nafsham*) for the sanctity of the land and sanctity of the Zionist ideal." As he explained, "the lips of these great dead men spoke from their graves" and called out to the audience, "Jews, go up to the Land and possess it with the blood of your hearts and the sweat of your brows; then, only then, will it be guaranteed to you that the Land will be yours for an inheritance."[66]

Others, including Rabbi Mordechai Aharon Kaplan (Max Aaron Kaplan), expressed similar sentiments. In an open letter directed towards other Orthodox rabbis and preachers, the rabbi of Harlem's Nahalat Tzvi synagogue explained that the British government could not realize Jewish millennial hopes unassisted: "It depends on our opinions and the desires of our hearts how and with what we will advance the British government's desire. A holy obligation is placed upon all Jews today to sacrifice their money and their blood for national resurrection."[67]

In contrast with Rabbi Kaplan, who would remain in America after the war, Ben-Gurion and Ben-Zvi wanted to be among the first to demonstrate their preparedness to sacrifice for creation of Jewish state in Palestine, a sentiment soon conveyed by a resolution passed by the Poalei Zion party branch where the two men were active:

> We the Hebrew workers, the flagbearers of the Hebrew language, resolve to join the vanguard

> camp that will go up first to our homeland, and we obligate ourselves to dedicate all our strength to continue the work of the Hebrew workers and guards who gave up their lives (*masru et nafsham*) to our nation's resurrection in its historic land, to the building up of our land and the renewal of our culture on the basis of Hebrew labor and Hebrew language.[68]

Regardless of Ben-Zvi and Ben-Gurion's declared willingness to spill their blood fighting for a Jewish homeland, they had been expelled from Ottoman Palestine. Only their active involvement in negotiations between the British government and various Zionist organizations to permit Jews to fight as a distinct group within the British military offered them a chance to align their rhetoric with their actions on the Palestinian front.

Ze'ev Jabotinsky viewed his people's participation in the Entente forces struggle against the Central Powers as a way to strengthen their position at the postwar negotiation table and he was among the first Zionist leaders to advocate such an approach. Initially, his efforts led to the establishment of the short-lived Zion Mule Corps, a logistical unit of Jewish soldiers that supported non-Jewish combatants, but the idea eventually found more significant expression. When the British government instituted conscription in 1916, it sought a way to enlist Russian Jewish immigrant men residing in Britain to their cause and it created the Jewish Legion. Ultimately, negotiations with various Zionist organizations led to creation of three battalions and the enlistment of five thousand Jewish men to serve in them. The 39th Battalion of the Royal Fusiliers recruited its members in the United States. When the opportunity to enlist presented itself, Ben-Gurion and Ben-Zvi volunteered for the American battalion and worked to get other American Hebraists to enlist alongside them.[69]

Ha-Toren voiced meaningful support for Ben-Gurion and Ben-Zvi's position throughout 1918. Full-page ads calling for "young Jews who are not required to serve in the American military" to volunteer for the Jewish Legion were the most visually striking examples of this. Yet featured articles and news digest sections also voiced support for the two men's position.[70] For example, a fictive dialogue between two young American Hebraists written by Reuven Brainin, who played an active role in the American battalion's establishment, appeared in *ha-Toren*. It voices his active support for the Jewish Legion, as well his approval of his sons Yosef and Moshe's enlistments. In the dialogue, a young Hebraist who has just volunteered for the Jewish Legion promotes his position by challenging his American Hebrew interlocutor's masculinity. In addition to castigating his interlocutor for not joining the Jewish Legion, the volunteer takes issue with his interlocutor's failure to either laud his voluntarism or acknowledge that the volunteer's behavior proves more laudatory than his own. The volunteer rejects the assertion that "a live dog is better than a dead lion;" he asserts that if his cowardly counterpart was truly young he would "be overjoyed with the great opportunity before him to be one of the first to endanger his life for his and his nation's honor, for his homeland and its futures."[71] If not, the volunteer tells him, "cowardly young Zionists like him should stay at home, on their dais and on their watch, and receive their salaries, so that they will be able to go to Zionist gatherings and celebrations to applaud speakers who lecture eloquently about Israel's resurrection in the Land of Israel."[72]

Mainstream American Hebraists were not immune to the challenge put before them by proponents of a martyrial form of Hebrew masculinity.[73] They felt required to either actively heed the call to arms or speak out in favor of it. Thus, soon after the first enlistment group of the Jewish Legion left for Palestine, the Hebrew Club of City College proudly announced the departure of its members Frishkof and Grossman, and the *"Pirhei Tzion"* (Flowers of Zion) club of Perth Amboy, New Jersey, blessed their departing members.[74] New York's *"Bnei Am Hai"* (Sons of the Jewish People Live) club did their counterparts one better. It held a banquet in honor of its enlisting members.[75] Thereafter, one finds the Hebrew club Masada wishing its member S. Likhterman the best as he set off for Palestine. Its members declared their hope to see him "in our land as part of a nation free and healthy in body and soul."[76] By advertising that its members Aharon Frankel, Mordechai Halevi, Nun Mandelblat, Mem. Neiman, Zeev Pavzner, A. Rabinovitz, and Aleph Tabak had volunteered for the Jewish Legion, "Histadrut Ahi'ever" conveyed a sense of superiority grounded in its members' decision to take up the call to arms.[77]

Reports in *ha-Toren* of successful recruiting efforts and parades accompanying departing recruits to their boats made it seem like the enlistment goal of 10,000 American Jewish men would be easily reached and Hebraists would constitute the bulk of this number.[78] Yet this goal was never met and the reality of Jewish Legion recruitment proved radically different from *ha-Toren*'s presentation of it. British military representatives in America physically examined roughly 2700 Jewish men and deemed them physically fit for service.[79] Among actual recruits, only a third were members of Zionist organizations. Furthermore, many were members of groups like the Yiddish-speaking Labor Zionist Jewish National Workers' Alliance (Yidish Natsionaler Arbeter Farband), one hundred members of which reportedly joined the Jewish legion, and exiled Palestinian Jews, who used their enlistments as a cost-free way to return home.[80]

Only a small number of American Hebraists considered Jewish Legion service as the best way to advance national needs and embraced the risks of fighting on the battlefield for the establishment of a national home in Palestine. Even before recruitment for the American battalion started in March 1918, the British had taken Jerusalem and their conquest of Palestine was largely complete. Furthermore, the last recruits to enlist in the Jewish Legion were only sent off to Palestine in October, the same month the British signed an armistice with the Ottoman empire. Many legionnaires never saw combat, few were placed in situations where they faced imminent danger, and most recruits returned to the United States having accomplished very little on behalf of the Jewish people. Nonetheless, Ben-Zvi, Ben-Gurion, and other Zionist leaders assigned great importance to the Jewish Legion; they viewed it as a demonstration of a global Jewish commitment to fight and die for a Jewish national home and strengthen the Zionist claim to Palestine. By contrast, Hebraists who stayed in America to further Zionist-oriented education viewed their time as more wisely spent than if had they enlisted in the Jewish Legion. For them, positive educational and ideological outcomes trumped symbolic accomplishments.

Even after many of the most vocal Hebrew supporters of the ideal of martyring oneself for the nation had joined the Jewish Legion, and the British and the Ottomans had signed an armistice that precluded Jewish legionnaires' martyrdom, belief in the importance of martyrdom in defense of the nation continued to reverberate in *ha-Toren*'s pages. In October 1918, a thirteen-year-old Jewish girl living in Harlem decided to fly the Zionist flag from her parent's fire escape during a neighborhood block party. Immigrant Irish boys, neighborhood adults, and the police responded derisively to Sadie Dellon's innocent act of Jewish patriotism. After confronting a group of Irish youths, who pelted the flag with stones and broke a window in her parents' apartment, Sadie was attacked by a group of boys and a woman. A policeman saved Sadie from serious harm at her attackers' hands, but he blamed her for what happened. In her humiliation, Sadie committed suicide. Overlooking the evidence, the Jewish press, including *ha-Toren,* represented Sadie's death as murder and portrayed her as a heroine who died defending Jewish honor and sense of peoplehood through her defense of the flag.[81]

The Sadie Dellon case proved exceptional. The American Hebraist community was beginning to assume a more unified character as prominent proponents of political Zionism who glorified mortal sacrifice on behalf of the nation left the United States. Overwhelmingly, proponents of Hebrew committed themselves to a spiritual Zionist agenda and were prepared to dedicate their lives to intertwined Hebrew educational and cultural programs in America.

There were Hebraists in the United States who prioritized practical steps towards the construction of a Jewish national home in Palestine who maintained nationalist views quite different from those advanced by Ben-Gurion and Ben-Zvi and who remained in America in late 1918. Nonetheless, most of them eventually decided that America was an inappropriate place for them. They acknowledged their disinterest in the tedious mission that American Hebraists were assuming. When opportunities arose to head to Europe or Palestine to engage more directly with issues of Zionist state-building and more immediate redemptive possibilities, they seized them. For example, one reads in December 1918 that Shemaryahu Levin was preparing to return to Europe, where he would assume leadership of the Zionist movement's central committee. He would no longer be penning *ha-Toren*'s editorial column *Parshat ha-shavu'a*.[82] In a less overtly political way, Eliezer Ben-Yehuda and Nahum Slouchz later immigrated to Palestine, where they could combine their desire to spread Hebrew and Jewish culture with their commitment to the building up of the land.

As Hebraists possessed of an action-oriented Zionist approach emigrated from the United States, American Hebraists redoubled their efforts to build an educational infrastructure that would transmit Hebrew and Jewish culture to new generations of Jews. This reflected their affinity with cultural Zionism and their prioritization of spiritual redemption. This affinity also found expression in American Hebrew publications, such as *ha-Toren* and its successor *ha-Do'ar*. Geopolitics and international Zionist affairs in Palestine and Europe played a less significant role in these publications moving forward, and their focus increasingly shifted to the American Hebrew orbit, issues of Hebrew education in America, and the publication of Hebrew literature produced by authors residing in the United States.

CONCLUSION

During the World War I era, the belief that the United States constituted the only viable contemporary location for Hebrew culture and Jewish nationalism brought individuals with divergent Zionist views into the American Hebraist camp; this helps account for *ha-Toren*'s big tent nature on the eve of the Balfour Declaration. Yet, when the Balfour Declaration raised hopes for spiritual and earthly redemption among American Hebraists, previously obscured tensions surfaced. Most American Hebraists, who were proponents of cultural Zionism, chose to remain in the United States. By and large, they pursued spiritual redemption through the development of American Hebrew culture and the construction of a coherent Jewish educational system that could disseminate it and its associated values to American Jewish youth. Meanwhile, Hebraists living in the United States who prioritized construction of an earthly Jerusalem interpreted the Balfour Declaration as a sign that practical efforts could lead to the construction of a Jewish national home in Palestine. This interpretation led many to sever their ties with America and emigrate to Palestine to participate in nation-building or to Europe to advance a Palestinocentric Zionist agenda. Their departure left the American Hebrew camp with a more unified character and consequently a sharper strategy for the pursuit of a cultural Zionist and Hebraist agenda. Over time, their achievement of spiritual Zionist goals has been forgotten, but it constitutes an important page in American Jewish history.

Endnotes

1 On *ha-Toren* and its important role in American Hebrew culture's development, see Alan Mintz, "A Sanctuary in the Wilderness: The Beginnings of the Hebrew Movement in America in *Hatoren*," in *Hebrew in America*, ed. Alan Mintz (Detroit, MI: Wayne State University Press, 1993), 29–67.

2 On Berkowitz, see Avraham Holtz, *Isaac Dov Berkowitz: Voice of the Uprooted* (Ithaca, NY: Cornell University Press, 1973), 15–26. On Levin, see Judah Bernstein, "A Preacher in Exile: Shemaryahu Levin and the Making of American Zionism, 1914–1919," *American Jewish History* 102:3 (2018): 323–50.

3 On American Hebraists' distinctive form of Jewish national identity, see Michael Weingrad, *American Hebrew Literature: Writing Jewish National Identity in the United States* (Syracuse, NY: Syracuse University Press, 2011). On this distinctive Hebrew national vision's emergence in contradistinction to Jewish nationalism in Palestine, see Philip Hollander, "Voicing Alternative Hebrew Cultural Visions: Menachem Ribalow and *Antologiyah shel ha-shirah ha-ivrit be-Amerikah* (Anthology of Hebrew Poetry in America)," in *Russkie evrei v Amerike* (Russian Jews in America), ed. Ernst Zaltsberg (St. Petersburg: Akademichesky Proect, 2008), 16:71–89. Cf. Stephen Katz, *Red, Black, and Jew: New Frontiers in Hebrew Literature* (Austin: University of Texas Press, 2009); Alan Mintz, *Sanctuary in the Wilderness: A Critical Introduction to American Hebrew Poetry* (Stanford, CA: Stanford University Press, 2012).

4 For an eyewitness account of the east European Jewish heartland's devastation, see S. Ansky, *The Enemy at His Pleasure: A Journey Through the Jewish Pale of Settlement*, trans. Joachim Neugroschel (New York: Metropolitan Books, 2002). For an accessible discussion of Jewish life in wartime Palestine, see Abigail Jacobson, *From Empire to Empire: Jerusalem Between Ottoman and British Rule* (Syracuse, NY: Syracuse University Press, 2011), 22–52.

5 Jacob Kabakoff, "Hebrew Culture and Creativity in America," in *Jewish Life in America*, ed. Theodore Friedman and Robert Gordis (New York: Horizon Press, 1955), 194.

6 Ya'akov Kabakov, "Eliezer Ben Yehuda be-Amerikah," in *Sefer ha-do'ar: mivhar ma'amarim le-yovel ha-shishim tarpav-tashmav*, ed. Ya'akov Miklishanski and Ya'akov Kabakov (New York: ha-Histadrut ha-'Ivrit be-Amerikah, 1982), 203–4.

7 Shabtai Teveth, *Ben-Gurion: The Burning Ground 1886-1948* (Boston: Houghton Mifflin, 1987), 89–142.

8 On Brainin, see *YIVO Encyclopedia of Jews in Eastern Europe*, s.v. "Brainin, Re'uven," by Stanley Nash, http://www.yivoencyclopedia.org/article.aspx/

Brainin_Reuven. On his eventual marginalization within the American Hebrew community, see Ya'akov Kabakov, "Parshat Brainin be-Amerikah," pts. 1 and 2, *ha-Do'ar* 61.9 (January 8, 1982): 140; 61.10 (January 15, 1982): 149–50.

9 "Le-Hithadshut 'ha-Ivri,' le-Inyane ha-sha'ah," *ha-'Ivri*, January 7, 1916.

10 On the founding of *ha-histradrut ha-'Ivrit be-Amerikah* and its efforts at self-definition in its first years, see Moshe Pelli, *ha-Tarbut ha-'Ivrit be-Amerikah: 80 shnot ha-tenu'ah ha-'Ivrit be-Artzot ha-brit 1916–1995* (Tel Aviv: Reshafim, 1998), 21–78.

11 On the development of the American Hebrew press, see Shai Nehushtai, "ha-'Itonut ha-'Ivrit ha-Amerikayit, 1871–1914: megamot u-tekhanin," *Keshet* 4 (1988): 31–49; Michael Brown, "All, All Alone: The Hebrew Press in America from 1914–1924," *American Jewish Historical Quarterly* 59:2 (1969): 138–77. On this specific journal and organization, see Kabakoff, "Hebrew Culture and Creativity in America," 171–85; David Mirsky, "Hebrew in the United States, 1900–1920," in *Herzl Year Book* 5 (1963), ed. Raphael Patai, 84.

12 Gerald Sorin, *A Time for Building: The Third Migration, 1880–1920* (Baltimore, MD: Johns Hopkins University Press, 1992), 58.

13 Kabakoff, "Hebrew Culture and Creativity in America," 186; Mintz, "A Sanctuary in the Wilderness," 41–45; Dan Miron, *Ben ha-'ayin ha-nivka' la-'olam ha-nirka': ha-shira ha-'Ivrit be-Amerikah: parshat Avraham Regelson*, in *ha-Shirim*, by Avraham Regelson (Jerusalem: Mossad Bialik, 2013), 304–5.

14 Mintz, "A Sanctuary in the Wilderness," 32–33.

15 Women possessing Hebrew language proficiency and nationalist sentiment participated in the American Hebrew community. Nonetheless, scholars have yet to clarify their place within it. Already in the 1890s, one finds women writing in the American Hebrew press and struggling to ward off exclusion. Discussions of Hebrew clubs in *ha-Toren*, however, point to women's active participation in the American Hebrew community in 1917. Whatever the case regarding efforts to exclude women from the American Hebrew community, the literary community was an overwhelming male bastion. In deference to this fact, I will employ "men" to refer to its members. Mintz, *Sanctuary in the Wilderness*, xiv; A. R. Malakhi, "Toldot ha-tenu'ah ha-'Ivrit be-Amerikah," in *Hagut 'Ivrit be-Amerikah*, ed. Menakhem Zohari, Arieh Tartokover, and Hayyim Ormiyan (Tel Aviv: Hotza'at ha-brit ha-'Ivrit ha-Olamit, 1974), 3:221–24.

16 On the role of newspapers and novels in the creation of an imagined sense of national community among people who could never have all met face-to-face, see Benedict Anderson, *Imagined Communities* (London: Verso, 1997), 22–46.

17 On the breakdown of traditional Jewish society in East Europe and East European Jewish society's transformation, see Israel Bartal, *The Jews of*

Eastern Europe, 1772–1881, trans. Chaya Naor (Philadelphia: University of Pennsyl-vania Press, 2005). On the production of a Hebrew national community, referred to as a Hebrew literary republic, through production and consumption of Hebrew journalism and literature, see Dan Miron, *Bodedim be-mo'adam: li-deyoknah shel ha-republikah ha-sifrutit ha-'Ivrit bi-thilat ha-me'ah ha-'esrim* (Tel Aviv: 'Am 'Oved, 1987), 56–111; Dan Miron, *From Continuity to Contiguity: Towards a New Jewish Literary Thinking* (Stanford, CA: Stanford University Press, 2010), 57–133.

18 Miron, From *Continuity to Contiguity,* 72.

19 A. R. Malakhi, "Hayye Ab. Goldberg," in *Sefer Avraham Goldberg: kovetz ma'amarav ve-divre ha'arakhah al hayyav u-pe'ulotav* (New York: 'Ogen, 1946), 51–55.

20 On Persky's life, see Daniel Persky, "Teshuvot le-she'elot ha-mekhon ha-bio-bibliographi 'Genazim' Tel Aviv, Medinat Yisrael," in *Genazim: kovetz le-toldot ha-sifrut ha-'Ivrit be-dorot ha-ahronim,* ed. Barukh Karu, vol. 5 (Tel Aviv: Masadah, 1965), 20–35.

21 The Pool of Siloam was built during the reign of King Hezekiah. It provided a water supply to the walled city of Jerusalem and thereby contributed to its ability to withstand external sieges. Like the ancient water source, the journal's founders envisioned it as something capable of sustaining the Jewish people.

22 On Ahad ha-Am and *ha-Shiloah,* see Steven Zipperstein, *Elusive Prophet: Ahad Ha'am and the Origins of Zionism* (Berkeley, University of California Press, 1993), 105–69; Ali Attia, *The Hebrew Periodical ha-Shiloah (1896–1919): Its Role in the Development of Modern Hebrew Literature* (Jerusalem: Magnes Press, 1991).

23 Sa'adyah Maximon, "Hayye Avi," in *Sefer Maximon,* ed. Yohanon Tversky (Tel Aviv: Hotza'at ha-histadrut ha-morim veha-menahalim be-Amerikah, 1935), 89–97.

24 On *landsmanshaftn* and their role in Jewish acculturation in America, see Daniel Soyer, *Jewish Immigrant Associations and American Identity in New York, 1880–1949: Jewish Landsmanshaftn in American Culture* (Detroit, MI: Wayne State University Press, 1997).

25 For a fuller discussion of this phenomenon's late-nineteenth-century development, see Malakhi, "ha-Tenu'ah ha-'Ivrit," 212–36.

26 Reuven Brainin, *Senunit* (New York: Ahi'ever, 1910), 7–10.

27 *Ibid.,* 7.

28 The buying power of five dollars in 1913 is equivalent to more than 131 dollars today.

29 Mintz, "Sanctuary in the Wilderness," 33.

30 *Ibid.*, 33–34.

31 "ha-Besorah ha-rishonah le-ge'ulah," Parshat ha-shavu'a, *ha-Toren*, November 16, 1917.

32 "ha-Mo'atzah ha-Tzionit be-Baltimor," ha-Tenu'ah ha-le'umit, *ha-Toren*, December 28, 1917.

33 Advertisements, *ha-Toren*, December 21, 1917.

34 Advertisements, *ha-Toren*, September 6, 1918.

35 Israel Efros, "Mit'orerot tikvot noshanot," *ha-Toren*, December 14, 1917; December 28, 1917.

36 Mintz, *Sanctuary in the Wilderness*, 123–24.

37 For more on this schema, as well as Hibbat Tzion poetry's overlooked beauty, see: Rut Karton-Blum, "Introduction" to *ha-Shirah ha-'Ivrit bi-tekufat hibbat Tzion*, ed. Rut Karton-Blum (Jerusalem: Mossad Bialik, 1969).

38 Hayyim Nahman Bialik, *Shirim, 1890–1898: Mahdurah mada'it be-leviyat mevo'ot ve-hilufe nusah*, ed. Dan Miron (Tel Aviv: Dvir, 1983), 127–34.

39 Efros, "Mit'orerot tikvot noshanot," *ha-Toren*, December 14, 1917.

40 Efros, "Mit'orerot tikvot noshanot," *ha-Toren*, December 28, 1917.

41 *Ibid.*

42 *Ibid.*

43 Zipperstein, *Elusive Prophet*, 33–104.

44 Alan Mintz, "American Hebrew Literature," in *Cambridge Companion to Jewish American Literature*, eds. Hannah Wirth-Nesher and Michael Kramer (New York: Cambridge University Press, 2003), 92–109.

45 On Yiddish's role in traditional East European Jewish education, see Benjamin Harshav, *The Meaning of Yiddish* (Stanford, CA: Stanford University Press, 1999), 9–24.

46 David Kaufman, *Shul with a Pool: The "Synagogue-Center" in American Jewish History* (Hanover, NH: University Press of New England, 1999), 144.

47 Jonathan Krasner, *The Benderly Boys and American Jewish Education* (Waltham, MA: Brandeis University Press, 2011); *The Women Who Reconstructed American Jewish Education 1910–1965*, ed. Carol Ingall (Waltham, MA: Brandeis University Press, 2010).

48 Kaufman, *Shul with a Pool*, 128–63.

49 *Ibid.*, 146.

50 David Kaufman, "Jewish Education as a Civilization: A History of the Teachers Institute," in *Tradition Renewed: A History of the Jewish Theological Seminary*, ed. Jack Wertheimer (New York: Jewish Theological Seminary, 1997), 567–80.

51 On this report, see Meir Ben-Horin, "From the Turn of the Century to the Late Thirties," in *A History of Jewish Education in America*, ed. Judah Pilch (New York: National Curriculum Research Institute, 1969), 67–70.

52 On Friedland, see Emanuel Gamoran, "Abraham H. Friedland," *American Jewish Year Book* 42 (1940-41):145–52; Menahem Ribalov, ed., *Sefer zikaron le-Het Aleph Fridland* (New York: ha-Histadrut ha-'Ivrit be-Amerikah, 1940); Michael Shields, "Abraham H. Friedland: American Hebraist and Jewish Educator," rabbinic thesis, Hebrew Union College-Jewish Institute of Religion, 2008.

53 Ben-Horin, "From the Turn of the Century," 64–65.

54 For a fuller discussion of these books and their relationship to Friedland's pedagogical approach, especially after his move to Cleveland in 1920, see Shlomo Haramati, "Sippure ha-yeladim shel H"A Friedland: ha-ma'avar min ha-sippur ha-didakti le-sippur ha-'omanuti be-sifrut ha-yeladim be-'Artzot ha-Brit," in *Migvan: Sefer ha-yovel le-Ya'akov Kabakof* (Lod: Mekhon Haberman le-mekhkere Sifrut, 1988), 141–71.

55 On the school's production of skilled Hebrew teachers, see Gamoran, "Friedland," 146; "Bayit hadash le-bet sefer ha-'Ivri ha-le'umi," ha-Tenu'ah ha-le'umit, *ha-Toren*, November 30, 1917; advertisement, *ha-Toren*, November 30, 1917; "le-Takanato shel bet-sefer ha-le'umi le-na'arot be-Nyu York," ha-Tenu'ah ha-le'umit, *ha-Toren*, December 7, 1917; advertisement, *ha-Toren*, December 7, 1917.

56 Joseph Eron, Joseph Barondess, Reuven Brainin, Zvi Hirsch Masliansky, Shimon Melamed and Isaac Straus, letter to the editor, *ha-Toren*, December 14, 1917.

57 Me-Hayye ha-agudot, *ha-Toren*, January 4, 1918.

58 "Hanukat bet-ha-sefer ha-leumi be-Nyu York," Shonot, *ha-Toren*, May 3, 1918.

59 Eron et al., letter to the editor, *ha-Toren*, December 14, 1917.

60 *Ibid.*

61 *Ibid.*

62 *Ibid.*

63 For more on Zionism as a supplemental nationalism employed by Western Jews to overcome a sense of marginalization in Western Europe and the United States, see Michael Berkowitz, *Zionist Culture and Western Jewry Before World War One* (Chapel Hill: University of North Carolina Press, 1996).

64 "Roshem ha-deklaratziyah ha-Britit be-'artzot shonot," ha-Tenu'ah ha-le'umit, *ha-Toren*, December 7, 1917.

65 *Ibid.*

66 *Ibid.*

67 Mordechai Aharon Kaplan, letter to the editor, *ha-Toren*, November 30, 1917.

68 "Me-Hayye ha-agudot," *ha-Toren*, December 28, 1917.

69 For a brief discussion of the Jewish Legion, see Derek J. Penslar, *Jews and the Military* (Princeton, NJ: Princeton University Press, 2013), 196–99. On the dynamics behind the American battalion's establishment embedded within an authoritative study of the Jewish Legion, see Yigal Elam, *ha-gedudim ha-'Ivriim be-milhemet ha-'olam ha-rishonah* (Tel Aviv: Ma'arakhot, 1973), 178–93; for reminiscences of American Jewish legionnaires, see Michael Keren and Shlomit Keren, *We Are Coming, Unafraid: The Jewish Legions and the Promised Land in the First World War* (Lanham, MD: Rowman and Littlefield, 2010).

70 Advertisement, *ha-Toren*, March 22, 1918.

71 Reuven Brainin, "Tze'irenu-giborenu (me-sihot ha-yom)," *ha-Toren*, March 8, 1918.

72 *Ibid.*

73 For more on the contemporary contestation of Zionist masculinity, see Philip Hollander, *From Schlemiel to Sabra: Zionist Masculinity and Palestinian Hebrew Literature* (Bloomington: Indiana University Press, 2019).

74 "Me-Hayye ha-'agudot," *ha-Toren*, March 8, 1918; advertisement, *ha-Toren*, April 19, 1918.

75 "Me-Hayye ha-'agudot," *ha-Toren*, March 15, 1918.

76 Advertisement, *ha-Toren*, April 19, 1918.

77 "Me-Hayye ha-agudot," *ha-Toren*, April 26, 1918; "Hadashot u-meora'ot," *Ha-Toren*, August 30, 1918; "Hadashot u-meora'ot," *ha-Toren*, September 20, 1918; "Hadashot u-meora'ot," *ha-Toren*, October 11, 1918.

78 For a discussion of parades seeing off Jewish Legion recruits, see "Hadashot u-me'ora'ot," *ha-Toren*, August 9, 1918; "Hadashot u-me'ora'ot," *Ha-Toren*, August 9, 1918.

79 Elam, *ha-gedudim ha-'Ivriim*, 190.

80 Penslar, *Jews and the Military*, 197; "Hadashot u-me'ora'ot," *ha-Toren*, July 12, 1918.

81 "'Al kiddush ha-degel ha-'Ivri," Shonot, *ha-Toren*, November 8, 1918; for a fuller discussion of this incident, see Gil Ribak, "'Beaten to Death by Irish Murderers': The Death of Sadie Dellon and Jewish Images of the Irish," *Journal of American Ethnic History* 32:4 (2013): 41–74.

82 *Ha-Toren*, December 6, 1918.

Frederick Burr Opper and Joseph Keppler, *The Modern Moses*, 1881

Source: Frederick Burr Opper and Joseph Keppler, "The Modern Moses," *Puck*, 1881, Cornell University Library, Digital Collections.

Roughly 2.5 million eastern European Jews fled tsarist Russia for the United States at the turn of the nineteenth and twentieth centuries. Titled "The Modern Moses," the illustration reprinted here, which appeared in the humor magazine *Puck* eight months after the assassination of Tsar Alexander II, is signed "O & K" for Frederick Burr Opper (1857–1937), a pioneer of American political cartoons and comic strips, and Joseph Keppler (1838–1894), an Austrian-born American caricaturist and political satirist. The cartoon depicts a seemingly endless column of Jewish immigrants, portrayed in starkly antisemitic terms (hooked noses, men with beards and earlocks, plump women clutching their children, a mix of paupers with knapsacks, wealthy men in top hats, even a radical in workers' cap carrying a mysterious lockbox), crossing the parted Atlantic Ocean (read: Red Sea) whose waters are marked "Oppression" and "Intolerance." The mixed multitude is greeted by a smiling Uncle Sam at the shore of the new Promised Land, a veritable "modern Moses" dressed in sandals, rays of light emanating from his head, who holds aloft a staff on which is written "Liberty." Notwithstanding the contrast between tsarist (read: pharaonic) oppression (threatening militaristic and ghoulish shapes populate the dark clouds) and the new Promised Land (a rising sun marked "Western Homes" signals America's radiance), the cartoon includes a mix of ambivalent and negative ideas about European Jewry.

— M.A.R

Abraham Walkowitz, *Four Heads*, 1904

Source: Abraham Walkowitz, *Four Heads*, 1904. Rose Art Museum at Brandeis University. Gift of Mrs. Teresa Jackson Weill, New York, 1975.283W.

Abraham Walkowitz (1878–1965), a pioneer of American modernist art, immigrated from Russia to the United States at the age of eight years old with his family. The Walkowitz family initially settled on New York's Lower East Side, where young Abraham went to public school and took to sketching scenes of his Jewish ghetto neighborhood. He soon began to study art at the Educational Alliance, then Cooper Union, and later the National Academy of Design. By 1900, his work was exhibited at the University Settlement House. In 1906, he traveled to Europe and spent extended time in Paris where he studied at the Académie Julian and was profoundly influenced by European modernist trends.

After his return to the United States, Walkowitz gravitated to a network of radical artists, thinkers, and activists in the New York area, notably "The Eight," a cohort of avant-garde painters that included Arthur B. Davies (1862–1928), William Glackens (1870–1938), Robert Henri (1865–1929), Ernest Lawson (1873–1939), George Luks (1867–1933), Maurice Prendergast (1858–1924), Everett Shinn (1876–1953), and John Sloan (1871–1951). Walkowitz's work first came to widespread public attention with the Armory Show, a landmark 1913 art exhibit in New York City of American and European painting and sculpture that included controversial works by The Eight as well as several leading European artists including Marcel Duchamp (1887–1968), Henri Matisse (1869–1954), and Pablo Picasso (1881–1973). Though the exhibit attracted 87,000 visitors and later came to be regarded as the dawn of American modernism, in its day it was considered scandalous by prevailing American standards. When it traveled to the Midwest, it was described by the local Chicago press as "profane," "blasphemous," "obscene," and "vile." The noted art critic Harriet Monroe (1860–1938) of the *Chicago Daily Tribune*, on the other hand, championed the "radical artists" as "profound" and "right." "They represent a search for new beauty," Monroe declared, "impatience with formulae, a reaching out toward the inexpressible, a longing for new versions of truth observed."[1]

Walkowitz is arguably best known for his sketches and paintings of the American dancer Isadora Duncan (1878–1927), many of which were exhibited by the famous American photographer Alfred Stieglitz (1864–1946) at Stieglitz's 291 Gallery located in midtown Manhattan. Duncan was "a muse," Walkowitz later recalled. "She had no laws. She didn't dance according to the rules. She created. Her body was music. It was a body electric, like Walt Whitman [1819–1892], his body electric... [Whitman's] *Leaves of Grass* [1855] is to me the Bible."[2]

In a related vein, Walkowitz's "Four Heads" (1904), reproduced here, depicts a seemingly casual encounter of four graceful figures. The two figures at left appear to be female, the figure third from left is male, and at right (only partially rendered) is an indeterminate profile. The alternating position of each head creates a sense of rhythm: looking right, left, straight, and right. As one surveys the figures, it is apparent they share certain general features. Their nontraditional apparel, fashionably short hairstyles, the hint of makeup, the man's dapper mustache, the figures' clear-eyed gazes, and their close physicality suggest a modern sensibility and even a hint of sensuality. Meanwhile, the seeming randomness of the moment is belied by the diligent composition and the figures' distinctive expressions underscore their individuality. In sum, "Four Heads," the product of an American Jewish artistic worldview rooted in New York's immigrant and cosmopolitan cultures, is an animated portrayal. Breaking with traditionalism, rigidly constructed social categories, and conventional artistic trends, the figures illustrate a complex and multilayered sensibility that reaches beyond notions of ethnicity, religion, nationality, and social status. Though Walkowitz would later opine, "I have no laws and no rules to make up [as an artist]," "Four Heads" stands out as a fine example of an American Jewish outlook that betokens a hopeful sense of belonging and confidence about the future.[3]

— M.A.R

Endnotes

1 Quoted in James Panero, "The Armory Show at 100: The Lessons of the 1913 International Exhibition of Modern Art," *New Criterion* 31 (December 2012), 10.

2 Quoted in "Oral History Interview with Abraham Walkowitz, 1958 December 8–22," Archives of American Art, Smithsonian Institution, 17.

3 *Ibid.*, 16.

Maurice Becker, *How Un-Jewish! The Campaign for the American Jewish Congress*, 1916

Source: Maurice Becker, cover art depicting campaign for the American Jewish Congress, (1916), Hathi Trust. Courtesy of University of Illinois at Urbana-Champagne, Urbana, IL.

In 1916, the nationwide American Jewish Congress campaign took center stage in American Jewish life. As noted else where in this volume, the congress movement, a loose coalition of left-leaning pro-Zionist forces, galvanized public opinion in favor of a nationwide American Jewish plenary.[1] Led by the liberal Zionist "Brandeis group," an elite cohort grouped around Louis D. Brandeis (1856–1941)—the so-called "People's Attorney" appointed in 1916 to the US Supreme Court by President Woodrow Wilson (1856–1924)—the congress movement grew into a significant political force on the American scene. In the wake of two years of dizzying political campaigning, it successfully galvanized American Jewish public opinion in favor of a democratically elected communal plenary. When the unprecedented American Jewish Congress finally convened in 1918 and 1920, it served as American Jewry's celebrated wartime flagship and ushered in a new era in organizational Jewish politics.

The image reprinted here appeared in January 1916 on the cover of the *Maccabean* (later renamed *New Palestine*), the first English-language Zionist periodical published in the United States. Drawn by Maurice Becker (1889-1975), a secular Jewish painter and political cartoonist of eastern European origin whose work was featured in mainstream periodicals like the *New York Tribune* and *Harper's Weekly* and socialist flagships like *The Masses* and *The Liberator*, the sketch depicts the spirited campaign for the American Jewish Congress. The illustration shows a confrontation between (at left) a throng of confident and vigorous young Jewish men and women, dressed in working- and middle-class garb, and (at right) tall, portly men in dark suits and top hats. The youthful marchers, their right feet indicating forward movement in unison, presumably represent the Jewish masses. They appear to be clear-eyed and determined, and they carry banners adorned with stars of David and labeled "nationalism," "democracy," and "Zion." Atop each banner a star of David ornament is also visible. By contrast, the well-heeled gentlemen in their long black overcoats, no doubt symbolizing American Jewry's elite "Fifth Avenue aristocracy," appear to be alarmed—their hands outstretched in what seems to be a futile effort to halt the marchers—"How un-Jewish!" they exclaim.

The illustration is also telling for its portrayal of the male and female marchers as equals. Indeed, the elections for the American Jewish Congress were open to "every Jew and every Jewess, twenty-one years of age or over."[2] The enfranchisement of women, itself a radical departure from patriarchal Jewish tradition and American norms, fundamentally altered the terms of the national conversation about the future of American Jewry. This development mirrored, in part, the broader trend of inclusivism that animated pro-congress grassroots forces, particularly Jewish immigrant and workers groups, who insisted on full participation and equal representation in organized American Jewish life. If the congress movement reflected the changing political consciousness of American society at large, it is nonetheless noteworthy that the congress elections enabled women to participate fully in American Jewish affairs three years prior to the passage of the Nineteenth Amendment. In sum, the cover illustration offers an intriguing glimpse of the American Jewish Congress—the controversy, the campaign, and the election—and can be viewed as a barometer of changing American Jewish attitudes to gender and political power.

— M.A.R

Endnotes

1 For detailed information, see chapter 5 of this volume: Mark A. Raider, "'President Wilson Speaks for America': The Brandeis Group, the American Jewish Congress, and the Balfour Declaration."

2 "The Call for the American Jewish Congress," *American Jewish World* 5, no. 7 (May 25, 1917), 160.

Djemal Pasha—Another Ivanoff?, 1917

Source: "Djemal Pasha—Another Ivanoff," *Maccabaean* (1917), Hathi Trust. Courtesy of Cornell University, Ithaca, NY.

As World War I escalated, the Ottoman regime became increasingly wary and suspicious of Palestine's burgeoning Jewish and Arab nationalist communities in the Turkish-controlled province of "Greater Syria." Ahmed Djemal Pasha (1872–1922), Palestine's military governor and a central figure in the Armenian genocide of 1915–16, served as the key official responsible for implementing the regime's draconian and violent policies. In 1915, Jews and Christians, traditionally exempt from military service, were suddenly subjected to forced military conscription and consigned to labor battalions. Many Jewish immigrants, now considered by Turkish authorities to be enemy alien nationals—a category broadly applied to eastern European Jewish colonists and pioneers despite their antipathy for the tsarist Russian regime—were forced to Ottomanize or leave the country. In due course, 18,000 (out of roughly 90,000) Jews were expelled from Palestine. Throughout 1915 and 1916, Arab nationalists, particularly politicians, journalists, and academics, were pressured by the Turkish regime and targeted in waves of mass arrests and hangings. In the early spring of 1917, Pasha, fearing the *Yishuv* was inclined to support the British war effort—in fact, British military forces were months away from the conquest of Palestine—brutally expelled tens of thousands of Jews from the coastal cities of Tel Aviv and Jaffa and banned Jews from Jerusalem and other major towns. "The joy of the Jews on the approach of the British forces would be short-lived," Pasha publicly declared, and they risked "shar[ing] the fate of the Armenians."[1]

News of developments in Palestine swiftly appeared in the American general and Jewish press, prompting widespread alarm and concern in real time. Indeed, by World War I, the historian Jonathan R. Winkler explains, advances in the science of telecommunications, namely, the proliferation of technology related to trans-Atlantic cable and intercontinental radio transmissions, were a ubiquitous feature of the West. "Together with domestic telegraph lines," Winkler notes, "information could move around the world within the space of 30 minutes to 1 hour."[2] That the American Zionist organization, headquartered in New York City, played an instrumental role in channeling information picked up by the American news media is demonstrated by the following items:

> *Daily Gate City and Constitution-Democrat*, New York, May 7, 1917.[3]—The same paths that Christ walked, teaching peace on earth and good will to men, are being filled today by thousands of terror-stricken, starving Jews, driven from their homes by Turkish bayonets, according to cablegrams received today by the Zionist organization here.
>
> With the British under General [Archibald James] Murray pounding at the gates of Gaza in their advance on Jerusalem, the Turks are herding the Jews northward, determined they shall not remain to see the holy land taken from the sultan.
>
> The eviction began in March, the message said, when 300 Hebrews were expelled from Jerusalem amid scenes of looting and pillage.
>
> Djemal Pasha, military governor of Palestine, declared he would make them suffer the fate of the Armenians. April 1, Djemal Pasha ordered eight thousand Jews driven from Jaffa. They were given forty-eight hours to leave. Even Jews owing allegiance to the Central Powers were included.
>
> The cablegram described terrible scenes when the Turkish troops went from house to house, driving the terrorized inhabitants into the streets. Crowds of Arabs and Bedouin women followed the troops, sacking every home. Two Jews from Yemen resisted. They were hanged at the entrance to Tel Aviv, and scores of fugitives streamed through the arch as their bodies dangled there.

Roads leading northward, away from the region where British guns were roaring from the Dead Sea to the Mediterranean, were lined with starving men, women, and children. The rich paid 200 francs for transportation nine miles to Petach Tikwah [*sic*].

Information here said many Jews crawled into the desert and died. Bandits attacked the refugees and stripped them of everything. Small forces of young Jews armed with knives and cudgels organized for defense. The Turks arrested them.

No Jews were known to have been killed by Turkish soldiers, but robbers were given free reign. Arabs on donkeys and camels hung on the flanks of the fleeing population, while the troops coming up behind beat the stragglers on.

American Jewish World, May 11, 1917.[4]—Some days ago warnings had come from England to this country that the Turks and Arabs were planning massacres and other acts of dire vengeance upon the Jews of Palestine. Since then news dispatches in the general press have confirmed the fears on which those warnings were based. We hope that the reports of brutal massacres of the Jews of Jaffa were exaggerated. But even so, their expulsion from that city on short notice must have worked untold hardships and in many cases complete ruin on the poor Jewish population. And who knows whether other Jewish settlements of that vicinity will not soon suffer a similar fate?

What may be the reasons for this outburst of brutality on the part of the [Muslims] of Palestine? We suppose that it is simply the result of war-panic that generally strikes blindly and furiously.

> It may have been brought on or intensified by the approach of the English in that direction, and the fear of the [Muslims] that Palestine would soon be taken from them. As usual, the Jews are the first victims of the populace's panic and fury. Jemmal [*sic*] Pasha, the military governor of Palestine has never been very friendly to the Jews. Yet the native or naturalized Jews of the Ottoman empire have always been loyal subjects. If the atrocities perpetrated upon the Jews of Palestine have the encouragement of connivance of the government authorities, Turkey may yet rue the day when it joined the lists of our persecutors.

Responding to the events described above, the *Maccabean* (later renamed *New Palestine*), an English-language Zionist periodical, published the political cartoon reprinted here. The unsigned image, titled "Djemal Pasha—Another Ivanoff?," equates Pasha's brutality with that of Nikolai Yudovich Ivanov (1851–1919), a Russian general who infamously engineered the mass deportations and expulsions of Jews in 1914 and 1915 from the war zone separating the tsarist empire from Germany, Austria-Hungary, and Romania. The illustration depicts an Ottoman official seated on a horse as he charges and beats a crowd of helpless men, women, and children. In the background, what appears to be the coastal city of Jaffa (a few seemingly ancient structures are visible) goes up in flames and plumes of dark smoke fill the sky.

— M.A.R

Endnotes

1 "Letters from Abroad: Jaffa (Special to the *American Jewish Chronicle*)—All Jews Expelled from Jaffa," *American Jewish Chronicle* 3, no. 1 (May 11, 1917), 11.

2 Jonathan R. Winkler, "Telecommunications in World War I," *Proceedings of the American Philosophical Society* 159:2 (June 2015), 163.

3 Quoted from "Driven Out of Jerusalem by Bayonets of Turks, Jews Flee from the Holy Land Along Paths Where Once Walked Preacher of Peace on Earth Centuries Ago," *Daily Gate City and Constitution-Democrat*, May 7, 1917, 1.

4 Editorial, "The Sad News from Palestine," *American Jewish World*, May 11, 1917, 120.

United War-Work Campaign, *Keep Them Smiling*, 1918

Source: United War Work Campaign, "Keep Them Smiling" (1918), World War I (1914–18) Nearprint, Special Topics, Jacob Rader Marcus Center of the American Jewish Archives, Cincinnati, OH.

In November 1918, seven major American organizations—the American Library Association, Jewish Welfare Board, National Catholic War Council (Knights of Columbus), Young Men's Christian Association (YMCA), Young Women's Christian Association (YWCA), Salvation Army, and War Camp Community Service—banded together to create the United War Work Campaign, a national fundraising drive to support the US military. The impetus for the coalition—known as the "Seven Sisters"—came from President Woodrow Wilson (1856–1924) who asked that these "accepted instrumentalities" be enlisted to assist "men in the ranks... in many essential matters of recreation and morale."[1] "It is my judgment," Wilson wrote to Raymond B. Fosdick (1883–1972), chairman of the War Department's Commission on Training Camp Activities, "that we shall secure the best results in the matter of the support of these agencies if these seven societies will unite their forthcoming appeals for funds, in order that the spirit of the country in this matter may be expressed without distinction of race or religious opinion in support of what is in reality a common service."[2]

The United War Work Campaign, which raised over $203 million and lasted into 1919, benefited from broad public support, especially from white ethnic, religious, and immigrant groups that sought to demonstrate their fidelity to the United States. It also reflected an ongoing investment by liberal American Protestant, Catholic, and Jewish communal and religious leaders in the ecumenical effort to promote the "tri-faith" ideal of America as a nation rooted in Judeo-Christian values and traditions. The developing conception of the nation's pluralistic religious character, including equality among Christians and Jews, was particularly visible in the US military where Protestant, Catholic, and Jewish chaplains worked closely together and provided pastoral care to soldiers of differing faith traditions.

The poster shown here is remarkably similar to another titled "Keep 'em smiling! Help War Camp Community Service—Morale is winning the war" (1918), designed by Murray Leone Bracker (1885–1937), an illustrator for *Scribner's*, *Hearst's Interna-*

tional, and *Collier's*.[3] Unlike Bracker's poster, however, this one, which also depicts a smiling soldier, Marine, and sailor, includes the emblems of the United War Work Campaign's constituent organizations. Moreover, it adumbrates the themes of equality and belonging by pairing the phrases "Keep them smiling" and "This home is helping our boys over there." In other words, the poster informs the viewer, all of the servicemen without exception are "our boys" and they are reliant upon and fighting for a shared "home," namely, American society writ large. This inclusive and patriotic outlook is reinforced by the poster's red, white, and blue border, as well as the symmetry of the constituent groups' emblems whose positionality forthrightly suggests the different faith communities are equal and interdependent.

— M.A.R.

Endnotes

1 Woodrow Wilson to Raymond Fosdick, October 10, 1918, Library of Congress, Woodrow Wilson Papers, http://presidentwilson.org/items/show/27576.

2 *Ibid.*

3 See "Keep 'em smiling! Help War Camp Community Service," Library of Congress Prints and Photographs Division, cph 3g09658 //hdl.loc.gov/loc.pnp/cph.3g09658.

Sabbath Evening Services at Camp Hancock, Augusta, Georgia, 1918

Source: "Friday Eve Services, Camp Hancock, Augusta, Georgia" (1918), Jewish Welfare Board Photos, PC-2077, Jacob Rader Marcus Center of the American Jewish Archives, Cincinnati, OH.

During World War I, the US military created a network of cantonments and training camps across the continental United States. Against this backdrop, there arose a "soldier press" that aimed to support enlistees, "fresh from civilian occupations... undergoing the difficult processes of adjustment and assimilation attendant on the transition to military life."[1] At its height, *Trench and Camp*, a weekly newspaper sponsored by the National War Work Council and the Young Men's Christian Association (YMCA), boasted a circulation encompassing thirty-eight US military cantonments and training camps with over 380,000 readers. In addition to national and local news, the newspaper included reports on military matters and the daily experience of life in the camps. Seeking to boost the morale of trainees and regiments stationed in the camps, it featured patriotic and inspirational material such as content produced by soldiers (poems, stories, and cartoons). Although some Catholic and Jewish critics complained that the YMCA used *Trench and Camp* as an "advertising scheme" to promote a Protestant worldview, the newspaper highlighted a substantial quotient of material concerning non-Protestant themes, including a trove of information supplied by the Jewish Welfare Board on American Jewish affairs.[2]

In December 1918, *Trench and Camp* reported on the lives of Jewish servicemen stationed in Camp Hancock, a sprawling military compound in Augusta, Georgia. Located on nearly 14,000 acres, the camp's tent city of 1,777 acres accommodated over 35,000 troops monthly. Interestingly, the following description of Jewish life in the camp appeared on the eve of the gathering of the American Jewish Congress in Philadelphia:

> ...The Sabbath hospitality nights [at Camp Hancock] still hold the interest of the [Jewish Welfare Board] audiences and even gain in popularity.[3] Last Friday evening an elaborate and enjoyable program was carried out under Rabbi Spitz, who made the attempt to transport to the evening the religious Sabbath hospitality atmosphere. Private Mallamed of the Medical Detachment, a lover of traditional Jewish melodies, rendered several selections and interpreted their spirit and traditional significance. Candidate Israel Gottlieb gave a reading from Sholom Aleichem, the renowned Yiddish humorist, to the hearty and evident delight of the audience. Mrs. Joseph Freifield, a longtime favorite at [Camp] Hancock, recited in fine style, and Private Meyer Weisgal led in the enthusiastic singing of Yiddish and Hebrew songs of the New Palestine. The Jew-

ish Welfare Board orchestra, with Sergt. Magrill and Pvt. Weizman at the violin and [Pvt.] M. Levy at the banjo, furnished the orchestra… Levy also rendered solos on the violin.

The most significant feature of the evening was an enthusiastic demonstration in honor of the First American Jewish Congress, which is held in Philadelphia the week of December 5. The entire audience rose on their feet and sang the *Hatikvah* [The Hope], the Jewish national hymn, and Corporal Margulis, delegate-elect to the [American] Jewish Congress, responded with a stirring address on the "Aims and Significance of the Congress," which is the first congress ever held by a united American Jewry...

The entertainment schedule will be carried through during the coming week along the same lines as in the preceding weeks. The speaker at the Sabbath hospitality evening will be Dr. Wilkinson, religious director of the YMCA at [Camp] Hancock and a large and appreciate[ive] audience is expected to receive him and to take part... Arrangements will also be made to report to the men the proceedings of the All-American [*sic*] Jewish Congress.[4]

— M.A.R.

Endnotes

1 Arthur M. Schlesinger, "The Khaki Journalists, 1917–1919," *Mississippi Valley Historical Review* 6:3 (December 1919), 350–51.

2 Quoted in *ibid.*, 353.

3 During World War I, the Jewish Welfare Board coordinated a variety of spiritual, educational, and recreational support for Jewish servicemen, including the provision of kosher food and worship and holiday services.

4 Quoted from "Jewish Welfare Board," *Trench and Camp*, December 18, 1918, 4.

James N. Rosenberg, *Return of the Troops*, 1919

Source: James N. Rosenberg, "Return of the Troops" (1919). Rose Art Museum at Brandeis University. Gift of the Estate of Thelma Sachar, 1997.3.

Born in Allegheny City, Pennsylvania, James N. Rosenberg (1874–1970) was the son of Henrietta Naumberg Rosenberg (1850–1944), a first-generation American, and Henry Rosenberg (1846–1927), an immigrant to the United States from Bavaria. In 1879, the Rosenberg family relocated to the Upper West Side of Manhattan and Henry joined his brothers-in-law as a partner in M & W Naumburg, which became in time one of the country's largest and most successful wholesale high-quality men's clothing firms. Young James grew up in wealth and comfort, and he attended Manhattan's liberal Ethical Culture School and the Gunnery Preparatory School, a boarding school in rural Connecticut. In 1895, he graduated from Columbia College and in 1898 he earned a Bachelor of Law degree from Columbia Law School. Thereafter, he enjoyed a meteoric rise in the arena of New York's legal community. In 1900, he opened a law practice with Joseph M. Proskauer (1877–1971), who later emerged as a prominent judge, political figure, and philanthropist. Rosenberg swiftly developed a reputation as an expert in bankruptcy law, and in 1901 he and Proskauer joined Abram I. Elkus (1867–1947), an elite Jewish communal figure and successful attorney (later appointed by President Woodrow Wilson as the US ambassador to Turkey) in the law firm of James, Schell & Elkus. In 1905, Rosenberg married Bessie Herman (1875–1979), with whom he had three children. In 1912, he left James, Schell & Elkus to open a new firm called Rosenberg and Levis, which specialized in bankruptcy law and took on major American corporate clients including Maxwell Motor Company (predecessor to the Chrysler Corporation).

In the 1910s, Rosenberg's artistic passion blossomed into a serious preoccupation and his sketches and paintings attracted attention and critical acclaim for their "poetic sense," "sensitive and quietly impressive" style, and "subtle handling of themes."[1] Between 1911 and 1917, his work was featured in solo exhibitions at Manhattan's well-known Louis Katz Art Galleries and Brooklyn's Arlington Art Galleries. He also participated in exhibits sponsored by the New York Water Color Club and the Society of Independent Artists.

What one observer in New York's *Sun* appreciatively described as Rosenberg's display of "much feeling" and "agreeable pastels in refined color" is amply evident in the image reproduced here, "Return of the Troops" (1919).[2] Depicting the March 25, 1919 victory parade of the 27th Division of the American Expeditionary Forces, the painting captures the moment when 20,000 servicemen, led by General John F. O'Ryan (1874–1961), the division commander, marched from lower Manhattan's Washington Square—where its towering marble arch, designed by noted architect Stanford White (1853–1906), was bedecked with balloons, streamers, patriotic bunting, and American flags—along Fifth Avenue. Ten thousand policemen were on hand to control the "happy, good-natured crowd" of some two million observers who cheered the triumphant procession.[3] "Those who had heard of the saying that an army marched on its stomach," reported the *New York Times*, "lost no time in giving the soldiers hot coffee, sandwiches, fruit —"[4]

> There was no dearth of cigarettes, and those who did not smoke found plenty of candy waiting for them... The arrival of a picked squad of men bearing aloft the service flag of the division containing 1,972 gold stars was the signal for the first prolonged outburst of applause by the thousands of spectators. The wounded men who began arriving in ambulances and touring cars immediately after this were greeted with ringing cheers. Spectators showered them with cigars and cigarettes and not a few doughboys received flowers from young women in the crowd.
>
> A temporary hush came over the multitude as a caisson, banked with floral tributes from the governor [Alfred E. Smith, 1873–1944], mayors of several cities, and the men of the 27th Division

> themselves, was driven by eight horses to Washington Arch, where it stood on view until the march began…
>
> …While the preparations for the parade were being carried into effect, airplanes hovered over the neighborhood and provided thrills aplenty for the crowd by the maneuvers of the pilots. The whirring of the engines in the planes excited many of the horses of the division and men in charge of them had difficulty in quieting them…[5]

The end of the Great War marked an important transition in Rosenberg's personal and professional trajectory. For at this juncture, Felix M. Warburg (1871–1937), the elite Jewish communal leader and investment banker, prevailed upon him to assist in the Joint Distribution Committee's (JDC) efforts to aid hundreds of thousands destitute Russian and Polish Jews whose communities were decimated during the Bolshevik Revolution and the fighting in the eastern war zone. Rosenberg took time away from his law practice for one year to devote himself fully to working with American Relief Administration, headed by Herbert Hoover (1874–1964), who soon became secretary of commerce under President Warren G. Harding (1865–1923). Shortly thereafter, Rosenberg became director of the American Jewish Joint Agricultural Corporation (Agro-Joint) and president of the American Society for Jewish Farm Settlements in Russia, in which capacity he oversaw the JDC's collaboration with the new Soviet regime and the disbursement of $8 million used to resettle 80,000 non-Jewish peasants and 300,000 Jewish refugees in rural areas, primarily Crimea.

In the 1920s, 1930s, and 1940s, Rosenberg would go on to serve in key leadership roles in American Jewish affairs, Jewish-Christian interfaith efforts, and humanitarian initiatives related to the League of Nations and the United Nations. As reflected in the artistry and vibrant color palette of "Return of the Troops," Rosenberg cherished his identity as a patriotic American. Meanwhile, in his work with the Agro-Joint he offered a glimpse of his personal outlook as an American Jew and commitment to serving the Jewish people. "I wish only to emphasize," he stated, "that to my mind this is as great a moment as history has ever offered to Jewry. If we let this great moment pass by, we may never again have such an opportunity for service…"[6]

— M.A.R.

Endnotes

1 "Two New Exhibitions in the Picture Realm," *Brooklyn Daily Eagle*, November 4, 1911, 12.

2 "Art in Galleries," *The Sun*, December 15, 1913, 9.

3 "Thousands Watch as Parade Forms," *New York Times*, March 26, 1919, 4.

4 *Ibid.*

5 *Ibid.*

6 Quoted in "James N. Rosenberg Urges Action on Crimean Colonization Plan," *Jewish News of Northern California* 57:22, March 28, 1924, 3.

Chapter 5

"President Wilson Speaks for America": The Brandeis Group, the American Jewish Congress, and the Balfour Declaration[1]

Mark A. Raider

> The importance of the [American Jewish] Congress can hardly lie in demonstration, it can only lie in the fact that it will put forward a body of men whom it will empower to act on Jewish questions as duly constituted representatives of the whole of American Jewry. —Horace M. Kallen (November 1915)[2]

> The granting of the mandate by the Peace Conference to Great Britain under the conditions which assure the establishment of Zion as a Jewish national homeland brings to a dramatic climax the long struggle for the regaining of Jewish nationhood. In that struggle the Jews of America have played a most important role, first in extending generous aid to the Zionist Organization over a period of many years and second in the organization during the time of the War

> of the American Jewish Congress which speaking in the name of the whole of American Jewry backed up and strengthened the demands of the Zionist movement and of the Jews from various lands placed before the Peace Conference for a Jewish homeland in Palestine. —*Reform Advocate* (May 1920)[3]

Major studies of Chaim Weizmann, Louis D. Brandeis, and the emergence of modern Jewish politics in the early decades of the twentieth century contribute significantly to our understanding of Zionism's impact on Europe, America, and global affairs. Weizmann, identified by Jehuda Reinharz as "a statesman without a state," understood "the fate of Zionism was bound with that of England" and proved uniquely adept at building "sufficient consensus in the Zionist ranks to back his particular point of view."[4] For its part, the British government appreciated Weizmann's ingenuity as a "one-man ministry of propaganda, foreign affairs, and strategic planning" and sought to capitalize on his global connections. "From the British point of view," Reinharz notes, Weizmann "freed" the British government of "responsibility for mobilizing the [wartime] Jewish support that was deemed so valuable by the Foreign Office."[5] With respect to the American scene, Melvin I. Urofsky points out Brandeis recognized "it would have done no good at all" for the Zionists to seek formal US government recognition of Jewish national aspirations in Palestine; unlike Great Britain, the United States "had no territorial ambitions in the Middle East."[6] Instead, Brandeis placed his faith in Wilson's personal pledge to support the Zionist project[7]—he "had made a promise and he would keep it in due time"—and "left Weizmann to pressure the British, while he urged American Zionists to build up organization and resources so that at the proper time they could back their colleagues overseas."[8]

The symmetrical nature of Weizmann's and Brandeis's wartime strategies, Ben Halpern observes, hinged on a "fully shared" synthetic Zionist vision that balanced "political action" with the *Yishuv*'s "social-economic construction" as "organically related aspects of a single endeavor, each aspect depending on success in the other."[9] To this challenge, each man brought a distinctive personality and leadership style. Weizmann, the "lobbyist as diplomat," projected "an image of himself as the spokesman for world Jewry," his success depended on "being accepted as a recognized leader" by "both the government and the Jewish public."[10] Brandeis, on the other hand, assumed command of American Zionism at the behest of a cadre of talented Progressive-era American Jewish lawyers, rabbis, and scholars, namely Stephen S. Wise, Julian W. Mack, Felix Frankfurter, Horace M. Kallen, and Jacob De Haas, who came to be known as the "Brandeis group." In contrast to American Zionism's lackluster old guard, led by the Semitics scholar Richard J. H. Gottheil,[11] Brandeis professed a new brand of Zionism coterminous with American progressivism and espoused "Zionist work as a project of soberly defined dimensions."[12] Brandeis generally preferred the role of "counsel for the situation" and "democratic consensus" to "party organization and power-brokerage," but neither he nor his inner circle shied away from the rough-and-tumble of American and Jewish politics.[13] In fact, they proved to be adept partisans and highly effective political operatives. Nowhere was this better illustrated, as Jonathan Frankel demonstrates, than Brandeis's shrewd leadership of the American Jewish Congress movement which "grew into a major force" and produced the unprecedented countrywide plenary (1918, 1920) that served as American Jewry's celebrated wartime flagship.[14]

It is also useful to note that American Zionism, the American Jewish Congress, and other American Jewish communal projects which arose in the Progressive era were buttressed in no small measure by the special place reserved for the Jewish people in Protestant America's sensibility and President Wilson's Christological worldview.[15] Though in some quarters of American society, as Eric L. Goldstein notes, Jews were viewed with suspicion and hostility, many Progressive-era "commentators" maintained they were also "part of the 'Great Caucasian family.'"[16] "They are not Jews in America," Wilson, the Democratic Party's standard bearer, declaimed in 1911 to an overflow crowd at New York City's Free Synagogue, "they are American citizens… We are not here to express sympathy with our Jewish fellow-citizens, but to make evident our cause of identity with them."[17] In brief, Wilsonian Progressivism included support for Jewish citizens at home, Jewish minority rights abroad, and new opportunities for Jews to participate fully in the modern world. Moreover, American Zionism benefited directly and indirectly from what Ira Katnelson has described as Wilson's predisposition to fight "for democracy and ethnic self-determination abroad without threatening the system of segregation at home."[18]

If championing Brandeis and Zionism elevated Wilson "to the status of a hero in Jewish history books," it is also clear, as Daniel J. Tichenor observes in chapter 1, that Wilson's "conceptions of liberal democratic reform were fused with deeply entrenched commitments to white supremacy," earning him an inglorious place in the history of American racism.[19] Certainly, W.E.B. Du Bois's characterization of Black Americans during the World War I era as being caught "in a difficult position" and "disappointed in President Wilson and the Democrats" was a colossal understatement.[20] In point of fact, as Nancy Weiss Malkiel argues, for Americans of color Wilson's New Freedom translated into "a new bondage," "disenfranchisement," and "the birth of full-scale state-level Jim Crow legislative discrimination."[21] Deprived of fundamental rights and civil liberties, Cara Lea Burnidge explains, minorities of all stripes were undercut and disadvantaged by Wilson's belief that "social stratification based on distinctions of race, class, and gender was not counter to the spirit of democracy but rather an integral part of it by providential design."[22]

In sum, the present study seeks to revisit the interrelationship of the Brandeis group, American Jewry, and the Wilson administration against the complex backdrop of Progressive-era America and the dynamic global arena of World War I. It argues that but for the synergy of the Weizmann camp and the Brandeis group, the complex negotiations leading to the Balfour Declaration, which stalled on several occasions, might well have unraveled completely. Even after Great Britain announced the declaration the Wilson administration's vision of postwar reconstruction was hardly a foregone conclusion. Despite uncertain and fluid conditions, Brandeis and his lieutenants—who faced fierce opposition and periodic setbacks—harnessed the empowering and democratizing force of American Zionism to unify American Jewry and press the case for a Jewish national home in Palestine under a British protectorate. Their efforts drove forward the fitful process that eventually yielded President Wilson's public endorsement of the Balfour Declaration. The ensuing symmetry of British and US government foreign policy objectives, bolstered by American society's increasingly favorable attitude to the Zionist cause, paved the way for the campaign for Jewish statehood.

American Israel and *Klal Yisroel*

With the outbreak of World War I, a tidal wave of popular support for democratization in American Jewish life surged forward, driven by the traditional notion of *kol yisrael arevim zeh bazeh* (all of Israel are responsible for each other) and desperate concern for the welfare of "suffering Jews in the war zones."[23] "We are perforce our brothers' keepers," declared Louis D. Brandeis, chair of Provisional Executive Committee for General Zionist Affairs (PEC), echoing the sentiment of many American Jewish leaders.[24] Judah L. Magnes, the charismatic rabbi and fair-haired boy of American Jewry's uptown patricians, called on "the leaders of the American Jews" to embrace an actionable agenda dedicated to the security, protection, and sustenance of *klal yisrael* (Jewish peoplehood).[25] "The whole Jewish world looks to American Jewry," Magnes noted, "for material help, for political and moral help during the war and at its conclusion..."[26] "The one hope of our coping with these problems," he insisted, "of doing justice to the Jews and to this country, is to set in motion a democratic, nation-wide Jewish movement that will place upon every Jew in the land a portion of the responsibility for the future."[27]

The call for unity in American Israel was not new. As early as 1903, the Reform synagogue movement's Union of American Hebrew Congregations (UAHC) called for a "permanent body, with a permanent organization," to be known as the American Jewish Congress, "to meet such problems as the Russian Jewish question, the Rumanian Jewish question, the Galician Jewish question, the evils of overcrowding in our large cities, the immigration question, etc., etc."[28] In 1905, the newspaper *Yidishe tageblat,* reacting to the Kishinev pogroms (1903–5), issued an impassioned plea for "a Congress of all the Jews in America" to bring together "Jews from all classes, be it Orthodox or Reform or Freethinking... It must be a people's congress, not an assembly of self-appointed 'representatives'..."[29] The same year witnessed the creation of the National Relief Committee (a fundraising campaign aid to Russian Jews) and the Jewish Defense Association (for the purchase of weapons for Jewish self-defense forces in Russia) to rally and centralize American Jewish philanthropic work.[30] In 1908, the Kehillah of New York City, a nondenominational experiment in urban Jewish confederation, advanced the idea of American Jewry as "one people with a common history and common hopes"; the Kehillah lasted for fourteen years.[31]

But the war, in the words of the historian Arthur A. Goren, "upset all the old canons."[32] For American Jews, particularly those of eastern European origin, the vexing plight of parents, siblings, and extended family caught in the eastern war zone was worrisome and traumatizing and many suffered from survivor's guilt. A groundswell of anxiety and fervor prompted the creation of the American Jewish Relief Committee, the Central Relief Committee, and the People's Relief Committee, created between 1914 and 1915 as philanthropic arms of, respectively, New York's elite Jewish patrons of central European ancestry (centered on the American Jewish Committee), the traditionalist eastern European Jewish immigrant community, and the

Jewish labor movement. Subsequently united under the banner of the American Jewish Joint Distribution Committee (JDC) and led by Felix M. Warburg, a partner in the investment bank Kuhn, Loeb & Company, the groups held mass gatherings and fundraising meetings in cities across the country and generated millions of dollars in contributions from poor and wealthy Jews alike for "war chests" and "patriotic funds."[33] The philanthropist Julius Rosenwald, president of Sears, Roebuck & Company, alone pledged one million dollars to the American Jewish Relief Committee "on condition that others raise the remaining nine million dollars."[34] The campaign was embraced by the leadership of American Jewry's evolving synagogue movements, namely, the UAHC, the Conservative movement's United Synagogue of America, and the Orthodox movement's Agudat Harabonim, as well as nonreligious entities including the Independent Order of Bnai Brith, the Federation of American Zionists, the cosmopolitan Workmen's Circle (Arbeiter Ring), and the National Council of Jewish Women.[35] In a related development, twenty-two national Jewish organizations established the National Jewish Welfare Board in 1917 and sustained close contact with the US military to care for Jewish soldiers, sailors, marines, and chaplains.[36]

The range of quasi-national American Jewish efforts on behalf of distressed Jewish communities overseas illustrates the extent to which the "Jewish differential"—a collective sense of the "Jew poised on the margins of gentile society"—became the animating consensus of American Jews during World War I.[37] Diverse figures from across the Jewish social, religious, and political spectrum gave voice to a collective vision of *klal yisroel politik* (Jewish political solidarity). Consider, for example, the case of Zvi Hirsch Masliansky, a traditionalist and Zionist figure who electrified crowds with "his remarkable artistry in oratory" in a public career that spanned tsarist Russia and the United States.[38] The self-described *matif haleumi* (national preacher) "preached a love of Judaism and a pride in Jewish peoplehood" to mixed audiences who, as Gary P. Zola notes, never expected to see the Land of Israel but "hungrily devoured

[his] words all the same."[39] In 1916, Masliansky addressed a mass gathering in St. Louis and stated "the Germans are suffering, the French are suffering, the English are suffering, the Russians are suffering":

> ... But ask the Jew in the trenches... Who is the Jew fighting for? ... In the theater of war, there [are] miles and miles of battlefields... there were the homes of most of our brothers and sisters....They are Jews! They are our brothers and sisters! They need bread! They cry to you who have a home... You who have shoes upon your feet and clothes upon your backs have a duty to perform... When one dies here, immediately his lodge brothers are notified... But there where thousands fall upon the battlefield of hunger and desolation, where shall we find a large enough lodge? The lodge of Israel – *Kol yisroel* – must pay its dues! Dues for the dead members of the Lodge of Israel... our lodger brothers cry out to us in America to help! ... Pay your dues! Dues! Dues![40]

Masliansky exemplifies the galaxy of "leader-orators" who crisscrossed the American Jewish scene calling for *klal yisroel politik*—equality for Jews worldwide, relief and rescue for Jewish communities in eastern and central Europe, and Jewish national unity.[41] Together with other uptown and downtown luminaries, including Joseph Barondess, Shmarya Levin, Magnes, Nahman Syrkin, Stephen S. Wise, and Chaim Zhitlowsky, he played a pivotal role in forging a Jewish national consensus among disparate immigrant and nonimmigrant circles. The "wider American wartime context," explains Judah M. Bernstein, provided the scope for such ethno-national leaders "to harness the growing the concern of American minority groups for the fates of their homelands."[42] Possessed of bountiful talent and adaptive dispositions, including the capacity to straddle theological, ideological, and economic barriers, they emerged as influential figures in (to borrow a phrase from Carolyn Eastman) the "platform culture" of the American Jewish communal arena.[43] Reflecting the turn-of-the-century pattern of leader-orators—that is, charismatic and powerful speakers who knew how to use the stage and deploy performative strategies ("words, gestures, facial expressions, and vocal tones") to enthrall audiences—they offered a common framework for people to digest and comprehend "complicated, contradictory cultural movements and political change" in their everyday lives.[44] In real time, they charmed diverse audiences with their "silver-tongued" oratory, embrace of Jewish and Western values, critique of Jewish life in America, and idealization of Palestine as the guarantor, if not the *summum bonum*, of an "authentic, full-blooded Jewish life."[45]

A fractious and hard-fought intracommunal battle raged for much of 1915 and 1916 over holding an American Jewish Congress. With the fate of eastern European Jewry hanging in the balance, the "chasm between different groups in [American] Israel" widened, resulting in the polarization of "masses and classes" and "democracy and oligarchy."[46] Opponents assailed the pro-congress movement as an East Side affair, brushing off its appeal beyond New York City and implying the very premise of a Jewish national assembly smacked of an alien mindset. The "great world," declaimed Mayer Sulzberger, a distinguished judge and former American Jewish Committee president, is untroubled about "your nationalism, or your Zionism, or your conferences, or your congress, or your democratic representation—not a bit of it."[47] "For them you are one," Sulzberger emphasized, "indivisible, inside and outside, a Jew."[48] Louis Marshall, the formidable New York lawyer and American Jewish Committee leader, privately disparaged the congress proposition as "deplorable, ridiculous, and inept," and railed against the PEC-forged Zionist coalition as "men who have no sympathy with Judaism and who are avowedly atheists or agnostics."[49] At the other end of the political spectrum, the radical Jewish advocates of class warfare voiced a heated antinational critique of the congress. "The [Jewish] workmen, the real champions of freedom and justice," a writer protested in a letter to the editor of *Der tog*, "cannot go hand in hand with the bourgeoisie Zionists of all shades."[50] The *Forverts* journalist Moyshe Olgin dismissed "the utopianism and dreams" of a *klal yisroel* organization as "untimely" and insisted "the idea of a Jewish Congress, of a Jewish parliament" had "faded before it has flowered."[51] In a word, neither the Marshall camp nor the cosmopolitan leaders of the Jewish labor movement saw any advantage in submitting their authority to a larger constellation of factions, organizations, and parties. Led, respectively, by the American Jewish Committee and National Workmen's Committee—dubbed by the Marxist Zionist theoretician Ber Borochov as the "capitalist-socialist bloc"—they opposed the congress on a mix of ideological and political grounds.[52] They also contended the PEC's efforts were a ruse to achieve unwarranted sway in American Jewish affairs.

Yet American Jewry's democratic impulse was "anything but muted" and the values of liberty, freedom, and democracy, which, as Jonathan D. Sarna argues, profoundly shaped the American Jewish experience, were on full display.[53] In public utterances and published articles, the Brandeis-led coalition framed the congress debate as a choice between "the old regime in American Israel" and the "Jewish masses [who] are determined at all costs to be the masters of their own fate," between the "anti-democratic," "un-Jewish," and "un-American" sensibility of a "small, self-chosen group of men" and the "collective spirit" of "a Congress democratically chosen and truly representative and faced in such a spirit withal as would represent the soul of Israel."[54] In statements calculated to allay concerns about Jewish patriotism and court the Yiddish-speaking milieu—American Jews of central European ancestry were suspected of sympathizing with the Kaiser, many leading American Jewish communal figures identified with pacifism (Gotthard Deutsch, Judah L. Magnes, and Stephen S. Wise stood out in this regard),[55] and large numbers of eastern European Jewish immigrants, antipathetic to tsarist Russia, populated the ranks of radical political and labor groups—Brandeis himself asserted the natural "kinship of Jewish and American ideals."[56] Of the eastern and southern European Jewish masses, he argued, Jews were especially well suited to the New World environment. Democracy, he confidently stated, is among the world's Jews "not an ideal merely" but rather "a practice" stemming from "qualities of mind, body, and character" developed over centuries.[57] "Is it not a striking fact that a people coming from Russia," he asked, "the most autocratic of countries, to America, the most democratic of countries, comes here, not as to a strange land, but as to a home?"[58]

> The explanation lies mainly in the fact that the twentieth century ideals of America have been the ideals of the Jew for more than twenty centuries... We are bound not only to use worthily our great inheritance, but to preserve and, if possible, augment it; and then transmit it to the coming generations... Shall we with our inheritance do less than the Irish, the Servians [*sic*], or the Bulgars? ...Zionism seeks merely to establish in Palestine for such Jews as choose to go and remain there, and for their descendants, a legally secured home, where they may live together and lead a Jewish life; where they may expect ultimately to constitute a majority of the population, and may look forward to what we should call home rule.[59]

In contrast to the *noblesse oblige* of American Jewry's so-called "Fifth Avenue aristocracy" and the class warfare of Yiddish-speaking radical leaders, Brandeis and his lieutenants unapologetically defied rising countrywide anti-immigrant sentiment while making a compelling case for eastern European Jewish immigration to the United States and Palestine. The Brandeis group also publicly challenged and rebuked the American Jewish Committee, the National Workmen's Committee, and other political adversaries opposed to democratization in Jewish communal life. Brandeis and his lieutenants used their visibility on the American scene and unabashed pride in their American Jewish identity—liberal, fully acculturated, and, in large measure, non–religious—to make the case for a secularized brand of *yiddishkayt* (Jewishness) that appealed to a diverse array of native-born and foreign-born Jews. Nor were they deterred, as reported in the Detroit *Jewish Chronicle*, by the fact that "the proposal to hold a Jewish Congress" spawned "great diversity of opinion and a feeling of considerable bitterness among American Jews."[60] American Jewry's changing demographic profile and budding national consciousness, the Brandeis group reasoned, warranted new political leadership. They framed the issue of democratization as a moral imperative and sought to rally a national consensus for the congress. As a structural matter, they argued, the need to up-end and reconstruct American Jewry's established order was a matter of *klal yisroel politik* and Jewish survival. To this end, the Brandeis group—powered by a loose coalition of Jewish immigrant and middle-class support in a variety of urban centers—joined forces with eastern European advocates of Jewish nationalism in a carefully orchestrated campaign to champion the movement for an American Jewish Congress.

The American, Anglo-Jewish, and Yiddish press closely tracked the pro-congress advocates' movements and utterances and "gave columns to the agitation of Zionism."[61] In a highly publicized display of cross-cultural comity, Brandeis and Shmarya Levin undertook a joint speaking tour throughout the Northeast and Midwest that attracted huge crowds.[62] "The coming of Mr. Brandeis and Dr. Levin found its way into all the papers," reported the *Maccabaean*, "and the English dailies made it their business to interview [them]... Thus Zionism literally became the talk of the town."[63] A headline in Chicago's *Sentinel* noted "Zionists Cannot Supply Demand Seats—Brandeis and Levin Arrive."[64] "More Successes from the Levin-Brandeis Tour" reported *Dos yidishe folk*.[65] Fanning out across the country, the Orthodox publicist Gedaliah Bublick, the journalist Bernard G. Richards, the writers Charles A. Cowen and Abraham

Goldberg, the socialist Zionist theoretician Nahman Syrkin, the Labor Zionist leaders Meyer Brown and Baruch Zuckerman, and the Yiddish journalist and playwright Abraham S. Schomer likewise generated excitement and enthusiasm through countless speaking engagements. With arguments couched in terms befitting their respective religious, ideological, and philosophical orientations, they expanded the lexicon of democratization and Zionism in modern Jewish life. Chaim Zhitlowsky, for example, called for support of the congress in the name of the Jewish worker, the Jewish people, and overturning the status quo:

> The vital question before the Jews now is whether or not they want to live like every other nation, a free and independent life in a country of their own... The Land of Israel of the past must be the Land of Israel of the future... The American Jewish Congress which we are now organizing will have to voice the views of the American Jews... [not] those leaders with a narrow, hobbled conception of Jewish affairs, whose political methods are like those of Tammany politicians, and who exercise an unrestrained power over the Jewish workingmen. The present convention shows that the Jewish workingmen are of national sentiments and respond to our call. We will go to the masses over and above the heads of their leaders, and I am certain the masses will be with us.[66]

The distinctive appeal and energy of key figures associated with Jewish national revival in Palestine reinforced the pro-congress movement. Akin to the romantic pride taken in Aaron Aaronsohn, Palestine's debonair Jewish agronomist and Zionist champion who, as Matthew M. Silver observes, had an "electrifying effect" on Henry Morgenthau Sr., Louis Marshall, Julius Rosenwald, Louis D. Brandeis, and other elite American Jews, the presence in the United States of the Poalei Zion ideologist Ber Borochov, the Jewish Legion advocate Pinhas Rutenberg, and the Zionist pioneer leaders David Ben-Gurion, Yitzhak Ben-Zvi, Alexander Hashin, Shlomo Kaplansky, and Yaakov Zerubavel—each of whom spent extended time in the country during World War I—injected the American Jewish scene with inspired nationalist discourse and first-person accounts of the *Yishuv*.[67] "There are among the representatives of the Poalei Zion [party]," commented the *American Jewish Chronicle*, "brilliant writers and scholars and journalists..."[68] The energetic and passionate public relations activity of these colorful Zionist figures, lauded as representatives of Palestine's heroic pioneering movement, offered a bold alternative to the Brandeis group's businesslike American orientation.[69] "They spoke about the Jewish Legion," recalled Golda Meir, then a young woman living in Milwaukee, arguing "an effective Jewish claim could be made to the Land of Israel after the war if only the Jewish people played a significant and visible military role, *as Jews*, in the fighting..."[70]

> They told us in detail about the fifty-odd Jewish agricultural settlements that had already been established... in a way that made it seem real and populated by flesh-and-blood people, not mythical heroes... They told us about Tel Aviv, which had just been founded on the sand dunes outside Jaffa, and about Hashomer, the Yishuv's self-defense organization... But most of all, they talked about their hopes and dreams for an Allied victory over the Turks...[71]

The networking efforts of these left-wing Zionist activists vis-à-vis Jewish nationalist, Hebraist, and socialist groups in the United States, notes the historian Jonathan Frankel, their contributions to a variety of Yiddish newspapers and periodicals, and their tireless lobbying for the American Jewish Congress helped to "arouse maximal public interest" in the role of Zionism in American Jewish life.[72] In this period, Ben-Gurion, Ben-Zvi, Hashin, and Zeruvabel published two editions of *Yizkor*

(Remember), a commemorative volume honoring fallen Hashomer watchguards in Palestine, and Ben-Gurion and Ben-Zvi also published *The Land of Israel in Past and Present*.[73]

The American Jewish Congress campaign also benefited from the growing public support of prominent non-Jews. Business, clerical, communal and philanthropic leaders and elected officials—despite fears stoked by nativists and xenophobes who derided southern and eastern European immigrants as "beaten men of beaten races" that would "cause general moral degeneration as sure as night follows day"[74]—endorsed Palestine's new Jewish society-in-the-making as a corollary of Wilson's vision of the "self-determination of nations."[75] The Chicago evangelical Methodist William E. Blackstone, for example, who in 1891 presented President Benjamin Harrison with a petition calling for Jewish restoration in the Land of Israel, submitted a memorial to Wilson in May 1916 "to consider the condition of the Jews and their right to a home in Palestine."[76] Signed by Newton W. Thompson, acting governor of California, C. E. Sebastian, mayor of Los Angeles, Shailer Mathews, the University of Chicago theologian, Abram W. Harris, president of Northwestern University, Andrew D. White, president of Cornell University, John Wanamaker, the Philadelphia merchant and former US postmaster general, and dozens of other celebrated names, the memorial helped to put wind in the sails of the Brandeis group. After its formal adoption by the Federal Council of Churches, the Los Angeles Baptist Ministers Conference, the Methodist Episcopal Church of Southern California, and the Presbyterian Ministerial Association of Los Angeles, Stephen S. Wise met with Wilson to discuss the Blackstone memorial.[77]

In spite of the era's prevailing social and political divisions, supportive expressions of pro-Zionist sentiment emerged from various corners of the American landscape. Former president Theodore Roosevelt, Henry Cabot Lodge of Massachusetts, Samuel Gompers of the American Federation of Labor, and other influential political figures vouched for the legitimacy of the Zionist project and the credibility of the American Jewish

Congress campaign.[78] Typical of such statements was that of Oregon's George E. Chamberlain, former governor and chairman of the US Senate's committee on military affairs. Interviewed in March 1917 by Max Rhoade, a young Washington lawyer and Jewish activist (later a founder of the Zionist college group Avukah), Chamberlain lamented "the fact that in the twentieth century of ours there are still bigots in the world—quite a few in high places—who are fools enough to have the medieval antipathy toward the Jew."[79] Taking note of "organized prejudice against the Catholics" and "other relics of past centuries of narrow-mindedness," he pondered, "Jewish problem? Yes, assuredly, there does still remain a great deal to do for the Jew in according him justice..."[80]

> The Jewish people must first work out a definite programme as to what they want themselves. The United States, and other nations that stand for justice and equitable treatment in favor of all peoples and nationalities, cannot be expected to take any move in behalf of the Jews without knowing exactly what they desire... The Jewish Congress is just exactly what [is] needed to clarify and ultimately indicate these desires of the Jewish people...
>
> The President has pointed out that America stands ready to help, and should help, the oppressed of all nations. The United States has done so in the past. She did it for the Filipinos. She did it for the Cubans. So far as the Jewish people is concerned, we have already more than one instance of this country's special interest. The United States revoked her treaty with Russia because of her indignation at Russia's treatment of the Jews. There are other instances in which the United States has helped the Jews of foreign countries.

> I have always been in sympathy with [the Zionist] movement. It seems quite natural to me that Jews in this country should be supporting this movement to help their coreligionists abroad; to improve their condition. I must say, I see no reason why the Jews should not have a land of their own to work out their own ideals, own aspiration, own way of life, like any other people...
>
> Before the Jews try to get a land of their own, however, they must try to secure all their rights as citizens in those lands where they still labor under restrictions. The rest will then be easier. Yes, you may say, I am in full sympathy with the Jews for wanting a home of their own. I hope they will succeed in establishing one. I think they *will* succeed.[81]

Chamberlain's statement is noteworthy, of course, because of his influential role in US military affairs during World War I. An ally of Wilson, Chamberlain supported the administration's preparedness and mobilization efforts, and he was instrumental in the creation of the Selective Service Act. His statement also highlights the adaptation of the Brandeisian synthesis of democratic values and Jewish nationalism, in terms readily understandable to non-Jews, for the orbit of American political discourse. Like other Progressive-era public figures, Chamberlain upheld the Monroe Doctrine, including America's presumed responsibility to "retain the Philippines, control the Panama Canal, and dominate the Pacific," as fundamentals of "manifest destiny" and Wilson's vision of liberal internationalism.[82] He viewed the prospect of an American Jewish Congress as a manifestation of modern American society's willingness to assume "the responsibilities of leadership of a community of nations pledged to peace through collective security, even if it means going to war to preserve it."[83] Jewish political solidarity, he averred, opened a pathway to combating anti-Jewish hostility, which he equated with other forms of antimodern and anti-American bigotry, and securing the liberty and freedom of Jews in other lands was the predicate to securing Jewish national aspirations in Palestine.

Rise of the Brandeis Group

Woodrow Wilson surprised the American political establishment and the nation in January 1916 by nominating Louis D. Brandeis to be an associate justice of the US Supreme Court. Wilson, whose own renomination as president was, as yet, uncertain, hailed Brandeis as "a lover of the right" and "a friend of justice" imbued "to the very heart with our American ideas of justice and equality and opportunity."[84] In early June, the US Senate confirmed Brandeis's appointment and a couple weeks later Wilson accepted the Democratic Party's mantle for a second term. Not only was Brandeis the first Jew appointed to the Supreme Court, but his elevation was also achieved over the opposition of key Wilson advisers and powerful political adversaries. Wilson's predecessor William Howard Taft, for example, denounced Brandeis as "utterly unscrupulous... a man of infinite cunning... of great tenacity of purpose, and, in my judgment, of much power for evil."[85] The Boston patrician William F. Fitzgerald disdainfully sniffed "the fact that a slimy fellow of this kind by his smoothness and intrigue, together with his Jewish instinct can [be appointed to the court] should teach an object lesson" to all true Americans.[86] In contrast to Wilson's opponents who decried Brandeis's "radical character" and characterized him as "fiery disturber" of the "public welfare and the prosperity of the country," supporters hailed Wilson's selection as "a master stroke" and "evidence [the president] does not consider creed or nationality in selecting men for public office."[87] In the American Jewish arena, newspapers and periodicals carried banner headlines celebrating Brandeis's nomination. Even Brandeis's conservative political opponents, who seethed behind closed doors over his liberal and Zionist commitments, appreciated the groundbreaking nature of his selection for the highest court in the land. American Jewry's aristocrats "[James] Speyer, [Jacob H.] Schiff, [Otto H.] Kahn, [and] Louis Marshall," Taft shrewdly observed, "all have to praise the appointment and all hate Wilson for making it."[88] Brandeis himself deemed the nomination evidence that "in the opinion of the President there is no conflict between Zionism and loyalty to America."[89]

The choice of Brandeis came after Wilson had already decided in 1913 against including him in his cabinet. It appears, as Melvin I. Urofsky suggests, that Brandeis's reputation as an "economic radical" weighed especially heavily in Wilson's decision-making.[90] In fact, notwithstanding the appointments of Oscar S. Straus as secretary of commerce under President Theodore Roosevelt and (a generation later) Henry Morgenthau Jr. as secretary of the treasury under President Franklin D. Roosevelt, it is evident that Jews faced barriers to high office until the mid-twentieth century.[91] Wilson's choice of Brandeis for the US Supreme Court was thus a statement of philosophical principle and a matter of political calculus; Brandeis won the support of Progressives and social reformers in Democratic and Republican circles, and his appointment enabled Wilson to leave an indelible footprint on the American judiciary.

Brandeis's heightened political authority coincided with a maelstrom of domestic and international crises that jolted American Jewry. First, the Russian Revolution, as the *American Jewish Chronicle* stated, although "expected for a long time by friends of progress and liberalism" struck in March 1917 like "a thunderbolt out of a blue sky."[92] Raising hopes for the equality and citizenship of Russian Jews and an end to the tsarist regime's antisemitic policies, including termination of the Pale of Settlement, the revolution fanned pent-up hopes among American Jews.[93] Many understood it "as the means to the final settlement of the Russian Jewish question."[94] Others anticipated its repercussions would "revolutionize the entire Jewish political life," "call into being new political energies... from the point of view of Jewish nationalism," help to "place Israel on a firm footing," and "create a Jewish national center."[95] Next, Wilson's call in April for the United States to join the Allied war effort (following the resumption of unrestricted German submarine warfare and the sinking of US merchant ships) generated widespread American Jewish patriotism. Together with the overthrow of Russian tsarism, which neutralized the Yiddish-speaking milieu's animus to the Triple Entente, Wilson's idealistic vision ("the world must be made safe for democracy") captured the hearts and minds of native-born Jews and eastern European Jewish immigrants alike.[96] Virtually overnight, American Jewish support for pacifism disappeared as the country rallied to the national standard. Between 1917 and 1918 more than 250,000 Jews enlisted in the US military. (Some 2500 Jewish immigrants living in the United States also joined the 39th and 40th Battalions of Royal Fusiliers, known as the Jewish Legion, and served under British auspices in Palestine.) Finally, news of the *Yishuv*'s precarious situation alarmed American Jews. The American Jewish press reported on the "pillage, murder, robbery, and starvation [in Palestine] caused by [Ahmed] Djemal Pasha," the Ottoman military governor of greater Syria.[97] Pasha, a central figure in the Armenian genocide of 1915–16, publicly threatened "the joy of the Jews on the approach of the British forces would be short-lived as he would make them share the fate of the Armenians."[98] In another instance, he announced the "intention of authorities to wipe out Jewish population of Palestine."[99]

In the wake of the Turkish commander's "barbarities" and "black plans of destruction to new Jewish settlement," Palestine's Jewish population dropped from 94,000 in 1914 to 60,000 in 1918.[100] Meanwhile, American Jews drew comparisons between Pasha's draconian treatment of the *Yishuv* and former tsarist General Nikolai Ivanov's expulsion of hundreds of thousands of Russian Jews from the eastern war zone.[101] The mix of famine, disease, expulsions, and outmigration prompted a steady drumbeat of American Jewish relief efforts. By the close of 1918, the JDC had transferred approximately $35 million in aid to the *Yishuv*, including deliveries "courtesy" of the American navy colliers USS *Vulcan* and USS *Sterling* of "nine hundred tons of provisions" in 1915 and "a consignment of drugs and other medical supplies" in 1916, respectively.[102] Much of the success in this regard, which required deft navigation of the Washington bureaucracy and the American government's complex wartime relationships with Berlin and Constantinople, was due to the intercession of the Brandeis group with Secretary of the Navy Josephus Daniels and Secretary of State William Jennings Bryan. The Brandeis group, which maintained a variety of channels with American officials, also enlisted the assistance of Henry Morgenthau Sr. and Abram I. Elkus, who served consecutively as Wilson's US ambassadors to the Ottoman empire.

Viewed in its totality, the successful mobilization of American Jewish resources to ensure the *Yishuv*'s wartime survival was nothing short of remarkable. Even in the spring 1917, despite the Central Powers' blockade of ocean passage to the Middle East, Brandeis and Wise prevailed upon Col. Edward M. House, Wilson's close friend and personal adviser, to seek the president's direct approval for an American medical unit to travel to Palestine on humanitarian grounds. Denied assistance by Robert Lansing, Bryan's successor as secretary of state, the president personally authorized the request. In due course, notwithstanding the complexity owing to the severance of official ties between the United States and Turkey, including detention of the USS *Des Moines* in the port of Alexandria, the American medical unit arrived in Jaffa in the summer. Led by Dr. Isaac Max Rubinow, a well-known Progressive social insurance theorist, statistician, and physician, the forty-four-person unit included medical doctors, specialists, nurses, and staff. The JDC equipped the unit with an operating budget of $400,000 and a start-up delivery of $25,000 worth of medical supplies.[103]

The confluence of developments noted here strengthened the "magnetic pull" of the American Jewish Congress campaign.[104] After two years of countrywide publicity and stormy debate, as Jonathan Frankel observes, "the idea of the congress had struck deeper roots in [American Jewish] public consciousness than even its advocates had realized."[105] "The Russian republic and America's intervention in the world war," the *Bnai Brith Messenger* stated, "are bound to bring about the greatest relief to Israel... Zionism has gotten such a hold on many of our people that the recent freedom in Russia... has made our people still more sanguine for the restoration of the land of our forefathers."[106] A groundswell of support for postwar national self-determination, including "internationally guaranteed, public recognized institutions for the free, national development of the Jews in Palestine," now took hold of the American Jewish scene.[107] In April 1917, for example, a national convention of Jewish socialists resolved:

> Whereas, the recent [Russian] revolutionary developments, as a consequence of the world events, have placed the full liberation and self-government of all nationalities as the basis for universal peace,
>
> Be it, therefore, resolved that in this historic moment the Jews throughout the world proclaim and demand the full measure of national liberation and a publicly secured home for the Jewish people in Palestine, and,
>
> Be it further resolved, that in the elections to the American Jewish Congress... all delegates supported by this organization do not vote against placing the Palestine question in its entirety on the agenda of the Congress, and... that they be obligated to vote for Palestine as a publicly secured home for the Jewish people.[108]

Many of American Jewry's most visible and influential community figures played key roles in promoting the cause of the American Jewish Congress. Nathan Straus, the influential co-owner of the R.H. Macy and Abraham & Straus department stores and a celebrated New York Jewish philanthropist, appeared at a mass meeting that "jammed" New York City's

Cooper Union "to the legal limit."[109] Announcing his support of a resolution (adopted by the "great audience with a whoop") pledging allegiance to the "fundamental object of the Zionist movement to obtain for the Jewish people 'a publicly secured and legally secured home in Palestine,'" Straus declared:[110]

> I have been in Palestine several times... I expect to go again soon. (Applause.) If you prove to me that you are good Zionists but haven't got your fare and want to go, I'll take you. (Then the roof came off.) I am especially glad... that we are witnessing the spectacle of the whole world applauding, approving, and supporting our great purpose to reestablish the Jewish people on their own soil. For the whole world has come to recognize the justice of our righteous demand—that our dearly beloved Palestine, the land of Jewish heart desires, shall be restored to us. I am happy that [the anti-nationalist] opposition [to the congress] is rapidly transforming itself into approval and support. No longer have the Zionists to battle within Jewish ranks, and no longer are the Zionists, who have always understood the real hope and the real need of the Jewish people, compelled to debate their principles...[111]

In the spring of 1917, following months of intracommunal wrangling, political jockeying, and protracted negotiations among rival Zionist, non-Zionist, and Jewish labor leaders, the Jewish Congress Organization Committee (JCOC), comprised of representatives of American Jewry's key factions, groups, and organizations, produced a framework for countrywide elections. The pro-Zionist forces, led by the Brandeis group, insisted on the principle of one-person, one-vote, and a straightforward majority election system. "What is good enough for the American congress," proclaimed the *Yidisher kemfer,* "is good enough for the Jewish congress."[112] In due course, the JCOC "issued a public call "earnestly request[ing]" the Jews of America "to select representatives to an American Jewish Congress which shall meet on September 2, 1917 at Washington, D.C., exclusively for the purpose of defining methods whereby, in cooperation with the Jews of the world, full rights may be secured for the Jews of all lands and laws discriminating against them may be abrogated."[113] The announcement defined the phrase "full rights" in terms that underscored the difference between the status of American Jewry and that of other diaspora Jewish communities:

> 1. Civil, religious, and political rights, and in addition thereto.
> 2. Wherever the various peoples of any land are or may be recognized as having rights as such, the conferring upon the Jewish people of the land affected, of like rights, if desired by them, as determined and ascertained by the Congress.
> 3. The securing and protection of Jewish rights in Palestine.
> 4. The question of economic reconstruction of the Jewish communities in the war zones.[114]

The JCOC further maintained "every Jew and every Jewess, twenty-one years of age or over, shall be qualified to vote for representation to the Jewish Congress."[115] The enfranchisement of women, itself a radical departure from patriarchal Jewish tradition and American norms, fundamentally altered the terms of the national conversation about the future of American Jewry. This development mirrored, in part, the broader trend of inclusivism that animated pro-congress grassroots forces, particularly Jewish immigrant and workers groups, who insisted on full participation and equal representation in organized American Jewish life. In other respects, it reflected the changing political consciousness of American society at large energized by the National American Woman Suffrage Association, the National Woman's Party, and the National Birth Control League. As Melissa Klapper points out, by this time women's suffrage was "a frequent topic of discussion in virtually all American Jewish periodicals in both English and Yiddish."[116] The congress elections opened a distinctive pathway for Jewish women in the United States to participate fully in American Jewish affairs without the need "to compromise any aspect of their identities or communal affiliations."[117] It is noteworthy, of course, that the call for women to vote for and participate in the congress as delegates occurred three years prior to the passage of the Nineteenth Amendment. In sum, the American Jewish Congress—the controversy, the campaign, the election, and the event itself—serves as an important barometer of changing American Jewish attitudes to gender and political power. In contrast to conservative opponents of the congress movement, who were closely tied to the Republican Party, advocates of the congress echoed the Wilsonian idealism of the Democratic Party.

In June, with roughly 350,000 votes accounted for in total, including 125,000 votes cast in New York City and hundreds of thousands cast by Jewish immigrants nationwide, the pro-Zionist forces scored an overwhelming victory in the congress elections.[118] Declaring the elections "a success," *Di naye velt* noted "the broad Jewish public showed much greater interest in the elections to the Jewish Congress than one could have expected."[119] A sizable number of candidates "known to the Jewish masses" as "Jewish public workers of high grade," including a majority of "outspoken nationalists," were elected.[120] The "influence" of women in "Jewish affairs and how important a part they play," stated the *American Jewish World*, "was clearly demonstrated at the polling places" in the election to the American Jewish Congress.[121] "That the successful candidates owed... their election to the votes of the women was clearly to be seen. Prominent women throughout the country were also candidates..."[122] In the event, the Brandeis group owed its triumph to a broad national coalition of immigrants, workers, middle-class professionals, and women.

Coming on the heels of the US government's war declaration, American Zionism's victory paradoxically proved to be a strain on plans for the American Jewish Congress. On the one hand, the Brandeis group's sway in American Jewish affairs was fully vindicated. On the other, contrary to the populist will of the American Jewish masses, it became evident that convening the congress presented potential pitfalls and hazards. Many Jewish leaders openly feared the plebiscite—potentially riven by public debate between pacifists and prowar advocates—risked accentuating intracommunal tensions, raising the specter of "the charge of disloyalty on the part of the Jews toward America," and resulting in inflammatory public statements about the fate of the Jews in Europe and Palestine.[123] "It is no time for us Jews," an associate of Bernard G. Richards cautioned, "to clamor for our rights apart from the right we have of manifesting our devotion to the nation under whose protection we live."[124] The Brandeis group, publicly committed to democratization in Jewish life, itself became divided over the best strategy to manage the congress's raw and unformed political power while safeguarding its authority. Julian W. Mack and Felix Frankfurter, among Brandeis's closest advisers, believed the congress's pro-Zionist majority coalition could not afford to diverge from the Wilson administration's wartime agenda. Others (in particular Horace M. Kallen) argued delaying the congress could hand the Brandeis-led coalition's adversaries (Bnai Brith, the American Jewish Committee, and internationalist labor) a new opportunity to derail plans for the gathering. The deep suspicion and acrimony between the Brandeis group and the Marshall camp was palpable.[125] Mack, a founding member of the American Jewish Committee who sustained amicable relations with Marshall and other non-Zionists, attempted to build bridges between the rival communal leaders. Unsuccessful in his efforts to persuade Cyrus Adler that "a democratic congress was inevitable," he and other members of the Brandeis group understood the Marshall camp, albeit temporarily cowed, if given the opportunity, would not hesitate to try and undermine the Zionist leadership's political standing.[126]

WAR AND REALPOLITIK

As the debate over the American Jewish Congress unfolded, the fluid wartime context shaped the Brandeis group's trajectory. With the collapse of the tsarist regime, a new wave of pogroms engulfed the eastern war zone, decimating villages and towns proximate to the front. (The pogroms, including the slaughter of Jews by Ukrainian units of the Red Army, continued sporadically until 1921.) News of anti-Jewish violence now became a ubiquitous feature of the Jewish press—including the murder in 1920 of Israel Friedlaender and Bernard Cantor as they traveled in Ukraine on behalf of a JDC commission—shocking American Jewry and highlighting the urgent need for large-scale relief, rescue, and emigration.[127]

The British military campaign in the Middle East reached a turning point in the spring of 1917. Following the winter Battle of Rafah, when the British seized control of the northern section of the Sinai Peninsula, Ottoman forces lost ground and the British steadily advanced into southern Palestine. It was at this juncture Chaim Weizmann, who sustained close contact with highly placed British officials and communal figures, learned of the Sykes-Picot Agreement (a secret Anglo-Franco compact formulated in 1916 dividing the wartime spoils of the doomed Turkish empire) and the British war cabinet's plan to take control of much of the Middle East.[128] He also learned a "memorial was being prepared on the whole question" of Palestine—a proposition for which Weizmann had vigorously lobbied since 1915—and for which it was generally believed "very important to obtain American Jews' support."[129]

The British government's eagerness to cultivate the Wilson administration's support, Josephus Daniels would recall years later, and "attract to the Allied cause the moral and material resources of the Jewish communities of the world," infused Anglo-American wartime relations with a special dimension.[130] Collaboration between the Zionists in London and Washington now assumed new urgency. On the Zionist front, Weizmann "pinned his hopes on Brandeis as the person most capable of influencing President Wilson" and entreated his American colleagues to court the Wilson administration's pro-Zionist associates and allies.[131] Writing to Brandeis in early April 1917, Weizmann asserted, "the position here is developing fairly rapidly and one may say without exaggeration very satisfactorily."[132]

> Since the invasion of Palestine by the British army our problem has become much more tangible and *actuel*. I think that everybody here realizes the importance of the Palestinian campaign and the press on the whole is extremely favorable to a Jewish Palestine under a British protectorate…
>
> From the documents which accompany this letter you will be able to see how far the negotiations have progressed and I hope you will be satisfied that the work has been carried out with the necessary circumspection and care. Allow me to supplement the information contained in these documents by the following remarks:
>
> I had an opportunity of seeing Mr. Balfour on the 22nd March and of discussing with him the Zionist position, and I have no hesitation in saying that the Secretary of State for Foreign Affairs is in full sympathy with our aspirations and I am sure that we may reckon on his support. We may also reckon on the full sympathies of the Prime Minister with whom I had the honor of discussing the question on the 3rd of April. The main difficulty seems to be the claims of the French. I hope to be in a position soon to send you a separate report on that question.

> We look forward here to a strengthening of our position, both by the American government and American Jews and on that point I had a conversation with Mr. [Norman] Hapgood… An expression of opinion coming from yourself and perhaps from other gentlemen connected with the government in favor of a Jewish Palestine under a British protectorate would greatly strengthen our hands.[133]

The synergistic if somewhat frenetic communication that transpired between Weizmann and Brandeis from April to November 1917 defined British and American Zionist wartime strategy. It also had the immediate effect of supplying a detailed view of Weizmann's activity in London, information that substantively informed the Brandeis group's discussions in Washington with Wilson, Edward M. House, and government officials. Weizmann, as Jehuda Reinharz observes, was a "relentless and single-minded" figure of rare diplomatic and political talent who recognized the fortuitous convergence of British policymakers' quest "to tip the scales of the war in their favor" and the Zionist movement's need "to win international recognition and respectability as a national movement."[134] Buoyed in part by his relationship with Brandeis—British officials believed Weizmann's access to American Jewish leaders could help sway American opinion and boost support for Britain's wartime needs—Weizmann boldly and strategically pressed the Zionist case to full advantage. In contrast, the Brandeis group, engaged publicly in the American Jewish Congress campaign and privately in lobbying the American government for humanitarian assistance of the *Yishuv,* appreciated the exponential value of the proposed British declaration but was, as Ben Halpern notes, "decidedly restrained" in its efforts to "influence American policy at the fountainhead."[135] As a matter of political strategy, Brandeis "no doubt realized" that "policy declarations by governments had no binding force" and the "critical moment for Zionist hopes… would come at the peace conference."[136]

Although the perspectives of the Weizmann camp and Brandeis group were roughly complementary, the dynamics of their cultural-political settings differed greatly. "The British 'used' the Zionists," Reinharz explains, and "the Zionists [under Weizmann] 'used' Britain"—both sides "needed each other, and they benefited from one another."[137] Zionism, in the words of Mark Sykes, was "the key to the lock" and would ultimately determine Turkey's fate and the future of Palestine.[138] The Wilson administration, by contrast, was not compelled to define US national interest in terms of a future British protectorate in Palestine or assisting the Zionist cause. In fact, notwithstanding the Progressive impulse and the rise of ethnic politics in the American setting, Washington, dominated by a Protestant establishment, generally displayed striking indifference to the desires and interests of minorities. American Jewish leaders, irrespective of the exaggerated British assessment of their influence, historically operated at the margins of the public square. The rise of immigration restriction and the Red Scare made American Jewry, among other minority groups, painfully aware of its limited political capital. The Immigration Act of 1917, twice vetoed by Wilson and passed by Congress over his objections, created an "Asiatic Barred Zone" and reinforced the American gatekeeping notion of maintaining classifications of "desirable," "undesirable," and "excludable" immigrants.[139] It prefigured the Emergency Quota Act of 1921 and the Johnson-Reed Act of 1924 which in effect ended immigration to the United States from southern and eastern Europe and non-European countries. The closing of America's "golden door" accentuated the desideratum for an alternative pathway for eastern European Jewish immigration.[140]

Scholars who have closely studied Wilson's attitude to Zionism and the prospect of a Jewish national home in Palestine offer competing explanations for the crystallization of the president's behind-the-scenes support of the Balfour Declaration in fall 1917 and his public affirmation of it in August

1918.[141] Leonard Stein suggests Lansing persuaded Wilson "to keep silent" when initially asked for a public expression of his approval of the declaration.[142] Stein argues Lansing objected to the declaration because "the partition of the Turkish empire formed no part of [American] war aims," but also "seems to have disliked the declaration on other grounds."[143] He ultimately counseled Wilson "to resist the pressure of American Zionists."[144] As a result, the president was "headed off from his original intention and, for the time being at least, dropped the idea" of a public endorsement.[145] When Wilson decided "to give the Zionists some open encouragement" ten months later, it was, Stein notes, in response to "urgent representations" from Wise who "reminded him" the declaration was "silent on the subject" of Palestine's suzerainty and left this matter to "determination at the peace table."[146] Thus, he posits, Wilson, "preoccupied with other matters which interested him more," did not generally give "the Zionist question much serious thought."[147] As a counterpoint, Richard Ned Lebow argues Wilson "personally favored Zionism" but was no less motivated than his British counterparts by "considerations of grand strategy" and temporized in anticipation of "differing circumstances" in the war's progress.[148] Wilson, he asserts, deliberately offered a "noncommittal response" to initial British inquiries about his "sympathy with the Zionist movement" and "if the president favors [a British] declaration."[149] By early October, against the backdrop of Turkey's military and territorial incursion into the Caucuses, which undermined Turkish defenses elsewhere and portended the collapse of the Palestine front, "Wilson had found a way to get around the obstacle" of becoming entangled in the Turkish-British struggle over the Middle East. Without rocking relations between the United States and Turkey, he decided to "approve the declaration but insist that his approval not be made public."[150] Stein and Lebow represent two poles of the scholarly spectrum: the former asserts Wilson's Palestine agenda was largely shaped by those around him, the latter argues Wilson shrewdly assessed the overall situation and used only the most advantageous and productive opportunities to deploy America's outsized clout. In either case, it would appear American Jewry's pro-Zionist sensibility was at best a cognate factor in Wilson's wartime calculus.

The Brandeis group's centrality in this drama, as this essay contends, is actually hiding in plain sight and warrants rethinking. That is to say, because American Jewish power was on the whole more apparent than real, the true significance of the Brandeis group's role vis-à-vis Washington and London lay in the declaration's long-term implications for the *Yishuv*, plans for a British protectorate in Palestine, and helping to shape the future of US foreign policy in the Middle East. Given the urgency and the high stakes of the wartime crisis, the Brandeis group, reliant on American goodwill and power, necessarily focused on what was possible and attainable in the context of Wilson's presidency, but also laid the groundwork for driving forward the Zionist agenda in the future. This meant, above all else, harmonizing Zionism's political strategy with the emerging reality of Palestine in the postwar era. "The hope of democracy for ourselves and the nations of the earth," stated Stephen S. Wise, "lies in the triumphant prosecution of the war in which we are engaged."[151] Undaunted by changing circumstances, the Brandeis group resolutely pursued a tripartite Zionist agenda of mobilizing American Jewry, nimbly advancing Weizmann's pursuit of a British declaration, and deploying its lean political capital in tactical moves designed to win the endorsement of key players in the American government and ultimately the president himself. The historical record from 1917 to 1918 is replete with instances of the Brandeis group lobbying, coaxing, and otherwise appealing to the Wilson administration for expressions of support of the Zionist cause and the idea of a postwar British protectorate in Palestine.

An important turning point was reached on April 9, 1917, when Wise met with House. Wise subsequently informed Jacob De Haas:

> I have just had a long talk with Colonel House, and I cannot tell you how pleased I am. He understands the situation, and what is better yet, not only is it in his mind and not only did he realize the imminence of the British possibilities, but he said he is keeping our papers before him in order to move at the right moment.
>
> He said this that was significant: "Perhaps we can help to get the British government to make such concessions to France and Russia as will make it possible for them to grant the desired concessions in Palestine." It is almost too good to believe, and almost too important to put to paper. Of course, you will put this paper away as soon as you have read it.
>
> . . .Of course, we must trust him in the matter, we do. He is enlisted in our cause. There is no question about it whatsoever. The thing will go through Washington without a delay.
>
> He made this statement that is interesting: "Six months ago, I would have said that a British-American protectorate over Palestine and Syria would be impossible. Nothing is impossible any longer. Everything has broken down, and we can build up again almost as we choose." That side of things is evidently covered.[152]

Occurring just days after Wilson's call for a US declaration of war against Germany, the meeting illustrates the parameters of the Brandeis group's strategy. Though historians tend to regard Wise's record of the April 9 discussion with some skepticism, it is undeniable that House gave Wise reason to feel hopeful about the administration's general attitude to Zionism and future orientation. In the weeks and months that followed, Brandeis, Wise, Mack, De Haas, and Frankfurter sustained frequent (sometimes daily) contact with House and State

Department officials as communications between London and Washington transpired. Brandeis and Wise also met with Wilson privately on a few occasions to provide him with updated information about Weizmann's progress and to discuss developments related to Zionism, the *Yishuv*, and the Middle East. In doing so, they played indispensable roles as the Zionist Organization's foremost interlocutors with the citadel of American power. The net result was that Brandeis, who also held meetings with Foreign Secretary Arthur Balfour during his April-May 1917 official visit to the United States, "took the leading role personally" in elevating discussion of the Zionist cause to the level of an American foreign policy concern and engaging both leaders on the future of Palestine and the US-British wartime partnership.[153]

As the Brandeis group's efforts proceeded apace—punctuated but not derailed by Henry Morgenthau's ill-fated Palestine mission, a poorly managed smokescreen to engineer a separate peace treaty with the Porte (June-July 1917),[154] protracted but dead-end negotiations with Jacob H. Schiff about possibly joining the American Zionist movement (October 1917-January 1918),[155] and episodic attempts by House, Lansing, and other officials to tamp down or undercut the Zionist position—it navigated the shoals of America's entry into the war while attending to a host of communal, domestic, and international challenges. Looking beyond the welter of contemporaneous activity, the American Zionist leaders' overriding concern centered on the paramount issue of preserving the fragile political equilibrium between itself (on behalf of American Jewry) and the White House, which hinged in large measure on Wilson. Anticipating that Wilson's vision of a new world order would be adjudicated at the peace conference, the Brandeis group, as Ben Halpern points out, was "more than willing to share the responsibilities flowing" from a British declaration and accordingly it mobilized a broad coalition of communal forces that "left no doubt [American Jews] contemplated a scale of immigration that would yield a Jewish majority in Palestine."[156]

Even as the Brandeis group sought to court the Wilson administration and American government officials, a heated controversy was brewing in American Jewish circles concerning the idea "to postpone, not abandon the Congress."[157] In the public arena, Brandeis and his lieutenants endeavored to bolster the confidence of the proponents of the American Jewish Congress. Behind the scenes, Brandeis's inner circle used every arrow in its quiver to neutralize the anti-Zionist protestations and "near-hysteria" of the American Jewish Committee leaders.[158] Cyrus L. Sulzberger labeled the proposed congress a "calamity," Jacob H. Schiff lamented it would be American Jewry's "darkest day," and Simon Wolf bluntly informed Wilson that the Marshall-Schiff camp was "utterly opposed" to the congress.[159] From June through October 1917 it was actually Wise at the behest of Brandeis (who had by now largely withdrawn from the limelight of congress activity)—and with Wilson's tacit approval—who piloted the Zionist leadership's efforts to disabuse American Jewry's elected representatives of "the unwisdom of a congress at this time."[160] There is "a great deal of feeling about the Congress," Wise reported to Brandeis, "but I think we can explain why a postponement [has] to be, and I am hoping that the outcome of the negotiations... will ultimately more than satisfy our Zionist friends."[161]

Keenly alert to the fluidity and dynamics of the moment, the Brandeis group sought to reduce the intracommunal temperature while bolstering American Jewry's broader national interests and external political agenda. The floor debates at the congress, it was feared, would only amplify vigorous non-Zionist opposition to the Brandeis group's agenda and foment the spirited grassroots demands of Poalei Zion activists, likely to insist on a resolution denouncing the Turkish regime, who chafed under what Baruch Zuckerman called the American Zionist leaders' "monopoly on Palestine."[162] Among the most visible of Zionist dissident leaders, David Ben-Gurion took aim at the Brandeis group's allegedly deferential posture and caustically derided the

"Galut [exile]-like" and "servile" congress "born in impotence and shame."[163] The "so-called Jewish Congress," he insisted, represented the "moral bankruptcy of American Jewry" and ought to be replaced by the Zionist congress as "the preparatory parliament of the future home of the Jewish people."[164] Given the narrow range of options, the determination of Brandeis, Mack, and Wise to postpone the congress in fact enabled the American Zionists to maintain their tactical advantage. Postponement preserved the Brandeis group's democratically conferred political authority, forestalled a potential challenge to the dominance of the Brandeis-led coalition at the congress, and avoided a possible rupture with Wilson administration.

After several weeks of intense political battles—"Postpone the [American Jewish] congress and you annul it," warned Nahman Syrkin—Wise and Marshall, in what must have appeared to be an unholy alliance, brokered a decision by the JCOC executive committee to defer the congress until after the war's conclusion.[165] Fearful that "probable indiscretion at the great gathering would compromise the Jews of this country," Marshall noted the "ever-growing antisemitic feeling in America" and urged "that all sorts of precautions should be taken not to provoke it."[166] In addition to American Jewry's influential uptown *"shtadlonim"* (court Jews), the Brandeis group also used its political capital to enlist the White House in providing cover for postponement.[167] In a statement released on July 1, 1917 Wise publicly reported, "A contrary impression having gained currency":

> I am authorized to say that the President has learned with interest of the proposed American Jewish Congress. While it may seem necessary to the gentlemen who have called the Congress to postpone it for some little time from the date fixed—September 2—because of the urgency at this time of the public business, the President is persuaded that the American Jewish Congress will wisely and prudently serve Jewish interests

> and that its deliberations and policies will be in accord with and helpful to the aims and policies of the American Government.[168]

THE BALFOUR DECLARATION

Notwithstanding the irony of the JCOC's antidemocratic posture, the American Zionist leadership—now with Wilson's public blessing—handily dispensed with the issue of postponing the congress. Over the course of the summer and early fall of 1917, as Frankfurter (who took a leave of absence from Harvard Law School to serve as a special assistant to Secretary of War Newton D. Baker) kept a watchful eye on the Morgenthau mission (appointed by Wilson personally, Frankfurter dutifully reported on Morgenthau's "wild goose chase"),[169] the Brandeis group engaged in a series of communications with Weizmann and House concerning the drafting of a British declaration and prospects for its American support. The first major breakthrough in negotiations occurred on July 18, when Weizmann submitted an official text to Balfour and the Foreign Office on behalf of the Zionist movement. Two crucial months ensued during which time the text was subjected to close scrutiny and considerable pressure from all sides.[170] Underscoring the transnational nature of the Zionist enterprise, the Weizmann camp and Brandeis group embraced the sine qua non of a British protectorate of Palestine—dismissing the idea of an Anglo-American protectorate, an alternative floated by British observers concerned about French opposition to British geopolitical aspirations. As well, they understood the crucial significance of securing American support for a British declaration prior to the peace conference and the force of realpolitik at play in London and Washington.

On September 23, following weeks of intensive strategizing about the declaration—and cables to Brandeis in which Weizmann urged (not for the last time), "Would greatly help if President and yourself would support text"—Brandeis and Wise met with House in New York City.[171] House, who was secretly receiving British intelligence reports of the Weizmann-Brandeis transmissions, remained the central channel for discussing the British war cabinet's aims with Wilson. Whether or not bypassing Lansing and the State Department was a subterfuge to keep "the United States technically clear of any pledges," as the historian Frank E. Manuel muses, Lansing's implacable opposition to the Zionist cause certainly limited the Brandeis group's options.[172] House, by contrast, irrespective of his private misgivings about Zionism, generally kept open lines of communication with the Brandeis group and acted as Wilson's trusted broker concerning the British government and Zionist affairs. A curious mix of patrician antisemitism and respect for the Zionist leadership's capacious activity and influence, coupled with deference to Wilson's presidential authority, is evident in House's personal diary record of a September 23 meeting with Brandeis and Wise:

> They came to talk of the Zionist Movement. They had received a cable from Weitzman [*sic*] of London outlining in two paragraphs the views of the [Foreign Office] and the [Prime Minister] which they, the F.O. and P.M., were endeavoring to get the War Council to accept. I suggested against pressing the President for any public statement. I suggested they bring the French, Italian, and Russian Governments as near the attitude of Great Britain and the United States as was possible and then leave the matter there. *I confessed that the President was willing to go further than I thought advisable . . .*[173]

House, who enjoyed a close friendship with William Wiseman, head of British military intelligence in the United States, and counted Wiseman "a part of [his own] inner circle" and an "important intermediary in Anglo-American relations," was no doubt well informed of the Zionist movement's active efforts to court the Allied powers.[174] Like his British counterpart, House seems to have had a somewhat inflated sense of global Jewish political influence. He thus urged the Brandeis group to do its utmost, even though France and Italy had already signaled support of a Jewish national home in separate letters to Zionist diplomats. At the same time, as indicated by the communications between London and Washington, he understood that British officials expected the French, Italian, and Russian governments to accede to a British declaration concerning Zionism and a Palestine protectorate. What is particularly telling about this juncture is the mix of House's adroit perception of Wilson's orientation and his astute sense of timing in promoting the president's emerging vision of postwar global reconstruction. "You know of my deep interest in Zionism," Wilson had assured Wise a couple months earlier.[175] "Whenever the time comes," Wilson said, "and you and Justice Brandeis feel that the time is ripe for me to speak and act, I shall be ready."[176] It would have been unnecessary for Wise to relate this anecdote to House (though it is hard to imagine he did not do so).

As the probability of postwar British control of the Middle East (inclusive of Palestine) became imminent, Wilson's resolve to forge the region's future as part of a liberal New World order strengthened, and he quietly countenanced the actualization of Jewish national self-determination. Indeed, House followed suit by explicitly prompting the Brandeis group to follow up with Weizmann and other Zionist contacts, thereby effectively soft-pedaling Wilson's influence vis-à-vis British policymakers without tarnishing the administration's profile as an impartial actor. The Brandeis group, too, benefited from this arrangement, both with respect to helping shape the Wilson administration's agenda and boosting American Jewry's perceived status in international affairs. In a word, House knew he could count on the Brandeis group's assiduity and high level of contacts irrespective of his own view of Zionism. His readiness to share sensitive information with Brandeis and Wise was in fact part of a delicate dance between the White House and the American Zionist leadership. The Brandeis group, cognizant of House's unique gatekeeping role, supplied the Wilson administration with information and support as part of a broader agenda that simultaneously helped to advance American wartime and diplomatic interests. Against this backdrop, Brandeis felt confident in replying to Weizmann's cable of September 19 with a cable of his own on September 24, a copy of which was forwarded to House, stating: "From talks I have had with the President and from expressions of opinion given closest advisors I feel I can answer you that he is in entire sympathy with declaration… I of course heartily agree."[177] He sent Weizmann a second cable the same day recommending, "it would be wise for you to get French and Italians to enquire what attitude President is on declaration."[178] Brandeis next met with House on September 29; no record of the meeting exists but it is known Brandeis provided House with documentation of ongoing Zionist activity and Middle East affairs.

As the month of September drew to a close, news leaked from the Washington that House was enlisting Brandeis to assist with the Wilson administration's preparations for a future peace settlement conference.[179] Typical of the American press coverage, the *New York Times* cited "published reports" indicating Brandeis would be assisting House "in the compilation of data on peace."[180] In the Jewish public arena, weeklies like Denver's *Jewish News* carried editorials about "the appointment by President Wilson of Justice Louis D. Brandeis to assist Colonel House in gathering peace data."[181] Though the Wilson administration denied the media reports and Brandeis refused to comment on them, news of Wilson's long-term planning traveled widely and stirred the romantic hopes and patriotic zeal of American Jewry.[182] "This makes it almost certain," the St. Louis *Jewish Voice* repeated, that Brandeis "will sit at the peace conference… when representatives of all countries gather together to adjust matters at the termination of the world war."[183]

> Zionism will be officially submitted to members of the conference by Justice Brandeis. "This proves among other things," said [the Denver Zionist leader] William R. Blumenthal... "that Zionists are not considered as undesirable citizens, as some opponents would have us believe. And it means that Zionism will be an issue at the peace conference after the war."[184]

The notion that Wilson might consult Brandeis on domestic or international matters was hardly surprising. "Time and again," Melvin I. Urofsky observes, "Wilson had to make decisions about the organization of the war program that ran counter to his ingrained instincts, and he would turn to Brandeis for advice."[185] Quite apart from Brandeis's rapport with Wilson, however, it is intriguing to consider the timing of the leak that surfaced as Weizmann, in De Haas's words, was "looking for a public declaration" of American support but also signaling "his needs would be met if our government agreed that the British should make their position known."[186] News of Brandeis's purported involvement in Wilson's future planning, including the dispensation of the Ottoman empire's territories, had a strong ripple effect. (As evidenced by leaked reports of Morgenthau's secret diplomatic mission of July 1917, this was not the first time that White House and US officials "disavowed any responsibility for authorizing peace feelers."[187]) Wilson, as the historian Selig Adler observes, aware of "the cleavage in the Jewish ranks" over Zionism was likely unsurprised by the "avalanche of anti-nationalist feeling" that befell Washington.[188] His correspondence demonstrates that the president knew what it meant to be "caught between the division of ideas" that roiled the American Jewish scene.[189] It is also possible that Wilson, regardless of stated US government policy, essentially used this opportunity to tip his hat at the prospect of Jewish national self-determination in Palestine under a British protectorate. Indeed, that is precisely how opponents of American Zionism read the situation. "The Jews from every tribe,"

House complained on October 3, "have descended in force, and they seem determined to break in with a jimmy if they are not let in."[190] In London, Weizmann reached much the same conclusion. Referring to the Washington rumors and the machinations of Edwin Montagu and other anti-Zionist British Jewish communal leaders, he observed: "All that strengthens and encourages the movement and no amount of talk by Mr. Montagu or people like him will stem the tide."[191] Intentional or otherwise, it appears the sequence of events—that is, Brandeis's cable of September 24 to Weizmann declaring Wilson's and his "entire sympathy with declaration" and the widespread rumor of Brandeis's involvement in preparations for the peace conference—broke the logjam in the London-Washington negotiations and cleared the way for a new phase of Anglo-American collaboration.

On October 4, the British war cabinet approved a new draft of the British declaration known as the Milner-Amery text.[192] Weizmann immediately alerted Brandeis in this regard and warned him of efforts by Montagu and other "influential Jews" who while not in a position to "ruin the Zionist plan... might succeed in weakening it."[193] On October 6, Balfour sent the Milner-Amery draft to House. The American embassy in London, circumventing protocol, and bypassing Lansing, forwarded a copy of the text directly to the White House. Weizmann meanwhile cabled the text to Brandeis and urged, "It is essential to have not only President's approval of text but his recommendation to grant this declaration without delay."[194] Wiseman also reached out to House and prodded him for Wilson's approbation. In response to the flurry of communications, Brandeis instructed De Haas: "Suggest [Wise] see Col. House immediately and see what he can do. Have wired SSW today."[195] In a curious twist, on October 13 Wilson wrote a seemingly offhand note to House: "I find in my pocket the memorandum you gave me about the Zionist movement. I am afraid I did not say to you that I concurred in the formula suggested by the other side. I do and would be obliged if you would let them know it." On October 16, House responded to Wilson: "I will let the British government know that the formula they suggested to the Zionist movement meets with your approval."[196] Wilson's "much debated note," with its obscure reference to a "memorandum," has been alternately described by scholars as a "breezy reply," a byproduct of the president's wartime distraction, and possibly a sign of his general disinterest in Zionism.[197] Drawing conclusions on this score is at best a speculative exercise. We do know, of course, that Wilson was absorbed at this juncture by the threat of German submarine warfare, building up the US Navy (shortly to become "the most colossal conveyance of fighting men the world had ever known"),[198] the deployment of the American Expeditionary Forces on the western front under General John J. Pershing, and the creation of the War Industries Board under Bernard Baruch.

The historical record clearly shows that the Brandeis group knew how to get Wilson's attention despite such weighty matters. For example, even as the United States engaged on October 15 in its first battle with the Imperial German Navy, resulting in the first recorded enlisted American casualty of the war, House made time to meet with Wise and De Haas. In addition to seeking House's intervention with Wilson, Brandeis's advisers offered the Wilson administration recommendations for two specific emendations to the draft British declaration's phraseology. House informed Wise and De Haas "he had seen [the Milner-Amery text] previously, and that he had been instructed to approve it and had forwarded to London the expression of approval."[199] De Haas subsequently reported to Brandeis that House indicated his willingness "to have a message sent [to London] recommending the changes [the Brandeis group] proposed."[200] This included the idea of substituting the term "Jewish people" for "Jewish race" and adjusting the text's so-called safeguard clauses to affirm "the rights and status enjoyed by Jews in any other country."[201] Such modifications, they recommended, illustrated the legitimacy of Jewish national aspirations while amplifying the Zionist case as an expression of Progressive liberalism and enlightened British internationalism. The proposed language also ensured the declaration would align with Wilson's assertion that "no nation should seek to extend its policy over any other nation or people, but that every people should be left to determine its own policy, its own way of development, unhindered, unthreatened, unafraid, the little along with the great and powerful."[202]

Following the meeting with House, De Haas reported to Brandeis:

> [House] offered no objection to London publishing the declaration, thinking that there may be reasons why London desired to do so at this time, but expressed the belief that Weizmann wanted it as against the opposition, and, to use his own words, "seeing that you have all the governments with you, I don't see why you should worry about this opposition."
>
> He made it very clear that the [Wilson] administration's public approval of this declaration would not be made at present time, either here or in London, unless the President acted under pressure exerted by the British government, but that the president did approve... However, he felt that if the declaration was published by England, that such publication would be an excellent occasion for the presentation by us of our memorandum to the president, and securing a reply that would paraphrase this declaration in a form that would serve all our purposes. He told me that he would inform Dr. Wise about that later as events developed...
>
> We, therefore, advise you to cable to Weizmann that the president has already sent the message of approval to London, but believes public declaration by him would be injudicious...[203]

Three days later, Brandeis—who previously discussed emending the text with Wise, De Haas, and other close advisers—responded to De Haas's report indicating: "My disposition would be not to attempt to change the [declaration's] phraseology. Weizmann is probably doing the best he can, and the difference does not seem to me to be very important..."[204] It appears Wise and De Haas may not have fully resolved the issue of the suggested edits with Brandeis prior to their meeting with House. Although Weizmann later claimed the final changes to the British declaration "actually came from Brandeis," the sequence of events in real time suggests this was not the case.[205] As Jehuda Reinharz concludes, other historical actors proposed strikingly similar modifications, and in any case, "House does not seem to have sent on the American objections."[206]

The true significance of the encounter between House and the Brandeis group arguably had more to do with the question of public perception than the issue of causality. "On both points," Leonard Stein observes, "the declaration was amended in the sense desired by the American Zionists before its final approval by the war cabinet on October 31, and they were not unnaturally under the impression that this was the result of their representations to House."[207] Aware that Wilson approved the proposed formula "just as it is," House did not need to "definitely promise" that "the two corrections" desired by the Brandeis group would be factored into his London communication.[208] When Wise optimistically suggested to Brandeis, "I believe he will find it possible to make those suggestions," Brandeis offered a characteristically tempered response.[209] It appears that Brandeis's assessment of the key objective—namely, leveraging House to obtain Wilson's approval of the text regardless of the question of emendations—was at heart correct. At the same time, Wise's meeting seems to have pushed the door open more widely to the issue of how Zionist influence was perceived. Though House may not have delivered fully on the Brandeis group's requests, he did satisfy the Zionist movement's minimal requirement of codifying Wilson's approval and laying out a plan for "securing a [public] reply" to the Balfour Declaration "in a form that would serve all our purposes."[210] He also designated Wise as Wilson's chosen agent for a forthcoming presidential announcement, thus elevating the Brandeis group's stature in the eyes of Washington, London, and the general public. As a matter of protocol, House next passed on a White House communication to Wiseman who cabled the message to London: "Colonel House put formula before President, who approves of it but asks that no mention of his approval shall be made when His Majesty's Government makes formula public, as he has arranged that American Jews shall then ask him for his approval, which he will give publicly here."[211] In sum, undeterred by House's ambivalence, explicit opposition by Lansing and State Department officials, and the anti-Zionist lobbying of Morgenthau and other elite Jewish leaders, the Brandeis group kept alive the flame of Wilson's support for Zionism and his sympathy with British objectives in Palestine.

It would not be until September 1, 1918—on the eve of the Jewish New Year and Palestine's conquest by the British—that Wilson issued his landmark statement, addressed to Wise, indicating his public approval of the Balfour Declaration.[212] Framed as an appreciation of the Zionist leadership and support for the cornerstone ceremony of the Hebrew University of Jerusalem in July, Wilson's statement (which may well have been drafted by Wise) amplified the formula of the Balfour Declaration:

> I have watched with deep and sincere interest the reconstructive work which the Weizmann Commission has done in Palestine at the instance of the British Government, and I welcome an opportunity to express the satisfaction I have felt in the progress of the Zionist movement in the United States and in the Allied countries since the declaration by Mr. Balfour on behalf of the British Government, of Great Britain's approval of the establishment in Palestine of a national home for the Jewish people, and his promise that the British Government would use its best endeavors to

> facilitate the achievement of that object, with the understanding that nothing would be done to prejudice the civil and religious rights of non-Jewish people in Palestine or the rights and political status enjoyed by Jews in other countries.
>
> I think that all Americans will be deeply moved by the report that even in this time of stress the Weizmann Commission has been able to lay the foundation of the Hebrew University at Jerusalem, with the promise that that bears of spiritual truth.[213]

When the American Jewish Congress at last convened in Philadelphia in December 1918, following the British conquest of Palestine and the Allied Powers' armistice with Germany, some 400 delegates from 87 cities gathered at the Metropolitan Opera House for three days of impassioned public debates and stormy plenary negotiations. "Five thousand people were seated inside," Jonathan Frankel notes, while "another ten thousand milled around outside the building."[214] American and Zionist flags and welcome banners adorned the scene. Buoyed by the Balfour Declaration and anticipation of the Paris Peace Conference, the pro-Zionist forces arrived in the City of Brotherly Love with the wind at their backs. As a bloc, the American Zionist movement was also unified by the Pittsburgh Program, a Jeffersonian-inspired vision of the Jewish commonwealth in Palestine adopted at its June national convention. Written by Kallen, the Pittsburgh Program projected a Brandeisian strategy for the *Yishuv*'s development as "a model democratic Jewish nationality, following the guidelines of Progressive reform."[215] With broad support from the spectrum of American Jewry, including the eastern European Jewish immigrant community, the Brandeis group capitalized on the congress to publicly consecrate American Jewry's political priorities.

In an opening address, the venerable philanthropist and Zionist advocate Nathan Straus voiced the optimistic tone of the gathering: "The realization of our plans for this Congress—satisfactory to all elements of American Jewry—is a great triumph."[216] "We want not toleration," he continued, "but liberation for our brethren in all lands... The Balfour Declaration—standing out as unique, unprecedented in its liberal spirit—followed by the unqualified approval of our own President Wilson and by His Holiness, Pope Benedict XV, by France, Italy, and Serbia, has made certain the realization of our aspirations as far as Palestine is concerned."[217] Following a brief contest of political jockeying, during which the leftwing Zionist forces led by Syrkin, Zhitlowsky, and Zuckerman called for the installment of a congress presidium and, failing to overcome the will of the majority, nominated the famous Yiddish poet Yehoash (Solomon Blumgarten) to head the plebiscite, Julian W. Mack was elected president by a comfortable majority of 232 to 61 votes.[218] In a display of solidarity, Mack, who enjoyed a reputation among the *yahudim* and the *yidn* as a conciliating and unifying agent, was escorted to the platform by Marshall and the Zionist dissident leader Louis Lipsky. Taking the floor, Mack asserted, "President Wilson is at the peace conference..."[219]

> He stands for all that the Jewish people desire. His voice will be potent in the realization of their hopes. When this gathering in the world powers shall have eventuated into a League of Nations, the reestablishment of the Jewish nationality will be accomplished. An independent statehood at this time is an impracticable and impossible dream. Palestine must be placed under the trusteeship of one of the great powers, a power that stands for fundamental liberty and democracy. And if it shall be determined that Great Britain, whose armed forces have led in the liberation of the Holy Land from the oppressive rule of the Turks, shall exercise on behalf of the League of Nations the trusteeship in Palestine, then surely

> the aspirations of the Jewish people will find full and complete recognition.[220]

Mack's statement gave full-throated expression to the Brandeis group's assessment of Zionism's dependence on American presidential authority and the looming international agreements to be codified and implemented by the Allied governments. Laying out a vision of a British protectorate and a pathway to Jewish sovereignty, he underscored the symbiotic relationship between the critical importance of American presidential power and the end-goal of Jewish statehood. While support at all levels of the American government was crucial to the machinery of the Zionist cause, the president alone, invested with broad authority by the Constitution in foreign policy matters—in the words of the *Maccabean*— "speaks for America."[221]

It is also useful to consider the extent to which the American Jewish Congress, an impressive and historic phenomenon in its own right, signaled the rise of a new American Jewish consciousness. Underscoring a broad communal consensus, the congress made visible American Jewry's collective belief in the value and utility of a voluntary nondenominational and nontheistic national superstructure committed to the principles of freedom of expression, democracy, and unity. Although the gathering was an ephemeral event, viewed as a totality—the political maneuverings of various factions and groups, the polished and substantive addresses of Mack, Marshall, Zhitlowsky, and other luminaries, the impassioned floor debates, the several resolutions adopted, including major statements concerning the plight of Rumanian Jewry and a proposed "Jewish Bill of Rights"[222] (drafted by Marshall) to be presented at the peace conference—the three-day plenary demonstrated significant commonality of commitment and purpose. As an occasion, it also made visible the importance of "spoken-word performances" in the development of twentieth-century American Jewry's political sensibility.[223] Among its key resolutions, the plebiscite unanimously determined to "instruct its delegation in Europe to cooperate with the representatives of other Jewish organizations and specifically with the World Zionist Organization, to the end that the Peace Conference may recognize the aspirations and historic claims of the Jewish people with regard to Palestine" and affirmed its support of "the British Government's declaration of November 2nd, 1917, endorsed by the Allied Governments and the President of the United States . . ."[224]

Hailed as a landmark event by the American press, the plenary generated national attention and excitement. The *New York Tribune* mistakenly reported on "the realization of the Zionists' aims for a Jewish *state* in Palestine."[225] New York City's *Evening World* jubilantly declaimed "Jewish Congress Marks an Epoch in History of Race" and "Nothing Like It Since the Exile."[226] The *World* duly noted the Congress delegates' pilgrimage to Independence Hall. "All felt it was proper to visit the Liberty Bell," it reported, "because it represented American freedom and was housed in the city where both American freedom and the prospective Jewish freedom were proclaimed."[227] It also observed "the wealth of enthusiasm when Judge Julian Mack of Chicago struck his gavel" and the Congress concluded with the singing of "the Jewish national hymn [Hatikvah] . . . followed by "My Country 'Tis of Thee" and the American national anthem."[228]

It is evident, to paraphrase Carolyn Eastman, that "the dynamics that took place on stage and among attendees" at the American Jewish Congress "mirrored and commented directly" on the "social divisions and exclusions" experienced by American Jews in the turbulent World War I era.[229] The congress made visible American Jewry's robust communal profile and served as a generative vehicle for conducting public education, public business, and public policy. Led by a sparkling array of talented religious, secular, socialist, Hebraist, Zionist, and non-Zionist leaders—English, Yiddish, and Hebrew speakers—the plebiscite created a collective space for American Jews to think about their interconnected world, express the political will of ordinary men and women, and affirm their ethnic-national identity. Surveying the critical issues facing the congress and the give-and-take required of its participants, Louis Marshall celebrated "the free air of America" that informed the proceedings.[230] Marshall, originally opposed to the congress, now called on American Jews to set aside "controversies and misunderstanding" and "in the spirit that prompts reasonable men [and women]... to dispose of a practical business proposition which has led to differences and controversies," to unify in the common cause of "peace and harmony."[231] He threw his support behind the Jewish national cause and advised that consequential work lay ahead. "The future of Palestine is no longer a mooted question," he declared, "It has become a settled question."[232]

> The action of the British government, as announced by its eminent spokesman, Mr. Balfour, endorsed as it has been by France, Italy, Serbia, Greece, and other of the Allied nations—approved as it has been by the President of the United States—will undoubtedly receive at the Peace Conference which is about to assemble in Versailles, the sanction of all the nations of the world... It is not for us to say how the problem shall be worked out. [Julian W. Mack has described] the various plans which will be presented for consideration by the nations whose guarantee is essential in order to make effective the British Declaration... We here in America sympathize with every Jewish aspiration. Many of us who have in the past been disconnected with the Zionist organization, have nevertheless felt that it would be a privilege to assist in the rehabilitation of the land of our fathers... This is the accepted time and hour when the united will of the Jewish people must be heard at the peace table... It must be our purpose to protect the rights of our own people. That is our specific problem—a task sufficiently large to occupy our thoughts exclusively...[233]

In the final analysis, the congress underscored the political unity of American Jewry and the organized community's commitment to democratic values and principles and three cardinal priorities to be considered at the Paris Peace Conference: (a) Jewish minority rights, (b) Jewish postwar reconstruction, and (c) the development in Palestine of the Jewish national home. The net result was a broad-based platform and a new mandate for American Jewish leaders that reflected a massive restructuring and reorientation of American Jewry as a whole. In selecting Mack and Marshall as co-chairs of the delegation to accompany Wilson to Versailles, the congress placed its faith in two of American Jewry's most eminent, able, and trusted interlocutors. Well-equipped by virtue of their professional and political stature, they brought appreciable legal and diplomatic skill to the delegation which "symbolized unity" in American Jewish life.[234] Mack and Marshall personally embodied a conjoining of American Jewry's old and new guard and an apposite bridge between the community's principal factions. In practical terms, they promised to serve as a moderating and consolidating influence on the delegation's other distinguished members, partisan figures who spoke for "nearly all elements in the American Jewish community."[235] Though the display of solidarity was not without discord, Mack and Marshall, working closely with Barondess, Harry Cutler, Jacob De Haas, Bernard Levinthal, Nahman Syrkin, Morris Winchevsky, and Stephen S. Wise, attended to their shared task with a high sense of dignity and purpose. Interestingly, of the delegation members, it was Wise (who enjoyed a special rapport with Wilson, Brandeis, and Weizmann) that joined the president during his triumphal visit to England on the eve of the peace conference, including "tea at Downing Street."[236]

Conclusion

During World War I, American Jewry, guided by the determined savvy of the Brandeis group, attained a new level of national and international political prestige. The campaign for the American Jewish Congress, which brought to the fore a broad coalition of Yiddish-speaking immigrants and workers, middle-class professionals, and women from across the country, demonstrated the power of American Jewry's liberal humanitarian and pro-Zionist forces. The Brandeis group successfully mobilized and harnessed the community's sense of *klal yisroel politik* to "dethrone the select group represented by the American Jewish Committee," surmount anti-Zionist Jewish opposition from across the social, religious, and political spectrum, and achieve a dominant position in American Jewish affairs.[237] Under Brandeis's shrewd leadership, and with the indefatigable efforts of his inner circle (Wise, Mack, Frankfurter, Kallen, and De Haas), Zionism, formerly a parochial concern of a vocal American Jewish minority, emerged as a cornerstone of the organized American Jewish scene and integral to the Wilson administration's wartime and postwar geopolitical strategy.

The winding path from Wilson's philosemitic embrace of American Jewry to his public affirmation of the Balfour Declaration points up the Brandeis group's assiduous use of every opportunity to bring the Zionist cause into harmony with Wilson's political ambitions and presidential agenda. At each twist and turn, Brandeis and his lieutenants were careful not to overstep Wilson's political calculus. Their prudent assessment of the constraints faced by Wilson, first as a presidential candidate and then as president, reflected a keen awareness of the dynamism and high stakes of the political arena. Withal, Brandeis deftly and methodically forged a strategy that emphasized Zionism's value in domestic affairs and its promise for the future of American geopolitical interests. By contrast, consider the case of Brandeis's contemporary Henry Morgenthau Sr., the influential American Jewish lawyer and businessman. Morgenthau, who chaired Wilson's campaign finance committee—and like Brandeis was passed over for a cabinet position—was recruited by Wilson personally to serve as the US ambassador to Turkey, a position he held from 1913 to 1916.[238] Though Morgenthau and elite American Jews regarded the posting as a consolation prize, Wilson clearly viewed Morgenthau's Jewish credentials as an asset. "Constantinople is the point at which the interest of American Jews in the welfare of the Jews of Palestine is focused," the president explained, "and it is almost indispensable that I have a Jew at the post."[239] Indeed, during the war Morgenthau played a critical role in helping to secure and protect Palestine's defenseless Jewish community and exposing the Turkish genocide of the Armenian population (1914–15), famously reproaching the Ottoman minister Talaat Pasha: "Our people will never forget these massacres… You are defying all ideas of justice."[240] Yet despite Morgenthau's high profile, close connections with elite American Jewish figures, and personal investment in and access to Wilson, his political influence did not match that of Brandeis. No doubt, this was partly a matter of personal temperament and chemistry. It also appears Morgenthau's proclivity to act as a solo operator rather than a confederate forestalled his effectiveness. This proclivity was especially manifest in Morgenthau's "secret mission" to secure "a separate peace with Turkey" in the summer of 1917.[241] The ill-conceived and poorly managed diplomatic foray, which "annoyed" Wilson—he instructed House to inform the British war cabinet that "Morgenthau had not been authorized to express the President's views to anyone, nor to approach any Turkish leaders officially"—ended in failure and public humiliation.[242] In short, as the Brandeis and Morgenthau cases illustrate, American Jews played a distinctive role in Wilson's liberal brand of Christian internationalism, however, it was the Brandeisian Zionist orientation that most closely aligned with what the historian Cara Lee Burnidge identifies as Wilson's resolve to make "the social gospel a matter of U.S. foreign relations."[243]

Notwithstanding Wilson's physical decline in 1919 and American society's abandonment of the Wilsonian vision of a new world order, it is evident that World War I, which provided the scope and inducement for the convergence of the Zionist movement and the Allied powers, spawned a new era in modern Jewish politics. Wilson's attitude to Zionism's utility as an element of American wartime policy ebbed and flowed, but he never wavered in his attachment to the Zionist project and the idea of a Jewish national home in Palestine. His private discussions about Zionism with members of the Brandeis group were generally warm and encouraging; his public expressions and activity tended to oscillate between cryptic and straightforward displays of support. A particularly remarkable instance in this regard is Wilson's March 1919 letter, addressed to Wise and widely reprinted in the American and Jewish press:

> You may quote me as having said, as for your representations touching Palestine, I have before this expressed my personal approval of the declaration of the British Government regarding the aspirations and historic claims of the Jewish people in regard to Palestine. I am, moreover, persuaded that the Allied nations with the fullest concurrence of our own Government and people, are agreed that in Palestine shall be laid the foundations of a Jewish Commonwealth.[244]

In this statement, Wilson surpassed his previous utterances. In fact, the language here went considerably farther than the president's August 1918 letter to Wise; his use of the term "Jewish Commonwealth" outstripped the Balfour Declaration's ambiguous phraseology concerning a "national home for the Jewish people." Wilson, in effect, offered American Zionists a trump card. That such support was to become normative in American politics would be demonstrated the following year with the publication and widespread circulation of *The American War Congress and Zionism* (1919), a 240-page book published by the Zionist Organization of America that reprinted testimonials by Wilson and 300 members of the US congress, namely, sixty-one senators from forty-three states and 239 representatives from forty-four states and three territories.[245]

Neither the presidential election of 1920 (which brought Republican Warren G. Harding to power) nor the intra-Zionist Brandeis-Weizmann schism of 1921 (which sent the Brandeis group into exile for a decade) derailed American society's or American Jewry's pro-Zionist orientation. Furthermore, even as the United States descended into the postwar abyss of Jim Crow, isolationism, xenophobia, and anti-immigrant hostility—a decade dubbed the "tribal twenties" by John Higham—American Jewry was well equipped to mobilize a countrywide campaign in support of the Balfour Declaration's far-reaching implications.[246] Though the Harding administration displayed a cool attitude to Zionism—for example, Secretary of State Charles Evans Hughes treated American Zionist petitions with disdain and US officials demurred when the League of Nations debated the inclusion of the Balfour Declaration in the preamble to the British Mandate[247]—there was no question but that a sea change had occurred in the relationship of American Jewry, Zionism, and American society. This new reality was codified in September 1922 when Harding signed the joint Lodge-Fish Resolution into law, explicitly endorsing the Balfour Declaration on behalf of the US government. The legislation, which superseded Wilson's presidential statements, signaled a new trajectory in American foreign policy and a new phase in the campaign for Jewish statehood.

ENDNOTES

1 Quoted from an editorial in the *Maccabean* 30 (December 1917), 408, cited in Charles Israel Goldblatt, "The Impact of the Balfour Declaration in America," *American Jewish Historical Quarterly* 57, no. 4 (June 1968), 477. This chapter is dedicated to the memory of Dr. Martin B. Malin (1961-2020)—scholar, friend, and consummate mensch. Special thanks to Carolyn Eastman, Stephen Porter, Jonathan D. Sarna, Paul Stob, and David Stradling for valuable suggestions and criticism concerning this essay.

2 Horace M. Kallen to Louis D. Brandeis (November 23, 1915), Horace M. Kallen Collection, MS-1, 4/10, Jacob Rader Marcus Center of the American Jewish Archives (hereafter: "AJA").

3 "Role of American Jewish Congress in Furthering Claim for a Jewish Palestine," *Reform Advocate* 59, no. 14 (May 8, 1920), 314.

4 Jehuda Reinharz, *Chaim Weizmann: The Making of a Statesman* (New York: Oxford University Press, 1993), 211.

5 *Ibid.*, 210.

6 Melvin I. Urofsky, *Louis D. Brandeis: A Life* (New York: Pantheon Books, 2009), 518.

7 A. Scott Berg, *Wilson* (New York: G.P. Putnam's Sons, 2013), 588.

8 Urofsky, *Louis D. Brandeis*, 519.

9 Ben Halpern, *A Clash of Heroes: Brandeis, Weizmann, and American Zionism* (New York: Oxford University Press, 1987), 266–67.

10 *Ibid.*, 126, 128, 139, 147.

11 The journalist and Zionist leader Louis Lipsky disparaged Gottheil as "a student of dead languages" who "likes to take life leisurely… was never a platform speaker… and avoided the exciting issues of the day." Prevailed upon by "a small group of east coast Zionists," Lipsky recalled that Gottheil assumed "the office [of FAZ president] with reluctance and did not alter his interests or his way of life because of it… leading a cloistered life from which he emerged from time to time to intervene in the practical aspects of Zionism… As [FAZ] president he was troubled by the birth pangs of the new organization… Untrained in the art of raising money or creating a nationwide propaganda for the new movement… his official duties irked him beyond endurance… especially as the practical affairs of the [FAZ] made no visible progress." Quoted from Louis Lipsky, *Memoirs in Profile* (Philadelphia: Jewish Publication Society, 1975), 211–13.

12 Halpern, *A Clash of Heroes*, 106–7.

13 *Ibid.*, 112, 117.

14 Jonathan Frankel, *Prophecy and Politics: Socialism, Nationalism, and the Russian Jews, 1862–1917* (Cambridge: Cambridge University Press, 1984), 515.

15 On the spectrum of American Protestant attitudes to Jews and Judaism, see Egal Feldman, *Dual Destinies: The Jewish Encounter with Protestant America* (Urbana: University of Illinois Press, 1990), 240–46. For a useful discussion of liberal Protestant and Jewish encounters in the Progressive era, see Kevin M. Schultz, *Tri-Faith America: How Catholics and Jews Held Postwar America to Protestant Promise* (Oxford: Oxford University Press, 2011), 26–34.

16 Eric L. Goldstein, "The Unstable Other: Locating the Jew in Progressive-Era American Racial Discourse," *American Jewish History* 89, no, 4 (December 2001), 387.

17 Wilson's address, "The Rights of the Jews," concerning the proposed abrogation of the US-Russia Treaty of 1832, is reprinted in *The Public Papers of Woodrow Wilson: College and State – Educational, Literary, and Political Papers* (1875–1913), eds. Ray Stannard Baker and William E. Dodd, vol. 2 (New York: Harper & Brothers, 1925), 320–21. See also Naomi W. Cohen, "The Abrogation of the Russo-American Treaty of 1832," *Jewish Social Studies* 25, no. 1 (January 1963): 3–41; Clifford L. Egan, "Pressure Groups, the Department of State, and the Abrogation of the Russian-American Treaty of 1832," *Proceedings of the American Philosophical Society* 115, no. 4 (August 1971): 328–34.

18 Ira Katznelson, *Fear Itself: The New Deal and the Origins of Our Time* (New York: Liveright Publishing, 2013), 290.

19 Jonathan D. Sarna, "Woodrow Wilson Was a Hero to Jews: What Should We Do with His Racism?" *Forward* (July 2, 2020), https://forward.com/opinion/450092/woodrow-wilson-was-a-hero-to-jews-what-should-wedo-with-his-racism/; see Daniel J. Tichenor's essay in this volume.

20 W.E.B. Du Bois, "My Impressions of Woodrow Wilson," *Journal of Negro History* 58, no. 4 (October 1973), 457.

21 Nancy J. Weiss, "The Negro and the New Freedom: Fighting Wilsonian Segregation," *Political Science Quarterly* 84, no. 1 (March 1969), 61–62.

22 Cara Lea Burnidge, *A Peaceful Conquest: Woodrow Wilson, Religion, and the New World Order* (Chicago: University of Chicago Press, 2017), 74.

23 Babylonian Talmud, Shevuot 39a; "Million Dollars Raised for War Victims," *American Jewish World* 2, no. 17 (December 31, 1915), 323.

24 Louis D. Brandeis, "A Call to the Educated Jew," *Menorah Journal* 1, no. 1 (January 1915), 17.

25 "Memorandum for the President and Members of the Executive Committee of the American Jewish Committee" (May 9, 1915), in *Dissenter in Zion: From the Writings of Judah L. Magnes*, ed. Arthur A. Goren (Cambridge, MA: Harvard University Press, 1982), 139.

26 *Ibid.*

27 *Ibid.*, 143.

28 "A Forerunner of the American Jewish Congress: Union of American Hebrew Congregations Favored Plan of Permanent Jewish Congress in 1903—Important Document Just Brought to Light," *American Jewish Chronicle* 3, no. 1 (May 11, 1917), 20.

29 Quoted in Jonathan Frankel, *Prophecy and Politics*, 492.

30 *Ibid.*, 487–95.

31 Quoted in Gerald Sorin, *A Time for Building: The Third Migration, 1880–1920* (Baltimore, MD: Johns Hopkins University Press, 1992), 215–16.

32 *Dissenter in Zion*, ed. Goren, 161.

33 Naomi W. Cohen, *Not Free to Desist: The American Jewish Committee, 1906–1966* (Philadelphia: Jewish Publication Society of America, 1972), 85–86; Harry L. Lurie, *A Heritage Affirmed: The Jewish Federation Movement in America* (Philadelphia: Jewish Publication Society, 1961), 91–95.

34 Editorial, *American Jewish Chronicle* 2, no. 20 (March 23, 1917), 612. See also "Mr. Rosenwald's Letter to Mr. Marshall in which he offers $1,000,000 for Relief," in *ibid.*, 629.

35 Sorin, *A Time for Building*, 208–9.

36 Cyrus Adler, "The Jewish Welfare Board—Twenty Years Old," *American Jewish Year Book* 39 (1938), 149–50.

37 Lucy S. Dawidowicz, *The Jewish Presence: Essays on Identity and History* (New York: Holt, Rinehart and Winston, 1977), 127, 130.

38 Lipsky, *Memoirs in Profile*, 241. For a useful analysis of Maslianky's preaching and impact in the Jewish public arena, see Matthew M. Silver, *Zionism and the Melting Pot: Preachers, Pioneers, and Modern Jewish Politics* (Tuscaloosa: University of Alabama Press, 2020), 70–76.

39 Gary Phillip Zola, "The People's Preacher; A Study of the Life and Writings of Zvi Hirsch Masliansky (1856–1943)," rabbinic thesis, Hebrew Union College-Jewish Institute of Religion, 1982, 21.

40 "Synopsis of Speech by Rev. H. Masliansky" (March 21, 1916), *Jewish Voice* 60, no. 12 (March 24, 1916), 3.

41 Carolyn Eastman, "Oratory and Platform Culture in Britain and North America, 1740–1900," *Oxford Handbooks Online* (New York: Oxford University Press, 2016), 2, https://www.oxfordhandbooks.com/view/10.1093/oxfordhb/9780199935338.001.0001/oxfordhb-9780199935338-e-33?rskey=9S-GLhc&result=2.

42 Judah M. Bernstein, "A Preacher in Exile: Shemaryahu Levin and the Making of American Zionism, 1914–1919," *American Jewish History* 102:3 (July 2018), 329.

43 Carolyn Eastman, "Conclusion: Placing Platform Culture in Nineteenth-Century American Life," in *Thinking Together: Lecturing, Learning, and Difference in the Long Nineteenth Century*, eds. Angela G. Ray and Paul Stob (University Park, PA: Pennsylvania State University Press, 2018), 188.

44 *Ibid.*, 187, 188.

45 Ivri Onokhi, "The Influence of the American Rabbi," *American Jewish Chronicle* 5, no. 20 (September 27, 1918), 508; Bernstein, "A Preacher in Exile," 347.

46 Horace M. Kallen, "Jewish Quarrels and Unity," *American Jewish Chronicle* 1, no. 7 (June 23, 1916), 200.

47 Quoted in *ibid.*, 200.

48 Quoted in *ibid.*, 200.

49 Quoted in Silver, *Louis Marshall and the Rise of Jewish Ethnicity in America*, 286.

50 Quoted in Robert E. Park, *The Immigrant Press and Its Control* (New York: Harper and Brother, 1922), 172–73.

51 Quoted in Frankel, *Prophecy and Politics*, 513.

52 Quoted in Jonathan Frankel, "The Jewish Socialists and the American Jewish Congress Movement," *YIVO Annual of Jewish Social Science* 16 (New York: YIVO Institute for Jewish Research, 1976), 286.

53 Jonathan D. Sarna, "The Democratization of American Judaism," in *New Essays in American Jewish History: Commemorating the Sixtieth Anniversary of the American Jewish Archives* (Cincinnati, OH: Jacob Rader Marcus Center of the American Jewish Archives, 2010), 96.

54 Stephen S. Wise, *A Jewish Conference or Congress—Which and Why?* (New York: Bloch Publishing, 1915), 125–27, 129.

55 Sarah Panter, "Neutral Spectators from a Distance? American Jews and the Outbreak of the First World War," *Religions* 9:7 (2018), 5; https://doi.org/10.3390/rel9070218.

56 Brandeis, "A Call to the Educated Jew," 15.

57 *Ibid.*

58 *Ibid.*

59 *Ibid.*, 15, 17–18.

60 "The Jewish Congress as Seen by a Non-Jew," *Jewish Chronicle* 1, no. 6 (April 7, 1916), 6.

61 Morris Frommer, "The American Jewish Congress: A History, 1914–1950" (Doctoral Diss., Ohio State University, 1978), 60–61.

62 Bernstein, "A Preacher in Exile," 324–30.

63 A. Levinsohn, "The Knights of Zion Convention: A Summarized Report," *Supplement to the Maccabaean, Maccabaean* 28, no. 1 (January 1916), ii. See also: Schmarja [*sic*] Levin, "Take Care of the Organization!" *American Jewish Chronicle* 3, no. 1 (May 25, 1917), 4–5; Schmarja Levin, "Our Pioneers in Palestine," *American Jewish Chronicle* 3, no. 3 (May 11, 1917), 69–70.

64 "Zionists Cannot Supply Demand Seats—Brandeis and Levin Arrive," *Sentinel* 20, no. 14 (December 31, 1915), 2.

65 Cited in Bernstein, "A Preacher in Exile," 325.

66 Quoted in "From Coast to Coast," *American Jewish Chronicle* 2, no. 21 (March 30, 1917), 664.

67 Silver, *Louis Marshall and the Rise of Jewish Ethnicity*, 177–78; Michael Brown, *The Israeli-American Connection: Its Roots in the Yishuv, 1914–1945* (Detroit, MI: Wayne State University Press, 1996), 22; Henry Morgenthau III, *Mostly Morgenthaus: A Family History* (New York: Ticknor and Fields, 1991), 146–47.

68 "Editorial Notes," *American Jewish Chronicle* 1, no. 22 (October 13, 1916), 692.

69 Derek J. Penslar, *Zionism and Technocracy: The Engineering of Jewish Settlement in Palestine, 1870–1918* (Bloomington: Indiana University Press, 1991), 45, 69, 153; S. Ilan Troen, *Imagining Zion: Dreams, Designs, and Realities in a Century of Jewish Settlement* (New Haven, CT: Yale University Press, 2003), 9–10, 29–34, 152–54.

70 Golda Meir, *My Life* (New York: G.P. Putnam's Sons, 1975), 57, emphasis in original.

71 *Ibid.*

72 Frankel, *Prophecy and Politics*, 515.

73 Brown, *The Israeli-American Connection*, 204; Mark A. Raider, *The Emergence of American Zionism* (New York: New York University Press, 1998), 83–88.

74 Quoted in David R. Roediger, *Working Toward Whiteness: How America's Immigrants Became White, the Strange Journey from Ellis Island to the Suburbs*, revised ed. (New York: Basic Books, 2018), 66–67.

75 Wise also advocated appealing to the British government to grant "home rule to the Irish people." See Wise's letter to Woodrow Wilson (April 11, 1917) in *The Papers of Woodrow Wilson*, ed. Arthur S. Link, vol. 42 (Princeton, NJ: Princeton University Press, 1983), 41–42, 44–45.

76 Quoted from "Memorial to President Woodrow Wilson" (May 1916), 1–2, Wheaton College Billy Graham Center Archives, https://www2.wheaton.edu/bgc/archives/docs/BlackstoneMemorial/1916a.htm. See also letter

from William E. Blackstone to President Woodrow Wilson (November 17, 1916), Wheaton College Billy Graham Center Archives, https://www2.wheaton.edu/bgc/archives/docs/BlackstoneMemorial/1916LettertoWilson.htm. See also Yaakov Ariel, "An American Initiative for a Jewish State: William Blackstone and the Petition of 1891," *Studies in Zionism* 10 (1989), 125–37; and Yaakov Ariel, "William Blackstone and the Petition of 1916: A Neglected Chapter in the History of Christian Zionism in America," *Studies in Contemporary Jewry* 7 (1991), 68–85.

77 "Memorial to President Woodrow Wilson," 3–4.

78 Frommer, "The American Jewish Congress," 68.

79 Quoted in Max Rhoade, "Senator Chamberlain on the Jewish Problem," *American Jewish Chronicle* 2, no. 21 (March 30, 1917), 660.

80 Quoted in *ibid.*

81 Quoted in *ibid.*, emphasis in original.

82 "Points to Army's Needs," *New York Times* (September 8, 1913), 16.

83 Tony Smith, *Why Wilson Matters: The Origins of American Liberal Internationalism and Its Crisis Today* (Princeton, NJ: Princeton University Press, 2017), 12.

84 Letter from President Woodrow Wilson to the US Senate (May 5, 1916), *Congressional Record* (May 9, 1916), 7628, Louis Dembitz Brandeis Collection, Box 63, Series I.IV.a.1, Robert D. Farber University Archives and Special Collections Department, Brandeis University Library.

85 Quoted in Urofsky, *Louis D. Brandeis*, 438.

86 Quoted in *ibid.*, 440.

87 "Let the Thinking People Rule! Brandeis, the Firebrand," *Leslie's Illustrated Weekly Newspaper* (February 17, 1916), http://www.accessible.com.proxy.libraries.uc.edu/accessible/preLog?LinkType=SERIALSSOLUTIONS&ArticleID=FrankLesliesWeekly.FL1916021703.00003; "Praise Wilson's Action," *New York Times* (January 29, 1916), 3.

88 Quoted in Yonathan Shapiro, "American Jews in Politics: The Case of Louis D. Brandeis," *American Jewish Historical Quarterly* 55:2 (December 1965), 210.

89 Quoted in Jonathan D. Sarna, "'The Greatest Jew in the World since Jesus Christ': The Jewish Legacy of Louis D. Brandeis," *American Jewish History* 81:34 (Spring-Summer 1994), 358–59.

90 Urofsky, *Louis D. Brandeis*, 376.

91 Wilson's adviser Bernard Baruch reportedly lamented, "I could have been President of the United States—if I had not been a Jew." Quoted in Margaret L. Coit, *Mr. Baruch* (Boston: Houghton Mifflin, 1957), 359. See also Mark A.

Raider, 'To Secure Israel's Survival and Security: President Gerald R. Ford and Secretary of State Henry Kissinger Meet with American Jewish Leaders (1976)," in *New Perspectives in American Jewish History: A Documentary Tribute to Jonathan D. Sarna*, eds. Mark A. Raider and Gary Phillip Zola (Waltham, MA: Brandeis University, 2021), 331–32, fns. 1–5.

92 Editorial, *American Jewish Chronicle* 2, no. 20 (March 23, 1917), 609.

93 Tony Michels, "The Russian Revolution in New York, 1917–19," *Journal of Contemporary History* 52:4 (October 2017), 959–60.

94 Editorial, *American Jewish Chronicle* 2, no. 21 (March 30, 1917), 642.

95 "The Russian Revolution and Its Aftermath," *American Jewish Chronicle* 2, no. 20 (March 23, 1917), 614; Isidor Zar, "Israel and Triumphant Nationalism," *American Jewish Chronicle* 2, no. 21 (March 30, 1917), 648.

96 President Woodrow Wilson, Address Delivered at Joint Session of the Two Houses of Congress, April 2, 1917; U.S. 65th Congress, 1st Session, Senate Document 5.

97 "All Jews Expelled from Jaffa—Pillage, Murder, Robbery, and Starvation Caused by Djemal Pasha," *B'nai B'rith Messenger* 21, no. 23 (May 25, 1917), 3.

98 "Letters from Abroad: Jaffa (Special to the *American Jewish Chronicle*)—All Jews Expelled from Jaffa," *American Jewish Chronicle* 3, no. 1 (May 11, 1917), 11.

99 "Turkey," *American Jewish Year Book* 20 (1917), 318.

100 Levin, "Our Pioneers in Palestine," 69–70.

101 See "Djemal Pasha—Another Ivanoff," *American Jewish Chronicle* 3, no. 1 (May 11, 1917), 13. See also Eric Lohr, "The Russian Army and the Jews: Mass Deportation, Hostages, and Violence during World War I," *Russian Review* 60, no. 3 (July 2001), 409; Sean McMeekin, *The Russian Revolution: A New History* (New York: Basic Books, 2017), 67–68.

102 Caitlin Carenen, "Complicating the Zionist Narrative in America: Jacob Schiff and the Struggle over Relief Aid in World War I," *American Jewish History* 101 (2017), 2; "Jewish War Relief Work," *American Jewish Year Book* 19 (1917), 202, 207.

103 Mira Katzburg-Yungman, *Hadassah: American Women Zionists and the Rebirth of Israel*, trans. Tammy Berkowitz (Oxford: Littman Library of Jewish Civilization, 2012), 28–31; Jaclyn Granick, *International Jewish Humanitarianism in the Age of the Great War* (Cambridge: Cambridge University Press, 2021), 168–70.

104 Silver, *Louis Marshall and the Rise of Jewish Ethnicity in America*, 306.

105 Frankel, "The Jewish Socialists and the American Jewish Congress Movement," 299.

106 David I. Liksaltz, "Zionism and Its Development," *B'nai B'rith Messenger* 21, no. 19 (April 27, 1917), 2.

107 Quoted from "Jewish Socialists for Palestine—Convention Notes," *B'nai B'rith Messenger* 21, no. 17 (April 18, 1917), 3.

108 *Ibid.*

109 "Straus Sees Zion Near Realization," *Sun* (May 6, 1917), 7.

110 *Ibid.*

111 *Ibid.*, 7.

112 Quoted in Frankel, "The American Jewish Congress Movement," 294.

113 "The Call for the American Jewish Congress," *American Jewish World* 5, no. 7 (May 25, 1917), 160.

114 *Ibid.*

115 *Ibid.* See also: "Plan of Election for American Jewish Congress," *American Jewish Chronicle* 2, no. 23 (April 13, 1917), 752–53; Horace M. Kallen, "The American Jewish Congress: An Achievement of Americanism," *American Jewish Chronicle* 2, no. 23 (April 13, 1917), 740–41, 755, 758.

116 Melissa R. Klapper, *Ballots, Babies, and Banners of Peace: American Jewish Women's Activism, 1890–1940* (New York: New York University Press, 2013), 58.

117 *Ibid.*, 62.

118 The precise number of total votes cast in the election for the American Jewish Congress is a matter of dispute and estimates range from 330,000 to more than 400,000 votes cast. See "Over 400,000 Votes Cast in Jewish Congress Election," *American Jewish World* 5, no. 10 (June 15, 1917), 202; Frommer, "The American Jewish Congress," 103; Frankel, "The American Jewish Congress Movement," 301; Zosa Szajkowski, *Jews, Wars, and Communism*, vol. 1 (New York: Ktav Publishing House, 1972), 204.

119 Quoted in Frankel, "The American Jewish Congress Movement," 301.

120 "Editorial Notes," *American Jewish Chronicle* 3, no. 2 (May 18, 1917), 33.

121 "Over 400,000 Votes Cast in Jewish Congress Election," 202.

122 "'Votes for Women' Wins Out in Election," *American Jewish World* 5, no. 12 (June 22, 1917), 246.

123 Quoted in Frommer, "The American Jewish Congress," 106.

124 Quoted in *ibid.*

125 On the clash between Marshall and Brandeis over the American Jewish Congress, see Jonathan D. Sarna, "Two Jewish Lawyers Named Louis," *American Jewish History* 94:1-2 (March-June 2008), 14–16.

126 Cohen, *Not Free to Desist*, 98. Cyrus Adler vociferously opposed the congress and blamed the lack of American Jewish comity during and after the war on Zionist leaders. In particular, he detested Stephen S. Wise and refused to mention him by name in his memoir: "For several years, steps had been taken to create a new Jewish organization to be known as the American Jewish Congress... The attempt would I think have succeeded had it not been for one man who was determined it should fail, as he wished all Jewish life in America and the world over to be controlled by Zionists." Quoted from Cyrus Adler, *I Have Considered the Days* (Philadelphia: Jewish Publication Society, 1941), 306. Adler had a similarly jaundiced view of Louis D. Brandeis; see *Cyrus Adler, Selected Letters*, ed. Ira Robinson, vol. 1 (Philadelphia: Jewish Publication Society, 1985), 289–90, 308–9, 315, 392, and David G. Dalin, "Cyrus Adler, Non-Zionism, and the Zionist Movement: A Study in Contradictions," *AJS Review* 10:1 (Spring 1985), 79-80.

127 "The Late Drs. Israel Friedlander and Bernard Cantor," *Hebrew Standard* 76, no. 9 (August 27, 1920), 6.

128 With the concurrence of Russia and Italy, Britain and France signed the Sykes-Picot Agreement in 1916. The agreement laid out a postwar plan to partition the Ottoman provinces outside of the Arabian Peninsula into British- and French-controlled areas. Under the terms of the agreement, Palestine would largely come under British control.

129 C. P. Scott, editor of the *Manchester Guardian*, quoted in Stein, *The Balfour Declaration*, 365. In December 1915, Lucien Wolf, the Ango-Jewish writer, historian, and diplomat suggested: "I am not a Zionist and I deplore the Jewish national movement... Still, the facts cannot be ignored, and in any bid for Jewish sympathies today very serious account must be taken of the Zionist movement. In America, the Zionist organizations have lately captured Jewish opinion... This is the moment for the Allies to declare their policy in regard to Palestine... If, for example, they would say they thoroughly understood and sympathize with Jewish aspirations in regard to Palestine, and that when the destiny of the country comes to be considered, these aspirations will be taken into account... I am confident they would sweep the whole of American Jewry into enthusiastic allegiance to their cause." Quoted in Leonard Stein, *The Balfour Declaration* (New York: Simon and Schuster, 1961), 220–21.

130 Josephus Daniels, Wilson's secretary of the US navy, as quoted in Paul L. Hanna, *British Policy in Palestine* (Washington, DC: American Council on Public Affairs, 1942), vii.

131 Reinharz, *Chaim Weizmann*, 190.

132 Letter of Chaim Weizmann to Louis D. Brandeis (April 8, 1917), in Chaim Weizmann, *The Letters and Papers of Chaim Weizmann*, vol. 7 (August 1914–

November 1917), ed. Leonard Stein (Jerusalem: Israel Universities Press, 1975), 357.

133 *Ibid.*, 357–58.

134 Reinharz, *Chaim Weizmann*, 212, 214.

135 Ben Halpern, "Brandeis and the Origins of the Balfour Declaration," *Studies in Zionism* 7 (Spring 1983), 99.

136 *Ibid.*, 100.

137 Reinharz, *Chaim Weizmann*, 212.

138 Quoted in Lebow, "The Morgenthau Peace Mission of 1917," 285.

139 Erika Lee, "The Chinese Exclusion Example: Race, Immigration, and American Gatekeeping, 1882–1924," *Journal of American Ethnic History* 21:3 (Spring 2002), 40.

140 The phrase "golden door" was made famous by Emma Lazarus's sonnet "The New Colossus" (1883), which is inscribed at the base of the Statue of Liberty.

141 See, in particular, the following works: Selig Adler, "The Palestine Question in the Wilson Era," *Jewish Social Studies* 10:4 (October 1948), 303–34; Ben Halpern, "Brandeis and the Origins of the Balfour Declaration," *Studies in Zionism* 4:1 (Spring 1983): 71–100; Ben Halpern, *A Clash of Heroes: Brandeis, Weizmann, and American Zionism* (New York: Oxford University Press, 1987); Ben Halpern, "The Drafting of the Balfour Declaration," in *Herzl Year Book* 7 (New York: Herzl Press, 1971), 255-84; Richard Ned Lebow, "Woodrow Wilson and the Balfour Declaration," *Journal of Modern History* 40:4 (December 1968), 501–23; Frank E. Manuel, *The Realities of American-Palestine Relations* (Washington, DC: Public Affairs Press, 1949); Herbert Parzen, "Brandeis and the Balfour Declaration," in *Herzl Year Book* 5 (New York: Herzl Press, 1963), 309–50; Jehuda Reinharz, *Chaim Weizmann: The Making of a Statesman* (New York: Oxford University Press, 1993; Leonard Stein, *The Balfour Declaration* (New York: Simon and Schuster, 1961), 592–98; Melvin I. Urofsky, *Louis D. Brandeis: A Life* (New York: Pantheon Books, 2009).

142 Stein, *The Balfour Declaration*, 593.

143 *Ibid.*

144 *Ibid.*

145 *Ibid.*, 594.

146 *Ibid.*, 594–95.

147 *Ibid.*, 596.

148 Lebow, "Woodrow Wilson and the Balfour Declaration," 521, 523.

149 *Ibid.*, 523.

150 *Ibid.*, 523.

151 Quoted in Joseph Rappaport, "Zionism as a Factor in Allied-Central Power Controversy, 19141918," in *Early History of Zionism in America*, ed. Isidore S. Meyer (New York: American Jewish Historical Society, 1958), 313.

152 Quoted in Halpern, "Brandeis and the Origins of the Balfour Declaration," 83.

153 *Ibid.*, 84.

154 For a useful analysis, see Richard Ned Lebow, "The Morgenthau Peace Mission of 1917," *Jewish Social Studies* 32:4 (October 1970): 267–85.

155 Evyatar Friesel, "Jacob H. Schiff Becomes a Zionist: A Chapter in American Jewish Self-Definition, 1907–1917," *Studies in Zionism* 3:1 (1982): 55–92. See also folders titled "Kallen, Horace M." folder (453/13) and "Zionism" (455/25) in Jacob H. Schiff Papers, MS-456, Box 455, AJA.

156 Halpern, *A Clash of Heroes*, 180, 188.

157 Copy of letter from Simon Wolf to Nathan H. Straus (July 5, 1917), "Jewish War Relief" (453/4), Jacob H. Schiff Papers, MS-456, Box 455, AJA.

158 Cohen, *Not Free to Desist*, 92.

159 Quoted in Cohen, *Not Free to Desist*, 92; letter from Simon Wolf to Woodrow Wilson (June 11, 1917), "Wolf, Simon" (455/24), Jacob H. Schiff Papers, MS-456, Box 455, AJA.

160 Letter of Stephen S. Wise to Louis D. Brandeis (October 5, 1917), Louis D. Brandeis microfilm.

161 *Ibid.*

162 Quoted in Frankel, "The American Jewish Congress Movement," 310.

163 Quoted in *ibid.*, 311.

164 Quoted in *ibid.*, 311.

165 Quoted in "American Jewish Congress Postponed Indefinitely," *American Jewish Chronicle* 3, no. 24 (October 19, 1917), 705.

166 Quoted in *ibid.*

167 Quoted in *ibid.*

168 "President Approves of Jewish Congress," *American Jewish World* (July 6, 1917), 262.

169 Quoted in Joseph Adler, "The Morgenthau Mission of 1917," *Herzl Year Book* 5 (1963), 274.

170 See Halpern, "Brandeis and the Origins of the Balfour Declaration," 71–100.

171 Quoted in Lebow, "Woodrow Wilson and the Balfour Declaration," 510, fn. 40.

172 Manuel, *The Realities of American-Palestine Relations*, 167.

173 Quoted in Lebow, "Woodrow Wilson and the Balfour Declaration," 516, emphasis added.

174 Charles E. Neu, *Colonel House: A Biography of Woodrow Wilson's Silent Partner* (New York: Oxford University Press, 2015), 279.

175 Quoted in Wise, *Challenging Years*, 189.

176 *Ibid.*

177 Quoted in Lebow, "Woodrow Wilson and the Balfour Declaration," 514.

178 Quoted in Stein, *The Balfour Declaration*, 529.

179 "American Jewish Congress Postponed Indefinitely," 705; "Justice Brandeis to Represent United States at Peace Conference," *Sentinel* 28, no. 1 (October 5, 1917), 2.

180 "Brandeis Silent on Peace Reports," *New York Times* (October 2, 1917), 2.

181 Editorial, *Jewish Voice* (October 12, 1917), 4.

182 "Brandeis Silent on Peace Reports," 2; "Justice Brandeis to Represent United States at Peace Conference," 2.

183 Editorial, *Jewish Voice* (October 12, 1917), 4.

184 *Ibid.*, 4.

185 Urofsky, *Louis D. Brandeis*, 497–98.

186 Quoted in Lebow, "Woodrow Wilson and the Balfour Declaration," 511.

187 Lebow, "The Morgenthau Peace Mission of 1917," 275–76, 283–84.

188 Adler, "The Palestine Question in the Wilson Era," 312.

189 *Ibid.*, 311.

190 Quoted in Lebow, "Woodrow Wilson and the Balfour Declaration," 518.

191 Letter of Chaim Weizmann to Philip Kerr (October 7, 1917), in Chaim Weizmann, *The Letters and Papers of Chaim Weizmann*, vol. 7 (August 1914-November 1917), ed. Leonard Stein (Jerusalem: Israel Universities Press, 1975), 528.

192 The Milner-Amery text proposed by the British war cabinet stated: "His Majesty's Government views with favor the establishment in Palestine of a National Home for the Jewish race and will use their best endeavors to facilitate the achievement of this object, it being clearly understood that nothing shall be done which may prejudice the civil and religious rights of

the existing non-Jewish communities in Palestine or the rights and political status enjoyed in any other country by Jews who are contented with their existing nationality." Quoted in Halpern, "The Drafting of the Balfour Declaration," 276.

193 Quoted in Parzen, "Brandeis and the Balfour Declaration," 337.

194 Quoted in *ibid.*, 338.

195 Quoted in *ibid.*

196 Reprinted in Ezekiel Rabinowitz, *Justice Louis D. Brandeis: The Zionist Chapter of His Life* (New York: Philosophical Library, 1968), 73.

197 Halpern, "Brandeis and the Origins of the Balfour Declaration," 97; Manuel, *The Realities of American-Palestine Relations*, 169; Stein, *The Balfour Declaration*, 530.

198 Berg, *Wilson*, 461.

199 Letter of Jacob De Haas to Louis D. Brandeis (October 16, 1917), reprinted in Parzen, "Brandeis and the Balfour Declaration," 349.

200 Quoted in *ibid.*, 350.

201 Manuel, *The Realities of American-Palestine Relations*, 170; Halpern, "The Drafting of the Balfour Declaration," 281–82.

202 Woodrow Wilson, "Peace Without Victory" (January 21, 1917), in *The World's Greatest Speeches*, eds. Lewis Copeland, Lawrence W. Lamm, and Stephen J. McKenna, fourth ed. (Mineola, NY: Dover Publications, 1999), 353.

203 Letter of De Haas to Brandeis, reprinted in Parzen, "Brandeis and the Balfour Declaration," 350.

204 Quoted in *ibid.*, 338, fn 65.

205 Chaim Weizmann, *Trial and Error*, 207.

206 Reinharz, *Chaim Weizmann*, 201.

207 Stein, *The Balfour Declaration*, 531.

208 Quoted in *ibid.*, 532.

209 Quoted in *ibid.*

210 Letter of Jacob De Haas to Louis D. Brandeis (October 16, 1917), reprinted in Parzen, "Brandeis and the Balfour Declaration," 350.

211 Quoted in *ibid.*, 530.

212 For the authorized and final text of the Balfour Declaration, see Introduction, 20.

213 "Letter (Endorsing Zionist Movement)" of Woodrow Wilson to Stephen S. Wise (September 1, 1918), in *Supplement to the Messages and Papers of the*

Presidents, Covering the Second Term of Woodrow Wilson, March 4, 1917 to March 4, 1921 (Washington, DC: Bureau of National Literature, 1921), 8575.

214 Frankel, "The American Jewish Congress Movement," 318.

215 Sarah Schmidt, "Toward the Pittsburgh Program: Horace M. Kallen, Philosopher of American Zionism," *Herzl Year Book* 8 (1978), 31. For a useful discussion of Brandeis's modifications to Kallen's draft, see Jonathan D. Sarna, "A Projection of America as It Ought to Be: Zion in the Mind's Eye of American Jews" in *Envisioning Israel: The Changing Ideals and Images of North American Jews*, ed. Allon Gal (Detroit: Wayne State University Press, 1996), 51–54.

216 "Mr. Nathan Straus' Address," quoted in *Report of Proceedings of the American Jewish Congress, Philadelphia, PA, December 1918* (New York: American Jewish Congress, 1918), 11.

217 *Ibid.*, 13

218 *Ibid.*, 15.

219 "Judge [Julian W.] Mack's Inaugural Address," quoted in *ibid.*, 18.

220 *Ibid.*

221 See footnote 1 of this essay.

222 *Report of Proceedings of the American Jewish Congress*, 66–67.

223 Eastman, "Conclusion," 188.

224 *Ibid.*, 51.

225 "Programme Framed at Philadelphia Convention to Govern Proposed Nation," *New York Tribune* (December 17, 1918), 11, emphasis added.

226 "Jewish Congress Marks an Epoch in History of Race," *Evening World* (December 19, 1918), 16.

227 *Ibid.*

228 *Ibid.*, 16.

229 Eastman, "Conclusion," 196.

230 Quoted in "Address of Mr. [Louis] Marshall," *Report of Proceedings of the American Jewish Congress*, 26.

231 *Ibid.*, 30.

232 *Ibid.*, 23.

233 *Ibid.*, 23–24.

234 Sorin, *A Time for Building*, 213.

235 *Ibid.*, 213.236 Manuel, *The Realities of American-Palestine Relations*, 210.

237 Stein, *The Balfour Declaration*, 448.

238 Morgenthau, *Mostly Morgenthaus*, 101.

239 Quoted in *ibid.*, 103.

240 Quoted in Peter Balakian, *The Burning Tigris: The Armenian Genocide and America's Response* (New York: Harper Collins, 2004), 260.

241 Morgenthau, *Mostly Morgenthaus*, 179–94.

242 William Yale, "Henry Morgenthau's Special Mission of 1917," *World Politics* 1:3 (April 1949), 319. See also Lebow, "The Morgenthau Peace Mission of 1917," 267–85.

243 Burnidge, *A Peaceful Conquest*, 3.

244 "President Wilson Favors the Zionists," *Jewish Voice* 66, no. 11 (March 14, 1919), 1.

245 *The American War Congress and Zionism: Statements by Members of the American War Congress on the Jewish National Movement* (New York: Zionist Organization of America, 1919).

246 John Higham, *Strangers in the Land: Patterns of American Nativism, 1860–1925*, second ed. (New Brunswick, NJ: Rutgers University Press, 2002), 264.

247 The second and third paragraphs of the Palestine Mandate adopted by the Council of the League of Nations state: "...Whereas the Principal Allied Powers have also agreed that the Mandatory should be responsible for putting into effect the declaration originally made on November 2, 1917, by the government of His Brittanic Majesty, and adopted by the said Powers, in favor of the establishment in Palestine of a national home for the Jewish people, it being clearly understood that nothing should be done which might prejudice the civil and religious rights of existing non-Jewish communities in Palestine, or the rights and political status enjoyed by Jews in any other country; and, Whereas recognition has thereby been given to the historical connexion [*sic*] of the Jewish people with Palestine and to the grounds for reconstituting their national home in that country..." *Palestine Mandate (Full Text) as Finally Approved by the Council of the League of Nations at St. James's Palace, Monday, 24th July, 1922, and Accepted for Administration by H.B.M. Government*, Supplement to the *Jewish Guardian*, July 28, 1922, 2.

Portrait of Jacob Rader Marcus as a Doughboy, c. 1918

Source: Portrait of Jacob Rader Marcus as a Doughboy (c. 1918). Jacob Rader Marcus Photos, 1900–1920, PC-5005, folder 1, Jacob Rader Marcus Center of the American Jewish Archives, Cincinnati, OH.

After the United States declared war on Germany in April 1917, the Wilson administration instituted compulsory military conscription for all able-bodied men between the ages of twenty-one and thirty years old. In due course, some 225,000 American Jews served in the US military, including a sizable number of eastern European Jewish immigrants who only recently arrived in the country and declared their intention of becoming citizens. Though American Jews made up roughly 3.25 percent of the total US population, they supplied nearly six percent of servicemen and women in uniform. "Military service promised to be a context in which Jewish men could demonstrate their valor and value as American citizens," notes Jessica Cooperman, and purportedly demonstrated that Judaism was "an American religion, worthy of equal representation in military and government policy because of the many ways it reinforced American ideals."[1]

For Jewish doughboys like Jacob Rader Marcus (1896–1995), pictured here in uniform,[2] military service was an Americanizing process that pushed Jewish recruits and their families into the mainstream and boosted their sense of Americanness and belonging. A keen observer of world events, Marcus, who later became a distinguished scholar and "dean" of the field of American Jewish history, kept a wartime diary. As Gary Phillip Zola demonstrates in the chapter that follows, Marcus's diary testifies "to the many ways that [he] grew and matured as a Jew and an American."[3] Moreover, his "personal reflections and ruminations illuminate an array of social and spiritual challenges that engaged American Jews during the early decades of the twentieth century."[4]

— M.A.R.

Endnotes

1 See chap. 3 in this volume: Jessica Cooperman, "The Jewish Welfare Board and the Challenges of Zionism in Wartime America."

2 According to the memoir of another soldier, standard U.S. military issue consisted of "1 O.D. [olive drab] coat; 1 O.D. rousers, 2 khaki trousers; 1 khaki coat; 1 pair shoes; 1 pair puttees; 2 shirts; 1 overcoat; 1 poncho; 1 overalls; 1 jacket; 1 hat; 2 suits summer and 2 suits winter underwear; 6 pairs six; 1 belt." Quoted in Richard Rubin, *The Last of the Doughboys: The Forgotten Generation and Their Forgotten War* (Boston: Houghton Mifflin, 2013), 210.

3 See chap. 6 in this volume: Gary Phillip Zola, "'It's a Great Life if You Don't Weaken': Jacob Rader Marcus's Reflections on Being a Jewish Doughboy."

4 *Ibid.*

CHAPTER 6

"IT'S A GREAT LIFE IF YOU DON'T WEAKEN": JACOB RADER MARCUS'S REFLECTIONS ON BEING A JEWISH DOUGHBOY

GARY PHILLIP ZOLA

Scholarly interest in Jewish memoirs and autobiographies first developed in the nineteenth century as part of the central European Jewish movement known as *Wissenschaft des Judentums* (Science of Judaism). Leading practitioners of *Wissenschaft* including Leopold Zunz, Heinrich Graetz, and Moritz Steinschneider took an active interest in the lives of great Jewish personalities and thinkers and produced pioneering studies of Maimonides, Baruch Spinoza, Moses Mendelssohn, and others. Indeed, Graetz's personal diary and a biography of Zunz were later published by their devoted students Philipp Bloch and David Kaufmann, respectively.[1] While such works helped to pave the way for modern Jewish studies, they understandably lack the conceptual framework that today informs the academic study of biographies, memoirs, and hybrid forms of life writing. Yet, as historian Michael Stanislawski has observed, for all that the field of Jewish studies has developed in myriad ways, the genre of first-person record-keeping remains a complex, multifaceted, and frequently underappreciated phenomenon. He notes that many contemporary historians rely "quite unselfconsciously" on memoirs, autobiographies, diaries, and journals as "unproblematically reflective of historical truth."[2] A countervailing approach, which draws on the insights of historians, literary theorists, psychologists, and neuroscientists alike, holds that memoirists "implicitly and explicitly are writing histories of their times" and cannot but help becoming entangled in "dilemmas of facticity and historicity."[3] Put another way, what journaling and autobiographical writing lack in "formal cohesiveness," the literary scholar Felicity A. Nussbaum has asserted, can be understood to signify a "particular historical moment."[4] Quoting the literary critic Donald Stauffer, Nussbaum further explains that the medium makes "no pretense to artistic structure" and "no attempt to see life . . . whole" but rather accentuates "the immediate present."[5] The net result is that diaries, journals, memoirs, and autobiographies can be used productively to raise important questions about "experience and identity" and "expose the manifold meanings, silences, and discontinuities in the texts."[6] Arriving at a similar conclusion, Jehuda Reinharz, the leading biographer of Chaim Weizmann, asserts that the value of memoirs is not their "limited" factual value but rather the ways they illuminate the author's "state of mind" at the time the "recollections" were written.[7]

Elsewhere in this volume, scholars Sarah Imhoff and Pnina Lahav provide rich biographical analyses of Jessie Sampter and Golda Meir, respectively. Probing the memoirs, letters, and prose writings of these two remarkable women, each of whom left an indelible imprint on Zionism, the *Yishuv*, and the State of Israel, Imhoff's and Lahav's chapters demonstrate how profoundly Sampter and Meir were shaped by the American setting. Interestingly, as they point out, in neither instance did Sampter and Meir react at length or in a significantly visible way to the Balfour Declaration's announcement. It is nevertheless apparent, to paraphrase Nussbaum, Stauffer, and Reinharz, that Sampter's and Meir's silences and discontinuities are belied by a distinctive quality of mind that crystallized in a worldview prizing a synthesis of Jewish and Zionist commitments.

Along similar lines, this chapter contends that Jacob Rader Marcus's (1896–1995) wartime diary opens the door to a rich and generative case study. In a word, Marcus, who voluntarily enlisted in the Ohio National Guard in May 1917, produced a record of penetrating observations that help us to understand the critical impact of World War I on American Jews and the fluid nature of the American Jewish experience. In the fullness of time, Marcus would emerge as a leading American Jewish academician and a steward of Reform Judaism in the United States. His wartime diary, which contains but modest references to the Jewish national project, marks an early step in his journey and mirrors American Jewry's state of mind during this fateful period, providing us with a broader perspective on the absorption of a decidedly pro-Zionist orientation, a phenomenon that Marcus himself would later document.

A JEWISH DOUGHBOY

Writing in August 1917, only four months after his enlistment in the US military, Marcus vented his spleen on the pages of the diary he had just begun to keep:

> I have been working like a dog all day, not military work but that cursed stenographical stuff. I'm getting sick and tired of it . . . Why should I, a young, active man suffer, work 15 hours, day in and day out? Why should I suffer, for what? Thoughts such as these stirred me all the day and I felt disgruntled and disgusted. I'll have to watch those spells; they kill a man for life; "It's a great life if you don't weaken."[8]

Marcus's sockdolager, "It's a great life if you don't weaken," was a familiar catchphrase, a popular bromide particularly

among American servicemen during the Great War. Although it is difficult to pinpoint the precise genesis of this phrase, the slogan's increased usage derived from a popular cartoon strip drawn by a young illustrator named Eugene (Gene) Byrnes. "It's a Great Life If You Don't Weaken," debuted on April 15, 1915, in the *New York Telegram*, and the humorous strip quickly became a syndicated hit. Readers looked forward to the cartoon's recurring focus on ordinary human foibles that most people found familiar and relatable. For example, one strip began with an ordinary fellow standing in line to purchase a new cigarette lighter from a seller who promises the lighter will never fail to produce a flame. In subsequent frames, of course, the reader finds the man desperately attempting to ignite his new lighter using a variety of humorous gyrations, but without success. Finally, in the last frame, we see that the frustrated man has shimmied up a gaslit lamppost and is struggling to light his cigarette with the gas flame that is perched atop the streetlight! So much for the reliable cigarette lighter he purchased!

Week after week, Brynes made his audience smile by poking fun at familiar but exasperating daily frustrations and disappointments. The cartoon's slogan entreated readers to look past their daily aggravations, never "weaken," and try to remember that when all is said and done, "it's a great life"![9]

Marcus employed this popular saying more than sixteen times in the pages of his extraordinarily insightful and informative World War I diary. In the pages of this private journal, the future rabbi, scholar, and educator recorded a detailed and colorful accounting of his World War I activities, ruminations, and private introspections. Marcus repeatedly returned to this popular maxim because, as we will see, it constituted a fitting response to the many frustrations, challenges, and emotional valleys the diarist experienced as a Jewish doughboy serving in the American Expeditionary Forces (AEF) during the war.

Rabbi and Scholar

Jacob Rader Marcus was the first American-born, academically trained, historian of the Jewish experience in North America and the first to devote his scholarly energies full-time to the field of American Jewish history. Due to his trenchant research and prodigious erudition, Marcus's peers referred to him as the "dean of American Jewish historians."[10] Born in New Haven, Pennsylvania, Marcus's interest in Jewish scholarship emerged while attending religious school at Wheeling, West Virginia's Eoff Street Reform Congregation whose rabbi, Harry Levi, was an ordinand of Hebrew Union College (HUC) in Cincinnati. Levi was impressed by young Marcus's intellect, and he encouraged his student to enroll in HUC and study for the rabbinate. In the fall of 1911, a fifteen-year-old Marcus traveled by train to Cincinnati to begin his rabbinical training at HUC. Later in life, Marcus recalled that he cried all the way from West Virginia to Cincinnati. After a dramatic pause, he would say with tongue in cheek: "You would cry too if you were going to the Hebrew Union College!"[11] Aside from his two years of military service during World War I, and his years of graduate study in Europe, Marcus spent the remainder of his life at HUC in Cincinnati.[12]

Upon his ordination in 1920, Marcus was appointed to the HUC faculty by its president, the distinguished Jewish theologian Kaufmann Kohler. Initially, Marcus taught courses in biblical history and general Jewish history. Recognizing that his academic training was not adequate for his professorial role at HUC, Marcus traveled to Berlin in 1922 to pursue doctoral studies with the noted Jewish historian Ismar Elbogen. The University of Berlin awarded Marcus a PhD in 1925 and, in 1926, he resumed his faculty duties at HUC.

Prior to World War II and the Nazi Holocaust, all the great centers of Jewish life were in Europe. Consequently, scant attention had been paid to the history of the American Jewry. Marcus was among the first to recognize what he described as "the growing importance of American Jewish history." In the early 1940s, Marcus began to apply modern critical methodology to the writing of American Jewish history. At HUC in 1941, he began teaching what was, most probably, the nation's first required university-level course in American Jewish history.[13]

In 1946, Marcus recommended to Reform Judaism's rabbinical association, the Central Conference of American Rabbis, that American synagogues begin a systematic effort to preserve congregational records and documents relating to Jewish communal life. Recognizing the tremendous scholarly value in having a centralized institution to preserve and catalogue these documents, Marcus advocated the establishment of "an American Jewish Archives." In 1947, with the support of his friend and schoolmate, Nelson Glueck (1900–1971), who became HUC's newly elected president earlier that same year, Marcus convinced HUC's board of governors to establish the American Jewish Archives (AJA), a semi-autonomous national institution with its own building and staff on the school's Cincinnati campus. Marcus became the AJA's founding director, and he led the institution until his death in 1995. Under Marcus's dynamic leadership, the AJA grew into one of the world's largest and most significant catalogued collections of archival material documenting the history of Jewish life in North America.

Marcus's professional career was fundamentally an alloy composed of two cardinal elements: Marcus the rabbi and Marcus the scholar. His writings demonstrate that his concept of history was informed by a religious perspective; a secular, critical historian would not have written about the Jewish past in the way that Marcus did. Toward the end of his life, Marcus embraced this tension; he made no apologies for it. The historian, he noted, could not "jump out of his skin." He insisted that he was "devoted to the critical method" of scholarship, but simultaneously he declared himself a loyal partisan of his subject matter: "I like Jews," he wrote, "I am convinced that they are an unusually gifted lot."[14] Marcus consciously sought to maintain a proper balance between what he himself called a "pardonable filiopietism" and "the desire to create a new American historiography which will more truly reflect the growth of the American people."[15] In light of his prodigious scholarship, the many posts he occupied in the field of American Jewish history, and the impact he had on several generations of American Reform rabbis, Marcus unquestionably influenced the course of American Jewish life during the last half of the twentieth century.[16]

To Serve or Not to Serve

On April 2, 1917, President Woodrow Wilson went before a joint session of Congress to request permission to declare war on Germany, a request that was granted on April 6. Initially the Wilson administration believed that a large volunteer army could be recruited to prosecute the war "over there." This idea quickly fell by the wayside as generals and the ever-intensifying war persuaded the president that an immense force would be needed and only a general draft could bring such a massive army into being in a timely fashion. Congress passed the Selective Draft Act in May 1917, and shortly thereafter newspapers across the nation began to publicize "Registration Day," whereupon young Americans between the ages of twenty-one and thirty were encouraged to do their part by registering for military service in the AEF. Patriotic sentiment exploded across the nation. As one historian noted, "enthusiasm, approaching hysteria, ran high among the American people... a holiday spirit was evident as men... lined up to register. There were surely those who considered ignoring duty's call, but they must have had second thoughts when President Wilson informed the nation that those who failed to register or fled to Canada would be arrested and, if convicted, be sentenced to a year in prison. By early in June, over 9 million Americans had voluntarily registered for the draft."[17] Yet even before Registration Day, many young Americans wanted to join the war effort, so they did not wait to be drafted, but rather they enlisted as soon as possible. This is what Marcus did.[18]

Many of those who registered for the draft were immigrants, and this is particularly true of the Jewish servicemen. Millions of eastern European Jews had immigrated to the US between 1881 and the onset of World War I. Some had little interest in the war, and they had no desire to serve in America's new national army.

Many other Jewish immigrants, however, saw military service as a civic duty, and more than 225,000 Jews served in the US military during the Great War.[19]

The twenty-one-year-old Jacob Rader Marcus was only a year and a half away from completing his eight-year-long rabbinical curriculum. Like many of his American Jewish contemporaries, Marcus enlisted in the Ohio National Guard two and a half weeks before "Registration Day."[20] Never given to patriotic effusions or exuberant flag-waving, Marcus made it clear in his diary that he believed it was his civic duty to enlist in the AEF and to serve the nation. Years later, he jocosely explained that when America entered World War I, he had been a student at HUC for nearly seven years. "It was a long program," Marcus would blithely explain, "and I needed a break from the academic rigor. It was coming out of my ears! So, I decided to enlist in the army!"[21] If Marcus consulted with anyone about his decision to leave school and enlist, no written record of those exchanges has survived. His private ruminations intimate, however, that his decision to join the military was intertwined with his personal struggle to individuate from his family and make his own decisions as a mature adult.

Marcus's family members were horror-struck when they learned that the future rabbi was planning to enlist in the AEF after Congress voted to declare war on Germany. On April 17, 1917, Jennie and Aaron Marcus sent their son a terse, one-sentence telegram: "Don't do anything until you get our letter." Marcus received a second urgent telegram the very next day from his father with even more agitation: "Wire if you have enlisted already. Answer immediately. Mother coming." Clearly, Marcus's parents feared their son may have already enlisted or was planning to do so in the very near future. It is impossible to know whether Jennie and Aaron Marcus jumped to this conclusion because they anticipated that their dutiful son would take such a step or, alternatively, if they received word that Jacob intended to enlist should the US declare war on Germany. Regardless, Marcus's parents were dyspeptic.[22]

Marcus's parents and siblings refused to acquiesce to Marcus's decision, and they repeatedly urged their son and brother to abandon his plans to enlist in the AEF. On April 22, 1917, Isaac Marcus, Jacob's older brother corresponded and tried to convince his impetuous younger brother to bow to his parents' will. "We have been thinking things over," Isaac reasoned,

> and we thot [*sic*] it best that you come home at once and we will place you on a good farm where we know you will be doing your country, yourself, and us the most good. Instead of working in the supply department why not help to produce the supplies? It is easy enough to get sufficient men for the supply department but the farmers will suffer for lack of men and the country needs the farmer today more than they [*sic*] need the soldier. I am sure you will secure your credits from the university and the college providing you speak to the faculty and tell them what your plans are... Whatever you do, don't be in a hurry to enlist in the service. I believe our plan is about the best thing for you. Please let us hear from you.[23]

The family's pleadings were to no avail. Marcus enlisted in the AEF on May 1, 1917. Shortly thereafter, his parents traveled to Cincinnati and expressed their disapproval personally.[24] As late as November 1917, his family was still trying to persuade Jacob to withdraw from the military. Pulling back the curtain on the family's dynamics, Isaac's letter (signed by Isaac and Aaron) manifests a growing impatience with the rabbinical student's youthful obstinance:

> I note that the ages for the conscription have been agreed upon and I also read who are exempted, and to my surprise I see that "ministers and *students* of recognized divinity or *theological schools*, etc." are exempted. This means in plain

> words that you did not have to enlist but you "are in it" and now the problem is, father says, for you to try to get out of it. If you can, by all means, surely there is some way, and this exemption law may serve as a loophole for you. We do not like to say "I told you so" but if you had listened to our original plan you would not have enlisted and you would have been a free man. Mother does not know anything about this law exempting you, if I told her she would go into hysterics. For goodness sakes do the best you can to get out of this fix.[25]

Jacob had no intention of rethinking his decision and toward the end of the year, Marcus's family finally began to make peace with his decision to enlist—as long as their son remained as far away as possible from the front lines. Marcus's first assignment in Cincinnati was a desk job. From May through August, Marcus worked as a stenographer for the regiment's commanding officer, Congressman Victor E. Heintz.[26] This office job undoubtedly came as a relief to Marcus's worried parents and siblings. By late September, however, the job's tedium began to irritate Marcus, and he longed for a way to escape the ceaseless office work. One Sunday, late in August 1917, Marcus noted in his diary:

> This is Sunday, a day of rest. Willy-nilly it is a day of rest for the Jews, except those who put in "their best licks" playing pinochle and poker. But it had no semblance of a rest day to me not that I played poker, nor even bridge, but that I had plenty of work to do. I always have. I am now a stenographer, not a [battalion] Sgt. Maj.[27] I do all of Heintz's personal correspondence instead of learning how to prepare forms and learn army paperwork. The only reason that I am not objecting is that I cannot and in the second place this personal *correspondence,* mostly to Washington, will soon cease, I hope...[28]

For Marcus, relief from the stenographic monotony came in mid-October, when he was transferred to Camp Sheridan in Montgomery, Alabama, a new training facility established in July 1917 to house the Ohio National Guard regiments who would soon become the 37th Infantry Division, known as the "Buckeye Division." During their stay at Camp Sheridan, the soldiers were informed they would be trained for deployment in France.

A military assignment in France, even if it meant higher risk of death, appealed to the young and adventuresome Marcus. He confided to his diary that he longed to go to France with the military, though he never elaborates on why this assignment is so important. On some days, Marcus is hopeful that he will be sent to France. On other days, he feared he would not be chosen to go abroad with his battalion. At such times the diary bespeaks Marcus's flagging spirits. We can surmise that he shared his thoughts about going "over there" with his family and, in doing so, he rekindled his family's angst.

On November 12, 1917, Marcus informed his diary that he had received "a strong letter from home telling me to get a safe berth and keep away from France." In a revealing entry, Marcus sheds light on his attitude toward enlistment and military duty: "In this game you go where they send you and do your duty and ask no questions and that is just what I am going to do. I enlisted voluntarily and I am going to take just what I get. Be it good or bad. Let's hope it's all for the good."[29]

Three days later, a letter from Marcus' mother, written in Yiddish, arrived. "A Yiddish letter from home always means trouble," Marcus lamented, "I dread them."[30] Marcus's Yiddish may have become rusty, but he was able to discern that his mother was disconsolate over the possibility that her son might be sent to the front lines in France. Although he had tried his best to reassure her in his letters to home, Marcus realized that his "assurances have little weight since I joined the army against her express wishes."[31] Marcus's mother unleashed a torrent of guilt as she poured out her heart. She wrote that she would "go crazy" if her son ended up serving "in the trenches."[32] Her bitter criticism and heavy-handed disapproval crushed her son's spirit:

> [My mother wrote] that she wept all day, every minute of her day and night was spent in thinking of me and crying. I broke down. She also condemned my statement that I would become a buck-private, a statement that I do not think that I ever meant seriously. She implied, I believe, that the reason that I had joined the army was to expatiate for some miserable vicious sin.[33]

The letter devastated Marcus. After reading it a second time, he responded with unhemmed despair. The following day, he memorialized the experience in his diary:

> I took out mother's letter and started to read it. It broke my heart. For the first time in months if not in a year I wept until my eyes were red . . . I wrote as my heart prompted me. As I wrote I wept and my tears fell on the blotter under my fingers. I think I made a mistake in writing the letter that I did.[34]

A few days later, Isaac Marcus lovingly tried to bolster his younger brother's flagging spirits. Isaac opened Jacob's letter before his mother could read it, and he decided not to show her the doughboy's raw epistle. "You ought to know better than to write such a letter to your mother," Isaac scolded. "She is very sensitive and excitable." Isaac reminded his younger brother not to take his mother's histrionics to heart. "I have been with the folks all my life and I believe I understand Mother better than you do . . . she even told me herself that I did wisely in not taking her utterances seriously!"[35] Then, in a loving effort to buck up his little brother's bruised feelings, Isaac signs off by providing Jacob with some old-fashioned good advice:

> The sun is shining every day in Alabama so don't forget to look at it occasionally, it will help to drive away the blues. Buy some good joke books and have a good hearty laugh. At the rate you are going where will you be when you are a man of 40? If I get any more gloomy letters from you I'll take "that Choo-Choo to Alabama" and give you a good spanking. NIX ON THE WEEPS!... Take my tips and give Mr. Awful Gloom a good kick![36]

Reading the entirety of Marcus's World War I diary one finds that "Mr. Awful Gloom" did indeed make return visits from time to time, but regarding Marcus's decision to go wherever Uncle Sam wished to send him, the family finally conceded defeat. After their son arrived in France, the quarreling letters ceased. Marcus took note of their change of heart. "The greatest surprise to me was the way that they took my transfer over here. Not a word. Poor folks, possibly they have come to the conclusion that I know what is best for myself."[37]

SIGNIFICANCE OF MARCUS'S DIARY

Although hundreds of soldier-diaries have survived from the Great War—among them a fair number written by Jewish soldiers who fought on both sides of the conflict—Marcus's diary constitutes the only known sustained expression of personal reflections from a rabbinical student who was so keenly and personally interested in the future of Jewish life in the United States. As a result of its focus on American Jewry and American Judaism, Marcus's wartime diary is in many respects sui generis.[38]

To be sure, a few scholars have made note of Marcus's World War I diary in their historical analyses of this era. Christopher Sterba, for example, mentions Marcus's diary in his important volume *Good Americans: Italian and Jewish Immigrants during the First World War*. Sterba highlights Marcus's many references to antisemitism as well as the antisemitic behavior he witnessed while serving in the AEF during this period.[39]

Similarly, Jessica Cooperman's pathbreaking volume exploring the rise of religious pluralism during World War I makes beneficial use of Marcus's diary. Like Sterba, Cooperman points out that Marcus's diary sheds important light on the various forms of bigotry that Jewish doughboys confronted in the context of their military experiences. In addition, Cooperman draws on Marcus's personal reflections to deepen our understanding of the Jewish experience in the AEF during World War I.[40]

The unique historical significance of Marcus's diary lies in the fact that his youthful reflections offer researchers a rare glimpse into how a neophyte American rabbi, a young intellectual who had been Americanized through his educational experiences at Hebrew Union College in Cincinnati, experienced the hardscrabble life of the nation's military ranks. Marcus's status as a highly educated religiously liberal Jew shines through on every page. His ruminations about his service in the AEF are distinctive because they offer readers a rare opportunity to deepen their understanding of how Marcus's rabbinical education and his own personal ambitions influenced his understanding of the turbulent times he experienced.

The exercise of keeping a daily or regular journal served the writer in many ways. This is especially true for soldiers who recorded their experiences in real time. On the one hand, the diary was a trusted confidant, so the writer felt free to put down his or her true, uncensored feelings and thoughts. In addition, there was significant therapeutic benefit in this journaling activity. Keeping a diary during a war provided soldiers with "a place into which they could unload their fears and frustrations."[41] Marcus's World War I diary exemplifies these features vividly.

The diary is replete with instances of Marcus's self-doubt and self-criticism. For example, he confesses to his diary that after leading services on one occasion, he was "quite nervous," and the sermon he delivered was not well-received. He could see that he had not held his listener's attention, and he chastised himself saying, "I need more confidence in myself, a more fluent vocabulary, and better vocal control."[42] On another occasion, when he was attending a Passover seder, he returned home and disclosed to his diary that his hosts had invited him to lead the recitation of the traditional *Birkat Hamazon* (Grace after the Meal) during the seder meal. "[I] felt ashamed," the student rabbi privately admitted, "when they asked me to lead in the *mezuman* and I was not able to."[43]

The rich historical content of Jacob Rader Marcus's diary provides readers with a textured look at his day-to-day experiences during the strain of war. Knowing as we do the arc of Marcus's future career, one is struck by the young scholar's free-flowing ruminations; observations that run the gamut of the emotional and intellectual spectrum. The young writer's diary is filled with thoughts: prescient, prosaic, humorous, and heartbreaking. Through the lens of this 100-year-old diary, a reader discovers the many ways in which military service and, more specifically World War I itself, shaped Marcus's thinking about the challenges—both personal and professional—that he and his peers faced during this transformational era.

Marcus's notable reflections on four interesting and significant topics illustrate the diary's rich potential as a valuable primary source document regarding the history of Jewish life in America: (a) Zionism; (b) exogamy; (c) Jews and non-Jews; and (d) Jews and African Americans.[44]

ZIONISM

It is interesting to note that Marcus makes no mention whatsoever of the Balfour Declaration in his diary—even though he wrote in his diary every single day during the month of November 1917. This fact is more intriguing since Marcus does periodically share his thoughts on Zionism.

On May 1, 1918, for instance, Marcus makes note of an interesting encounter he had with Rabbi Bernard C. Ehrenreich, the rabbi of the Jewish congregation in Montgomery, Alabama, where Marcus was stationed.[45] Ehrenreich, a rabbi-educator who would become a pioneer of the American Jewish camping movement, invited Marcus to attend a lecture given by Itamar Ben-Avi, son of the renowned Hebraist of the Yishuv, Eliezer Ben-Yehuda, who was speaking to the Montgomery Jewish community that evening. In his diary, Marcus described Ben-Avi as "a delicate looking esthetic fellow with large black eyes, clear skin, black wavy hair falling over his temples." Despite Marcus's kind assessment of his physical appearance, he was not impressed with Ben-Avi's "sweet low passionate voice that ascends and breaks." In Marcus's view, Ben-Avi's talk on the Turks in Palestine was "not very strong," and he summarized his impressions of Ben-Avi with two colorful words: a "crazy nationalist."[46]

Toward the end of the evening, as people were departing, Marcus noted that "a little fat man with watery eyes" dashed into the room. The man had wanted to hear Ben-Avi's lecture, but he had arrived too late. The man told Marcus and Ehrenreich that he had wanted to attend the lecture so he could tell Ben-Avi and others that as a young man he had once met the great Herzl. Again, Marcus was nonplussed by the man's Zionistic effusions, and in his diary he summarized the man's idealization of "the early days of Zionism" with one succinct comment: "pathetic."[47]

Some months later, after Marcus had returned to the US from France, he was attending a Passover Seder in Chillicothe, Ohio. There he encountered a soldier named Hazen[48] who delivered "an impassioned appeal for Zionism" in Yiddish. "His philosophy," Marcus recollected, was "that the hatred for the Jew will always exist… [and he] was grieved by the fact that Jewish soldiers [were] fighting all over the world for their respective nations [yet] they [were] often subject to prejudice and persecution in those very countries." Marcus was mystified by Hazen's passion and, particularly, he noted that Hazen declared he was astonished by Jews who were "anti-Zionistic and [used] the formula America is good enough for me."[49]

During the 1920s, Marcus witnessed many changes that undoubtedly influenced his thinking about Zionism. First, Marcus personally observed nascent Nazi bigotry while studying for his PhD in Berlin during the early 1920s. Later in life, he recollected seeing young men affiliated with the Nazi party standing on a street corner and handing out propaganda in Berlin. The aging scholar would reflect back on that experience and admit he had not taken the menacing agitators seriously enough: "I thought those men were crazy, but *they* were not crazy. *I* was."[50]

Second, Marcus visited Palestine in 1926, after completing his PhD and before he returned to Cincinnati to resume his career on the faculty of HUC. Marcus spent three months exploring the *Yishuv* for himself. His reappraisal of Zionism reflects an objective scholarly analysis wherein Marcus attempts to describe the Zionist landscape accurately and fairly. Though he did not consider himself a Zionist per se (he never joined a Zionist organization), he forcefully emphasized Zionism's growing significance as a mass movement among Jews in every part of the world, including in the American Jewish community.

Interestingly, Marcus was one of the first historians to recognize that American Jews had embraced a unique form of Zionism. Like Zionists around the world, American Zionists believed that the establishment of a national homeland would serve as a much-needed refuge for "hundreds and thousands" of "physically downtrodden" Jews.[51] Similarly, the establishment of a Jewish national homeland would make Jews a people like all other peoples of the earth. At the same time, Marcus stressed, most American Zionists do not consider themselves to be personally in need of a safe haven or national homeland. Working for the Zionist cause, then, provided many American Jews with a venue for expressing their Jewish loyalties in the American political arena and not exclusively in the American synagogue. "The truth is" Marcus concluded, "the 'secular' Jew, who threatens to outnumber the 'religious' Jew, needs a sphere of activity in which he can express his Jewish affiliation."[52]

The views Marcus expresses on Zionism in his World War I diary serve as a baseline for future historians seeking to assess the ways in which Zionism became a mass movement in America. For Marcus, the gap between the attitudes of the Reform community in which he had been educated and socialized and his own Eastern European upbringing gradually closed as conditions in European Jewry steadily deteriorated in the 1920s and early 1930s.[53]

In sum, during his years as a doughboy Marcus displayed little recognition of Zionism's growing popularity among segments of the American Jewish community. However, the young rabbi's analysis of Zionism clearly evolved after World War I and his generally dismissive attitude during his years in the service took a complete turn by 1933 with the publication of his noteworthy scholarly essay "Zionism and the American Jew." This essay, which appeared in the second volume of Phi Beta Kappa's recently inaugurated literary journal, the *American Scholar,* forcefully demonstrates that changing world events had transformed Marcus's view of Zionism. The essay provides the reader with a general description of the Zionist landscape as it developed up to that point in time. In addition to identifying the various Jewish groups that supported and opposed Zionism, Marcus explains why so many American Jews had become attracted to the movement since the promulgation of the Balfour Declaration. "It may be," he opined, "that Zion's appeal to the American Jew lies in its incitation to purposeful activity. It offers a rounded-out, well-integrated national ideal . . . The Jew is tired of waiting for the Messiah; he has determined to create him—in Palestine."[54]

Exogamy

During his time in the US military, Marcus encountered several Jews who were romantically involved with non-Jews. These exogamous relationships surprised the young rabbinical student, and he frequently wrote about the topic in his diary. Shortly after arriving in Montgomery, for example, Rabbi Ehrenreich invited Marcus to his home for dinner. Among the guests the rabbi had invited were two of Marcus's fellow servicemen, who had recently married non-Jewish women. "The Jews of [Montgomery] are crazy about these two girls," Marcus conceded. "I am not! One I have heard is no good . . . the other I don't like."[55]

On another occasion, Rabbi Ehrenreich told Marcus about a non-Jew who had undergone circumcision so that he could marry a Jewish woman who belonged to Congregation Kahl Montgomery. Marcus disagreed with the rabbi's liberal approach in the privacy of his diary: "I believe," he wrote "that I am right when the ultimate good of the race and the religion is considered. It looks harsh but it is for the good, the ultimate good of all, I am sure."[56]

Marcus also took note of a fascinating exchange that transpired with an acquaintance he knew from Cincinnati, Leo Joseph Osburg. Marcus was caught off guard when Osburg revealed the fact that his mother was a Catholic and his father was a Jew and, additionally, Osburg's wife was a non-Jew. Osburg confided in Marcus telling him that none of his friends knew these details and, remarkably, he confessed that he was particularly careful to conceal this information from his Jewish friends and acquaintances. Osburg told Marcus that he considered himself to be a Jew but, since many of his friends and family were unaware of the fact that his own parents were intermarried and that he, too, was intermarried, he found himself "chagrined and embarrassed" when he heard Jewish people attack intermarried Jews bitterly, "with curses."[57] Osburg shared this information confidentially with Marcus because he feared that Marcus might someday say such a thing, and he wanted his friend to know how it affected him. Recounting the story in his diary, Marcus reflected: "Poor fellow. He fears that it would change the attitude of his Jewish pals if he told them so he remains quiet. I object to intermarriage on racial and religious grounds; the boys object because they have found through experience that such marriages are always extremely unfortunate."[58] The reader will never know whether student rabbi Marcus comforted his friend by reassuring him that he would never be judgmental, or if he simply listened thoughtfully without responding one way or the other.

These entries by the diarist along with others illuminate the complicated social and cultural atmosphere that many Americanizing Jews like AEF soldier Marcus encountered. Jews were striving for social integration and equal footing, and many servicemen had their first chance to break out of their mostly Jewish world and engage with the allures of general society. Yet it is interesting to note that a religiously liberal Jew like Marcus—soon to be ordained a rabbi—was suspicious of these early exogamous stirrings which would, of course, foreshadow a profound American Jewish quandary that would intensify over the entire course of the twentieth century.[59]

As it was with Zionism, Marcus's views concerning rabbinical officiation would evolve over the course of his career. As a young soldier about to become a rabbi, Marcus repeatedly voiced suspicion that gentile women had ulterior motives for wanting to marry Jewish men. Yet later in his career, Marcus would voice his support for rabbis officiating at interfaith wedding ceremonies.

Jews and Non-Jews

Marcus's diary throws back the curtain on an array of conflicting emotions that Americanized Jews like himself experienced when compelled for the first time to associate with non-Jews in the close quarters of the AEF. Marcus vacillates between expressions of respectful admiration and bitter recriminations for the non-Jew. On the one hand, Marcus favors the Jew over the gentile because he is convinced the Jew has a higher level of morality and integrity than the non-Jew. On the other hand, the gentile often possessed characteristics that, in Marcus's opinion, the Jew should strive to emulate.

Young Marcus admired powerful gentiles, and he took pride in Jews who were muscular and capable of defending themselves both physically and verbally, just like non-Jews. For instance, Marcus wrote about a young man named Emerman, who joined Marcus's company in Montgomery.[60] Emerman possessed a fierce disposition that Marcus admired. The young Jew didn't "take anything from anybody." Marcus dubbed Emerman's style and approach a "fighting Judaism," and this, he wrote, was "the right idea any way you take it."[61]

In another entry, Marcus mused about the psychological differences he believed distinguished Jews from non-Jews:

> We Jews are racially sensitive I really believe. We are damned conscientious about our work; we worry all the time. If we have too much work, we do it and then complain; if we don't have enough we complain all the same. And we complain bitterly. I have always done so even knowing that it was wrong of me to kick. It always is but it must be the nature of my people never to be satisfied. We are too ambitious for that. We are not dull and phlegmatic and unambitious, far from it. We like to make good and if we can't we feel bitter about it. We have a crying sense of injustice. If things aren't exactly right we murmur and raise our voices to the skies. We are not satisfied at [*sic*] anything. Never. This is our blessing and incidentally our curse.[62]

Marcus occasionally attributed the disdain that Jews received at the hands of their commanding officers to an unwillingness to respond unthinkingly to directions or commands. This intolerance along with the "perverted ideas the non-Jews have about us [Jews]" irked Marcus. He told his diary their behavior toward his people was "absolutely nonsensical. Nobody really understands the Jew" Marcus wrote. "He doesn't understand himself.[63]

Marcus came to believe that "the boys who stick up for their rights have little trouble though they meet the A.S. [antisemitism] invariably." Weak Jews, he wrote, "suffer a great deal [and] even [in] the fighting divisions right on the lines the Jewish boys had trouble. It exists at all times and under all circumstances."[64]

A corollary to the muscular or "fighting Jew" was the self-effacing or self-denying Jew. Marcus held Jews of this ilk in utter disdain. Philip Rosen was one such soldier. According to Marcus, Rosen "tried to deny his Judaism" but his disavowals backfired because the gentiles easily saw through his attempts to conceal his Jewish heritage. "He was a poor Jehuda known throughout the Bn. [battalion] as 'Murphy,'" a popular slang expression at that time meaning "a potato" or a dolt.[65]

In another entry, Marcus writes again about Leo J. Osburg, who was married to a non-Jew. Marcus accused Osburg of being "a coward and deceitful." The Jews in the battalion tried to help Osburg "in every way" and Osburg would repay their loyalty by tattling on them to the Commanding Officer. "All the Jew boys are sore at Osburg," Marcus wrote, because he "tells the C.O. sometimes, that he is a Jew and then again he says that he is a gentile. Evidently he forgets to tell the C.O. that he is also a damn fool."[66] Marcus summarized his attitude about Jews like Rosen and Osburg by noting how odd it is that "birds who have the [Jewish] 'map' all over them try to deny themselves."[67]

In the privacy of his diary, Marcus also gave voice to stereotypical remarks about non-Jews. After a non-Jewish officer scolded Marcus publicly for looking over his shoulder while he typed, Marcus unleashed a condescending rant against all non-Jews:

> I take it for granted that all people are as decent as I try to be and always forget that I am nothing but a hook-nosed Jew and no right to associate with a decent American (Christian). How interesting. It is only a Jew who can be a real gentleman under all occasions. A gentile with a little power is a tyrant. He has not the spiritual depth to appreciate the responsibility of power.[68]

Marcus's diary is peppered with his vacillating thoughts about Jews and gentiles. On the one hand, he idealizes Jews. Addressing himself sternly, Marcus adumbrates a philosophy that remained with him for the rest of his life:

> Marcus, remember that wherever you go you are a Jew. Whether you will or not always publish it and exult in it. It won't do you a damn bit of good

> if you don't. [Gotthard] Deutsch and [Moses] Hess have the right idea. Hess' [*sic*] conclusions are wrong that's all: Be a Jew for you have to be any-how. The "Nations" won't let you forget it. This is the worst way of looking at it from the Jews' point of view. The best way is to honestly glory in the greatest "discipline" despite the occasional rebuff it may now and then call forth.[69]

On the other hand, he often extolled non-Jews for providing American Jews with a worthy example of behavior to which they should strive to emulate:

> Since I have been in the Army I have forgotten how to worry. I have learned to do my duty and take it easy at the same time. I have learned as I wrote in my last letter that the best things in life should not be forgotten. That all is not sorrow or fear but that there should be laughter and joy in life. We ought to take an example in life from our gentile neighbors. They don't worry. We worry too much, we take life too serious.[70]

JEWS AND AFRICAN AMERICANS

The presence of armed African American soldiers trained in the North was a flashpoint of tension in the deeply segregated and pervasively white supremacist atmosphere of the American South. Black soldiers such as those in the 369th and 370th Infantry Regiments were constantly confronted with what must surely have seemed to be foreign and constricting Jim Crow regulations, which some of them accidentally transgressed and others purposefully ignored. The disdainful and condescending treatment of the Black community in the southern city of Montgomery shocked Marcus, and he frequently recorded his thoughts on this subject.

Shortly after arriving at Camp Sheridan, Marcus had a haircut at a shop where the barbers were African Americans. The fact that Marcus selected this barber shop bespeaks something of his own benign attitude toward people of color. Conversing with one of the barbers, Marcus was told about a "Negro Major named Fuldon.[71] "I've seen him," Marcus noted in his diary, "and I certainly like his looks and wouldn't object working under him.[72]

Marcus repeatedly recorded his positive impressions of the African American soldiers. "There was a Negro captain here today; fine type, fine accent, no brogue. They surely have some splendid men."[73] In the privacy of his diary, however, Marcus describes the horrific consequences of the South's systemic social racism, to which the US military often turned a blind eye:

> We are given orders to keep away from Negroes, not to speak, [or] be spoken to by them. Not to patronize their establishments. Their wash women cannot even come to our shacks for clothes . . . The men swear they will not salute the Negro officers and there is a lot of hard feeling against them. Byers, who is so pious, he is a devout High Churchman, surprised me by his vindictive attitude toward them.[74]

Marcus also took note when a regiment of African American troops from Ohio arrived at Camp Sheridan. "Fine looking bunch," he wrote. Yet witnessing the appalling ugliness of racism in the American South shocked the young Jewish officer: "Two of [the troops were] shot to death the other day in town for insulting a white woman. I don't believe it. I believe that they were murdered to intimidate the others. These Southerners hate Negroes."[75]

Interestingly, Marcus slowly became convinced that the prejudice and blinkered bigotry aimed at the African American was comparable to the mindless antisemitism that the Jew suffered. "I am forcibly impressed everyday by the fact that a Negro is not considered as being human in this South. He is like the Jew, extra-human."[76] On another occasion, Marcus recalled hearing a white officer telling his soldiers "that no self-respecting white man would be seen talking to a Negro woman in the South." Pondering that comment in the pages of his diary, Marcus wrote: "I sometimes think that there is a wonderful similarity between the sufferings of the Jews and the Negro. Yet if one would put the two in the same class down here in the South, there would be nothing short of a riot. Nothing short of a riot."[77]

The longer Marcus remained in the South the more the bigotry toward African Americans tormented him. Eventually, the frustrating injustice of the Jim Crow society he experienced persuaded him that something needed to be done to rectify the systemic wrongs he witnessed:

> As I went out I saw a Negro beggar moaning for money and murmuring something about "slave days." I don't think she was ever a slave but I do believe that she certainly was a miserable sight. The Negro problem came back to me with great force. Here is a people, a vast people, crushed, its moral backbone crushed, its girls—young and old—prostitutes to an alarming extent. Its men without any manhood. Why? No pride. No education. Without these two which are linked they will never improve. Yet they must. They are in bondage; they must be freed?[78]

CONCLUSION

For historians of the American Jewish experience during World War I, Jacob Marcus's World War I diary constitutes a treasure-trove of interesting data on the American Jewish experience during that consequential epoch. It possesses several distinctions which, considered collectively, render Marcus's real-time reflections remarkable and unique.

First, Marcus's personal reflections and ruminations illuminate an array of social and spiritual challenges that American Jews serving in the AEF encountered during World War I. At the same time, the diary provides us with a deeper understanding of the general social and cultural factors that shaped Marcus, a young man who was destined to become a prominent historian and, as a teacher of rabbis, an important American Jewish influencer. These are the qualities that imbue Marcus's diary with unique historical value. Many Jewish doughboys kept diaries that have been published or preserved in archival collections. Jewish chaplains also kept diaries that have survived, like the reminiscences published by Lee J. Levinger (1890–1966) or the wartime diary of the French historian, Marc Bloch (1886–1944).[79] Yet these documents are not comparable to Marcus's writings.

Levinger's reminiscences are administrative and informational in contrast to Marcus, who relentlessly probed interpersonal relations along with an array of contemporary Jewish issues. Bloch's diary shares some of the same historiographical texture as Marcus's reflections in that they are both interested in memorializing the many kinds of men with whom they had not previously had social contact. As one scholar noted, Bloch was clearly aware that his diary might one day serve as "witness and narrator" to the experiences about which he was journaling.[80] Yet these two future scholars lived in two completely different contextual realities: American versus France. Marcus's status as a *future* rabbi and budding scholar along with his ability to disclose his own developing thoughts and private emotions add tremendous richness to his diary.

As noted above, Marcus was meliorating two identities. He was an American and a Jew. His reflective struggles to navigate and negotiate these two demanding loyalties shed light on Marcus's generation: eastern European immigrants or the children of eastern European immigrants for whom the Great War was a transformational experience. Future historians may usefully employ Marcus's diary to the reminiscences of the American Jewish men (mostly immigrants) who served in the Jewish Legion—the latter was intensely focused on Zionism and the future of the *Yishuv*.[81]

Many scholars have examined aspects of Marcus's career. He has long been acknowledged for his incomparable work as the "dean" of American Jewish historians, his determination to build a great American Jewish Archives mirroring his own his visionary sense of the field, and his personal commitment to American Reform Judaism and, especially, to the Reform rabbinate. The fact that Hebrew Union College in Cincinnati was the *only* rabbinical seminary in America to make primary source research in American Jewish history a core course in its curriculum bespeaks the uniqueness of Marcus's philosophy. Yet, in all that has been written about the "Doctor," his service in the AEF has escaped close examination. Marcus's diary pulls back the curtain on this formative period in his life. It illuminates how his experiences as a young American Jewish soldier in World War I shaped his thinking about the modernization of the American Jewish experience. In this sense, Marcus's diary anticipates the central issues of American Jewish life in the twentieth century, and his personal experience prefigures America's transformation to an urban society, American Jewry's impact on the American academy, and the rise of rabbis and scholars as Jewish thought leaders.

Finally, Marcus's diary testifies to the many ways that Marcus grew and matured as a Jew, as a man, and as an American. Like the 225,000 of his coreligionists who served as soldiers during World War I, Marcus's time in the AEF proved to be a crash course in learning how to balance one's American aspirations together with one's Jewish loyalties. Marcus's diary demonstrates the extent to which he was himself cognizant of this dialectical tension as he lived it. Perhaps this is what he meant whenever he reiterated the exclamation that became his watchword as a doughboy: "Now is a chance for me to work out my own motto... It's a great life if you don't weaken."[82]

Endnotes

1 See Philipp Bloch, "Memoir of Heinrich Graetz," in Heinrich Graetz, *History of the Jews*, vol. 6 (Philadelphia: Jewish Publication Society of America, 1898), 1–86; and David Kaufmann, "Die Familie Zunz," in *Monatsschrift für Geschichte und Wissenschaft des Judentums* 38 (N. F. 2), no. 11 (Karlsbad, 1894): 481–93.

2 Michael Stanislawski, *Autobiographical Jews: Essays in Jewish Self-Fashioning* (Seattle: University of Washington Press, 2004), 8.

3 *Ibid.*, 6, 7.

4 Felicity A. Nussbaum, "Toward Conceptualizing Diary" in *Studies in Autobiography*, ed. James Olney (New York: Oxford University Press, 1988), 128–29.

5 *Ibid.*

6 *Ibid.*, 129.

7 Jehuda Reinharz, *Writing the Biography of Chaim Weizmann* (Rehovot, Israel: Yad Chaim Weizmann, 1992), 8.

8 Jacob Rader Marcus Diary (hereafter: "JRM diary"), August 27, 1917, MS-210, box 70, folder 2, The Jacob Rader Marcus Center of the American Jewish Archives, Cincinnati, OH (hereafter: "AJA").

9 Sara Duke, *Biographical Sketches of Cartoonists & Illustrators in the Swann Collection of the Library of Congress* (Arlington, VA: Comics DC, 2012), 44–45. Also available online at https://archive.org/details/DukeBioSketchesOfCartoonistsInSwannCollAtLOC/Duke-Swann2017/page/n45/ mode/2up?view=theater. The catchphrase also became the title of a popular song written in 1917. See "It's a Great Life If You Don't Weaken" by Arthur Spaulding (1877–1953) and Joseph M. Daly (1883–1968). The song was recorded in the mid-1920s by two different bands: Sam Lanin's (1891–1977) Famous Players and Singers, and George Olsen (1893–1971) and his Orchestra. See Brian Rust, *The American Dance Band Discography 1917–1942*. 2 vols. (New Rochelle, NY: Arlington House, 1975).

10 Marcus's best-known volumes include, *The Jew in the Medieval World* (1938), *Memoirs of American Jews* (1955), the three-volume *The Colonial American Jew, 1492–1776* (1970), *The American Jewish Woman: A Documentary History* (1981), *The Concise Dictionary of American Jewish Biography* (1994), and *The Jew in the American World* (1996). His four-volume magnum opus *United States Jewry, 1776–1985* (1990–1993) remains the definitive reference work on the history of the Jew in North America.

11 Jacob R. Marcus Oral History Interview with Nick Clooney, Sept. 28, 1986, CD-394, AJA.

12 On Marcus, see Jon Butler, "Jacob Rader Marcus and the Revival of Early American History, 1930–1960," *American Jewish Archives Journal* 50:1-2 (1998): 28–39; Stanley F. Chyet, "Jacob Rader Marcus—A Biographical Sketch" in *Essays in American Jewish History to Commemorate the Tenth Anniversary of the Founding of the American Jewish Archives Under the Direction of Jacob Rader Marcus* (Cincinnati, OH: American Jewish Archives, 1958), 1–22; Randall M. Falk, *Bright Eminence: The Life and Thought of Jacob Rader Marcus: Scholar, Mentor, Counselor, for Three Generations of Rabbis and Lay Leaders of American Jewry* (Malibu, CA: Joseph Simon Pangloss Press, 1994); Jeffrey S. Gurock, "Jacob Rader Marcus, Salo W. Baron, and the Public's Need to Know American Jewish History" *American Jewish Archives Journal* 50:1-2 (1998): 22–27; Jonathan D. Sarna, "Jacob Rader Marcus (1896–1995)," in *The Dynamics of American Jewish History: Jacob Rader Marcus's Essays on American Jewry*, ed. Gary Phillip Zola (Hanover, NH: University Press of New England, 2004), 3–12; Lance J. Sussman, "'Historian of the Jewish People': A Historiographical Reevaluation of the Writings of Jacob R. Marcus," *American Jewish Archives Journal* 50:1-2 (1998): 10–21; Gary Phillip Zola, "Jacob Rader Marcus and the Dynamics of American Jewish History," in *The Dynamics of American Jewish History: Jacob Rader Marcus's Essays on American Jewry*, ed. Gary Phillip Zola (Hanover, NH: University Press of New England, 2004), xiii–xxxi.

13 *Essays in American Jewish History, to Commemorate the Tenth Anniversary of the Founding of the American Jewish Archives under the Direction of Jacob Rader Marcus*, ed. Bertram W. Korn (Cincinnati, OH: American Jewish Archives, 1958), 16. See HUC Bulletin (1941), HUC nearprint, AJA.

14 The foregoing quotes are from *United States Jewry*, ed. Jacob Rader Marcus, vol. 1 (Detroit, MI: Wayne State University Press, 1989), 15.

15 The foregoing quotes are from *Memoirs of American Jews, 1775–1865*, ed. Jacob Rader Marcus, vol. 1 (New York: Ktav Publishing House, 1974), 5.

16 See Jonathan D. Sarna, "Jacob Rader Marcus (1896–1995)," *American Jewish Year Book* 97 (1997): 633–40.

17 Warren S. Tryon, "The Draft in World War I," *Current History* 54:322 (June 1968), 339, 344.

18 *Ibid.*

19 For an especially useful analysis of Jews and the draft during World War I, see Christopher M. Sterba, *Good Americans: Italian and Jewish Immigrants During the First World War* (New York: Oxford University Press, 2003), 53–81. See also Alexander M. Bielakowski, *Ethnic and Racial Minorities in the U.S. Military: An Encyclopedia* (Santa Barbara, CA: ABC-CLIO, 2013).

20 See Jacob Rader Marcus's "Officer's Record Book" and his Discharge Papers from the National Guard "by reason of being drafted into U.S. Service," August 5, 1917, Jacob Rader Marcus Papers, MS-210, box 71, folder 6, AJA.

21 Nick Clooney interview, CD-394, AJA.

22 Jacob Rader Marcus Papers, MS-210, box 65, folder 4, AJA. Marcus's father, Aaron Marcus (nee Markelson, 1865–1932), and his mother, Jennie Rader Marcus (nee Reider (1870–1971), immigrated to the United States from Vidz (Widzy), which was in the Lithuanian province of Kovno. Marcus recounted his father's story in the fourth volume of *United States Jewry* (1993), 97ff.

23 Isaac Marcus to Jacob Rader Marcus, April 22, 1917, MS-210, Box 65, Folder 4, AJA. This letter is signed "Isaac and the folks."

24 JRM diary, May 5, 1917, MS-210, box 70, folder 1, AJA. "Mother took my enlistment—wept + moaned. Inconsolable. Father quiet but displeased."

25 Isaac Marcus to Jacob Rader Marcus, November 11, 1917, MS-210, Box 65, Folder 4, AJA. This letter is signed "Isaac and Father."

26 Heintz was a prominent local figure. A graduate of the University of Cincinnati Law School, Heintz was elected as a Republican to serve in the US House of Representatives from Ohio. His term began in March of 1917 but, as soon as the US entered the war, Heintz received a commission to serve as a captain in the US Infantry. He absented himself from the work of Congress for the remainder of his term. He chose not to run for reelection in 1918. For more on his distinguished career, see *Cincinnati Enquirer*, December 29, 1968, 1 and January 9, 1969, 6. See also *Cincinnati Post* and *Times Star*, December 28, 1968, 1.

27 In the diary, Marcus writes using the abbreviation "Bn." for battalion.

28 JRM diary, August 26, 1917, MS-210, box 70, folder 2, AJA.

29 JRM diary, November 12, 1917, MS-210, box 70, folder 2, AJA.

30 JRM diary, November 15, 1917, MS-210, box 70, folder 2, AJA.

31 *Ibid.*

32 *Ibid.*

33 JRM diary, November 15, 1917 and November 16, 1917, MS-210, box 70, folder 2, AJA.

34 JRM diary, November 16, 1917, MS-210, box 70, folder 2, AJA.

35 Isaac Marcus to Jacob Rader Marcus, November 20, 1917, MS-210, Box 65, Folder 4, AJA.

36 *Ibid.*

37 JRM diary, February 22, 1918, MS-210, box 70, folder 2, AJA.

38 There exists an extensive body of historical literature on Jews and World War I, and informative studies have shed much light on Jewish participation in the military, on Jewish attitudes toward the war, on the Jewish chaplaincy, on antisemitism, and on an array of political consequences that affected world Jewry in aftermath of World War I. In addition to

Cooperman and Sterba's work on Jewish soldiers during World War I, see also, Michael Adler and Max R. G. Freeman, *British Jewry Book of Honour* (London: Caxton Publishing, 1922); David J. Fine, *Jewish Integration in the German Army in the First World War* (Boston: De Gruyter, 2012); Paula Kitching, *Britain's Jews in the First World War* (Stroud, UK: Amberley Publishing, 2019); and Edward Madigan and Gideon Reuveni, *The Jewish Experience of the First World War* (London: Palgrave Macmillan, 2019). On the Jewish chaplains and chaplaincy during World War I, see Lee J. Levinger, *A Jewish Chaplain in France* (New York: Macmillan, 1921); Ronit Y. Stahl, *Enlisting Faith: How the Military Chaplaincy Shaped Religion and State in Modern America* (Cambridge, MA: Harvard University Press, 2017); and Albert Isaac Slomovitz, *The Fighting Rabbis: Jewish Military Chaplains and American History* (New York: New York University Press, 1999). On antisemitism and World War I, see Peter C. Appelbaum, *Loyalty Betrayed: Jewish Chaplains in the German Army During the First World War* (Portland, OR: Vallentine Mitchell, 2014); Joseph W. Bendersky, *The "Jewish Threat:" Anti-Semitic Politics of the U.S. Army* (New York: Basic Books, 2000); William Brustein, *Roots of Hate: Anti-Semitism in Europe before the Holocaust* (New York: Cambridge University Press, 2003); Brian E. Crim, *Antisemitism in the German Military Community and the Jewish Response, 1914–1938* (Lanham, MD: Lexington Books, 2014); Michael Geheran, *Comrades Betrayed: Jewish World War I Veterans under Hitler* (Ithaca, NY: Cornell University Press, 2020); Tim Grady, *The German-Jewish Soldiers of the First World War in History and Memory* (Liverpool: Liverpool University Press, 2011); and Lee J. Levinger, *Anti-Semitism in the United States* (New York: Bloch Publishing, 1925). Regarding the influence of the Great War on Jewry, see Jason Crouthamel, Michael Geheran, Tim Grady, and Julia Köhne, *Beyond Inclusion and Exclusion: Jewish Experiences of the First World War in Central Europe* (New York: Berghahn, 2019); and *World War I and the Jews: Conflict and Transformations in Europe, the Middle East, and America*, eds. Marsha L. Rozenblit and Jonathan Karp (New York: Berghahn, 2017). In addition to this vast corpus of research, dozens of World War I diaries are readily accessible to the reading public. Among the cornucopia of published diaries and correspondences, one finds an interesting selection of logs or journals written by Jewish soldiers. For a roster of diaries and memoirs, see http://www.firstworldwar.com/diaries/index.htm. See also, https://wwi.lib.byu.edu/index.php/Diaries,_Memorials,_Personal_Reminiscences

39 See Sterba, *Good Americans*, 194–95.

40 Jessica Cooperman's excellent doctoral dissertation on the Jewish Welfare Board (JWB) during World War I draws extensively from Marcus's diary, as well as from his correspondence with his parents and siblings; see Jessica Cooperman, "'A Little Army Discipline Would Improve the Whole

House of Israel': The Jewish Welfare Board, State Power and the Shaping of Jewish Identity in World War I America," PhD diss., New York University, NY, 2010, 248–55. See also Jessica Cooperman, *Making Judaism Safe for America: World War I and the Origins of Religious Pluralism* (New York: New York University Press, 2018).

41 See "World War I: Diaries and Memoirs," Veterans History Project Collection, Library of Congress online website: https://www.loc.gov/collections/veterans-history-project-collection/serving-our-voices/ world-war-i/world-war-i-rememebered-100-years-later/wwi-remembered-diaries-and-memoirs/

42 JRM diary, April 18, 1919, MS-210, box 70, folder 2, AJA.

43 See JRM diary, April 18, 1919 and Tuesday, April 15, 1919, MS-210, box 70, folder 2, AJA.

44 There are more than four important topics worth exploring in Marcus's wartime journal, but these four themes appear frequently in the pages of his diary.

45 Bernard Calonius Ehrenreich (1876–1955) received his rabbinical ordination from the Jewish Theological Seminary in New York and a baccalaureate degree from New York University in 1900. Prior to becoming a rabbi, Ehrenreich helped to establish the first Jewish college fraternity, Zeta Beta Tau. Ehrenreich served congregations in Atlantic City, New Jersey, and Philadelphia, Pennsylvania, where he completed a PhD at the University of Pennsylvania. In 1906 Ehrenreich took the pulpit of Congregation Kahl Montgomery in Montgomery, Alabama. In 1915, Ehrenreich founded Camp Kawaga, located in Minocqua, Wisconsin. The Ehrenreich collection is preserved at the American Jewish Historical Society, New York, NY. See Byron L. Sherwin, "Portrait of a Romantic Rebel: Bernard C. Ehrenreich" in *Turn to the South: Essays on Southern Jewry*, eds. Nathan M. Kaganoff and Melvin I. Urofsky (Charlottesville: University Press of Virginia, 1979), 1–12; Harold Wexler "Rabbi Bernard C. Ehrenreich: A North Progressive Goes South," in *Jews of the South: Selected Essays from the Southern Jewish Historical Society*, eds. Samuel Proctor and Louis Schmier (Macon, GA: Mercer University Press, 1984), 45–64.

46 JRM diary, May 1, 1918, MS-210, box 70, folder 2, AJA.

47 *Ibid.*

48 Hazen, Marcus noted, was attached to the 114th Machine Gun Battalion of the 30th Infantry Division. There are no Hazens on the roster of this battalion, though there are two men named Hanson (Charles and Harry). In any event, Marcus recollected that Hazen made an impassioned appeal for Zionism in Yiddish. To justify his belief that Zionism was essential for the survival of world Jewry, Hazen recounted how, when he was in a military

hospital recuperating from an attack of poisonous gas that had damaged his eyesight, he was bedded next to a fellow Jew who had just come out from under the ether after having a leg removed. The man with the amputated leg was moaning loudly, so another [evidently non-Jewish] neighboring patient yelled out: "Hit that Jew with a club and stop his yowling." Marcus noted that the injustice of this remark so angered Hazen that even though he was in agony, he started to rave and curse, and though he was blinded by poisonous gases, he dared any blankety-blank to come over and repeat that and he would kill him.

49 JRM diary, April 15, 1919, MS-210, box 70, folder 2, AJA. According to Marcus, Hazen then cited an incident that occurred when his company was on a march to the front line: "...In a company of 130 or more entire squads dropped out in sheer exhaustion but one squad with a Jewish non-com stuck it out just to show the *Goim* [*sic*] that as Jews they could stick [it out]. Hazen said that if one Jew would have dropped out remarks would have at once been made about the Jew and his courage."

50 Marcus repeated this story frequently to his students.

51 Zola, *Dynamics of American Jewish History*, 72.

52 *Ibid.*

53 *Ibid.*, 61–75. See also Jeffrey S. Gurock, "Jacob Rader Marcus's and Salo W. Baron's Prognostications about the Fate of European Jewry, 1933–1939," *American Jewish Archives Journal* 73:1 (2021): 1–19.

54 Jacob Rader Marcus, "Zionism and the American Jew," *American Scholar* 2:3 (July 1933): 290–91.

55 JRM diary, November 3, 1917, MS-210, box 70, folder 2, AJA.

56 JRM diary, December 31, 1917, MS-210, box 70, folder 2, AJA.

57 During the period of 1900–1920 in the US, only two percent of Jews were intermarried according to the National Jewish Population Study. This number did not grow significantly until after 1960. Fred Massarik and Alvin Chenkin, "United States National Jewish Population Study: A First Report," *American Jewish Yearbook*, 1973 (New York: American Jewish Committee, 1972), 264–315. Leo Joseph Osburg (1891–1968) was a 1st Lieutenant in the Infantry. He is mentioned in *The Official Roster of Ohio Soldiers, Sailors and Marines in the World War, 1917-1918*, vol. 13 (Columbus, OH: F.J. Heer Printing Company, 1926): 12905.

58 JRM diary, August 25, 1917, MS-210, box 70, folder 2, AJA.

59 *Ibid.*

60 Marcus is referring to a man named Allen H. Emerman (1899–1958), although in his diary he spells the name "Emmerman." In referring to Emmerman, Marcus almost always omits the man's first name, but based

on the details he includes in the diary, it is almost a certainty that the Emmerman to whom he refers is Allen H. Emerman who was raised in Ohio but settled in Erie County, Pennsylvania after the war. See John Elmer Reed, *History of Erie County Pennsylvania* (Indianapolis, IN: Historical Publishing Company, 1925), I:547.

61 JRM diary, December 17, 1917, MS-210, box 70, folder 2, AJA.

62 *Ibid.*

63 JRM diary, December 26, 1917, MS-210, box 70, folder 2, AJA.

64 JRM diary, December 6, 1917, MS-210, box 70, folder 2, AJA.

65 JRM diary, November 15, 1918, MS-210, box 70, folder 2, AJA. Phillip Rosen (1896–1969) immigrated to the US from Hungary. The son of an Orthodox rabbi named Bezalel Rosen (1872–1929), Phillip was a prominent dressmaker in Scranton, PA.

66 JRM diary, October 4, 1917, MS-210, box 70, folder 2, AJA.

67 *Ibid.*

68 JRM diary, September 3, 1917, MS-210, box 70, folder 2, AJA.

69 JRM diary November 16, 1918, MS-210, box 70, folder 2, AJA. Marcus is referring to his revered teacher Gotthard Deutsch (1859–1921) and the prominent German-Jewish philosopher, socialist, and founder of labor Zionism, Moses Hess (1812–1875).

70 Jacob Rader Marcus to "Folks" (parents), September 9, 1918, MS-210, box 65, folder 4, AJA.

71 John C. Fulton (1894–1978) was born in Morristown, Tennessee. He became a major in the infantry in August of 1917 and served in the 9th Training Battalion of the 37th Infantry Division as well as the 372nd Infantry Division. He was stationed at Camp Sheridan, Alabama and Camp Stuart, Virginia. Honorably discharged in April of 1918, Fulton became a leader in both the military and in politics, especially in the African American community. See *Official Ohio Roster of Ohio Soldiers and Sailors*, 6: 5735; "Administration's Attitude: Toward Negro Candidate for Delegate at Large is Changed, "Tis Said." *Cincinnati Enquirer*, April 6, 1916: 9.

72 JRM diary, September 15, 1917, MS-210, box 70, folder 2, AJA.

73 JRM diary, October 25, 1917, MS-210, box 70, folder 2, AJA.

74 JRM diary, October 11, 1917, MS-210, box 70, folder 2, AJA. Arthur Hamilton Byers (1893–1918) was born in Crewe, England. During his short career he became a 2nd lieutenant and served as both bandleader and in the cavalry. He died of influenza at Fort Bliss, Texas in 1918. *Official Roster of Ohio Soldiers, Sailors and Marines*, 3: 2395.

75 JRM diary, October 14, 1917, MS-210, box 70, folder 2, AJA. Marcus uses the "N-word" slur four times in his diary. He employs this term when he is speaking in the voice of some bigot he has heard or, alternatively, when he is mocking the hatred Southern whites have for African Americans.

76 JRM diary, November 17, 1917, MS-210, box 70, folder 2, AJA.

77 JRM diary, December 7, 1917, MS-210, box 70, folder 2, AJA.

78 JRM diary, December 12, 1917, MS-210, box 70, folder 2, AJA.

79 On Levinger, see n. 31, supra. See also, Marc Bloch, *Memoirs of War, 1914–1915* (Ithaca, NY: Cornell University Press, 1980).

80 Daniel Hochedez, "Un Historien au Front: Marc Bloch en Argonne (1914–1916)," *Horizons d'Argonne* 89 (2012): 61–66.

81 See Martin Watts, *The Jewish Legion and the First World War* (New York: Palgrave Macmillan, 2004), 138–59.

82 JRM diary, September 10, 1918, MS-210, box 70, folder 2, AJA.

Your Old-New Land Must Have You! Join the Jewish Regiment, c. 1917

Source: Reprinted from David Ben-Gurion, *The Jews in Their Land*, trans. Misha Louvish (Garden City, NY: Doubleday, 1966), 286; original in Haganah Historical Archive, Tel Aviv, Israel.

James Montgomery Flagg's (1877–1960) signature World War I recruitment poster featuring Uncle Sam is arguably one of the most iconic works of Americana ever created. A talented American illustrator and artist, Flagg's captivating design features a half-length portrait of a determined Uncle Sam in a white top hat adorned with a blue band of American stars, and wearing a white shirt, red bow tie, and blue overcoat. His chiseled features are accentuated by silver hair, a white goatee, bushy eyebrows, a piercing gaze, and an index finger pointed directly at the viewer. The bold lettering beneath Uncle Sam exclaims, "I want YOU for U.S. army: Nearest recruiting station."[1]

Given that such propaganda played a critical role in World War I—"celebrating the loyalty of new citizens" and conferring "public legitimacy" on their status as new Americans—it is perhaps unsurprising to find that Flagg's Uncle Sam was imitated in the American Jewish setting.[2] In fact, even before the United States formally joined the Allied Powers, the war's escalation prompted calls in the Jewish public arena for the creation of a British-sponsored military auxiliary force that would fight in Palestine. Although the Jewish Regiment's contribution to the total Allied war effort was minimal, it had great symbolic value for American Jews who relished the image of a Jewish military force that combated the stereotype of immigrant Jews as rootless, cowardly, and defenseless.

The image reproduced here bears a striking resemblance to Flagg's profile of Uncle Sam and hints at that other iconic symbol of the American experience, Columbia. In this instance, a young female figure burnishing the words "bat-Zion" (daughter of Zion) emerges from a large star of David; her posture and facial expression mirror that of her defiant Yankee counterpart. The blue and white color scheme, reminiscent of the Zionist flag, underscores the theme of Jewish national identity. Bat-Zion's flowing hair, crowned by an ornate medieval warrior queen headband with a star of David, is matched by a flowing Oriental tunic with an embroidered collar and sleeves. The totality of the image betokens a sense of classical nobility and conjures up images of Maccabean warriors and ethereal Jewish female figures common in the period's romantic Zionist iconography.[3] In yet another parallel to Flagg's design, the Yiddish phrase at the top of the illustration ("Your Old-New Land must have you!") is completed by the call for able-bodied Jewish men and women to enlist ("Join the Jewish Regiment").

— M.A.R.

ENDNOTES

1 James Montgomery Flagg, "I Want You for U.S. Army," 1917, Library of Congress Prints and Photographs Division, Washington, DC, https://www.loc.gov/pictures/item/96507165/.

2 John Higham, "America in Person: The Evolution of National Symbols," in John Higham, *Hanging Together: Unity and Diversity in American Culture*, ed. Carl J. Guarneri (New Haven, CT: Yale University Press, 1992), 51.

3 Ephraim Moses Lilien (1874–1925), a leading European Jewish illustrator and printmaker, played a key role in shaping early Zionist iconography. Synthesizing biblical and religious themes with non-Jewish artistic ideas, he updated the traditional Jewish "woman of valor" concept as a "modern Jewess" and created a distinctive "Jewish Oriental style" and a "New Jewish Woman" paradigm. (Lynne Swarts, "Lilien's Sensual Beauties: Discovering Jewish Orientalism in Ephraim Moses Lilien's Biblical Women," *Nashim* 33 [Fall 2018], 90, 113.) Some notable examples in this regard are "The Silent Song" (1900); "The Sabbath Princess" (1901); cover art of *Ost und West* (1901); "An Allegorical Wedding, Sketch for a carpet dedicated to Mr. and Mrs. David Wolffsohn Triptych: Exile, Marriage, Redemption" (1906); and "Courting in Spring" (1909). In 1906, Lilien helped to establish Jerusalem's Bezalel Academy of Arts and Design.

CHAPTER 7

JESSIE SAMPTER'S PACIFISM AND THE CURIOUS INVISIBILITY OF WOMEN ZIONIST THINKERS

SARAH IMHOFF

"How to square myself with myself?"[1] Zionist Jessie Sampter asked in "The Speaking Heart," her unpublished autobiography from the early 1920s. She was a woman of paradoxes. When she was twelve years old, she had polio, which permanently affected her hands and back; she also had what we now call "post-polio syndrome," which left her exhausted and in pain for much of her adult life. Sampter never married, she wrote of homoerotic longings in her unpublished autobiographies, and after she moved to Palestine she lived and made financial decisions with a fellow Zionist named Leah Berlin. Sampter, then, was disabled and perhaps queer, and yet she also outspokenly supported Zionism, a movement that championed both physical production and reproduction. Yet this intersection was only part of the paradox. When she asked how to square herself with herself, she was responding to a pressing political situation in 1917 and 1918: "How to reconcile my Americanism, my internationalism, my Zionism?"—and how to reconcile all three with her pacifism.

This chapter focuses on Sampter's thought as to the coexistence of these seemingly incongruous ideologies: pacifism, Jewish nationalism, and internationalism. If internationalists saw the ideal society as one that crossed national boundaries, decried isolationism, and defied any nationalistic chauvinism, how could an internationalist also be a nationalist? Even if the two were compatible, which nationalism would she choose, or did she think it was possible to hold more than one nationalist position simultaneously? A pacifist who opposed the United States entry into the Great War, Sampter accused President Woodrow Wilson of duping the nation and her fellow Americans of going "war-mad."[2] But how could a Jewish nationalist living in Palestine—however its boundaries were drawn, a place in which Jews were a small minority of the population—be in favor of state-building and remain a devoted pacifist?

This essay uses Sampter as a lens for considering the relationship among nationalism, internationalism, and pacifism in the period of the Great War not because any one of her individual positions was wholly unique. In fact, her Zionism was similar to that of Judah L. Magnes, Louis D. Brandeis, and Hadassah leaders such as Irma Levy Lindheim. She shared her dual commitment to internationalism and Jewish nationalism with a small group of American Jews and a strong sense of pacifism with some other prominent Zionist women including her friends Henrietta Szold, Alice Seligsburg, and Lotta Levensohn. Taking Sampter as the central figure shows us something beyond the particular content of her ideologies: her embodied life and political life were profoundly characterized by apparent tension, and yet, she was content—more than content, committed—to living with seemingly incongruous tensions. Presumably competing ideas, values, and attributes were actually fundamental to her intellectual and embodied life.

Surely, we know many people, both historically and in the present, who hold incongruous views. Many, however, take pains to explain why any incongruity only seems to exist. Philosophers and political figures often articulate how apparently tension-filled ideologies can be made to fit together.[3] Sampter occasionally did the same thing, working to show how ideologies, such as nationalism and internationalism, could be harmonized. But more often, instead of trying to banish all tension, she sat with it. She named the friction, and she grappled with the meaning of holding political and religious positions that did not easily mesh. In this way, Sampter's writing is particularly valuable in a larger context of intellectual history because it helps us see that the project of being a thinker need not always be about trying to smooth over tensions. It can also be about thinking with those tensions.

This chapter also stakes the claim for women's philosophies to take their places alongside the men's philosophies currently at the center of Jewish intellectual history.[4] There is already a rich scholarly literature about women Zionists, detailing their contributions to philanthropy, health initiatives, education, and local organizing. Historians have traced Zionist women's activities in the United States, Europe, and Palestine, as well as the effects of Zionism on Jewish women of North African descent.[5] Through this literature, a number of women Zionist activists of this time are relatively well known. Henrietta Szold helped established Hadassah and remained its leading personality even after she stepped down from its presidency. Irma Levy Lindheim became a Zionist at age 31, and moved herself, her children, and her mother-in-law to Palestine five years after her husband's death. Then she joined a kibbutz.[6] Lotta Levensohn was a writer, a Hadassah leader, and an activist. These women participated more in political activism and wrote less than Sampter, and yet they were her peers and friends, and they shared political concerns. They were also some of the leading lights of American Zionist projects, both in the United States and in Palestine.

Sampter's singular story also might inspire us to consider the story of each of these women as Zionist *thinkers* in her own right—to see each not only as an organizer, educator, fundraiser, or "mother of the Yishuv," as Szold was sometimes called. Many of these women were also these things, but that should hardly exclude them from more intellectual matters. Women participated in Zionist philosophy and political thought, though their presence in those arenas was not always recognized, or even uncontested.

To this day, the canon of what counts as Jewish thought is still overwhelmingly a list of men's writings—and the canon of important Zionist writings is even more so.[7] This is in part because there were relatively few women writing publicly in the vein of Zionist thought. But this scarcity is no accident. Women were actively excluded from the ranks of influencers by Zionist men. The Federation of American Zionists (FAZ), and its successor the Zionist Organization of America (ZOA), wanted Hadassah to function as a place for middle-class women to fundraise, not to think or work independently. Historian Mary McCune writes, "Much of the FAZ leadership considered Hadassah a collection agency, a philanthropy, or, worst of all, an insignificant charity, despite the fact that raising funds and distributing them was precisely the role the men had planned for a national women's Zionist organization."[8] Henrietta Szold herself registered her frustration with this contradiction: "There has been constant criticism because [Hadassah] was not political enough, or because it was too political[;] either it didn't think or it thought too independently."[9] It seemed that the FAZ wanted money and women "recruits" but "not their minds," she reflected.[10] Sampter too complained: "Yet the men, with all their appreciation of her personality, never gave Szold the place she deserved on their councils."[11] When historians write about Zionism, however, they should not follow the male Zionists' sexist exclusion. Even if there were fewer women writers, there were some, such as Sampter, Szold, Levensohn, and Lindheim. And even if they were not as widely read as the men, they surely contributed to Zionist discourse and education.

To include some of these women, we might have to broaden our ideas of what counts as a thinker—perhaps by including what they wrote in letters, newsletters, or other Hadassah documents, and not just books and widely circulated articles. We might even consider positions worked out together through interpersonal relationships, such as weighty matters addressed on both sides of continued correspondence, as the pacifism and politics of Szold and Sampter developed. For women who did not write philosophical tomes, we might have to look elsewhere to analyze their thoughts fully.

For other cases, like that of Sampter, the answer is even easier. Sampter should be part of this canon—after all, she published eleven books, dozens and dozens of poems, translations of poetry (including a book of Hayyim Nachman Bialik's poetry in translation), and more than a hundred articles in both English and Hebrew.[12] She also headed the education committee for Hadassah, historically the most successful American Zionist organization by almost any measure. She corresponded with Mordecai Kaplan, Horace Kallen, and others who already appear as part of American Jewish intellectual history. Studying Sampter and her writings also suggests ways that other women might be assessed as contributors to Zionist thought: her thought often emerged through conversations, letters, and others' responses to her writing, as well as her reflections on her own body and emotions. Although Sampter's thought can help us better understand Jewish men's thought about Zionism, internationalism, and pacifism, this chapter tells Sampter's story with reference to the women around her.

Sampter grew up in an Ethical Culture family; they were Jewish by heritage but participated in Felix Adler's religious movement. Adler had abandoned his rabbinical path to found the movement, which emphasized morality apart from specific traditional theologies and whose motto was "creed not deed." As she grew into adulthood, Sampter learned about a vast array of religious philosophies and texts, but she also struggled to find a religious community where she felt intellectually at home. While attending a Unitarian church, she met a Zionist poet named Hyman Segal. The two went to Zionist lectures together, and he encouraged her to think about the importance of Jewish nationalism. Through Segal she soon came to know other Zionists, including the American Zionist leader Henrietta Szold, who would become a lifelong friend and mentor.

Szold brought Sampter into the Hadassah fold, where she became involved in propaganda and Zionist education. Though she noted the Balfour Declaration in 1917, in her words, "it came as no surprise to those of us who had been close to the center, who knew what persuasive personalities had worked with the personalities in power,"[13] in particular, Chaim Weizmann, Albert Einstein, and Louis Brandeis. Yet in spite of her acknowledgement of its potential importance, she still declared "imperialism" immoral. "If chances of war brought us salvation, we should thank God, not Britain," she wrote.[14] Even a new Jewish civilization in Palestine was not enough to justify the violence of war.

A pacifist who grew disillusioned with American politics during World War I, she moved to Palestine in 1919 without any family and with only a one-year employment contract with Hadassah. Shortly thereafter she gave up her American citizenship. In subsequent years, her letters do not mention the Balfour Declaration—instead, citing the 1920 San Remo conference as a more pivotal moment—and she came to be quite critical of the British government in Palestine. Through it all, she retained her complex commitment to Jewish nationalism, internationalism, and pacifism.[15]

Sampter thought deeply and with complexity about the political positions she held. She thought about their ideals, their structures, how individual experience should relate to them, how societies should work if following these ideals, and how different philosophies fit together. She thought about the relationship of God and history. Other American Jews were both Zionists and internationalists, for example, and yet Sampter's writing about these ideologies was particularly articulate and extensive, and she was especially reflective about what it would mean to hold both positions.

In this way, Sampter is unlike Theodor Herzl or Leon Pinsker, whose Zionist writings influenced many people to change their minds and to do political work. She published many dozens of essays and poems in English and Hebrew, but most of her books sold poorly, and she sometimes had trouble placing articles or getting publishers to agree to take on her manuscripts. Politicians did not come to her asking for advice or help. Rather, her writing is compelling because she was articulate and deeply reflective about the philosophies she held, why she held them, and what it meant to hold them together.

NATIONALISM AND INTERNATIONALISM

In the spring of 1914, Szold, having recognized Sampter's intellect, asked her to prepare a speech for a Hadassah gathering. Sampter chose the topic of Zionism and internationalism, and she admitted that there might seem to be a conflict but ultimately emphasized how one could subscribe to both. Her speech, later published as a pamphlet, began by voicing a position she herself would have sympathized with several years before: "We want universal brotherhood. We want to do away with nations. Then why try to establish another nation?"[16] We are internationalists, her imagined interlocutors said. Why should we consider Zionism? Sampter explained:

> The reason I find it hard to quarrel with them is that I agree with them in their main contention. I, too, want universal brotherhood. As a Jew I see that the idea of universal brotherhood is the crowning of Jewish prophecy. And yet the Jewish prophets were all nationalists. If I had to choose between universal brotherhood and the Jewish nation, I should of course choose universal brotherhood. But I do not believe that I have to make that choice.[17]

The philosophies need not conflict, but could coexist in a tiered system, she continued, and this tiered system worked to create peace. Internationalism should not mean the destruction of nations and ushering in of one vast undifferentiated humanity, but instead the cooperation of nations in a society of nations. Different nations have different gifts, and they should work together by each contributing according to its strengths. Sampter's vision paralleled Horace Kallen's well-known metaphor of the multiethnic United States as a symphony of different instruments, though her essay predated his by a year.[18] "Nations are the units in internationalism as individuals are the units of society," she told her audience. "Evolution is from the family to the tribe and free city, from the city to the nation to the international tribunal. Each one of these is a step towards peace."[19] Far from conflicting with one another, the existence of internationalism required the existence of nations, just as families required the existence of individuals. Moving to higher tiers meant moving toward peace—a subject that was becoming increasingly pressing for Sampter as international tensions escalated in Europe.

She poetically imagined a flag, typically a symbol of nationalism, which would represent this new internationalism. Published in 1919, "The New Flag" placed each nation on equal footing.

> I beheld a white flag with a circle of red stars
> upon it,
> And I asked: What is this flag with the circle of
> red stars upon it?
> Then he said: This is the flag of all the nations,
> With a star for every nation;
> Great or small, strong or weak, every nation has a
> star like every other,
> And none can tell which nation has which star.[20]

It was a white flag, as one might see in surrender. But while this flag marked the beginning of peace, it did not mark loss or the relinquishing of freedom.

Sampter's own Jewish nationalism, as she perceived its place in the world, aligned with her commitment to internationalism. After all, in her view, each person should have a nation and therefore a national culture and history because it was these distinctive things that they brought to the internationalist table. In a 1915 essay entitled "The Ideal of Peace in Jewish Thought and Life," Sampter even suggested that the distinctive Jewish message was internationalism: "Every nation has its message. The Jew believes in nationalism, in internationalism."[21] The result of all nations bringing their own cultural assets together would be a better life for all, she explained in her Hadassah speech: "I hope for a confederacy of all nations, for a world-wide solution of economic problems, for universal free-trade, for internationalism, for the fulfillment of Jewish prophecy."[22] Here using a style that characterized much of her writing, Sampter discussed political ideas (economic problems, free-trade, internationalism) seamlessly together with theological ideas (prophetic fulfillment). In the speech, Sampter also told her audience the Hebrew Bible was the source of both internationalism and Jewish nationalism: "What kind of universal brotherhood did the prophets teach? Was it not international righteousness, international morality? Universal brotherhood includes the brotherhood of nations."[23] In later years, Sampter continued to ground her internationalism in the biblical narrative, as she wrote in 1918: "I believe with the prophets that humanity is one as God is one... But also with the prophets I believe that internationalism implies the existence of free, orderly, self-respecting nations, of which the normal Jewish nation is to be one."[24] She described the "mission" of the Hebrew Bible "as a nation, a people, that shall carry out the laws of God in its national life and so be a constant historical spectacle—a sort of morality play—for the nations of the world until they, too, shall walk in the way of the Lord."[25]

Five years after Sampter's Hadassah speech, her fellow Zionist and friend Lotta Levensohn expressed a similar position on the relationship of Jewish nationalism and internationalism. She wrote to *The Nation* in response to an article critiquing Jewish nationalism: "'The Jew' does indeed aspire to lead humanity to brotherhood by the path of internationalism. But his method is that of demonstrating a righteous commonwealth in action. Nations are a necessary and inevitable part of the scheme of things."[26] Sampter and Levensohn, like many historians since, saw ethnic nationalism as a root cause of World War I, and, seemingly incongruously, also promoted Jewish nationalism. But it did not seem incongruous to them. As Levensohn wrote in a review of Sampter's *Book of the Nations*, "Not nationalism, but imperialism, is the heaven-crying iniquity."[27] Levensohn, like Sampter, vehemently opposed the United States' entry into the Great War. She admired the *Book of Nations* because it correctly identified the evils behind the war: chauvinistic nations trying to impose their own cultures and political rule on others. Embracing a national identity was good and natural, but mistaking that nationalism for what was universally best was not.

Before Palestine came under British rule, Levensohn articulated the meaning of Jewish nationalism as something not necessarily identical with statehood: "The Zionists do not aim at the establishment of an independent Jewish state. Zionism does not go beyond the political requirements of the Prophets: the right to self-government in all inner and local matters—that is, national autonomy. Full and unqualified allegiance to the Ottoman Government has been a matter of course in the Zionist program," she wrote in a Zionist primer. Like Sampter, she based her Zionist vision on the Hebrew Bible's prophetic sources: "In this autonomous national center Zionism will strive to realize the prophets' vision of Israel as a 'light unto the nations,' reflecting to all mankind the glory of the presence of God."[28]

Though the Hebrew Bible was the source of the ideal of the coexistence of nationalism and internationalism in Levensohn's and Sampter's eyes, history and sociology also strongly supported the mutual embrace of nationalism and internationalism. (Sampter also saw them in connection: she wrote, "In history, God is revealed to man through his own acts."[29]) In a pamphlet about Jewish history, Sampter wrote: "In America we have begun to see that one can be loyal to more than one country. We can work for both America and for Zion. Indeed the truer Jews we are the truer Americans we can be, for America needs what religion and social ideals the Jew can give her through her love for Zion."[30] Her proclamation sounded a lot like that of Brandeis, who famously declared: "To be good Americans, we must be better Jews, and to be better Jews, we must become better Zionists."[31] Both declarations rested on the idea that the United States benefited from cultural pluralism, in which each cultural group has something special to contribute to the country. Sampter also went one step further and insisted that each nation had something to contribute to humanity as a whole. Many years later, on the occasion of then-Supreme Court Justice Brandeis's eightieth birthday, Sampter remembered him saying something very similar about the broader value of a Jewish national culture: "Working with Jews in labor disputes, seeing their peculiar genius for democracy, I had the wish that this people should be given the chance to develop its own commonwealth, to let the world see this new thing it would create in democratic institutions."[32] A Jewish nation could be an exemplar of democracy, both Sampter and Brandeis hoped, a culture for others on the international scene to emulate.

PACIFISM AND NATIONALISM

"To be a pacifist at war! There is no fiercer struggle," she exclaimed.[33] As Sampter's self-searching query suggested, it was more than just the coexistence of nationalism and internationalism that made her feel at odds with her fellow Americans and fellow Zionists during World War I: there was also her commitment to pacifism. The war's effects made her think long and hard about the political realities in Palestine where Jews wanted to build a Jewish nation but confronted Arabs who saw the land as theirs—a situation that could not be wished away merely by writing about the land as if it were empty, as some Zionists seemed to think.[34] Through a conversation with Mary Antin, Sampter articulated a strong pacifism: if there were a war between Palestine and the US, she wrote, "I should not have to choose" because "I should be against both, as I am against all the combatants now."[35]

For Sampter, war was a product of people's immoral actions; it was neither a historical necessity nor a divinely sanctioned event. Even more: in a poem called "Punishment," she suggested that war was not the solution to evil, but rather a direct consequence of immoral actions and the immoral complicity with those actions. After describing sins with biblical language, she exclaimed, "If I have done these things, what is my punishment? If I have seen these things and held my peace, what is my punishment? This is your punishment: that you must kill."[36]

From the outbreak of war in Europe, Sampter began publishing pacifist essays and poetry. Many are particularly notable because they use martial imagery to describe Zionists, but they explicitly turn the images of war into images of peaceful advocacy and creation. A poem in the *Young Judaean* showed her acknowledgement of the appeal of war and soldiering and her simultaneous desire for her generation and the ones to follow to engage in peaceful nation-building:

> Children, have you read of soldiers/ Bravely marching to the fight?/ Lances bristling, bullets whistling/ Could not fill their hearts with fright?… Have you wish a chance at courage/ Just as great, as hard—and still/ Have you asked: Must every hero/ Hate and maim and burn and kill?/ Children, you are Young Judaeans,/ You are soldiers, if you will,/ Fighting for your exiled nation,/ Yet you need not hate nor kill./ … Live or die to serve your people,/ Not like soldiers, burn and kill,/ But as fearless and as noble/ Serve the world with kindness still.[37]

She hoped the appeal and romanticism of martial images would capture her readers, and that they would then turn their sights to peace. The *Young Judaean*, however, did not share her pacifist stance, and so after the United States joined the war, it continued to print her poetry on other Zionist themes but steered clear of overtly pacifistic poems.

Yet she continued to write them. "The Little Nation," for example, published in the *Maccabaean* in 1919, emphasized that war would not win either territory or ideals: "But I said: I am God's people. The sword cannot destroy and the sword cannot create. But the word of the Lord shall create and destroy... What is gained by knowledge and justice is from everlasting to everlasting; But what is gained by the sword shall be lost by the sword"[38] Later that year, "The Hero" celebrated the figure of a Jew whose strength came not from weapons but from religion and heritage: "This hero bears no shield of brass, no sword of steel. He bears a sack upon his back/ that's bent with toil and shame/ His shield a beard, a visage weird/ His sword—A Name!"[39] Sampter also used theological language and biblical allusion in her pacifist poetry. Another 1920 poem in the *Maccabaean* ended: "Their sin is full, saith the Lord/ They have reaped its fruit with the sword/ The shout of the reapers shall cease,/ No more shall their harvest increase/ The quick shall be as still as the dead/ For over them I will spread/ My tabernacle of peace."[40] A poem from her 1920 collection *Around the Year in Rhymes for the Jewish Child* also used biblical imagery to describe Jewish colonists in Palestine: "These were soldiers pioneering/ with the plowshare, not the sword/ Fighting for the right of nations/ Promised by the nations' Lord."[41] Another poem from the same collection described *yeshivah* students in the following terms: "The nations have/ Their soldiers brave/ That die on battle's field; But Israel's soldiers are her sages,/ Whose swords are words, whose forts are pages;/ They fight and never yield."[42] Thinking plows into plowshares was a cornerstone of Sampter's Zionism, whether her audience was *Maccabaean* readers or children.

Although pacifism was an unpopular position, Sampter was not alone in holding it, and she did not articulate her pacifist philosophy in isolation. Sampter read her draft of *The Book of Nations* to Szold, who discussed its ideas with her and encouraged her to publish it.[43] Attending to her reflections on her deep conversations with others encourages us to think about philosophies as not just the product of a single mind, but of a whole person, including her relationships with others. Sampter and Szold found themselves with similar political conundrums when it came to combining pacifism and Zionism in the United States. In the early 1920s, Sampter recalled her life at the outset of World War I: "War had broken out. I was with the vehement opposition; I had long been a member of the Women's Peace Party; now I joined the People's Council formed at the last moment to plead for a plebiscite, to keep us out of the slaughter."[44] As its name suggests, the Women's Peace Party formed in 1915 in response to World War I, and the People's Council was founded in 1917 to oppose Woodrow Wilson's decision for the US to enter the war. Henrietta Szold also joined both organizations. Szold wrote to Richard Gottheil, a second-generation American Zionist leader and professor of Semitics at Columbia University: "I am afraid you will have to bracket me with Dr. [Judah L.] Magnes and Miss [Lillian] Wald. I am anti-war, anti-this-war, and anti-all-war . . . My position—for me—is the essence of my religious and philosophical makeup."[45] Magnes was a prominent American Zionist who would eventually also move to Palestine and become president of the Hebrew University in Jerusalem. Wald was a well-known progressive activist and settlement house worker. The two had made their antiwar stances known, much to the chagrin of many of their American Jewish associates. Other Zionists wanted to spare the Zionist movement any additional embarrassment or fodder for accusations of anti-Americanism.

Pacifists had good company in the upper ranks of Hadassah: Six of the nine members of Hadassah's central committee were pacifists (Sampter, Szold, Lotta Levensohn, Nellie Straus Mochenson, Gertrude Rosenblatt, and Alice Seligsburg).[46] Yet they were the minority among American Zionists.[47] When Szold wrote a letter representing the pacifist group, Zionist leaders on the (wartime) Provisional Executive Committee for Zionist Affairs asked them not to resign from all official positions, including those in Hadassah. But that was not the end of the story: Szold, Sampter, Levensohn, and the others were asked to resign from the People's Council for Peace and Democracy because it engaged in "anti-government" activities.[48] Around the same time, Gotthard Deutsch narrowly averted being dismissed from his position as a professor at Hebrew Union College for his own membership in the People's Council.[49]

Szold and Sampter were not being paranoid when they agonized over their associations and worried that others were questioning their Americanism because of their pacifism. After they were asked to resign from the People's Council, Sampter wrote to Szold: "I believe we should refuse to discuss the merits of pro-war or anti-war, and insist that as moral beings our moral convictions are ultimate things which we cannot subject to any authority, any more than we could steal or murder to advance the Zionist cause."[50]

Szold explained her views in similar terms:

> Why, if I think that belonging to the Peace and Democracy movement is a way of expressing my Americanism, should I sit quietly by while the Zionist ideal is being travestied, and say I will withdraw because my participation may be 'damaging to the movement?'... The movement has gone to war. We are prepared to win by the sword and as a conquest the land which is to be for a sign of peace and justice.[51]

But cowed by Brandeis, Rabbi Stephen S. Wise, Judge Julian W. Mack, and other male Zionist leaders at an official meeting on September 23, 1917, Szold and Sampter resigned from the People's Council.[52] Sampter had already been critical of some aspects of the People's Council, so the decision to resign her membership from it came at only a small cost to her. But the seeming conflict among her support for a Jewish society in Palestine, her United States background, her internationalism, and her pacifism weighed on her heavily. "While I know my position is inevitable," she wrote to Szold, "I am not happier for having relinquished my pacifism." Szold replied, "You have described my state of mind."[53] In her memoir, Sampter decried "this madness of war, this howling discord in the symphony."[54] Some of her poetry in this time reflected the senselessness of war, as the opening poem in *The Coming of Peace* shows: "Brother, I slew thee with my hand/ And spilt, to serve a righteous cause, thy blood upon the land:/ Brother, my brother, I cannot understand/ Why I, to keep the Lord's command, must break the Lord's command."[55] "A time of paradoxes, of vast crossing passions," she called it.[56]

These paradoxes weren't merely intellectual: they often created conflict in her personal life. Jewish women across the political spectrum began to support the war: the National Council for Jewish Women moved its position from peace advocates to lukewarm war supporters, and some communists such as Rose Pastor Stokes thought that war might be the best means to better societies.[57] And many Jewish women also found camaraderie and social fulfillment in the war effort. Irma Levy Lindheim, Sampter's fellow Hadassah leader, joined the Motor Corps in 1917.[58] Lindheim later recalled:

> Whereas I had sought unsuccessfully for such a niche in peacetime, in wartime I had found my place in a group with a purpose, serving as a group in a common cause... The satisfaction I had longed for but never before found—of belonging to a group, and working, moreover, in service necessary to my country—was very great.[59]

In sum, Sampter's continued commitment to pacifism even after the United States entered the war was remarkable, especially since opposition to a war tends to decrease once a country enters it.[60] After Wilson's Fourteen Points speech, in which he laid out his peace plan for Europe and the US after the war, Sampter briefly wondered if she had been mistaken; perhaps war was the only way. But she soon returned to pacifism and expressed her frustration toward politicians like Wilson who used the drumbeat of war to seduce Americans. "How lonely was the pacifist!"

Sampter remarked. While her sister Elvie knitted socks for Allied soldiers, she knitted baby caps for Palestine.[61] After the United States entered the war in April 1917, she reported that she was a lonely "no" vote on whether the ZOA should encourage enlistment in the US armed forces.[62]

Later that year she used her own prophetic voice; she published *Sefer ha-Goyim* (The Book of the Nations) which used a prophetic style to decry the evils of pitting nation against nation. In place of a traditional author credit, the book said it was "transcribed by J. E. Sampter," suggesting not so subtly that its true author was God and Sampter was his messenger. Using biblical verses and imagery, Sampter excoriated modern nations for imperialist and economic sins that led the world into war: "I shall destroy the nations with their own weapons, saith the Lord."[63] She later summarized its warning:

> God would destroy the nations by their own weapons, as he destroyed in the flood, but Israel reminds him of his ancient promise to make of it a nation to save the nations. And he spares the nations for the sake of that hope, and he repeats the promise, in the face of despair, in the face of groveling, destroyed degenerate Jewry.[64]

God had kept the nations from destroying one another, Sampter asserted, not because they were behaving well but because of a promise to a small and "destroyed" nation.[65]

Though few shared her views, Sampter held firm to her conviction that pacifism and Zionism were not only compatible, but also logically intertwined. Before the war, in "The Ideal of Peace in Jewish Thought and Life," she had written, "two thousand years of wandering have left the Jewish people, the Jewish nation, firmly based as ever on the religious national ideal"—the ideal of peace.[66] "Not by power and not by might, but by my spirit, saith the Lord," she declaimed.[67] Though Jews loyally fought in the wars of their adopted countries, they did not fight on behalf of their own nation for the fundamental reason that war was not the Jewish answer, she explained. Jewish history often meant suffering, but it also meant keeping this peace-loving tradition: "Long suffering, non-resistance, and the healing peace of their religious life—this has been the existence of the exiled people among the oppressive nations."[68] Zionism, as the national movement of the Jews, was then fundamentally grounded in peace. Theologically and historically, the Jewish tradition from the biblical era to the present sustained a peace-loving Jewish nationalism.

Sampter connected ideas of nationalism and freedom with a fundamentally antiwar stance, and she saw all three as central to Jewish philosophy. War was "an enslavement of the spirit of man."[69] At its opposite was the "Jewish vision of freedom, of coming forth from Egyptian bondage to self-determination, of casting off the laws of others and accepting the laws of our own God, of our own ideal, is the vision that shall save the world, the salvation of nations as of individuals. It runs all through Jewish thought."[70]

Sampter also considered Zionism a practical solution to worldly issues. She saw it as substitute for the collective feelings provoked by war: "The Zionist movement... has solved for the Jew at least the problem of how to arouse all the nobility, loyalty, emotion, and self sacrifice aroused by war without the hate and brutality of war."[71] Sampter also envisioned that "the Jewish commonwealth, guaranteed by all nations... would stand as a watchman of peace between the East and West, at the very center of international strife."[72] Zionism and pacifism were two sides of the same coin for Sampter—though not everyone shared her view.

Americanism and Zionism

Amid both the war and Jewish nationalist hopes, the British government issued the Balfour Declaration: a document that might seem to be Zionists' dream come true. Sampter, however, wrote of it as a dark time. The land of Palestine suffered, and Jews settled there worried for their lives: "At the same time, the British offensive in Palestine, war crashing through the land of our hope, the Turks threatening a Jewish massacre, and then on November third, in the midst of this blackest anger, the Balfour Declaration, Great Britain's promise to the Jewish people that so far as her power lay, Palestine should become the homeland of the Jews."[73] The content of the declaration "came as no surprise to us who had been close to the center, who knew what persuasive personalities had worked with the personalities in power."[74] But her expectations were still high: "It was no surprise, and yet it came as an event of astounding import. Empires crashed, mighty men hurled peoples against each other, the Jews shattered among them; and out of this ruin the Jewish people was to be saved in its own land... So I thought. I was a fool, not knowing the barterings of politicians, the visionless opportunism of my own people. I was soon disillusioned."[75] The ZOA promoted pro-Allies war propaganda. Zionists fought alongside the British. The Balfour Declaration itself changed little for the better, as far as she could see.

With these developments, she asked:

> How to square myself with myself? How to reconcile my Americanism, my internationalism, my Zionism? It was not my Americanism and my Zionism that clashed; on the contrary they were in league. Soon President Wilson himself declared that he was a Zionist. The hyphen in America, that spectral proof for a new witchcraft persecution, was only used against our enemies, not against our friends: One dared not be a German-American, or later, an Irish-American, for fear of dire consequences, but no one heard of an English-American. Many Jews with German names took the opportunity to change them to fine-sounding English ones, such as West or Ford,

> yet the only American names I can think of at this moment are Pocahontas and Manhattan, and no one chose them.[76]

Although her Zionism and Americanism might in this moment seem to be good bedfellows, they now clashed (in the light of changed geopolitical circumstances) with her internationalism and pacifism, and she saw the United States in a starkly critical light. English settlers had taken the land from Native Americans, and then their descendants had erased Native people from the notion of what it meant to be a real American and replaced them with white Englishness. Even German-Americans and Irish-Americans found themselves excluded. This was no picture of internationalism, in which each nation brings its own gifts to the whole of humanity. This was a zero-sum nationalism, in which my nation is better than yours. Sampter reeled from the conflict.

In the months after the Balfour Declaration, she continued her Zionist work in the United States, but she began to wonder if she might be intellectually and politically happier in Palestine. In 1918, Mordecai M. Kaplan offered to pay her for two hours of assistance each day, but then Henrietta Szold asked if she might work for the ZOA instead. Sampter chose Szold and the ZOA, even though the total pay for four hours a day was the same as what Kaplan had offered to pay her for two hours.[77] She felt both excited and challenged by the ZOA's request: Sampter's *Course on Zionism* primer for Zionist educators was out of print, and they asked her to create a revised and significantly expanded version that would be titled *A Guide to Zionism*. Part of her task was to write the Palestine chapters herself, but even after reading dozens of contemporary accounts in English and Hebrew she felt unprepared to write a comprehensive guide. "But what could I do?" she asked herself. Her answer was clear: "Go to Palestine."[78]

NATIONALISM AND PACIFISM IN PALESTINE

The secretary of the ZOA initially denied Sampter's request to go to Palestine, but the group eventually granted its approval. Brandeis, who was also initially reluctant for Sampter to leave, agreed in the end. The terms were straightforward, and not terribly generous. She would go for part of the price of her passage and continue to receive her "present salary"—about $2,000 a month in today's dollars. She moved in 1919, never again to live in the United States. In fact, by 1926, she had given up her American citizenship in favor of British-issued Palestinian documents—a supremely unusual move. Few others did so, apart from Simon Agranat who very reluctantly gave up his citizenship to take up his role as a justice of the peace in Mandatory Palestine in 1941.[79]

Though living in Palestine would complicate her Zionism, she remained committed to pacifism, internationalism, and Jewish nationalism throughout her life.

Before the war and before her move, Sampter wrote confidently about the overlap of Jewish nationalism and peace: "Palestine, when it becomes a Jewish state, a sure legislative possession of the Jewish people, must be a neutral, international state, a citadel of peace."[80] But how could a land that was demographically less than 10 percent Jewish peacefully become a Jewish state? How could it be an "international" state? Though she did not fully grapple with those questions in her earlier years, her writings showed subtle ways she still sought to bring together her commitments to pacifism, internationalism, and a Jewish state.

Throughout the 1920s and 1930s, she promoted pacifism to English-language Jewish audiences. Though perhaps it might better be characterized as a policy of restraint rather than a thoroughgoing pacifism, Sampter never wavered from a commitment to Jews and non-Jewish Arabs peacefully living together. As her years in Palestine elapsed, she began to articulate the right of Jews in Palestine to defend themselves, even if that meant violence. After the rioting in Jerusalem in 1920, she wrote for *Young Judaea,* in the fictionalized form of a girl's journal:

> A *shomer* is a Jewish watchman who guards the fields at night against thieving Arabs. These watchmen are all strong, brave young men who ride horseback and carry pistols and are not afraid of anything. The Goldman girls know how to ride a horse and shoot a pistol, too, and they do not mind a bit going out alone at night. I like to think of American girls growing up that way in Palestine.[81]

In 1932, Sampter bought two guns. She hid them under the floorboards of the sitting room in her house in Rehovot, in case a member of a Jewish defense organization needed it for protection. She herself never learned to shoot a gun.

Historian Meir Chazan has written about Sampter's pacifism during her years at Kibbutz Givat Brenner (1934–38), when she wrote for both her community and the Hebrew-language newspaper *Davar.*[82] To both audiences, she cautioned restraint. Jews and Arabs were brothers, not enemies, she insisted, and they should build a new society together. Violence and domination were not the answer. In one newsletter, she chastened her readers to learn their history lessons:

> The goal of the French Revolution was to free human beings. It had wonderful slogans and enthusiastic fighters. Did it achieve its aim? It was also said about the World War [I] that it would bring an end to all wars. It was said that it would save democracy. But it brought the opposite, because love cannot come out of hate, or an improved society out of blood and fire. It is superstitious to believe that justice can grow out of

> killing, and that the benevolence of the next world can bloom out of the consuming fire. This is what the perpetrators of the Inquisition believed.[83]

No matter its noble aims, war did not create; it destroyed. Zionists should not repeat the mistakes of nations past.

Sampter idealized the *kibbutz* as a place that could model the peaceful upbuilding of the land, even when it meant turning the other cheek during attacks by Arabs. In 1938, she wrote a prose poem that was published in the English-language *Palestine Post* and *Davar.* "Something Happened" celebrated the *kibbutz* movement, but also insisted that restraint was a core component of its ideology: "Something happened. Shots were poured, from ambush, on our men on guard. A comrade fell before our eyes, bathed in his blood, who shall not rise. What did we do? We saw it through. Silently we veiled his face; with broken hearts, we kept our place. We stood on guard and so shall stand till peace and freedom bless our land."[84]

Sampter recognized that her Zionism and pacifism might not be ideally or philosophically at odds, but she saw how they created conflict for herself and others around her. In 1934, she published four poems in *Opinion*, an English-language Jewish journal. The poems each featured a woman living in Palestine, and each was accompanied by an illustration by Sampter's friend Ruth Light. These images showed intimate portraits of strong and determined women, yet they were also women who had known suffering. The poem "Sarah the Halutza [*sic*], Born in Russia, living in Galilee in a Kibbutz" dramatized the yearning for peace, its impossibility in the present, and a determined hope for it in the future.

> Peace, peace to the near and the far!
> Peace of the land, peace of stillness and emptiness.
> Those that are far long for it,
> Those that are near rejoice in it.

So still, so peaceful are the light-soaked hills,
The many-shaded vales, the many-starred deep firmament,
Peace like a cloak covers them, peace like a sleeping child breathes in them,
Their beauty is peace, their loveliness is a spirit.
But driven and restless we come to them and there is no peace in us...

We come to our land, we return!
Where is God? Where is our God?
We question the depth of the human heart seeking its fellow.
We will live together, a commune,
Work together, all equal, each lowly and noble;
Work close to the earth, break the heart of the earth
That it may give forth corn, fruit, bread and milk.
We come to find peace in labor and fellowship.
But we do not find it...

It will be different with our children.
They will have been born in this land,
They will have sucked their thoughts from its silence.
They will have plowed quietly above the earthquake.
Pastured their sheep from infancy among the thorns and the lilies.
They will know peace.[85]

In the drawing that appeared beside the poem, Sarah the *haluzah* (Hebrew for pioneer) appeared stern while children played behind her. She knew the violent past and the threat of violence always hanging over the present, but she believed that the future of Palestine would be one of peace. She felt it in the natural world around her—the "many-shaded vales, the many-starred deep firmament"—and she sought it in communal living, but peace eluded Palestine's new Jewish society. She lamented that the present was anything but peaceful and believed that the future could be one of peace if Arabs and Jews could learn to live alongside one another like the brothers they were.

What is missing from this poem is also telling; it waxes romantically about how peace is desirable but impossible at the current moment, all without directly saying anything about Arabs. Many American and European Zionists shied away from talking about Arabs—dramatized by slogans about "a land without a people for a people without a land"—or denounced them as savages. Even other settlers in the *Yishuv* could talk about peace while dancing around the issue, as the poetic voice of Sarah the *haluzah* did. Sampter, however, did write about the relationships between Jews and non-Jewish Arabs. In some ways she was more progressive than many other Zionists; in retrospect, we might call her a binationalist. But she also expressed condescending attitudes toward non-Jewish Arabs, depicting their culture as in need of refining and civilizing.

After years of living in Palestine, Sampter's pacifism remained idealistic, but she also managed to accommodate the idea of Jews using guns into her political commitments. She still saw the Jewish nation as a potential light unto the nations, but she also saw the darkness of the conflict around her.

CONCLUSION

In 1937, a year before her death, Jessie Sampter entered a contest for the best essay about how to combat antisemitism in the United States. The committee awarded her "Cure the Causes" an honorable mention and it was subsequently published alongside five other winners. The collected volume, edited by prominent Zionist leader Rabbi Stephen S. Wise and four other men, met with acclaim, including that of the novelist and translator Ludwig Lewisohn who praised Sampter's essay in a glowing review that concluded with twelve lines of her entry.[86] Those lines reiterated the necessity of Jewish nationalism for the sake of Jews but also for the sake of a contribution to internationalism, which she saw as the only path to peace.

> As a living entity, a Jewish community conscious of its national heritage, rich in the culture of its own people yet discharging with a full heart all the duties and labors of love of American citizens, we challenge our foes, we call them out into the open to show cause why we should do otherwise. We shall not try to make ourselves liked by being agreeable according to the standards of our critics. We are what we are, an international people. Only internationalism—nations organized integrally—can overcome war. Only an international group with a national center can be strong enough to face the world in this new-old struggle for international and intra-national justice.[87]

Even at the end of her life, then, after living through World War I, moving to Palestine, and seeing the often disheartening realities of Jewish state-building, Sampter's vision still upheld nationalism, internationalism, and pacifism as a vision of the future.

Including analysis of women's thought in American Jewish intellectual history is not only more ethical; it is also more accurate because it helps us see a more complete picture. Sampter herself also deserves particular attention: she recognized—rather than always trying to resolve—incongruities in her intellectual and embodied life. She was a Zionist living on a *kibbutz* who could not work with her hands. She held a fundamentally antiwar political stance while she bought guns. Throughout most of her adult life, she was a nationalist, an internationalist, and a pacifist. She did not always acknowledge the extent to which her ideals might clash, but neither did she try to explain away those tensions. She grappled with them in both private and public writing. Seeing

Sampter as a part of American Jewish intellectual history allows us to see alternative ways that a thinker might handle tensions and even conflict among their ideological commitments. As an ideology, pacifism was complex and thorny. So were nationalism and internationalism. And Sampter refused to make them look easy.

Endnotes

1 Jessie Sampter, "Speaking Heart" (unpublished autobiography), Jessie Sampter Papers, A219, Folders 11 and 12, 417, Central Zionist Archives (hereafter: "CZA").

2 Sampter, "Speaking Heart," 244.

3 For a close comparison that pursues this harmonizing impulse, see Hermann Cohen's work on internationalism, nationalism, and war. Cohen's thought sought to resolve tensions. Hermann Cohen, *Deutschtum und Judentum: mit grundlegenden Betrachtungen über Staat und Internationalismus* (Berlin: De Gruyter, 1915).

4 See, for example, Nils Roemer's review article of seven books on German Jewish intellectual history, in which women or gender arise as only categories that male thinkers respond to. Roemer, "New Perspectives on German Jewish Intellectual History," *German History* 28:2 (2010): 219–27. Notwithstanding critiques as old as Carole Kessner (1994) and as new as Nancy Sinkoff (2020), the "New York Intellectuals" are still discussed as men, in spite of the participation of Hannah Arendt, Lucy Dawidowicz, and other women. See *The Other New York Jewish Intellectuals*, ed. Carole S. Kessner (New York: New York University Press, 1994); Nancy Sinkoff, *From Left to Right: Lucy S. Dawidowicz, the New York Intellectuals, and the Politics of Jewish History* (Detroit, MI: Wayne State University Press, 2020), 3. Specifically about the history of pacifism as an ideology, men play central roles in most scholarly works, including Tamar Hermann, "Pacifism and Anti-Militarism in the period surrounding the Birth of the State of Israel," *Israel Studies* 15:2 (2010): 127–48; Michael Young, "Facing a Test of Faith: Jewish Pacifists During the Second World War," *Peace & Change* 3:2-3 (1975):

34–40; David Aberbach, *Nationalism, War, and Jewish Education: From the Roman Empire to Modern Times* (New York: Routledge, 2019); *War and Peace in the Jewish Tradition*, eds. Lawrence H. Schiffman, Joel B. Wolowelsky, and Robert S. Hirt (New York: Yeshiva University Press, 2007). Similarly, biographies of Judah Magnes, Martin Buber, Steven Schwartzchild, and Albert Einstein discuss their political philosophies of pacifism. This is not to say that there is no scholarly work on women, but the study of women intellectuals has not constituted the center of gravity of the field of Jewish intellectual history.

5 For literature on other women Zionists in the US and beyond, see Rose Stair, "The Woman's Voice in Zionism: Disentangling Paula Winkler from Martin Buber," *Religions* 9:12 (Nov 2018); Gerald M. Berg, "Zionist Women of the 1920s: The Voice of Nation Building" *Journal of Israeli History* 25:2 (Sept 2006): 313–33; *American Jewish Women and the Zionist Enterprise*, eds. Shulamit Reinharz and Mark A. Raider (Lebanon, NH: University Press of New England, 2005); *The Plough Woman: Records of the Pioneer Women of Palestine—A Critical Edition*, eds. Mark A. Raider and Miriam B. Raider-Roth (Waltham, MA: Brandeis University Press, 2002). On Sampter's own education work, see Rebecca Boim Wolf, "Jessie Sampter and the Hadassah School of Zionism," in *The Women Who Reconstructed American Jewish Education, 1910–1965*, ed. Carol K. Ingall (Waltham, MA: Brandeis University Press, 2010), 46–52. On Jewish women of North African descent, see Ella Shohat, "Sephardim in Israel: Zionism from the Standpoint of Its Jewish Victims." *Social Text* 19/20 (1988): 1–35. Of these scholars, Stair in particular frames Winkler primarily within Jewish thought, whereas the others are more properly characterized as social history or labor history.

6 Shulamit Reinharz, "Irma Lindheim: An American Zionist Woman's Search for Truth," *Proceedings of the World Congress of Jewish Studies* 12 (1997).

7 For example, Arthur Hertzberg's classic anthology *The Zionist Idea* collects the writings of thirty-seven important Zionists writing from the mid-nineteenth century to the founding of the state of Israel. All thirty-seven are men. Arthur Hertzberg, *The Zionist Idea: A Historical Analysis and Reader* (Philadelphia: Jewish Publication Society, 1997). Michael Stanislawski's *Zionism: A Very Short Introduction*, published in 2017, mentions only four women—three are poets or singers, the fourth is Golda Meir. Stanislawski, *The Zionist Idea* (Oxford: Oxford University Press, 2017).

8 Mary McCune, *The Whole Wide World Without Limits: International Relief, Gender Politics, and American Jewish Women, 1893–1930* (Detroit, MI: Wayne State Press, 2005), 38.

9 Henrietta Szold, "Address to the Delegates at the Zionist Organization of America at Pittsburgh," June 11, 1928. 4, RG 3 Box 6, Folder 2, Hadassah Archives.

10 *Ibid.*

11 "Speaking Heart," 219.

12 Some of Sampter's books include: *The Seekers* (New York: Mitchell Kennerley, 1910); *A Course in Zionism* (New York: Federation of American Zionists, 1915); *The Book of the Nations* (Sefer ha-Goyim) (New York: E.P. Dutton, 1917); *The Coming of Peace* (New York: Publishers Printing Company, 1919); *Brand Plucked from the Fire* (New York: Jewish Publication Society of America, 1937); Hayyim Nahman Bialik, *Far Over the Sea*, trans. Jessie Ethel Sampter (Cincinnati, OH: Union of American Hebrew Congregations), 1939.

13 Sampter, "Speaking Heart," 243.

14 *Ibid.*, 244.

15 Meir Chazan, "The Wise Woman of Givat Brenner: Jessie Sampter on Kibbutz, War, and Peace, 1934–1938" in *The Individual in History: Essays in Honor of Jehuda Reinharz*, eds. ChaeRan Freeze, Sylvia Fuks Fried, and Eugene R. Sheppard (Waltham, MA: Brandeis University Press, 2015); Sarah Imhoff, "Jessie Sampter, Religion, and Relation," in *At Home and Abroad: The Politics of American Religion*, eds. Elizabeth Shakman Hurd and Winnifred Fallers Sullivan (New York: Columbia University Press, 2022), 115–29.

16 Jessie Sampter, *Nationalism and Universal Brotherhood* (New York: Hadassah, 1914), 2.

17 *Ibid.*

18 Horace M. Kallen, "Democracy Versus the Melting Pot," *Nation* 100, no. 2590 (February 18–25, 1915): 190–94, 217–20.

19 Sampter, *Nationalism and Universal Brotherhood*, 3.

20 Jessie Sampter, "The New Flag," *Coming of Peace*, 24.

21 Sampter, "The Ideal of Peace in Jewish Thought and Life," 8, A219\14, CZA.

22 Sampter, *Nationalism and Universal Brotherhood*, 7.

23 *Ibid.*

24 Sampter, "I Told You So," 80.

25 *Ibid.*, 81.

26 Lotta Levensohn, "Jewish Nationalism," *Nation* 113, no. 2938 (October 26, 1921): 476.

27 Lotta Levensohn, "The Book of the Nations," *Menorah* 5, no. 5 (October-November 1919): 297.

28 Lotta Levensohn, "The Forerunners of Zionism" in Sundel Doniger, *A Zionist Primer* (New York: Young Judaea, 1917), 34.29 Sampter, "Speaking Heart," 225.

30 Jessie Sampter, "What Our History Means," (New York: Judean Press, 1916) 15, CZA 219\5.

31 Quoted in Jacob de Haas, *Louis Dembitz Brandeis: A Biographical Sketch with Special Reference to His Contributions to Jewish and Zionist History* (New York: Bloch, 1929), 163.

32 Jessie Sampter, "Teacher," *Palestine Post* (November 13, 1936): 4. Sampter is quoting Brandeis from memory.

33 Sampter, "Speaking Heart," 242.

34 On various US Zionists' ideas about Arabs, see Raphael Medoff, *Zionism and the Arabs: An American Jewish Dilemma* (Westport, CT: Praeger Press).

35 Sampter, "Speaking Heart," 234.

36 Sampter, "Punishment," *Coming of Peace*, 29

37 Jessie E. Sampter, "A Letter in Rhyme to Young Judaeans," *Young Judaean* 6:2 (October 1915): 57.

38 Jessie E. Sampter, "The Little Nation," *Maccabaean* 23 (January 1919): 6.

39 Jessie E. Sampter, "The Hero," *Maccabaean* 23 (September 1919): 261.

40 Jessie E. Sampter, "The Tabernacle of Peace" *Maccabaean* 24 (August 1920): 41.

41 Jessie Sampter, "The Palestinian Pioneers," *Around the Year in Rhymes for the Jewish Child* (New York: Bloch, 1920), 32.

42 Sampter, "Yeshiba," *Around the Year in Rhymes*, 29.

43 Sampter, "Speaking Heart," 240.

44 *Ibid.*, 239.

45 Henrietta Szold to Richard Gottheil, May 13, 1917, CZA. Quoted in Joan Dash, "Doing Good in Palestine: Magnes and Henrietta Szold" in *Like All the Nations? The Life and Legacy of Judah Magnes*, eds. William M. Brinner and Moses Rischin (Albany: State University of New York Press, 1987), 101.

46 Sampter, "Speaking Heart," 245.

47 See Melissa Klapper, *Ballots, Babies, and Banners of Peace: American Jewish Women's Activism, 1890–1940* (New York: New York University Press, 2013).

48 Sampter, "Speaking Heart," 245.

49 Evelyn Wilcock, *Pacifism and the Jews: Studies of 20th-Century Jewish Pacifists* (Gloucestershire, UK: Hawthorn Press, 1994), 45.

50 Jessie Sampter to Henrietta Szold, September 16, 1917, A125\26N, CZA.

51 Quoted in Dash, "Doing Good," 101.

52 *Ibid.*, 102. The minutes of the meeting (September 23, 1917) are available in the Central Zionist Archives, A125\18N.

53 Joan Dash, *Summoned to Jerusalem: The Life of Henrietta Szold* (New York: Harper and Row, 1979), 120.

54 Sampter, "Speaking Heart," 224.

55 "Brother, My Brother," *Coming of Peace*, 6.

56 Sampter, "Speaking Heart," 239.

57 Klapper, *Ballots, Babies, and Banners of Peace*, 113–14. Derek Penslar explains that "among middle-class Jews, women took the lead in promoting pacifism;" see Derek J. Penslar, *Jews and the Military: A History* (Princeton, NJ: Princeton University Press, 2015), 155.

58 Shulamit Reinharz, "Irma 'Rama' Lindheim: An Independent Zionist Woman," *Nashim* 1 (Winter 1998): 106–35.

59 Irma L. Lindheim, *Parallel Quest: Search of a Person and a People* (New York: Thomas Yoseloff, 1962), 49.

60 See, for example, Adam J Berinsky, *In Time of War: Understanding American Public Opinion from World War II to Iraq* (Chicago: University of Chicago Press), 2009.

61 Sampter, "Speaking Heart," 245.

62 *Ibid.*, 250.

63 Jessie Sampter, *Sefer ha-Goyim* [Book of Nations] (New York: E.P. Dutton, 1917), 24.

64 Sampter, "Speaking Heart," 240.

65 *Ibid.*

66 Jessie Sampter, "The Ideal of Peace in Jewish Thought and Life" (1915), 8.

67 *Ibid.*

68 *Ibid.*

69 Sampter, "Speaking Heart," 224.

70 *Ibid.*, 223–24.

71 Sampter, "The Ideal of Peace in Jewish Thought and Life," 8.

72 *Ibid.*, 9.

73 Sampter, "Speaking Heart," 243.

74 *Ibid.*

75 *Ibid.*

76 *Ibid.*, 244.

77 *Ibid.*, 255.

78 *Ibid.*, 258.

79 Pnina Lahav, *Judgment in Jerusalem: Chief Justice Simon Agranat and the Zionist Century* (Berkeley: University of California Press, 1997), 63–65.

80 Sampter, *Nationalism and Universal Brotherhood*, 7.

81 *Young Judaea* 11 (October 20, 1920): 57. The narrator was describing her visit to the village of Poriyah.

82 Chazan, "The Wise Woman of Givat Brenner," 89.

83 "Yesha" [Sampter's pen name in Hebrew], *"Hirhurim," Alon Givat Brenner* (December 11, 1936), quoted in Chazan, "The Wise Woman of Givat Brenner," 91.

84 Jessie Sampter, "Something Happened," *Palestine Post* (May 31, 1938), 6, previously published in Hebrew in Davar (May 23, 1938).

85 Jessie Sampter, "Sarah the Halutza," *Opinion: A Jewish Journal* 5 (October 1934).

86 Ludwig Lewisohn, "The World's Window: Anti-Semitism Once More," *Sentinel* (October 6, 1937): 5.

87 Jessie Sampter, "Cure the Causes" in *How to Combat Anti-Semitism in America*, ed. Stephen S. Wise (New York: Jewish Opinion Publication Corporation, 1937), 77.

Passover Seder Sponsored by US Armed Services, Paris, France, 1919

Source: US Armed Services Passover Seder, Paris, France (1919). World War I, PC-4808, Jacob Rader Marcus Center of the American Jewish Archives, Cincinnati, OH.

Over the course of the Paris Peace Conference (January 18, 1919–January 21, 1920), a veritable parade of Jewish dignitaries, including representatives of the American Jewish Congress and the World Zionist Organization, spent considerable time in Europe working with and lobbying the victorious Allied Powers on the design of the Treaty of Versailles. With the arrival of the Passover holiday (April 14–22, 1919), the Jewish Welfare Board, in collaboration with the US military, organized Passover seders for American service members throughout France and Germany.

The US military issued a general order for Passover furloughs: "Where it will not interfere with the public service, members of the Jewish faith serving with the American Expeditionary Forces will be excused from all duty from noon, April 14th, to midnight, April 16th, 1919, and, where deemed practicable, granted passes to enable them to observe the Passover in their customary manner."[1] Among the celebratory seders, American and European Jewry's leading figures assembled in Paris for a "Great Seder." The photo reprinted here captures a Passover holiday gathering. Hanging at the rear of the hall are the French, American, and British flags, with a Zionist flag pinned to the American flag. The well-dressed group includes military officers and distinguished Jewish and Zionist leaders: (at left) Judah L. Magnes (1877–1948) and Menahem M. Ussishkin (1863–1941), (standing at rear, left to right) Chaim Weizmann (1874–1952), Julian W. Mack (1886–1943), Louis Marshall (1856–1929), Harry Cutler (1875–1920), and Cyrus Adler (1863–1940), and seated (center) Abe Cahan (1860–1951).

— M.A.R.

Endnote

1 *United States Army in the World War, 1917–1919*, vol. 15: "Reports of the Commanders-in-Chief, Staff Sections and Services" (Washington, DC: Center of Military History, United States Army, 1991), 486.

CHAPTER 8

GOLDA MEIR AND THE BALFOUR DECLARATION

PNINA LAHAV

In the mid-1970s, as Golda Meir was dictating her memoirs to her ghost writer, Rina Samuel, the Balfour Declaration was vivid in her memory. She said: "It goes without saying that the announcement filled me with elation. The exile of the Jews had ended. Now the ingathering would really begin, and Morris and I together would be among the millions of Jews who would surely stream to Palestine."[1]

Of the 444 pages of her autobiography, Golda devoted two paragraphs to the Balfour Declaration. Clearly, therefore, even if the declaration was an important event in Jewish history, its place in Golda's life was modest. This should not be surprising. Golda was nineteen years old when Lord Arthur James Balfour, the British Foreign Secretary, issued the declaration. She lived with her working-class parents in the Jewish ghetto in Milwaukee, Wisconsin, far from London, Washington, Paris, and Berlin, where powerful men deliberated, negotiated, and sealed the language of the declaration.[2]

The first part of this essay addresses "history from the bottom": the political and social reception of the declaration by ordinary American Jews, living far from the centers of power. Within two decades, Golda would become a central player in the politics of the *Yishuv*. As Zionist leaders were racing towards a proclamation of a Jewish state, the Balfour Declaration was progressively exhausting its normative relevance, and Golda, already a recognized Zionist leader, took a part in its burial. The second part of this essay addresses Zionist history from the top and presents Golda's fingerprints on the events that caused the Balfour Declaration to lose its relevance as a dynamic influence on foreign affairs.

HISTORY FROM THE BOTTOM

While Lord Balfour, Lloyd George, Chaim Weizmann, Louis D. Brandeis, and other members of the international elite were busily negotiating the fate of Palestine, the nineteen-year old Goldie (as she was known at the time) Mabovitch, living in her parents' small home, was preparing to get married. Her universe was dominated by raucous and contentious arguments with her mother. It was a Jewish intergenerational struggle, fought in many American Jewish homes in the early twentieth century. Golda and her fiancé Morris Meyerson were both born in eastern Europe, but both arrived in America at a tender age and were shaped by the progressive American culture of their adopted homeland. All they wanted was a simple, secular ceremony at Milwaukee city hall. They self-identified as members of the working class, adhered to socialist ideology and were distanced from what socialists termed (pejoratively) as "bourgeois" culture, they wanted "no guests and no fuss."[3] Golda's mother, Bluma Mabovitz wanted the most festive celebration her means could afford. And from her perspective, a wedding was not a wedding unless it conformed to Jewish religious law.

This story gives us further insight into Golda's emerging social identity. Golda was growing up in the immigrant Jewish world that rapidly moved away from the orthodoxy of the *shtetl* (Yiddish for hamlet)—the Old Country—seeking to integrate into the larger American culture of their new homeland. For Golda and Morris, a part of this transformation was the adoption of a secular worldview. As she explained: "We were socialists, tolerant of tradition, but in no way bound by ritual. We neither wanted nor needed a religious ceremony."[4]

Golda reported that Rabbi Solomon Scheinfeld, who officiated in her wedding ceremony, was "one of the true Jewish scholars of Milwaukee."[5] Strictly orthodox, we learn that he would not eat or drink outside his home, but also that on this occasion he did make an exception and tasted her mother's cake. Mother Bluma, it turns out, was known as an excellent baker.[6]

One faces the representatives of three American Jewish generations. First, the rabbi, representing the "Old World" of Jewish orthodoxy. At that time, the larger part of Jewish orthodoxy was opposed to Zionism and disapproved of the Balfour Declaration. Most orthodox Jews of the turn of the century did not expect either gentile governments or Jewish diplomatic efforts by prominent secular Jews like Weizmann, Brandeis, or Lord Rothschild to restore the Jewish National Home. From their perspective redemption was extra political, strictly in the hands of the Almighty.[7]

However, generalizations can be misleading. Rabbi Scheinfeld, born in Lithuania, was a member of the Haskalah movement, a Jew learned in Jewish sources and in addition well versed in the body of Western knowledge and ideas. He was known to have been supportive of Zionism and therefore one may assume that he belonged to the minority in the orthodox camp that did consider the Balfour Declaration as a positive development, maybe even as a signal that redemption in the present time could be on its way.[8]

Golda's mother, an uneducated shopkeeper moved by practicality, always struggling to make ends meet, represents the typical Jewish immigrant in America of the early twentieth century. Striving to blend into her new American environment and leaving politics to men, she was probably oblivious to this historic turning point. It is safe to imagine that she did not see any value in a sixty-eight-word document issued in London. One may also assume that the idea of a "national home" felt irrelevant in the context of her expectations. Bluma had moved too many times. She had been already uprooted from Pinsk in Belarus to Kyiv and then back to Pinsk, always under conditions of abject poverty and harsh authoritarianism. Furthermore, the trauma of the trip from Russia to America was still fresh in her mind. She would not (even though she later did, to join her daughters) consider packing her meager belongings again and moving to an unknown desert land called Palestine. Unlike her beloved Golda, Bluma did not assign high priority to national fulfillment. Her home and final destination were Milwaukee, Wisconsin and as far as her identity, being an American Jew was satisfying enough. Her Jewish identity was traditional and religious. Neither secularism (assimilationism) nor nationalism (Zionism) occupied an important space in her world view.

The nineteen-year-old Golda, by now awakening to the allure of Zionism, was already toying with the idea of moving to Palestine. She was developing a passion to rebuild that far away land, even though she knew very little about it. Moreover, the America of World War I was not too kind to socialists like Golda and her friends, and she might have felt that in Palestine, where capitalism and antisocialism were underdeveloped, she would be more easily accepted.

In her memoirs, Golda offered a pragmatic reason to welcome the Balfour Declaration with some enthusiasm. She recalled that she valued the declaration primarily because of its impact on Morris: "[Morris'] decision was undoubtedly influenced to some extent by the fact that in November, 1917, the British Government announced . . . the Balfour Declaration."[9]

There is tension between the terms "undoubtedly" and "to some extent." One may speculate that "undoubtedly" was how Morris probably felt. "To some extent" was how Golda, the enthusiastic Zionist, felt. Reading between the lines one may hypothesize that for Golda the British announcement had secondary value. What mattered most was the determination, as she fantasized it, of the Jewish masses to return to their ancient land. Foreign leadership was appreciated, but it was not decisive.[10]

Why would the declaration matter to Morris, whose Hebrew name was Meir and who Golda called "Meirke," and even move him to accept his young bride's plan to move to Palestine? Morris, born in Lithuania, was a bright young man, who rejected Jewish orthodoxy in favor of the enlightenment—the arts and the humanities. Like many Jews of his generation, Morris fell in love with European culture and the treasures of the tents of Japheth as distinguished from those (in his eyes) more austere assets in the tents of Shem (Gen. 9:27). Morris was passionate about the visual arts, literature, and philosophy and was especially enamored of classical music. Palestine as an integral part of the Ottoman empire, with all the negative connotations of the exotic or Byzantine Oriental culture (which he probably knew very little about) was not too appealing to him. So, too, Morris found unattractive the idea of nationalism, rising in Europe at the time and reflected in the Zionism of his wife. Morris was "an enlightenment cosmopolitan"—a citizen of the world, embracing universal values and western civilization. His Jewish identity was at best of secondary importance. In the wake of the Balfour Declaration, the thought of British rule in Palestine, therefore, nurtured in Morris the expectation that his cherished universal values and way of life might be exported to Palestine and thereby make his new life more bearable.

To summarize: In these two paragraphs of Golda's autobiography, one hears the chorus of ordinary American Jews, all immigrants, in 1917, reacting to the Balfour Declaration. We hear the ardent Zionists, like Golda, full of elation and determination to seize the moment. We also hear the modern orthodox, like Rabbi Scheinfeld, supportive but certainly not rushing to make fundamental changes in his personal life, and the skeptical cosmopolitans, like Morris, hoping for strong British influence on the course of events. Finally, we hear the apolitical and pragmatic voice of the majority, persons like Golda's mother, uninterested in the potential of the declaration and focused instead on the present. In Bluma's mind what mattered was not the declaration but rather the immediate goal of getting Rabbi Scheinfeld to officiate in her daughter's wedding and eat her cakes.

The Balfour Declaration was indeed received with enthusiasm in some sectors of the Jewish street. Rachel Rojanski, the leading historian of the Poalei Zion party, tells us that on November 29, Poalei Zion, Golda's party, held a big rally in support of the Balfour Declaration in the prestigious Cooper Union Hall in New York City. Poalei Zion was a tiny party and did not galvanize the majority of American Jewry, but its voice was heard in Golda's circles. At the rally, speakers urged President Wilson to support a Jewish national home in Palestine. Also, Poalei Zion passed a resolution pledging individual commitment to this idea: "We solemnly declare… that at this time it is the sacred duty of every Jew to devote his spiritual and material powers, his life if necessary, to the immediate implementation of Zionism and the revival of the National Home in Eretz Israel."[11]

One of the speakers at this rally was the man who led Israel to independence, David Ben-Gurion. Thirty-one years old at the time, he gave a blazing speech and wrote to his father that he was in ecstasy: "I only know that I hardly knew myself when I spoke, I only felt a storm erupting inside me—and this storm sent the words out of my mouth."[12]

It is not clear whether Golda was aware of these events in real time. She probably experienced the enthusiasm expressed in her home state, Wisconsin, where the *Daily Wisconsin* declared support of Zionism as appealing "irresistibly to the imagination."[13] It is reported that in 1918–1919 there were "4,961 applicants for emigration to Palestine from the United States and Canada," 86 percent of whom were under 45 years of age, and possessed an average capital of $3,115. Among them were seventy-one Wisconsin Zionists."[14] Golda and Morris were two of these seventy-one individuals. Clearly, the number of true enthusiasts compared to the American Jewish population at large, was miniscule.

Golda and Morris were married on Christmas eve, December 24, 1917, some seven weeks after Lord Balfour issued his declaration. Less than three weeks earlier, another famous couple got married in New York City: David Ben-Gurion, the future founder of the state of Israel, married Paula Munweis. Like Morris and Golda, Ben-Gurion rejected religion and insisted on a wedding at city hall. He was an adult, away from home, and Paula accepted his preference for a secular wedding. The leaders of socialist Zionism viewed Jewish orthodoxy as conflicting with modernity. Ben-Gurion, as we know, also thought of the Jewish religion and lifestyle as an impediment to the revival of the Jewish people. Golda, it appears, was less radical. She accepted tradition as a part of life and pragmatically cherry-picked what she was prepared to adopt and what she would discard. To her, Zionism and a secular lifestyle went hand in hand and yet, as she noted rhetorically, some violation of the principle was harmless: "What damage would fifteen minutes under the *huppah* [Hebrew for wedding canopy]... do to our principles?"[15]

To plan her trip to Palestine, Golda assembled a small group of friends who were dedicated enough to the cause. Among them was her sister Sheyna who decided to leave her husband Sam-Shamai behind, take her two small children, and join Golda on the journey. Most details of this journey come from Sheyna's memoirs.[16]

Upon arrival in Napoli, Italy, the group heard the bad news: violence erupted in Palestine. Palestinian Arabs rejected the British plans to open the gates of Palestine to Jewish immigration, gates that until then were closed by orders of the Ottoman government. Of the 82,800 Jews in Palestine at the time, forty-three were murdered and 146 were wounded. Shortly before the groups landed in Italy, riots erupted. In an effort to halt immigration, the Arab porters at Jaffa port declared a strike. They would not carry Jewish passengers from the boats to shore.[17]

The group therefore traveled to Brindizi and from there took another boat to Alexandria, Egypt. From Egypt they embarked on a train, arriving in Tel Aviv on July 14, 1921.

Based on this narrative, and in the absence of conflicting information, it is safe to say that these events were the first to inform Golda of the complications embedded in the Zionist dream and in the Balfour Declaration. The declaration promised a Jewish National Home, but the local Arabs saw Palestine as their home and considered the declaration as an illegitimate and colonialist plan to dispossess them. They were determined to thwart this plan, by violent means if necessary.

The British government appointed a commission to examine the unforeseen complications and halted Jewish immigration until the development of a new policy. From Tel Aviv Golda wrote Shamai Korngold, her sister Sheyna's husband, and her brother-in-law, in Chicago:

> I am no politician and I shall not report in detail about England's policies, but one thing is clear, if we do not leave, England will help us... we already see some good signs. The governor of Jaffa, who acted inappropriately during the riots was demoted, and in his place came a decent man, who applied force to end the Arab boycott on delivering passengers to shore. He sent government boats accompanied by armed police (many of them Jews, in Tel Aviv all policemen are Jews) and brought the pioneers to shore. And the Arabs stood there silently, even though following the riots they bragged about their heroic actions.[18]

From this paragraph we learn that Golda did understand that given the Arab opposition, the British government felt ambivalent about the implementation of its declaration. However, Golda was hoping for British good will and calculated that stubborn Zionist resistance would persuade the British government to stand by the Zionist cause.

We also learn that Golda understood that violence was not the only threat to the idea of a Jewish national home. The economy was no less important. It is not easy to find work, even if you are willing to engage in hard work, she informed her brother-in-law: "It goes without saying that Eretz Israel is not like America and one must be prepared to suffer immensely, economic hardships as well as physical violence."[19]

From her sister Sheyna's memoirs we learn that recent newcomers were getting cold feet and returning to the United States. Golda and Sheyna were expecting friends from Chicago to greet them when they arrived in Palestine, but ironically, or symbolically, at exactly these moments the friends were finalizing their plans to return to the United States. These friends came to Palestine in 1919, two years after the issuance of the Balfour Declaration. They opened a small locksmith shop and intended to stay. However, the shop was damaged during the 1921 riots and the family fell into economic hardship. Like many others, they decided to pack their belongings and return to America.[20]

There were other hardships associated with the hot climate: the absence of electricity, lack of drinkable water (immigrants were warned to drink only boiled water), the unfamiliar vegetables such as eggplants and zucchini they had never seen before, and the unavailability of the beloved potato, a staple of eastern European cuisine. The Jews of Palestine, they discovered, were not always kind and welcoming toward the newcomers. As is often the case, there is a difference between the abstract sense of solidarity one experiences and the actual treatment of the stranger. Jewish Palestine was turning into a typical immigration society with its own veterans and greenhorns. Besides, there was no central planning or organization to implement the lofty idea of nation-building. Sheyna remembered: "In the United States we were certain that in Eretz Israel there is a public address to care for the absorption of the immigrants… we were disappointed to learn that no one took the time to instruct us, no institution considered itself obliged to help us."[21] Like the *goldene medine*—the "golden land" as the US was known among Yiddish-speaking Jews—Palestine was a grand concept full of aspirations and expectations. In fact, both places presented a harsh, difficult, and often frustrating reality.

It was probably at that moment that Golda and her group of American immigrants discovered the truth in the age-old saying that you can take a person out of their culture (America, in this case) but you cannot take that culture out of the person. They may have thought of themselves as "strangers in America," strangers enough to wish to relocate to the "promised land." Once in Tel Aviv, however, they realized they were indeed Americans and being American had its advantages. In a letter to her husband, Sheyna explained how they managed to locate their luggage, lost on the trip from Alexandria to Tel Aviv: "But we are not just ordinary folks but Americans and American citizens, so Golda and Morris went to Jerusalem and there was a great to-do. The American consul and the High Commissioner sent telegrams and, finally, with God's help, the baggage came."[22]

It stands to reason that not only Sheyna was realizing that "they were Americans." Golda, too, who was the one negotiating with the American Consul (by virtue of her excellent verbal skills) probably understood at that moment how advantageous it was to hold an American passport and speak fluent English. Even though she had just left the United States she must have felt the satisfaction of being an American. So, too, the American Consul in Jerusalem treated these American Jewish immigrants as bona fide Americans and thereby enhanced their sense of well-being in the "unknown" land of Palestine. Identity is a complex matter and dependent on geographic circumstances. Perhaps in Milwaukee or even in New York City Golda felt as a "Jewess," perhaps as a "hyphenated American," but once removed to Palestine the discovery of a common language and sensibility with the American Consul must have provided a boost to her "American" identity. In this context, it is also worth remembering that until the end of her life Golda kept her American accent. It could not have been too difficult for her to adopt the Israeli or German or Yiddish sound of the throaty "r" spoken by Israelis. After all, she was fluent in Yiddish and German. Keeping her American accent was certainly a sign of attachment to her American identity.

To make life livable, the grand concept of the Jewish national home, therefore, had to be sweetened and fortified by the help of mighty, non-Jewish, political powers. Jewish nationality was not useful and Israeli nationality was yet to be born. It must have felt good to be an American citizen and have a consul protect you vis-à-vis local powers. The new American immigrants to Palestine joined the thousands of extraterritorial citizens spread across the Mediterranean, living in one country yet benefitting from the protection afforded by Western powers elsewhere.[23]

Being American and fluent in English was clearly an asset enjoyed by other members of Golda's group. It made the integration into Palestine's workforce, such as it was, easier.

Morris found work as a bookkeeper at a British military base. Best friend Regina took advantage of the stenographic and typing skills she had acquired in a vocational school in Milwaukee and found a job with the organization that later became the Jewish Agency. Golda gave English lessons. In her memoirs she wrote:

> In November 1917, the British government announced that it favored "the establishment in Palestine of a National Home for the Jewish People" and that it would use "its best endeavors to facilitate the achievement of this objective." The Balfour Declaration—so named because it was signed by Arthur James Balfour, who was then Britain's foreign secretary, was couched in the form of a letter addressed to Lord Rothschild. It came just at the time that British forces, under General Allenby had begun to conquer Palestine from the Turks, and although in years to come the ambiguous way in which it was worded was to be responsible for endless bloodshed in the Middle

> East, in those days it was greeted by the Zionists as laying the foundations at last for a Jewish commonwealth in Palestine."[24]

The voice here is that of Golda Meir, the seasoned and experienced fourth prime minister of Israel, in her seventies, not the nineteen-year-old bride from Milwaukee, even though this statement is placed in the chronological recounting of events in 1917. By and large, Golda's memory was accurate. The declaration was in fact a letter from Lord Balfour to Lord Rothschild; General Allenby was indeed en route to conquer Palestine, and the language of the declaration was certainly sufficiently ambiguous, as diplomatic language tends to be. However, there were subtle and nuanced differences. While the original language of the declaration stated that, "his Majesty's government views with favor," Golda remembered a much more robust, "his Majesty's government favored." As minister of foreign affairs and as prime minister and versed in the nuanced usage of diplomatic language, it is quite likely that Golda would agree that viewing a plan "with favor" is not the same as simply favoring the same plan. More important, her rendition omitted the declaration's crucial qualification: "It being clearly understood that nothing shall be done which may prejudice the civil and religious rights of existing non-Jewish communities in Palestine, or the rights and political status enjoyed by Jews in any other country."[25] Without delving into the nuanced content of this proviso, it is hard to deny that Golda's omission is a good example of the difference between history and memory and a reminder of how treacherous and self-serving memory can be.

It would be interesting to reflect on the various stages that the Balfour Declaration underwent in Golda's mind, from the first time she encountered the exact language of the declaration, to the final moment of its rendition in her memoirs.

Three events depict Golda's interaction with the declaration as well as with the political history of Palestine prior to Israel's Declaration of Independence in 1948.

1. The British debate concerning the final decision to recommend the partition of Palestine. The question of partition agonized the Zionist leadership throughout the 1930s and early 1940s. By that time Golda was already a power to contend with and she opposed partition vehemently. It is quite possible that her opposition was partially rooted in her American background. In her childhood, Golda, like every school child in the United States, opened the day by placing her hand on her heart and pledging "allegiance to the Flag… and to the Republic for which it stands, one Nation under God, indivisible, with liberty and justice for all." The emphasis should be on the notion of "indivisible." The idea that the union was indivisible was grafted deeply into the psyche of every American child, Golda included. The thought of partition, therefore, constituted a warning sign signaling danger. It is also important to realize that as time passed she changed her mind. She realized that a compromise resulting in a tiny state—"*medinonet*," she called it—might have enabled Jewish refugees to escape from the Nazi hell in Europe. However, when the partition plan was first debated hers was one of the louder voices opposing a compromise.[26]

2. In 1948, shortly before Israel declared independence, Golda was sent on a secret mission to King Abdullah of Jordan. Her task was to avoid the imminent war between the *Yishuv* and its Arab detractors. King Abdullah had been a party to the diplomatic negotiations that preceded the Balfour Declaration, and was already the beneficiary of a part of Palestine which came to be known as "Transjordan." He nursed hopes and expectations to restore the old dream of a unified Arab state, a "greater Palestine" under Hashemite rule. That territory included not only the two sides of the River Jordan but also parts of what now is Syria. During his meeting with Golda, he emphasized that he could not accept the *Yishuv*'s offer of a compromise and partitioning

of the territory west of the Jordan River. Golda, thereby, was again confronted with the historical memory of the early twentieth century, with territorial plans and controversies obtained prior to World War I as well as the redrawn borders by the Sykes-Picot agreement of 1916. She could have reflected on the interaction between history and geography and its powerful grasp over contemporary politics. The region was marching to its own drum, and it was not the Jewish drum. Golda and the leadership of the *Yishuv,* wished either to stir the region away from its history or had faith in the power of their more ancient (2,000 years old, asshe enjoyed repeating) history to change that music.[27]

3. Golda was one of the few who shaped Zionist foreign policy on behalf of the Jewish Agency before the end of the British Mandate. In the summer of 1946, she considered and rejected the American-British plan known as the Morrison-Grady plan to turn Palestine into a four-canton federation. By then, Chaim Weizmann, the architect of the Balfour Declaration, had lost power as leader of the Zionist movement. Favoring a diplomatic solution based on compromise, Weizmann anxiously watched David Ben-Gurion and Golda Meyerson take over, and firmly and confidently escalate the conflict, heading toward a unilateral proclamation of Jewish statehood. Thus, Golda was instrumental in transforming the promise of the Balfour Declaration, from a moderate expectation of communal Jewish life under British rule to life as a sovereign people in an independent and sovereign State of Israel. [28]

Conclusion

Could it be that Golda was ambivalent about the Balfour Declaration and, if so, why?

Historian Arye Dubnov offers the thesis that in contemporary Israeli historiography the Balfour Declaration has faded or been marginalized for the purpose of highlighting the role played by the *Yishuv* in bringing about the Jewish state. He suggests that Israel's elite did not view the narrative of indebtedness to a benevolent imperial power as valid or sufficiently attractive. Therefore, an alternative narrative was developed, highlighting the *Yishuv*'s activist organization, military action, and enormous self-sacrifice. As this narrative ascended, the significance of the Balfour Declaration as a critical moment declined.[29] It is arguable that as one of the founding mothers of the State of Israel, Golda preferred this alternative narrative. She increasingly amplified the perspective that the State of Israel came about not because of the good will of the British empire and its Balfour Declaration but rather because of the brave actions and sacrifices of the *Yishuv*. Dubnov's thesis sheds light on Golda's ambivalence about the language of the declaration, an ambivalence that culminated in her failure to recall the critical qualification inserted by Lord Balfour into the declaration, concerning the civil and religious rights of the local population.[30] It also explains her observation that "[Morris's] decision was undoubtedly influenced to some extent by the... Balfour Declaration."[31] From Golda's vantage point in the 1970s, as she was writing her memoirs, there was little need for Morris to think that the Balfour Declaration would bring about the westernization of Palestine. Jewish immigrants arriving from Europe would do it, just as well.

One may locate the varieties of Zionist theory along a continuum spanning from utopian Zionism to catastrophe Zionism. Utopian Zionism envisioned a Jewish state that would serve as a model society, based on universal values and communal solidarity. It is an idea imbued with idealism and faith in humankind. Catastrophe Zionism was skeptical of the goodness of humankind and viewed the world as hostile to Jews. Therefore, catastrophe Zionism held that Jews must have a haven they can call their own, where they have full charge of their destiny and defend themselves. Both, of course, are ideal types.[32]

Golda's philosophy included elements of both Zionist theories, but the presence of catastrophe Zionism in her political thought had always been dominant. She never forgot how as a young girl in Kyiv, her parents helplessly anticipated an impending pogrom. That pogrom never materialized but the feelings of fright and anxiety traumatized her tender soul forever. Successive events confirmed her worst fears. The violence against Jewish communities in eastern Europe (where she had many relatives) during and following World War I, the antisemitism of the US government in the early decades of the twentieth century, locking America's gates at precisely the time when other destinations were unavailable, the concerted refusal of the nations of the world to come to the Jewish rescue which she witnessed firsthand as a representative of the Jewish Agency at the Evian Conference in July 1938, Kristallnacht and the horrors of the Holocaust, Great Britain turning its back to the Balfour Declaration and shutting the gates of Palestine at the time of utter Jewish misery—all of these events and more confirmed her world view that without a Jewish state there would be no relief.

Therefore, even though we do not have enough sources to shed light on her views as a young woman, it is safe to say that she saw the Balfour Declaration through the lens of the dire need of the Jewish people for a safe haven and political power. It was nice and good that the British Government looked upon that "Jewish National Home" with favor, but what really mattered was the steadfast Zionist determination to use all means to secure that national home. It is safe to say that her leadership had always been fueled by this philosophy.

At the end of the 1973 Yom Kippur War, days before she announced her retirement from the prime ministership, Golda was reflecting on her war-related traumatic experiences. From her perspective, Egypt and Syria's simultaneous attack on Israel were an inevitable continuation of the Arab determination to destroy Israel. Looking back, she could draw a line between the Arab boycott of her fellow Jewish immigrants to Jaffa in 1921 and the attacks on Israel in 1973. As prime minister, she probably experienced the refusal of the nations of Europe to allow the arms airlift from the US to Israel—at the height of Israeli vulnerability—as similar to the vulnerability of her own family during the days of the pogroms in Ukraine. Reporting to the cabinet about the heated arguments between Secretary of State Henry Kissinger and Secretary of Defense James R. Schlesinger about that crucial air lift of essential armaments to Israel, Golda reportedly stated that Schlesinger had commented to the Israeli ambassador "everyone hates you."[33] She was not surprised. She believed all along that Jews, and by extension, Israelis, were universally hated. From her perspective, that was the reason why the British government recognized a Jewish National Home in Palestine, and not much has changed since. During the tense 1974 negotiations with Kissinger, she confessed the depth of her despair in a stream of consciousness. She said:

> One thing drives me crazy when I address audiences in the U.S.... some very good friends... get up and say with great pathos "and Israel shall live forever." I once said to someone in Canada: "What would you think if I rose to say, out of friendly sentiments to Canada, 'Canada will live forever!'" When they say such a thing, with utter sincerity and out of true friendship to Israel, somehow in the back of their mind they think as a matter of fact I do not know whether Israel will live forever. I want her to exist and I want to encourage her, that's why I say she will live forever. This is the only state in the world about which such statements are made.[34]

Golda did not articulate the complex history leading from the Balfour Declaration to the establishment of the State of Israel, nor did she seek an in-depth comparison between Canadian and Israeli history. She merely envied the fact that Canada became such a fait accompli while the existence of Israel remained in doubt. It is safe to say that in her mind, the State of Israel would have been created regardless of the Balfour Declaration or that the original good will of His Majesty's Government was not necessarily the sine qua non in the long process that brought about the Jewish state. Her focus was always on necessity—the need for a Jewish state as a haven to her persecuted and misunderstood people. Golda's practical mind was not inclined to contemplate the question as to whether this haven could have been created without the policy implemented by the British in the aftermath of the Balfour Declaration. As she liked to say, she was too busy with real problems to speculate on events based on "what if."[35]

Endnotes

1 Golda Meir, *My Life* (Dell Publishing, 1975), 61.

2 For an overview of the acceptance of the Balfour Declaration in the United States and Canada, see Derek Penslar, "Declarations of (In)dependence: Tensions within Zionist Statecraft, 1896–1948," *Journal of Levantine Studies* 8 (2018): 13–34. On the history of the declaration, see Jonathan Schneer, *The Balfour Declaration* (New York: Random House, 2010).

3 Meir, *My Life*, n1, 61.

4 *Ibid.*

5 Ibid. For an elaboration on Rabbi Scheinfeld, see Louis J. Swichkow and Lloyd P. Gartner, *The History of The Jews of Milwaukee* (Philadelphia: Jewish Publication Society of America, 1963), 208.

6 In Pinsk, Belarus, Bluma supported her three daughters by baking and selling her goods.

7 See Schneer, *The Balfour Declaration*, supra n. 2. Reflecting the sexist consciousness of the time, Sir Mark Sykes, one of the architects of the Declaration, proclaimed "gleefully" "It's a boy." Id., 345. See also Itzhak Kraus, *The Theological Response to the Balfour Declaration* (Ramat Gan, Israel: Bar Ilan University Press), 28–29, 81 (Hebrew).

8 See, e.g., Swichkow and Gartner, *History of The Jews of Milwaukee*, 208; Jeffrey S. Gurock, "American Orthodox Organizations in Support of Zionism, 1880-1930," in *Zionism and Religion*, eds. Shmuel Almog, Jehuda Reinharz, and Anita Shapira (Waltham, MA: Brandeis University Press, 1998), 225.

9 Meir, *My Life*, n1, 60.

10 See *ibid.*, 65.

11 Rachel Rozanski, *Conflicting Identities: Poalei Zion in America, 1905–1931* (Sde Boker, Israel: Ben-Gurion Research Institute, 2004) (Hebrew). Rozanski also notes that the implementation of these commitments did not match the enthusiasm with which they were made, see 261.

12 Tom Segev, *David Ben-Gurion: A State at All Costs* (Jerusalem: Keter, 2018) (Hebrew), 138.

13 Swichkow and Gartner, *History of the Jews of Milwaukee*, n5, 255.

14 *Ibid.*

15 Meir, *My Life*, n1, 61.

16 Also joining were Golda's best friend Regina Hamburger and Regina's first husband Yossel Kopilov who was also Morris's best friend.

17 The ancient port of Jaffa was shallow and boats could not reach the shore. Passengers would be individually lowered from the boat and carried through the waves to shore by Arab porters.

18 Letter from Golda Meir to Shamai Korngold (August 24, 1921) reprinted in *Golda: In Memoriam*, ed. Nachman Tamir (Tel Aviv: Am Oved, 1981), 107.

19 Hard labor was also the lot of many Jewish immigrants to the United States. In her memoirs Sheyna recalled the hard work her fiancé Shamai engaged in upon arriving in Milwaukee. He found work in a shoe factory, was given a heavy hammer and asked to beat large sheets of leather. His hands were instantly covered with bruises and infected wounds and he had to abandon the work. Sheyna Korngold, *Memoirs* (Tel Aviv: Am Oved, 1968) (Hebrew),108.

20 *Ibid.*, 145.

21 *Ibid.*, 148.

22 Letter from Sheyna to Shamai reprinted in Marie Syrkin, *Golda Meir: Israel's Leader* (New York: G.P. Putnam and Sons), 70. Note that the erstwhile revolutionary Sheyna, who insisted on a secular wedding at city hall, nevertheless (perhaps subconsciously) mentions "God's help." American Jews experienced a strong tie to Judaism even if in practice they leaned toward a secular lifestyle.

23 See Wansbrough, J., H. Inalcik, A. K. S. Lambton, and G. Baer. "Imtiyāzāt." In *Encyclopedia of Islam*, edited by P. Bearman, T. Bianquis, C. E. Bosworth,

E. van Donzel and W. P. Heinrichs. (Leiden: Brill, 2003), 3: 1178–89. I thank Professor Jessica Marglin for this reference. See also: United States-Great Britain Treaty, United States Department of State Papers Relating to the Foreign Relations of the United States, 1924, vol. II (1924), Palestine Mandate Convention between the United States of America and Great Britain, Signed in London, 3 December 1924, 221. Palestine_Mandate_Convention_between_the_United_States_of_America_and_Great_Britain.pdf

24 Meir, *My Life*, n1,60.

25 Quoted in Schneer, *The Balfour Declaration*, n7, 341.

26 Meron Medzini, *Golda: A Political Biography* (Tel Aviv: Miskal, 2008), 101–4 (Hebrew).

27 *Ibid.*, 193–95.

28 See *Golda Meir: The Fourth Prime Minister*, ed. Hagai Tsoref (Jerusalem: Israel State Archives), 51.

29 Arye Dubnov, "Vertical Alliances, Informal Imperialism and Perfidious Albion: 100 Years to the Balfour Declaration," *Theorya U-Vikoret* 177 (2017), 49 (Hebrew).

30 Meir, *My Life*, 65.

31 *Ibid.*, n 1, 60.

32 See generally Shlomo Avineri, *The Making of Modern Zionism* (New York: Basic Books, 1981) and Gideon Shimoni, *The Zionist Ideology* (Waltham, MA: Brandeis University Press, 1995).

33 *Golda Meir*, ed. Tsoref, 541.

34 *Ibid.*, 626

35 Quoted in *Golda: A Documentary*, dir. Shani Rozanes, Sagi Bornstein, and Udi Nir (2019).

Rebuilding the Land of Israel: A Haven for the Jewish Wanderer, A Homestead for the Jewish Pioneer, 1927

Source: United Palestine Appeal, *Rebuilding the Land of Israel: A Haven for the Jewish Wanderer, A Homestead for the Jewish Pioneer* (1927). Courtesy of the American Zionist Movement, New York, NY.

Established in 1925, the United Palestine Appeal (UPA) sought to unify American Jewish philanthropic and relief efforts on behalf of the *Yishuv*. In practice, it operated as the American branch of the Jewish Agency for Palestine's key fundraising organizations, the Jewish National Fund and the Keren Hayesod. In 1939, the UPA partnered with the American Jewish Joint Distribution Committee to create the United Jewish Appeal. After the creation of the State of Israel in 1948, the UPA was renamed the United Israel Appeal.

In the image reprinted here, the cover art of a booklet titled *Rebuilding the Land of Israel: A Haven for the Jewish Wanderer, A Homestead for the Jewish Pioneer* (1927), two modern youthful figures, presumably *haluzim* (Hebrew pl., Zionist pioneers), stand shoulder to shoulder atop a hill overlooking a verdant Palestine landscape. A vista of fields, dotted with trees, and what appears to be a city or rural colony stretches before them. The man and woman both appear relaxed and confident as they gaze out upon the scene before them. Wearing a brimmed hat and a buttoned-down shirt with an open collar and rolled up shirtsleeves, the man points at the valley with his left hand and holds a pick-axe in the other. The woman, dressed in semi-modest attire including a headwrap (in Yiddish, *tichel*), grasps a rake with a long handle. Though the man appears to be a head taller than the woman, their relaxed posture and healthy countenance suggests an air of friendly camaraderie and equality, and the implied undertaking of shared physical labor underscores their identity as pioneers who represent a fruitful future. The booklet's title accentuates the young couple's investment in the modern Zionist project, even as it invokes the biblically inflected designation "Land of Israel" instead of "Palestine." Indeed, while the couple's appearance hints at a respectful attitude to a traditionalist sensibility (relatively modest attire and head coverings), there is nothing distinctively religious, Jewish, European, or class-conscious about the rendering, leaving open the possibility the image may appeal to a broad cross-section of American Jews.

— M.A.R.

CHAPTER 9

BEYOND PHILANTHROPY AND STATE-BUILDING: THE TRANSNATIONAL IMPACT OF AMERICAN ZIONISM ON POSTWAR JEWISH RECONSTRUCTION

ZOHAR SEGEV

The existential crisis of European Jewry, which began in the 1920s and reached its horrible climax in the Holocaust, led to a significant change in the relationship between American Jewry and the Zionist movement and subsequently between the American Jewish community and the State of Israel. The net result in this regard was the development of American Jewry's overwhelming support for a Jewish state. This process, which originated with the Balfour Declaration in 1917 and grew steadily until the end of World War I, reached a crescendo with the Nazi regime's rise to power in Germany followed by the shocking news of the Final Solution. The climax came with American Jewry's unprecedented political and economic support for establishing the State of Israel and for supporting the state during its first decade. Indeed, it is hard to imagine how the state could have come into being without American Jewish support.[1]

But backing for Jewish sovereignty in Palestine was just one element of American Zionist identity, and not necessarily the most important factor. It should be emphasized that after 1948,

Israeli policy was a key factor in what emerged as a widening gap between the American Zionist movement and Israel, beginning with the refusal of the Israeli establishment led by David Ben-Gurion to promote a meaningful partnership between Israel and American Zionist groups who had played a constructive role in the campaign for Jewish statehood. Ben-Gurion's approach shrewdly exploited the political and economic advantages that American Jewry could help to obtain for Israel while avoiding a genuine partnership and preserving Israel's absolute authority in Zionist affairs and American Jewish-Israel relations. This policy totally alienated Reform Judaism in Israel and strengthened Israeli political policies that were contrary to the sensibilities of most American Jews.[2]

Just how minor the issue of a Jewish state was in the United States, was clear, historically, even among American Jews who defined themselves as part of the Zionist movement. Thus, for example, Professor Richard Gottheil, a professor of Semitic languages at Columbia University, founder of American Zionism, and president of the Federation of American Zionists (1898–1904), asserted in his book *Zionism* (1914) that Herzl's Basel plan did not aim to establish a Jewish state in Palestine. This was indicated, Gottheil explained, by Herzl's use of the term "national home" rather than "Jewish state" in his public statements. Gottheil maintained that Herzl omitted the term "national home" from the Basel plan in order to widen the Zionist movement's reach and reduce the possibility of international opposition to the fledgling movement's objectives. This omission demonstrated, in Gottheil's view, that Herzl and the founders of Zionism did not consider the creation of an independent state to be a paramount goal.[3] In fact, although Gottheil was well aware that many Zionists worldwide believed an independent state to be the movement's ultimate objective, he argued that the unauthorized views of Zionist activists did not represent Zionism's actual strategy or true purpose.

Gottheil also recognized how difficult it was for European Zionists to understand the American reality. He understood that

Zionism arose within the distinctive context of hardships faced by eastern European Jewry, a situation largely irrelevant to the Jews of the United States, and that Reform Judaism's opposition to Zionism illustrated how complex it would be to integrate Zionism into American Jewish life. At the same time, he realized that while American Jews did not need Palestine as a haven, this did not necessarily mean Herzlian Zionism had no place in the American setting. Gottheil saw Zionism's main function as a modern secular movement, not as a means to concentrate the Jews of the world in Palestine. This was impractical in any case and did not answer the needs of Western Jewry in general or the needs of American Jewry in particular. As he saw it, Zionism was first and foremost a means to sustain Jewish solidarity wherever Jews lived, especially given the diminishing role of religion as Western Jewry became increasingly secularized and adopted the customs and language of the countries in which they lived. Over time, he believed, this seemingly inevitable process would threaten Jewish life in the United States and the entire Western world. Gottheil warned American Jews that the mass waves of Jewish immigration from eastern Europe prevented them from noticing the existential threat to their continued Jewish survival. Once the stream of traditional Jews from eastern Europe stopped, he cautioned, Jewish existence in the United States would be at risk unless American Jews adopted an American version of Zionism as their guiding ideological framework.[4]

Gottheil's view of Zionism as an ideology for Jews in the West and for American Jews in particular must be seen in the light of his previous attitudes. In December 1900 he defined Zionism as "a tremendous yearning to be better Jews in order to be better men."[5] To belong to the Zionist movement, according to Gottheil, goes beyond the narrow limits of the Jewish people, extending to humanity in general and especially to those countries that are home to Jews as individuals. It is hard not to see the similarity between Gottheil's perspective in 1900 and Louis D. Brandeis's famous definition of Zionism a generation later:

"To be good Americans, we must be better Jews, and to be better Jews we must become Zionist."[6]

Chaim Weizmann, with his sharp political instincts, understood that American Zionists would relate to Jewish nationality as just one element of modern Jewish existence and even oppose the establishment of a Jewish state. This is abundantly clear in an August 1919 letter from Weizmann to Felix Frankfurter, a future associate justice of the US Supreme Court.[7] Weizmann, arguably the most important European Zionist leader of this period and later president of the Zionist Organization, wrote to Frankfurter as part of his struggle against Louis D. Brandeis, the titular head of American Zionism and the first Jew appointed to the Supreme Court, regarding the issue of fundraising. The American Zionist movement's economic support was crucial to Weizmann's ability to bring the Balfour Declaration to realization. In his letter to Frankfurter, Weizmann presented his views on the fundamental principles of Zionism and contrasted them with those of Brandeis and Frankfurter. Zionism, Weizmann stressed, was built around one basic principle: international Jewish activity within a national framework to return the Jews to the land of Israel and there to rebuild Jewish life. This, Weizmann insisted, was the primary goal of Zionism as an international movement, for which all its attendant political and economic endeavors were required. His own Zionist views differed from those of Brandeis and Frankfurter because their Zionist activity focused on America, whereas Weizmann's strategy focused on Palestine. Inter alia, he wrote:

> You are fearful because you don't enter the depths of the Jewish question. You aren't in it over your heads as we are: you can afford to take it step by step, looking on from the sidelines. You can't afford to take any risks because you have got positions to lose, in contradistinction to us who have nothing to lose. Baron Edmond Rothschild and Sylvain Levi speak like you do. You

> are willing to reduce Zionist activity to a chartered company without profits, but not willing to lift it to a great movement capable of shaking the very foundations of the Galouth [*sic*] and shaking the eternal slavery to pieces![8]

In conclusion, Weizmann pointed out that his life centered intellectually and organizationally on Zionism, while for Brandeis and Frankfurter it was just a part, and not necessarily the most important aspect, of their lives. Reinforcing this point, he wrote: "Brandeis could have been a prophet in Israel. You have in you the making of Lassalle. Instead, you are choosing to be only a professor in Harvard and Brandeis only a judge in the Supreme Court."[9]

In addition to Gottheil, Brandeis, and Frankfurter, Abba Hillel Silver, the outstanding American Zionist leader of the late 1940s, criticized the political dimensions of Zionism. In an article entitled "Herzl and Jewish Continuity," published in a special 1929 issue of *New Palestine* commemorating the twenty-fifth anniversary of Herzl's death, Silver did not ignore Herzl's unique contribution to the emergence of Jewish national consciousness. However, together with his appreciation, he sharply criticized Herzlian Zionism for emphasizing the political process in the regeneration of the Jewish people. In doing so, Silver explained, Herzl elevated concepts from nationalist European doctrines of the nineteenth century and ignored the universal, prophetic elements of Jewish history.[10] Arguing this approach was contrary to the spirit and the essence of the Jewish people, Silver supported Herzl's opponents, particularly Ahad Haam, who stressed the moral and intellectual elements in the emergence of Jewish nationality, rather than the focus on exclusively territorial questions including Jewish national concentration in Palestine. Silver made it clear he did not oppose establishing a Jewish national home in Palestine and moreover asserted it would be impossible to achieve the universal goals of Zionism without life as a nation, but he pressed the case for the centrality of Judaism's prophetic and moral elements in Jewish nationalism. He saw this not as a pipe dream of a few romantics, but a guiding vision of active Zionists. He concluded his article by noting he hoped there would be no further need to stress nationality in the Jewish context: "In the future, Jews must avoid attaching so much importance to the national issue. They should confront not the absence of nationality in the fabric of Jewish life, but rather the influences of nationality on the Jewish world."[11] In sum, Silver took advantage of the periodical's anniversary issue to sharply criticize the very forms of national expression that had arisen to date and presented an alternative rooted in Herzl's work. He emphasized the prophetic and moral elements of Herzl's thought in accordance with his own views as an American Reform rabbi and an American Zionist.[12]

As noted above, the peripheral position of Palestine in relation to the American Jewish experience was, in part, a product of activities and attitudes of the Zionist leadership in Palestine and Israel, headed by Ben-Gurion. Keenly aware of the dramatic changes in American Jewish life in the wake of the Holocaust, he recognized that American Jewry played a central role in the long-term struggle for the Jewish state: both politically, by lobbying the Truman administration to support statehood, and economically, by generating desperately needed support for US loans and aid to the new nation. At the same time, Ben-Gurion, who viewed American Jewish leaders principally as rivals, took great care to prevent any real involvement of American Jewry in the governance of the Zionist enterprise.[13] Consider, for example, the following statement by Ben-Gurion about Silver to a meeting of the Mapai executive committee on the eve of the Twenty-second Zionist Congress (1946):

> The Jewish world changed. We have a new Jewish people. The only significant Jewish community is the American Jewish community. The American Jewish community has unique political importance in the Zionist movement and tremendous

> financial importance in the movement. Those two pacts constitute great danger to the Zionist movement. There is a danger that the Zionist movement would become an American Joint [Distribution Committee] with American supervisors who will control the entire Zionist movement and the Zionist enterprise.[14]

Later Ben-Gurion added:

> Until now the Right hasn't had a Zionist leader in the country [Palestine]. They have a local leader, [Israel] Rokach, but not an outstanding Zionist figure. Now the Right [in Palestine] has found its leader. Silver will not be foolish to appear as the leader of the Right, but he's tied to the Right. He's tied to the Revisionists. He could even take over the next Congress. He is not [Zeev] Jabotinsky. While he lacks some of Jabotinsky's preferences, neither does he have Jabotinsky's failings. He has no war record against the workers. He will send his officials to London and Jerusalem. It will be a government by officials... Silver is the most important leader in the American Jewish community. I am not sure that we can consider Silver as a fascist but we cannot ignore the possibility that Silver will lead with fascist tendencies.[15]

Golda Meyerson (Meir), later the fourth prime minister of Israel, also spoke to her fellow Mapai members in 1947

following the Zionist congress about her deep concerns regarding the American Zionists. Meir served as acting head of the Jewish Agency's political department following Moshe Shertok's departure in 1947 for the United States. She maintained that that congress was a defeat for Mapai: "In the four days I was in the country I managed to speak to a few members only briefly, but the dominant feeling was depression."[16] In her view, the American Zionists were the main reason that "there's not much good to say about the Congress."[17] She insisted that the American Zionists were the strongest political force there only because of the catastrophe that befell the Jews of Europe. American Zionism, despite its numerical strength, she insisted, was not prepared to take on the great task of the hour: "They were the opposite of modest and had no sense that their weight in the Congress was a matter of circumstance, the outcome of the great Jewish catastrophe."[18]

In the late 1940s, following the Holocaust and parallel to American Jewry's intensive engagement in the campaign to establish the State of Israel, Zionist and pro-Zionist sentiment plainly constituted only part of American Jewry's emerging ethnic identity. Two significant episodes help to illustrate this development. The first was the tremendous effort by the World Jewish Congress to rehabilitate the surviving remnant of European Jewry and, in effect, to reestablish and reinforce Jewish life in the diaspora. The second, closely connected with the latter, was the widespread use of the memory of the Holocaust to strengthen American Jewish communal identity.

The founding convention of the World Jewish Congress (WJC), attended by 280 delegates from thirty-two countries, took place in Geneva, Switzerland in August 1936. While the organization itself was new, its ideological roots lay in the transformations experienced by the Jewish communities in the United States and Europe in the wake of World War I, including the British government's dramatic promulgation of the Balfour Declaration. Stephen S. Wise, the Reform rabbi and a foremost American Zionist leader, was the WJC's lead founder and first president. The WJC defined itself as an international organization although, in fact, it primarily operated as an American Jewish enterprise. With headquarters located in the United States, its European and South American offices were financed by American sources and reported on their activities to the WJC directorate in New York City.[19]

The dramatic events of the Holocaust and World War II did not change the WJC leaders' views of a diaspora with an enhanced Jewish identity that would coexist with the emerging Jewish state. They were deeply concerned for European Jewish survivors and felt that rehabilitation was not just a solution for the individual but would also significantly impact the postwar Jewish world. Wise told the European branch of the WJC in 1945 that there should be a division of roles in the Jewish world between the WJC and the Zionist movement. He felt that world Jewry should be defined as one people with a common belief and a common future. Their main postwar problem was obtaining free immigration to Palestine and renewing Jewish life in countries liberated by the Allies. He added that the WJC was placing itself in the service of the Zionist Organization's just struggle and mobilizing all its resources to open the gates of Palestine to Jewish immigration. He praised the Zionist movement and especially the *Yishuv* and asserted the tremendous importance of increasing the size of Palestine's Jewish population to 600,000 as a basis for post-Holocaust Jewish existence. Together with the importance of the Zionist movement's efforts to resettle Jews in Palestine, Wise declared that the WJC was the only Jewish institution interested in and capable of renewing Jewish life throughout Europe. His emphasis on this parallel process challenged those who considered Zionism to be the sole solution to the postwar challenges facing the Jewish people, including many dogmatic Zionist leaders who opposed efforts to rebuild and institutionalize Jewish life in the diaspora. Wise did not believe his Zionism prevented him from dealing with the existential problems of Jews everywhere in the world, including Palestine. Throughout his speech, he drew parallels between the Zionist movement and the WJC, explaining that many Jews and non-Jews were opposed to both. The need for the Zionist movement, he argued, became evident in the early twentieth century and in the future the need for the WJC would likewise take root in Jewish collective consciousness. The parallel drawn by Wise illustrated his desire to fashion the

WJC in the likeness of the Zionist movement, namely, as an internationally recognized world organization with highly competent institutions representing world Jewry.[20]

In practice, the WJC engaged in wide-ranging activities with a view to renewing community life and resettling Jewish survivors who chose to return to their previous homes. It organized programs for community activists and social workers in the United States and in Europe. It produced educational lesson plans for new and renewed Jewish communal institutions in Europe that aimed to help children and adults integrate into postwar European life. There was also a complex legal project to recover communal property seized during the war, particularly in eastern Europe, as the material basis for community renewal. That the WJC endeavored to create a shared postwar national identity among a broad constituency of European Jewish communities, is manifest in numerous position papers, countless speeches, and organizational records and correspondence that underscore its self-appointed role as the representative body of the majority of post-Holocaust world Jewry. Hence, WJC institutions and committees maintained close contact with UN institutions and agencies, and in 1947 it was recognized by the United Nations as a nongovernmental organization with consultant status, giving legal backing to its unique position among Jewish organizations worldwide.[21]

Along with the WJC's intracommunity projects and activity vis-à-vis the United Nations, it operated a research program that compiled data about world Jewry for its own use and that of governments and other international groups seeking to integrate Jews into the new postwar reality. This research was carried out primarily by the Institute of Jewish Affairs (IJA), which was established in 1941 by Dr. Jacob Robinson, who served as a legal adviser to the Jewish Agency, the WJC's representative at the United Nations, and adviser to Justice Robert Jackson, head of the American prosecution in Nuremberg Trials (1945–46). Robinson's pioneering work involved the collection of a vast trove of hitherto unavailable data on the fate of the Jews in Europe. At the same time, IJA researchers worked to create a foundation for discussions between Jewish and international leaders concerning the postwar Jewish future. As the WJC archives reveal, such efforts went well beyond interest in pure research and were intended to provide the organization's leaders with a solid foundation for reestablishing Jewish life in Europe.[22]

Robinson's extensive public career beyond the WJC reflects the far-reaching implications that followed from the IJA's founding. If the legal, historical, and political data amassed by Robinson and his associates highlights the worldview of the WJC during and after World War II, they also point to their keen desire to be intensively involved in shaping and governing the postwar Jewish world. They believed the establishment of a Jewish state to be a central and critical element of world Jewry's postwar political realignment, and they sought to reinforce minority rights and human rights in general as necessary aspects of the continued survival of an international ethnic Jewish diaspora. Thus, while Robinson worked at the United Nations toward the establishment of an independent Jewish state, this was not his exclusive goal. Indeed, he advocated for minority rights in general and fought to protect the status of diaspora Jewry in particular.

In 1941, Robinson introduced the IJA to readers of the *Congress Weekly*.[23] He explained that every European power had established a dedicated research institute whose role was to conduct studies and collect factual data to enable decision-makers to operate more effectively. By contrast, he stated, the world's 17 million Jews had not succeeded in creating similar research institutes, despite the complex existential problems faced by the Jewish people. The Jews' overwhelming existential hardships and the complexity of global Jewish life (particularly war-torn European Jewry), he argued, warranted the founding and operation of a research institute charged with providing vital information to the leaders of the Jewish people and to the international bodies responsible for postwar Jewish reconstruction. Robinson was, of course, aware of the existence of academic research institutes in Palestine and elsewhere in the Jewish world, but argued that they had not provided the necessary data in the past, nor would they be able to act as information providers for the Jewish people's decision-makers in the future. Robinson preempted those who favored establishing the institute in Palestine rather than the United States, arguing that since the IJA was to operate in the diaspora, it was both ideologically and practically preferable that it be housed in New York City. Being located in New York City, he said, would more readily facilitate the IJA's collection of research data and enable it to maintain ongoing contact with Jewish and non-Jewish international institutions and organizational leaders it was expected to advise.[24] Robinson insisted that the IJA's work would not be merely theoretical. The staff, he explained, would examine European developments daily and offer practical plans intended to meet the needs of world Jewry and European Jewry in particular. Its research department would also consider a wide range of Jewish historical themes from the previous twenty-five years, examine present-day Jewish existence from legal, political, and economic standpoints, and propose solutions for Jewish immigration and rehabilitation in a variety of settings.[25] Robinson's fascinating presentation reveals the significance of the IJA's founding vision. It was not by chance that he invoked the research institutes of European powers to explain the need for the IJA. While the Jewish people had no European state of their own, they did possess national attributes and a well-developed political and bureaucratic system, justifying the establishment of a research agency similar to those of the European states. The IJA was thus important not only as a symbol of Jewish nationality in the diaspora, but also because of its activity and the fact the data it collected added tangible content to the abstract notion of Jewish nationality in the diaspora.[26] European Jewry's catastrophic plight in the early 1940s did not deter WJC leaders from driving forward their plans to establish the IJA. On the contrary, the emergency situation and the burgeoning antisemitic propaganda reinforced their awareness of the pressing need for such an entity. The crisis made it imperative to provide the most reliable data possible and to prepare contingency plans for the postwar reconstruction period they believed would follow the defeat of Nazism. Moreover, they asserted that it was precisely the ideological and physical attacks on world Jewry that required the establishment of an academic research institute to contribute to the reinforcement of a national identity in the diaspora and respond in a structured, effective, and rational manner to the enemies of world Jewry.

In 1941, Robinson set out a work plan for the IJA in a secret document that provides an important indication of the reasons for founding the research institute and the areas it would address. He was aware that the creation of a Jewish research institute in 1941, in the midst of the war, could be regarded as a superfluous luxury, given the travails of the war and the dire plight of European Jewry. He stressed that although the war had reached its fiercest moment thus far, it behooved the heads of the WJC to fulfill their responsibility as leaders of world Jewry by preparing for the postwar period. The current Jewish distress underscored the WJC leadership's responsibility to present the Jewish cause adequately and appropriately in the new world order that would emerge after the war. The research to be undertaken by the IJA would provide the WJC with the data, statistics, and work plans necessary for the organization's heads to present the Jewish perspective to international bodies and governments in the most effective manner possible. Robinson emphasized that victory over Germany would eventually be achieved and that only this assumption facilitated any sort of planning for the future. Yet from the Jewish point of view, victory was neither the sole nor the overriding objective. Robinson termed it "naïve" to assume that an end to the terrible suffering endured by the Jews of Europe would "automatically" result in a solution of the Jewish issue. The Jewish leadership had to be prepared to confront the nations of the world to ensure the future of the Jews. This would require painstaking preparation that took into account the dramatic transformation in the status of world Jewry over the preceding twenty-five years, as well as careful study of the mistakes made by Jewish organizations that had represented the Jews in the international arena in the past.[27]

Robinson noted that the proposal to establish the IJA was initially floated in April 1939 and authorized by the relevant WJC institutions. The original intention had been to locate the IJA in Geneva, but with the outbreak of World War II the enterprise was relocated to New York City, where it began operation on February 1, 1941. The WJC granted the IJA an annual budget of $100,000 and the institute quickly assembled a team of four researchers. Its primary objective was the collection of facts and data pertaining to the condition of European Jewry since 1914, with particular emphasis on the fate of European Jews under the Nazi regime. The IJA's scholars were tasked with establishing an extensive archive and library to contain relevant literature, journals, newspapers, government publications, and economic and statistical data on the Jews in the various communities, with close attention to those countries which had imposed economic restrictions on their Jewish minority. In addition, the IJA's researchers would collect any other written material that might contribute to an understanding of the situation of the Jews generally or provide specific information about the plight of European Jews. The IJA's scholars would analyze and process this information and present their findings in the form of publications and position papers. The researchers would focus on the legal and political status of European Jews in light of the sweeping changes since the Nazi regime's accession to power in Germany and the outbreak of the war. Robinson was most concerned about the legal status of the Jews and its impact on their right to participate, through representative organizations, in the political process that would follow World War II. Two years after the IJA was founded, Robinson stressed that even the Jews' possible self-identification as a separate group would be insufficient to guarantee that their representatives could participate in the political process that would shape the postwar world order. He maintained that affording the Jews appropriate international juridical expression and finding a singular formulation that would incorporate both their uniqueness and their legal right to participate in international processes would require the IJA's concerted and strategic efforts. Robinson argued that neither a legal solution nor an organizational structure capable of applying the necessary legal principles was yet in place, since the Jewish Agency, which possessed a recognized status under international law, represented the Jewish people only with respect to Palestine.[28]

In addition to their research foci, the IJA scholars monitored the discussions and preparations by governments and international organizations in anticipation of the global agreements to be concluded in the postwar period. A practical example of this aspect of the IJA's work can be found in attempts by WJC leaders to foster cooperation between the IJA and the research arm of the State Department. For example, in a meeting of Nahum Goldmann and Stephen S. Wise with Undersecretary of State Sumner Welles in February 1941, Welles promised the State Department's facilities would maintain an ongoing and formal working relationship with the WJC's new research institute.[29]

The work plan of the IJA devotes noticeable attention to its projected research on migration and colonization, about which Robinson wrote:

> The Institute, therefore, proposes to study the records of migration during the past twenty-five years and the experiences of that period, especially in connection with the refugee problem. It will study the attempts by governments, free organizations and individuals to bring order and system into an unplanned migration. Open spaces throughout the world and limits of city and country settlement will be carefully studied. Closely related to the migration question is that of colo-

> nization. Efforts at Jewish colonization in the past will be studied and a plan for Jewish colonization formulated in addition to the rehabilitation of the Jewish National Homeland in Palestine. Looking ahead the Institute will study all available data relative to the form which postwar Europe is to take, such as greater units (Federations), etc. The opportunities for Jews in this new world order will be considered in detail.[30]

The plan, with its emphasis on the issue of migration and colonization, represented the view of the WJC leadership during the 1940s and reinforced the impression that the organization did not regard the establishment of Jewish sovereignty in Palestine as its overriding mission, but sought to promote the twin goals Jewish migration to Palestine and the rehabilitation of Jewish life in Europe. The importance of the IJA, however, goes further than this. Its founding during the crisis years of the early 1940s and the breadth of the tasks with which it was charged indicate the belief of the WJC leaders that, after the war, they and their organization would be called upon to play a decisive role in determining the status and shaping the fortunes of world Jewry as an ethnic minority in the family of nations. Robinson and his associates came to realize that the collection and analysis of so great a variety of data and the preparation of appropriate work plans required broad research activity and extensive organizational efforts beyond the capacity of any other organized Jewish body in the world.

In 1951, the WJC directorate in New York City dispatched a memorandum to all the organization's branches in the United States and around the world. The document was part of the preparation for the eighth anniversary of the Warsaw ghetto uprising and traced the main outlines of a commemoration event to be held in WJC branches worldwide. It included the following passage:

> In all parts of the world, wherever there exists a nationally conscious Jewry, this great national day of mourning should be observed with becoming dignity and impressiveness. At large public gatherings an appraisal should be given of those cruel days and of the valor and self-sacrifice of the heroic Jewish men and women of the Warsaw ghetto uprising. Those heroes of ours bequeathed a mission to future generations, namely, to safeguard Jewish existence and to fight for Jewish rights... This year, more than ever before, we must make it clear to the whole world that our brothers and sisters of the Warsaw ghetto and elsewhere *did not die for our people only, but for all mankind* in the battle against forces which are preparing to rise up again not only against our people, but against the triumph of morality and humanity in general.[31]

The foregoing memorandum elaborates on the tendencies that surfaced years earlier in the preparations for the 1944 conference. The events organized to commemorate the Holocaust, especially those pertaining to the Warsaw ghetto uprising, held broader significance than similar events conducted to commemorate the Nazi regime's victims. These ceremonies were part of a broad organizational and ideological strategy promoted by the WJC, the practical significance of which was to create an ambience of nationalism among the Jews of the diaspora in the years following World War II. The memorandum explicitly defines the uprising's anniversary as a national day of commemoration and emphasizes its importance as a universal symbol of the Jewish people's struggle for liberation. In keeping with the worldview espoused by the WJC leaders, it proclaims that the ghetto fighters' war against the Nazis was waged not only on behalf of the Jews, but also as part of an all-encompassing endeavor in the interests of morality and humanity.

The WJC's New York City office advanced its efforts to elevate the Warsaw ghetto uprising as a major component of Holocaust commemoration in the 1950s by instructing its emissaries to ensure that memorial ceremonies marking the rebellion's anniversary be held not only in state capitals across the country, but also in other cities and even small communities. A circular dispatched in 1955 declared that the commemorations were meant to ensure that the memory of the uprising would become etched forever among wide swathes of the Jewish people. WJC offices in Europe and in the United States were required "to send to our office not later than the end of April all material which may serve as a report about what was done in your community as a dignified link in Jewry's world girdling chain, in order that this anniversary may become a perpetual memorial to the greatest manifestation of sacrifice and heroism in our history."[32] The memorial ceremonies were to become part of a broad educational endeavor among Jewish communities and schools including lectures, distribution of historical background material, and plans for discussions on the topic—all with the intent to ensure collective memory of the Holocaust would pass from one generation to the next and such events, denoted by the slogan "Reconstruction after the *Churban*" [Hebrew for destruction], might be invested with a sense of sanctification and empowerment of Jewish life akin to the communal day of mourning of Tisha Beav, marking the destruction of the ancient Temple in Jerusalem and other tragedies in Jewish history.[33]

To facilitate the WJC's comprehensive efforts of inscribing the Warsaw ghetto uprising as a key moment of contemporary Jewish historical memory, the New York office produced a flood of educational materials and circulars intended to generate and support widespread programmatic activity. In 1955, for example, it produced a lengthy document titled "Warsaw Ghetto Uprising: Remembering and Rebuilding."[34] The first section of the document contained a report on a comprehensive survey of the Warsaw ghetto uprising memorial ceremonies and commemoration activities conducted in large urban centers and in small communities in forty-seven countries. The survey generated substantial data pertaining not only to the ceremonies themselves, but also to ongoing educational and community projects concerning the uprising. The report's second section offered an analysis of the survey's findings, as well as guidelines for future programmatic efforts intended to synthesize commemoration of the Warsaw ghetto uprising and activity designed to reinforce Jewish identity. As stated in the introduction:

> In the light of the facts brought out in this survey, the anniversary of the Warsaw ghetto uprising will remain a permanent national or world Jewish memorial day. As the time goes on, the element of mourning will tend to become suffused with a spirit of contemplation and marked by an element of education and the building up of new cultural strongholds. But never will the element of mourning vanish altogether. This will be, as it should, the affirmative answer of a people with thousands of years of history behind it to the uprising of its heroic sons and daughters in the Warsaw ghetto.[35]

In the report's second section, the authors addressed the WJC's efforts to shape patterns of collective memory concerning the uprising. In a series of fourteen carefully composed questions and answers, the authors probed a variety of issues ranging from the involvement of Orthodox Jewish elements in communal memorialization activities to observations of countries with Jewish populations in which no such ceremonies were held at all. Of particular interest is the question concerning the status of memorial ceremonies in the State of Israel:

> *Question*: Is it true that in Israel the commemoration of the Warsaw ghetto uprising receives little

> attention because of an alleged indifference to Jewish affairs outside Israel and owing to a tendency not to have the struggle for today impaired by mourning for yesterday? *Answer*: According to our observation, the reply is clearly no. It is simply not true. It may be true in some measure that the commemorations of the uprising in the Warsaw ghetto are of a less pensive character in Israel than in the diaspora. They are more focused on the idea of rebuilding than of mourning, and this is only natural.[36]

This question indicates that many WJC members believed there were significant differences between the status of the Warsaw ghetto uprising in the collective memory of diaspora Jews and the meaning attributed to it by Israeli society in the 1950s. This impression is reinforced by the answer to the question. From the authors' perspective, the uprising was not accorded the status it deserved in the State of Israel. Moreover, they asserted, significantly different patterns of commemoration had evolved in Israel and among diaspora Jewry.

Determining if and why commemorative activity related to the Warsaw ghetto uprising was accorded a sufficiently meaningful place in Israeli society of the 1950s goes beyond the scope of this chapter. For our purposes, it is important to simply note that the WJC leadership in New York City believed significantly different patterns of Holocaust memorialization were taking root in the diaspora and in Israel and they believed it was the WJC's role to champion meaningful activity designed to ensure the Warsaw ghetto uprising's hallowed status in the Jewish public arena. They were particularly concerned that the distinctive patterns of Israeli Holocaust memory, in contrast to the sensibility of diaspora Jewish communities, consigned memorialization of the Warsaw ghetto uprising to a relatively marginal status.

In 1956, with a view to activating the WJC's global network of affiliates and broadly disseminating knowledge of the Warsaw ghetto uprising among diaspora Jews, the WJC's organizational division published and circulated a wide-ranging booklet in English and Yiddish titled "The Warsaw Ghetto Revolt: Climax of Jewish Heroism and Resistance in the Last 1800 Years."[37] The publication's title is self-explanatory; it establishes the authors' aim to use events commemorating the Warsaw ghetto uprising to shape the ethnic identity of diaspora Jews, and it hints at the idea of a Jewish community fighting for its existence rather than functioning as a passive entity. This perspective is also reflected in the booklet's introductory remarks penned by Isaac I. Schwarzbart, chair of the WJC's organizational division and a former member of the Polish government-in-exile during World War II:

> This year the WJC again addressed itself to Jewish communities the world over to observe this national memorial day. In this connection the Congress urged that the story of the Warsaw Ghetto Uprising be told this year as part of the glorious record of Jewish deeds of valor which adorn the pages of our long history. That the Warsaw Ghetto Uprising is not an isolated Jewish history which has frequently repeated itself, is clearly demonstrated in the accompanying survey entitled "The Warsaw Ghetto Revolt: Climax of Jewish heroism and Resistance in the Last 1800 Years." It is intended to serve first and foremost, our youth in our homes and schools. It might strengthen the ties between our youth and the spirit of Modiin, Jerusalem, Masada, Betar, and Warsaw.[38]

The WJC's organizational vehicle *Congress Weekly* played its part as well in transforming the Warsaw ghetto uprising into a major component of Holocaust memory among diaspora Jews. The issues of the weekly that appeared close to the memorial date carried testimonies and recollections of the uprising and encouraged readers to make the day of remembrance an integral part of public events related to the Passover festival. An editorial column in the March 1953 issue reads: "As we honor the memory of the Ghetto victims in this season of our Festival of Freedom, let us recall their invincible faith in the inevitable coming of liberation and in the ultimate triumph of justice. That is their legacy to us and to generations to come."[39]

The activity of the WJC in the three decades after World War II was quite different from that of other American Jewish organizations. Significant groups sought to structure the relationship between Israel and their own community in a way that would allow them to continue functioning as American citizens while maintaining strong relationships with Israel. Public discussion in this regard came to a climax in the 1950s with the agreement between Ben-Gurion and Jacob Blaustein, president of the American Jewish Committee. In principle, the Ben-Gurion–Blaustein agreement recognized the need for American Jews to show allegiance exclusively to the United States, and in tandem to acknowledge a special obligation to support the new State of Israel. In parallel fashion, Abba Hillel Silver, who emerged in the 1940s as American Jewry's most important leader and continued to hold considerable sway in the 1950s, sought to influence the State of Israel in general and shape American Jewish-Israel relations with an eye to sustaining American Zionism as a flourishing political movement.[40]

The WJC was unique not only in that it its leaders sought to structure relations between Israel and American Jews. It also worked tirelessly throughout the Jewish world, especially in the United States, to rebuild the European diaspora after World War II.

Conclusion

Rogers Brubaker has written about the complex challenges facing a voluntary organization that represents an ethnic minority dispersed among numerous countries. Such an organization strives to operate in a practical manner and to project itself as the exclusive representative of the majority of individuals who belong to the ethnic minority. According to Brubaker, such a situation cannot exist in reality for two reasons. First, the great variety that generally exists within the ethnic group precludes uniform representation; and second, members of ethnic groups dispersed throughout various lands are primarily concerned with existential problems that are not necessarily related to their group's minority status.[41]

The American Jewish community and its leadership did not know Brubaker. However, in their view the crisis of European Jewry created a new existential reality. The crisis and the attacks on Jews were not directed against isolated communities in separate countries. Rather, this was a general phenomenon that distinguished the Jews from the situation of other ethnic minorities and required a transnational response that crossed borders. The hopelessness of Jewish existence in the European diaspora led them to recognize that the only possible solution for continued Jewish existence in the modern age was to establish a Jewish state in Palestine. This view gained momentum and widespread public Jewish support following the Holocaust.

In response to the rise of the *Yishuv* and the changing status of European Jewry in the 1920s, 1930s, and 1940s, the American Jewish community developed an impressive and substantial network of philanthropic organizations, many of them devoted to Zionist activities in Palestine. The Zionist women's group Hadassah, for example, established in 1912, swiftly emerged as one of the World Zionist Organization's most important and impactful entities. Other American Jewish organizations became pro-Zionist or reversed their former anti-Zionist attitudes. The Reform movement is a clear case in this regard: it not only became "Zionized" but was the wellspring that produced the two most important American Zionist leaders of the 1930s and 1940s, namely, Stephen S. Wise and Abba Hillel Silver. Owing, however, to the unforeseen cunning of history, these organizations, originally created to strengthen the Jewish national home, resulted in a dynamic that reinforced the independence of diaspora Jewish life and spawned organizational and ideological alternatives to the Zionist imperatives of aliyah and the ingathering of the exiles.

ENDNOTES

1 For a useful analysis of American Jewish support of Israel, see Zvi Ganin, "The Blaustein Ben-Gurion Understanding of 1950," *Michael: On the History of the Jews in the Diaspora* 15 (2000): 29–57.

2 Ariel L. Feldestein, *Ben-Gurion, Zionism and American Jewry, 1948–1963* (London: Routledge, 2006), 1–29.

3 Richard J. Gottheil, *Zionism* (Philadelphia: Jewish Publication Society, 1914), 104–5.

4 *Ibid.*, 189–200, 201–8.

5 Richard J. Gottheil, speech, reported in American Zionist News (January 1, 1900), Stephen S. Wise Papers, record group A243, file 2, Central Zionist Archives, Jerusalem (hereafter: "CZA A243/2").

6 Quoted in Philippa Strum, *Brandeis: Beyond Progressivism* (Lawrence: University Press of Kansas, 1993), 114–5.

7 Letter from Chaim Weizmann to Felix Frankfurter (August 27, 1919) in *The Letters and Papers of Chaim Weizmann*, eds. Leonard Stein and Gedalia Yogev, vol. 9 (Israel: Israel University Press, 1975), 204–6.

8 *Ibid.*

9 *Ibid.*

10 Abba Hillel Silver, "Herzl and Jewish Messianism" in *Theodor Herzl, A Memorial*, ed. Meyer Weisgal (New York: Hyperion Press, 1929), 251–56.

11 *Ibid.*

12 The year 1929 was far from the last time Abba Hillel Silver criticized the national views of Herzl's Zionism. In fact, he voiced the same opinions in 1951. See Silver's lecture, "A Return Visit to Israel" (May 20, 1951), microfilm edition of the Abba Hillel Silver Archives, roll 4, file number 850.

13 Allon Gal, "David Ben-Gurion's Zionist Foreign Policy, 1938–1948: The Democratic Factor," *Israel Affairs* 1-2 (2004): 13–28; Allon Gal, *Toward a Jewish State, Political Preparation vis-à-vis the White Paper and the Outbreak of World War II, 1938–1941* (Sde Boker, Israel: Ben-Gurion University Press, 1985) (Hebrew); Zohar Segev, "Between Struggle and Cooperation: The Relationship between Ben-Gurion and the Zionist Leadership in the U.S.A. in the Early Forties," *State and Society* 2 (2002): 19–42 (Hebrew).

14 David Ben-Gurion's address to the Mapai executive committee (February 14, 1941), Labor Party Archives, Beit Berl (Kfar Saba, Israel).

15 *Ibid.*

16 Golda Meyerson at a meeting of the Mapai central committee (January 9, 1947), Labor Party Archives, Beit Berl (Kfar Saba, Israel).

17 *Ibid.*

18 *Ibid.*

19 For a full analysis in this regard, see Zohar Segev, *The World Jewish Congress During the Holocaust: Between Activism and Restrain* (Berlin: De Gruyter, 2014), 168–216.

20 Stephen S. Wise's speech to World Jewish Congress, European branch (August 18, 1945) (place not specified), World Jewish Congress Records, MS-361, Jacob Rader Marcus Center of the American Jewish Archives, Cincinnati, OH (hereafter: "WJC Records 361"), A9/10. This view of the WJC's purposes regarding Palestine and the diaspora was evident earlier. See, for example, World Jewish Congress Memorandum to the League of Nations (December 16, 1936), WJC Records 361, A1/2.

21 Memorandum of Dr. Robert Marcus, chairman of the World Jewish Congress Political Committee to the U.N. Committee on Genocide (April 6, 1948), WJC Records 361, 104B/3.

22 On Jacob Robinson and the Institute of Jewish Affairs, see the World Jewish Congress press release (undated) on Robinson's appointment to the UN Committee on Human Rights in 1947, WJC Records 361, C14/26. See also Mark A. Lewis, "The World Jewish Congress and the Institute of Jewish Affairs at Nuremberg: Ideas, Strategies, and Political Goals, 1942–1946," *Yad Vashem Studies* 2008 (36): 181–210. The WJC institutions sharply crit-

icized Jewish Agency activity at the Nuremberg trials. See: Stephen S. Wise's letter (October 17, 1945), WJC Records 361, B1/8#61; Jacob Robinson's report to the staff of the Institute of Jewish Affairs (December 6, 1945), WJC Records 361, C14/16.

23 Jacob Robinson, "The Institute of Jewish Affairs," *Congress Weekly* (February 21, 1941), 7, WJC Records 361, C86/1.

24 See confidential document by Jacob Robinson on the Institute of Jewish Affairs (April 29, 1939), WJC Records 361, A9/6.

25 See Robinson, "The Institute of Jewish Affairs," 8.

26 Anthony D. Smith, *The Nation in History: Historiographical Debates about Ethnicity and Nationalism* (Hanover, NH: University Press of New England, 2000), 52–76. Benedict Anderson highlights the importance of national leaders in colonial lands; see Benedict Anderson, *Imagined Communities: Reflection on Origin and Spread of Nationalism* (London: Verso, 1983), 141–47.

27 Jacob Robinson, Action Plan of the Institute of Jewish Affairs, 1941 (undated), WJC Records 361, A5/3.

28 Robinson's memorandum; see note 28 above.

29 Record of Wise's and Goldmann's meeting with Sumner Welles (February 17, 1941), WJC Records 361, D16/6.

30 See Jacob Robinson's memorandum (August 3, 1943), WJC Records 361, B95/8.

31 Memorandum dispatched from the World Jewish Congress's head office in New York titled "Eighth Anniversary of Warsaw Ghetto Uprising: An Appeal to All Our Affiliates" (February 19, 1951), WJC Records 361, H294/2.

32 Memorandum from the New York Head Office on the Occasion of the Twelfth Anniversary of the Warsaw Ghetto Uprising (January 25, 1955), WJC Records 361, H294/2.

33 *Ibid.*

34 "Remembering and Rebuilding, Survey and Analysis of the Twelfth Anniversary Commemoration of the Warsaw Ghetto Uprising" (July 1955) (no precise date specified), WJC Records 361, H294/2.

35 *Ibid.*

36 *Ibid.*

37 Booklet in English and Yiddish, 1956 publication (no precise date given), WJC Records 361, H294/2.

38 *Ibid.*

39 See *Congress Weekly—Tenth Anniversary of the Warsaw Ghetto Revolt* (March 30, 1953), WJC Records 361, H294/2. The weekly's editorial board also

devoted special issues to the topic of the Warsaw ghetto uprising in later years. See, for example, *Congress Weekly* (April 1, 1963), WJC Records 361, H294/2.

40 For a detailed analysis of Silver's Zionist perspective in the decades following the establishment of the State of Israel, see Zohar Segev, "American Zionists' Place in Israel after the Establishment of the State: Involved Partners or Outside Supporters," *American Jewish History* 93:3 (2007): 277–302.

41 Rogers Brubaker, *Ethnicity Without Groups* (Cambridge, MA: Harvard University Press, 2004), 22–24.

American Jewish Reactions to the Balfour Declaration and the San Remo Conference, 1918-1920

Source: Leon Israel (Lola), House of Israel rejoices at news of the San Remo Conference (1920). David and Fela Shapell Digitization Project, Jewish Historical Press, National Library of Israel and Tel Aviv University, courtesy of the Hebrew Union College Library.

The Balfour Declaration of 1917 inspired considerable Zionist enthusiasm in the American Jewish setting and garnered the support of many elected US officials. It also threw light on a variegated landscape of non-Zionists and anti-Zionist opponents from across the social, religious, and political spectrum. In the years immediately following World War I, the American Zionist movement—a loose coalition representing native-born and immigrant Jewish groups and communities—spearheaded an effort to unify American Jewry around three cardinal goals: the establishment of a democratically elected umbrella organization representing all American Jews, the promotion of Jewish minority rights in postwar Europe, and the establishment of an internationally sanctioned Jewish national home in Palestine. Against this backdrop, a talented cadre of elite Jewish communal leaders grouped around Louis D. Brandeis and Louis Marshall engineered a countrywide campaign that resulted in the convening of the American Jewish Congress in 1918 and 1920. In this two-year window, a vigorous public debate concerning the Balfour Declaration, Zionism, and postwar Jewish national reconstruction percolated in every corner of the American Jewish scene.

In April 1920, the Supreme War Council of the victorious Allied Powers, acting in concert with the newly established League of Nations, met in San Remo, Italy. The San Remo conference determined that the Middle East "territories" of Syria, Mesopotamia, and Palestine, formerly controlled by the Ottoman empire, were unprepared for independence and should be "subject to the rendering of administrative advice and assistance by a mandatory until such time as they are able to stand alone."[1] Among the resolutions taken at San Remo, the conference formally endorsed the Balfour Declaration and assigned the Mandate for Palestine to Great Britain. If the Balfour Declaration can be said to have electrified the American Jewish scene, the San Remo Conference and ensuing British Mandate might fairly be described as a galvanizing moment. The unprecedented reality of support for the Zionist project by the Allied Powers and League of Nations marked a sea change in modern Jewish politics. Zionist and even many non-Zionists responded to the prospect of the British Mandate with optimism and excitement. As Lola (pen name of Leon Israel, 1887–1955), the well-known New York City artist, suggests in the political cartoon reproduced here, even traditionalist Jews, for whom Zionism's this-worldly orientation was suspect, thrilled to news of the San Remo Conference as a step forward in an inscrutable divine plan. Directly above the traditional Jewish figure, identified as *"Beit Yisrael"* (House of Israel) in the windowsill, the Hebrew phrase *"Veatem amartem havtakhat shav he"* (And you said the promise was in vain) strikes a rhetorical blow at Zionism's detractors. Leaning out to address his listeners, he holds aloft a parchment labeled *"Hadeklaraziah shel Balfour nikdeshet al yadei agudat haamim"* (The Balfour Declaration is sanctioned by the League of Nations) and includes a ribbon seal that reads "San Remo."

To be sure, opposition to Zionism persisted in some quarters of American Jewish life, particularly the Jewish labor movement, classical Reform Judaism, and Orthodox Judaism. Reprinted below are statements by Isaac W. Bernheim (1848–1945), a successful businessman and founder of the I.W. Harper whiskey distillery, Jewish communal leader, and philanthropist, and Samuel N. Deinard (1873–1921), a Zionist rabbi, professor of Semitic languages, and editor of the *American Jewish World*, an English-language weekly. The commentary of Bernheim and Deinard exemplifies American Jewry's multifaceted response to Zionism in the waning months of the war and the postwar era, respectively.

Isaac W. Bernheim, "America First!" (1918)[2]

To the President and Members of the Central Conference of American Rabbis, Chicago, Ills.

Gentlemen: I realize that communication from a layman to a rabbinical conference is rather unusual, and I should hesitate to "break in" on your routine, were it not that the matter to be submitted by me is one in which every co-religionist, be he rabbi or layman, should be vitally interested. I am referring to "Zionism," which less than a generation ago appeared on the horizon as a tiny speck, a thing benevolent but utopian. It has grown and of late arrogated to itself the right to speak for all our co-religionists of every land, boldly asserting as its ultimate aim the creation of a national homeland for all Jews.

I shall not quarrel with any Jew who attempts to change his step-fatherland for a pleasant, congenial, and more promising real fatherland in Asia or elsewhere, but I deny most emphatically and with all the fervor within me that our American Reform Israelites are in that class. I solemnly affirm that to me Palestine or any section of the universe, save America, has only historical and cultural and human interest and meaning; that my home is in America, that my children are Americans, first, last and all the time, and that the men or set of men, who by act or deed or implication, may be disposed to becloud my title, or to create, in the minds of my fellow citizens of different faiths, a doubt as to my allegiance or to my rightful claim as citizen, can be considered by me only as enemies to my profoundest faith and my deepest loyalties.

The citizenship of my country with all the privileges and rights guaranteed to me by the Constitution of my country are to me and to mine priceless possessions which neither I nor my children would ever consent to surrender now allow any man or set of men to tarnish.

I am not unmindful of the fact that some,

indeed an insignificantly small percentage of the patriotic Americans of our faith, are identified with the Zionist movement. To question their motives would be as unjust as it would be undignified. They have a right to their opinion…

I am not disposed to take issue with people who claim we [Reform Jews] are at present a minority party nor do I deny that we will continue to be a minority for some time to come, but when that reservoir in Russia and Poland other sections of eastern Europe will cease to deliver thousands of fellow human beings of the Jewish faith, it will require no prophet to foretell that the orthodox Jews will gradually disappear because orthodoxy requires for its continued existence the ghetto and Orientalism; without it, it can neither exist nor grow.

American cities in the Middle West are furnishing proof of the truth of this assertion. Reform Israelites are rarely seeking orthodox religious affiliations, while the orthodox, in ever increasing numbers, are identifying themselves voluntarily with our Reform movement.

I am citing these facts merely to show that, if true to ourselves, we are the eternally fixed and that orthodoxy in America is a passing phenomenon.

The American Reform Israelite may modestly claim to have been the preserver of our religion in America, and to him destiny will likely assign the task of preserving and carrying forward those divine and unperishable principles, which have ever been the light and guide of our faith.

But in this we must hold fast the principle—America first!

Our children, now on the battlefields of France, will never consent to receive on their return a membership in your temples if, with it, you impose a citizenship of doubtful value...

America, that sun-kissed and God-blessed land, is just now engaged in the gigantic task of writing a new Torah of humanity; our boys are mingling their blood with the blood of children of other faiths, God bless them all! They are staking their lives to make it possible that this new dispensation may become a living reality...

On your return home, call the members of your congregation together; and let us know whether you are ready to participate in a conference in which the voice of the real American Israel may be heard, to be held in some city, centrally located, during the early fall.

My laymanship doubtless predisposes me to action... I admire your philosophic passion for unity in all Israel; but deliberations long spread out at the present time, when the whole world is agonizing for liberty and for the highest possible of all unities—the unity of America and mankind—would be, in my opinion, an historic blunder and nothing short of a crime. To you your tents, O Israel! The fate of the Jews, the world over, will be safe in the hands of an emancipated world, after this war of liberation is over. Our beloved country has entered the lists as champion of oppressed peoples, and the world will be made safe for Jews if it is made safe for democracy. But I dare to say that there is something more important to us than the safety of the Jews. It is the safety of Judaism. It is the safety of Judaism's spiritual heir—Americanism. As one of the rank and file of American Israel, I plead with you, say the strong and courageous word now, for the sake of our faith and our country.

The formation of the Reform Church of American Israelites has become an absolute and irrevocable and pressing necessity and its membership must consist of 100 percent Americans.

Cordially yours, Isaac W. Bernheim

Samuel N. Deinard, "Keep Cool," *American Jewish World* (1920)[3]

The wisdom of the golden mean, the virtue of moderation in thought and action—that should be our guiding principle... It is well to have this thought in mind as we contemplate the latest developments in the Zionist movement.

According to reports from San Remo, undoubtedly authentic, England has been given the mandate for Palestine, and in the peace treaty with Turkey the Balfour Declaration is given recognition and confirmation. Therefore, Palestine is henceforth a part of Britain's empire, just like Egypt or India. For that is what the mandate actually amounts to. But according to the Balfour Declaration the British government is pledged to help the Jews establish a national homeland in Palestine. How Britain will go about carrying out this pledge remains to be seen. There can be no doubt that Britain will primarily look out for British interests... If Jewish aspirations, plans, and activities coincide with them, well and good. If not, they will have to be modified according to British ideas and projects. Will Britain, for instance, allow a Jewish mass immigration to be immediately started into Palestine, assuming that the Zionist forces are able to manage, to finance, or otherwise to help and promote such an influx of the longing millions from eastern and central Europe? Will Britain allow and enable the Jews to acquire all the land necessary for colonization on such a huge scale? Will England at once allow the Jews a leading part in the government of the country, commensurate with Jewish capacity, energy, and intellect? These are questions that cannot yet be answered...

But we are not complaining. We shall be thankful for whatever boon England will grant us which shall bring us nearer the ultimate realization of our hopes. Providence has been very gracious to us. We have made wonderful progress as it is. Where would Zionism now be if Palestine were still a part of Turkey? What opportunities would we have for any approach to the establishment of a national homeland?

But see what our "cabinet," the administrative office of the Zionist Organization of America, has done in connection with the news from San Remo? It immediately set out to stampede the Zionist forces of the land. The shouting, the noise, the hurrahing, and the sundry theatricalities are calculated to sweep us off our feet. If the old idea of the mashiakh [messiah] had actually been realized during the last few days, our "cabinet" could not have devised any better schemes of arousing enthusiasm and excitement. A proclamation is sent out broadcast to all papers and all societies and their officers...

"Proclaim the Great Event.

"Our redemption has come! On the 7th day of the month of Iyar, 5680, 1850 years after the dispersion, Eretz Israel became once more the land of Israel, our land, and the land of our children. Arise! Our redemption has come!

"...Go out among the Jewish people wherever they gather, in their synagogues, societies, unions, and Hebrew schools, and proclaim the great event... It is urgent that in every district teams of Zionists generally consisting of two, one bearing the Zionist flag and the other the proclamation, should go out for this purpose... Wherever the Jews congregate, one should arise and proclaim the event... All this must be done between now and the 10th of May in order that every Jewish man, woman, and child in the United States should be acquainted with the great event..."

Does not all this sound like one of the antics of Sabbatai Zevi?[4] But that is not all. The "cabinet" is determined to take things by storm... And so it sends out a summons to an "Extraordinary Convention" to be held in the city of New York May 9 and 10... to take appropriate action on the new situation which confronts the Zionist Organization and to instruct the American Zionist delegates to the [Twelfth World Zionist Congress] to be held [in July 1921] at Carlsbad...

Now, we ask, what is the real object of it all? What "appropriate action" can the convention take "on the new situation that confronts the Zionist Organization"? What makes the situation so new? We have all along worked and raised funds in the expectation and hope that this very thing [which] has now come to pass, would actually happen—the English mandate and the Balfour Declaration... Is it not evidently a scheme to bring a large number of enthusiastic Zionists together for two days, to stir them up to a high pitch of excitement by flamboyant oratory, and by shouting and hurrahing and singing to carry them off their feet and to make them pledge themselves to almost anything demanded of them? We are given to understand beforehand that none of the regular organization questions will be taken up, which means that there will be no reports, no accounting, no discussion of desirable changes and improvements in the organization. The delegates will simply be sent home intoxicated with enthusiasm to do the bidding of the "cabinet." A fine scheme, worthy of the good old-time Republican or Democratic conventions.

Over against this excessive enthusiasm... we have the other extreme, the excessive belittlement of the event on the part of the old-time opponents of Zionism. For, after all, the news from San Remo should be very gratifying to every Jew. In the last issue of the *American Israelite*, Dr. David Philipson's[5] comment on the news is that it "dashes to the ground the Zionist program for the establishment of a Jewish state." And Dr. Louis Grossman[6] writes that "the phrase 'National Home for the Jews' is a juggling with words... A democratic Palestine is simply another English colony, and 'homeland' and 'Jewish commonwealth' are words of mere dreamers."

Between these two extremes, there is still the middle road, the golden mean, that all earnest and sincere Zionists will follow in the future... We shall give Britain the benefit of the doubt and trust her to deal fairly with us. We shall do our utmost to promote the Zionist cause in and outside of Palestine. We shall raise the necessary funds for actual work, for the building of the homeland in

> Palestine, but not for organization, publicity, and propaganda in America . . . Let us continue to work for Zionism, but keep cool at the same time.

Endnotes

1 San Remo Conference (April 1920), Syria, Mesopotamia, Palestine Mandates, United Nations, https://www.un.org/unispal/document/auto- insert-207297/.

2 Excerpted from Isaac W. Bernheim, *Yearbook of the Central Conference of American Rabbis* 28, ed. Isaac E. Marcuson (1918), 141–44.

3 Excerpted from Samuel N. Deinard, "Keep Cool," *American Jewish World* 8, no. 35, May 7, 1920, 8–9.

4 In 1648 Sabbatai Zevi (1626–76), a Sephardic rabbi and kabbalist born in Izmir (Smyrna), Turkey, proclaimed he heard a "heavenly voice" and declared himself to be the messiah. In 1654 he was excommunicated by the rabbis of Izmir and left for Salonica, where he attracted a large following. He next traveled to Rhodes, Tripoli, and Egypt before arriving in Gaza in 1665, where Nathan Benjamin ben Elisha Halevy (Nathan of Gaza) (1643–80) proclaimed him the messiah. Against the backdrop of rising messianic expectations, Zevi embarked on a grand tour via Jerusalem and Aleppo to Istanbul, where he was seized and imprisoned by the Turkish vizier. In 1666 he was taken to Adrianople, where the sultan forced him to choose between conversion to Islam or death. Following his conversion, Zevi assumed a new name and was granted a title and a government pension. Though he continued to practice Judaism secretly, Zevi's conversion undermined the Sabbatean movement and it quickly collapsed.

5 Ordained in 1883 by Hebrew Union College, David Philipson (1862–1949) served as rabbi of Congregation K. K. Bene Israel (Rockdale Temple) in Cincinnati (1888–1938). An ardent anti-Zionist and a champion of classical Reform Judaism, he chaired the Union of American Hebrew Congregations' board of editors of Religious School Literature (1903–24).

6 Louis Grossman (1863–1926), ordained in 1884 by Hebrew Union College, served as rabbi of Temple Beth El in Detroit (1884–1898) and Congregation Bene Yeshurun in Cincinnati (1898–1922). He was a professor of ethics and theology at Hebrew Union College (1898–1922). In 1909, he founded the Teachers Institute of Hebrew Union College and served as its principal until 1918.

AFTERWORD

THE BALFOUR DECLARATION IN HISTORICAL AND POLITICAL PERSPECTIVE

SUSANNAH HESCHEL

To the residents of the Mashriq and to Jews and Arabs throughout the world, the Balfour Declaration changed everything. Perhaps its importance was magnified because no one was certain what it really meant, not even the British government. The Balfour Declaration presented the world with a remarkable Rorschach test offering almost infinite ways to interpret its motivations and political significance. To some, it was a perfidious betrayal, while others rejoiced in its enormous commitment; some read "national home" and assumed Jewish immigration was intended, while for others "national home" was interpreted to mean "state." Did it express a British sympathy to Jews and Zionism or was it an assertion of the manly politics of British high imperialism in an era of demands for an end to colonialism? Jews and Arabs living in Palestine discovered within a few years that the reality of British rule was far different from the promises of a declaration. Within the United States, Balfour led to the emergence of a resilient, enduring "Congressional Zionism" seasoned with Orientalism, race, gender, and a distinctive American Protestantism.

Rarely has a paragraph as brief as the Balfour Declaration—which is a mere sentence—elicited such a vast historiography and produced such enormous international and historic consequences that continue to be debated to this day, consequences residing less in the declaration's words and authors than in the afterlife created by both its supporters and opponents and even by international observers. Of all the hundreds, even thousands of negotiations, promises, and treaties concluded and signed during that era, most are forgotten, while the Balfour Declaration rose from the ashes of World War I as a phoenix, transformed into a vital piece of international geopolitics, both celebrated and condemned to the present day, and persistently invoked in ideological debates.

For most of the Zionist leaders at the time, the Balfour Declaration stood as a watershed, establishing the "crucial international warrant for Zionism"[1] that put Zionism "on the international map and attested to its historical vitality"[2] without having defined Zionism. Indeed, precisely the lack of definition in the declaration opened the door for Zionist leaders to turn it into a warrant for Jewish statehood. Palestinian Arabs, described in the declaration as "non-Jewish communities," though they constituted 94 percent of its population in 1917, were coping with the collapse of the Ottoman empire following battles between British and Ottoman troops. Reactions to the Declaration from Palestinian Arabs are difficult to measure because the British "banned publication of news of the declaration [and] did not allow newspapers to reappear in Palestine for nearly two years."[3] Reports arrived via Cairo and Damascus, leading to a formal letter of protest, sent to the Versailles peace conference in December 1918, signed by thirty-three exiled Palestinian Arabs. At the same time, Ben-Gurion wrote, "We do not intend to push the Arabs aside, to take their land, or to disinherit them."[4]

Although the Balfour Declaration speaks of a "national home" and not a "state," Palestinians, understanding that it implied a promise of Jewish statehood in Palestine, demanded the Balfour Declaration be revoked. Indeed, a 2017 petition marked the 100th anniversary of the Balfour Declaration calling on Britain to "lead attempts to reach a solution that ensures justice for the Palestinian people."[5] The assumption of a promise of statehood was not misplaced; Jehuda Reinharz reports that at a small gathering of British government leaders, including David Lloyd George, the prime minister, and Winston Churchill, colonial secretary, at the home of Lord Balfour on June 22, 1921, Chaim Weizmann was assured that "by the Declaration, they always meant an eventual state." Weizmann's immediate concern was waning support for Zionism in the administration of Herbert Samuel, British High Commissioner for Palestine, who had called for representative government in Palestine. At this, Lloyd George told Churchill it must never happen. With that meeting, Samuel's political efforts were ended, reinforced by cabinet resolutions in August 1921.[6] In the United States, Zionists rejoiced over the Balfour Declaration and reconfigured Zionism as representing American ideals, a formula that has gained lasting support to this day from US presidents and, most important, cultivated a new American Zionism.

Historians debate interpretations of Balfour over the evidence they examine, the contexts in which they choose to place it, and the methods and questions they employ. Was the Balfour Declaration a necessary part of Britain's strategy to demolish the Ottomans and gain a foothold in the Middle East to expand its empire? Was Britain giving Palestine to the Jews or using the Jews to win American and Russian support for its war effort? Or was it an effort to preempt Germany from issuing a declaration in favor of Zionism?[7] Should Balfour be viewed among the many demands for independence from the British empire or as a strategy for British control of the Jews and the Arabs in Palestine? Was the Balfour Declaration the achievement of Chaim Weizmann, a "figure of rare diplomatic and political talent," as Mark A. Raider writes, and his Zionist colleagues in persuading Britain to advance Jewish nationalist interests?[8] Did Balfour resolve Europe's "Jewish Question" or exacerbate internal Jewish tensions? And what about the inhabitants of Palestine, Jews and Arabs, who were not unified ethnically, politically or religiously: how did they react? In the aftermath, Balfour may be viewed as the greatest political achievement in Jewish history or as undermining Jewish political stability by aligning Zionist interests with British imperialism and putting Jews at the mercy of unresolved political conflicts in the Middle East that were largely the creation of the European powers. These are among the problems debated by historians. The important achievement of this volume is to enlarge the historical context and examine the broad range of American Jewish involvement in the changes that occurred in American life resulting from World War I, including the negotiations leading up to the Balfour Declaration and its transformative impact on the American Jewish experience in nearly all dimensions.

Most scholars interested in the Balfour Declaration focus on the motivations of the British, though far more important were the consequences of the declaration. The popular Jewish narratives of the Balfour Declaration have long claimed it was Britain's gift to Zionism and the Jews, perhaps motivated by a philosemitic Christian theology of restoration, or brought about by the extraordinary achievement of brilliant Zionist negotiators. With the Jewish outpouring of gratitude for the Balfour Declaration, often misconstruing the declaration as a promise of statehood, many Jewish and pro-Zionist observers have assumed Britain was motivated by gratitude to Weizmann for producing synthetic acetone, used in explosives or by the Christian beliefs of Balfour and Prime Minister David Lloyd George.

Whatever sympathy for the Jews may have motivated British supporters of the declaration—and support was not unanimous among Britain's elected officials and elites—quickly disappeared during the Mandate era, to the grave disappointment of Zionist leaders. That has led to the antisemitic twist offered by some historians: the British were so antisemitic that they were convinced the Jews were all-powerful and could win support for the British war effort from the Americans and the Russians. While the Americans had joined the war in April 1917, the British were hoping for additional financial assistance. In Russia, the revolutionaries who had arrested the tsar in March 1917 were hesitant about joining the war; the Jews, as purported loyal Bolsheviks—so the British are said to have believed—could convince the Provisional Government to remain allied with Britain in the war effort. Or the Germans (so it was mistakenly believed in Britain) were on the verge of issuing their own Zionist statement, supposedly under Jewish pressure, that Britain wanted to pre-empt.

That the British believed Jews constituted an ethnically homogenous international Jewish community with a strong and unified commitment to Zionism was due, Mark Levene argues, to an antisemitic animus: "the origins of the Balfour Declaration are to be located less in the wartime policies and strategies of Britain in the Middle East and more in the murky waters of modern antisemitism."[9] After all, Alfred Balfour, as prime minister (1902–05), had promulgated the 1905 Aliens Act, to slow the immigration of Jewish refugees. Zionism, presumably, would also keep Jews out of England. Levene's emphasis on antisemitism explains what otherwise seems to be a striking shift in British policy away from Zionism once it received the mandate over Palestine and again during World War II. In a similar vein, James Renton emphasizes the British conviction in Jewish power but attributes it to the great success of Zionist propaganda.[10] Renton calls this "the Zionist masquerade" that convinced the British that the Jews were a racially homogenous and politically powerful group—a masquerade made easier by racist and Orientalist assumptions, seasoned with Christian traditions about Jews.[11]

Widening the historiographic framework allows historians to place the Balfour Declaration in a broader set of British political interests. For example, Danny Gutwein argues that

Weizmann aligned Zionism with a radical faction within the British government that sought to dismantle the Ottoman empire in order to extend British imperial hold on the Middle East; the Balfour Declaration was a piece of the strategy, promising to open Palestine to the Jews.[12] An even broader view of British politics is taken by Maryanne Rhett, who places the Balfour Declaration within the context of the many pressures on England from home-rule movements, especially from Ireland and India, as well as debates about the nature of nation and empire. In addition, Rhett looks at the roles of militarism, race, and gender in the shifting representations of Jews and Zionists during and after the negotiations.[13] Yuval Evri and Hillel Cohen add the important dimension of Palestine itself, which included staunch Arab opposition to Balfour, expressed in their annual protest march. European-born Zionist supporters of Balfour in Palestine wanted separation from the Arabs, and Sephardi Jewish intellectuals in Palestine "imagined Palestine not as a separate "Jewish Western kingdom" or a European settlement but as a shared Jewish-Arab space that would be part of the new Middle East yet found themselves caught between European Zionist settlers and native Arabs."[14]

While most historians, including Levene, Renton, Gutwein, and Rhett focus on the motivations of the British, they agree that Britain acted out of its own wartime interests, even if misguided by assumptions regarding Jews and Zionism, without much consideration of the impact Balfour would have in the future.[15] Yet the significance of the Balfour Declaration lies less in what it stated and primarily in what was created out of it. Most important, the declaration conferred enormous political prestige to the Zionist movement. Although some ideological debates were tolerated, the Eurocentric Zionist leadership suppressed Sephardi voices of dissent, focused on diplomacy with American and European governments while ignoring indigenous Arab leaders in Palestine, and rendered the movement male, white, and Orientalist.

To better understand who and what circumstances turned the Balfour Declaration into a powerful piece of international policy, we turn to this volume of essays on American Jews, Jewish nationalism, and World War I to learn a neglected element of the history: the role of ethnic Jewish political and Zionist activity in the United States. While Weizmann and his European Zionist colleagues certainly played crucial roles in promoting Zionism, this book demonstrates the particular kind of Zionism created in the United States and the unique support it received from officials at the highest level of the government. In addition, widespread popular support for Zionism brought additional publicity and transformed it from an expression of "favour" to a statement of political policy that ultimately won international support. Understanding the American context offers an important dimension that reframes both the motivation of the British government and the consequences of the Balfour Declaration.[16] Zionism had very strong support in Louis D. Brandeis and other elite American Jewish figures, and even from President Woodrow Wilson, who promoted the post–World War I promises to liberate nationalities and dismantle empires, and Zionist leaders pursued influence at the highest level, not unlike other social movements of the era, as Daniel J. Tichenor observes in his chapter. The leaders of racial justice and women's rights, Tichenor writes, even when discouraged, continued appealing to "the power and authority of the modern presidency to advance their cause."[17] Leaders of those movements may have struggled, however, as Raider observes, "Wilson's attitude to Zionism's utility as an element of American wartime policy ebbed and flowed, but he never wavered in his attachment to the Zionist project and the idea of a Jewish national home in Palestine."[18]

That raises the question of why support for Zionism prevailed in the United States, despite the American xenophobia and racism of the 1920s, and even increased, achieving a 1922 Congressional Zionist resolution. The Balfour Declaration became a turning point for American attitudes toward Zionism. Zionists aligned their movement with Wilson's principle of "self-determination of nations" to help Zionism escape the racist era of American nativism, setting the stage for many subsequent efforts to equate Jewish and American values, with Jews as fighting on their behalf. As Zohar Segev writes, the Warsaw ghetto uprising was later presented by American Jews as "waged not only on behalf of the Jews, but also as part of an all-encompassing endeavor in the interests of morality and humanity."[19] A World Jewish Congress 1951 memorandum cited by Segev outlined a message for commemorating the uprising:

> Our brothers and sisters of the Warsaw ghetto and elsewhere *did not die for our people only, but for all mankind* in the battle against forces which are preparing to rise up again not only against our people, but against the triumph of morality and humanity in general.[20]

In the wake of the Balfour Declaration, even the Warsaw ghetto uprising of 1943 was presented as a defense of American values, and Zionism was re-envisioned as a Jewish movement for the moral benefit of humanity, a vision aligned with American self-understanding as the moral beacon of world politics. Ultimately, the Zionist alliance with American power also shaped how American Jews subsequently presented themselves to the public.

While the British were wrong prior to November 1917 in believing that world Jewry was unified in support of Zionism, the Balfour Declaration became one of the most important factors in unifying Jews around the world in the conviction of the viability and importance of Zionism. A major contribution of this collection of articles is demonstrating some of the ways American Jewish engagement in Zionism became strong and widespread, in part thanks to a national campaign by the American Jewish Congress, led by Brandeis, but also thanks to smaller, local, and even peripheral communal efforts. American Jews supported both political and cultural Zionism, though not always under the same tent. Some, as Philip Hollander demonstrates here, worked for a revival of Hebrew culture and education in America, while others, spurred by the Balfour Declaration, emigrated to Palestine. As Jessica Cooperman notes in her chapter, American Jews presented Zionism as expressing key American political principles, such as self-determination, and, remarkably, claimed that Zionism made Jews better Americans; after all, Americans were not about to emigrate en masse to Palestine. Within the rampant xenophobia of the era, American Jews managed to largely avoid the accusations of dual loyalty and violent outbursts that targeted and victimized other ethnic groups.

The negotiators of the Balfour Declaration were heirs to nineteenth-century European liberalism who saw nothing wrong with imperialism—on the contrary, a Jewish homeland was viewed as a gracious gift to the Jews that redounded to Britain's benefit politically, militarily, and economically, while enhancing its self-understanding as the great colonial wellspring of Christian values. For the Americans, who were no less imbued with a colonialist mentality, Jews in Palestine would be a gift to Palestinian Arabs by creating infrastructure and economic development. Everyone would benefit—even, the Great Powers believed, the Arab peasants of Palestine, supposedly languishing in an underdeveloped corner of the world. The colonialist mentality prevailing in that era and long after, with all its racism, misogyny, and Orientalism, is inescapably obvious. Yet simply regarding the Balfour Declaration as a Zionist pawn in a new colonialist venture or as an extension of European colonialism ignores the mixture of geopolitical and religious complexities, conflicting motivations, and unanticipated outcomes so central to global and modern Jewish history.

The language of Balfour promised a "home" and not a "state" and failed to define the borders of that home or state, nor did it offer Jewish independent sovereignty. Balfour himself indicated that he intended "some form of British, American or other protectorate."[21] Moreover, it was to be a home "for the Jews" and not "of the Jews," as Zionist leaders had requested; had the British declared Palestine ontologically Jewish, they would have endorsed Zionism as a return to the ancient Jewish home where Jews were indigenous. The terminology was born of caution; "home," Ian Lustick points out, resonated in Britain with Irish demands for "home rule," that is, "national political autonomy and cultural self-expression," if not independent statehood.[22] Lustick also notes that while Theodor Herzl famously declared in his diary that he had founded the Jewish state at the First Zionist Congress in 1897, that same congress in Basel declared as its goal a "Heimstatt" [homeland] "for the Jewish people in Palestine secured under public law."[23]

Then as now, Zionism was not a united movement, but splintered among numerous factions, with statehood still in question for some, including the nature of that statehood. Then as now, almost no attention was given to the Arab population of Palestine. A small group of mostly German Jewish intellectuals living in the *Yishuv* formed Brit Shalom [Covenant of Peace] in 1925; calling for a binational Arab-Jewish state, they quickly became pariahs in the eyes of other Zionists for rejecting the Balfour Declaration.[24] For most Orthodox Jews at the time, Zionism was heretical, and Jews who felt at home in their native lands, from Germany to Morocco to the United States, viewed Zionism at best as a solution to other Jews' problems, not their own. Even the chair of the venerable Board of Deputies of British Jews protested the Balfour Declaration on the grounds that Jews were already at home in the diaspora, enjoying "religious liberty and the full rights of citizenship."[25] Arab leaders in Palestine responded to the Balfour Declaration by presenting a petition to the British government a year later, expressing sympathy for "the persecuted Jews and their misfortunes in other countries," but stating their opposition both to British and Jewish rule.[26] Sephardi Jews in the *Yishuv*, caught between the Arabs and appalled by the treatment of Palestinian Arabs by the European Zionist settlers, "criticized the arrogant and dismissive attitudes of the new Ashkenazi immigrants toward the Palestinian Arabs."[27]

Soon after the war, Arab leaders traveled to London and tried unsuccessfully to persuade British officials to rescind the Balfour Declaration.[28] The 1938 book, *The Arab Awakening,* by the Lebanese diplomat George Antonius presents the British as traitors to the Arabs and argued that Arab nationalism had arisen in the nineteenth century under the Ottomans.[29] A similar narrative about British duplicity quickly arose during the Mandate period among Jews in Palestine and Zionists in the West. The Balfour Declaration had become an article of Zionist faith that the Jewish nationalist movement would attain sovereignty and not simply British "sympathy." Clashes in the Mandate era between Jews and Arabs convinced both groups that Britain had betrayed them.

For Lloyd George, as Benny Morris writes, the year 1917 saw the Middle East at the top of Britain's agenda, culminating in Field Marshall Edmund Allenby's conquering entry into Jerusalem on December 11, 1917.[30] The British organized celebrations but excluded Arab participation, despite "a well-developed sense of Palestinian identity" that had emerged during World War I.[31] Earlier Zionist resolutions brought to the British government had been tabled in 1915 by Herbert Samuel and Lord Asquith, but Arthur Balfour and Lloyd George now made certain the declaration would be issued. Whatever the motivations, the Balfour Declaration's ambiguity offered polysemic propaganda, presented to the world as a British gift, and allowing Britain to conceal its Orientalism as well as its expansion of imperial power in Palestine under a veneer of Christian tribute to the Bible, a gift to the Jews (or to Europe for redirecting the Jews elsewhere) and a protection of the holy land.

Lord Balfour himself became a hero to the Jews and the declaration was celebrated by Jews around the world, generally under the misapprehension that a state had been promised. Public expressions of gratitude from Jews were abundant and long-lasting. In 1926, the prominent Cleveland Reform rabbi, Barnett Brickner, named his son Balfour. The son became a Reform rabbi and a leader in the Civil Rights movement and the effort to end the war in Vietnam. Public expressions of gratitude from Jews came in abundance and there was a sense, as Derek Penslar writes, of "joy, relief, and the ebbing of fear."[32] For many American Jews, the Balfour Declaration functioned as a wellspring of pride and inspiration, even if they had no intention of emigrating to Palestine. Not all Jews: Gary Zola presents the diary of the young Jacob Marcus, a "doughboy," fighting in the American army during World War I, who wrote with a dismissive tone about Jewish passion for Zionism in his diary entries of 1918.

While the Balfour Declaration was presented by Zionist leaders as a great victory for their movement, some worried whether a declaration issued by His Majesty's Government was the best way to achieve Zionist goals. The responses of Jewish socialists, Reform Jews, ultra-Orthodox Jews, and some leaders of the Jewish community in England ranged from strong misgivings to outright opposition, whether on political or religious grounds. In subsequent decades, as British support for Zionism cooled, some Jews wondered if the Balfour Declaration had been proclaimed not on behalf of the Zionist movement but for Britain's strategic political purposes that ultimately created a new set of conflicts for Zionism on the world stage. David Ben-Gurion warned, "Britain has made a magnificent gesture; she has recognized our existence as a nation and has acknowledged our right to the country. But only the Hebrew people can transform this right into tangible fact; only they, with body and soul, with their strength and capital, must build their National Home and bring about their national redemption."[33] Indeed, that is precisely the significance of Balfour's aftermath: how it was used to justify a Jewish project of state-building. To this end, as Zohar Segev demonstrates in his essay, American Jews made a significant contribution not only to providing important economic and political support, but refashioning Zionism into a movement that would appeal to Western regimes in the post–World War I era and beyond.[34]

Although Zionist negotiators of the Balfour Declaration had wanted a commitment to Jewish statehood, they nonetheless lauded the declaration and made a shrewd effort to turn it into a broader commitment. Their actual influence with the British government, however, was evanescent. Zionists felt betrayal after the British turned to Arab appeasement by appointing Haj Amin al-Husseini senior Muslim cleric in Palestine in 1921 and then radically limiting Jewish immigration to Palestine in the 1930s and during World War II, effectively abandoning six million European Jews to Nazi murder. While Zionist leaders had reached a zenith of political influence in 1917, they and all Jews proved powerless after 1933 to impel the American and west European governments to accept Jewish immigrants from Nazi Europe and, during the war, to secure protection for Jews in Nazi occupied territories and to convince the US government to bomb Auschwitz and the Nazi death camps.

Whatever the motivations in 1917 that produced the Balfour Declaration, once Britain received the Mandate over Palestine, Zionist pressure for statehood did not evoke similar support from the British; even "sympathy" for Zionism waned among British officialdom and took on bizarre political configurations. Thomas Reid, a member of Britain's Woodhead Commission, sent to Palestine in April 1938 to study partition plans, told a Jewish Agency Executive member that "Zionism was not a wise movement for the Jews to foster. It was the same nationalism that we objected to in Hitler. The solution of the Jewish problem was that adopted by the Bolsheviks—assimilation."[35] His words reflected the views of the British Foreign Office that the Jews "have waited two thousand years for their 'home'... they can afford to wait a bit until we are better able to help them get their last pound of flesh."[36]

The Balfour Declaration might be seen as the great achievement of a coalition of centrist and leftist Zionist leaders and groups, the beginning of the political road to establishing the State of Israel. Or was it, as the rightwing Zionist leader Vladimir Jabotinsky argued, a disaster because it transferred the keys to statehood from the Jews to a British government that ultimately fostered tensions between Jews and Arabs in Palestine, and blocked Jewish immigration after Hitler came to power.[37] Like Jabotinsky, but at the opposite end of the political spectrum, the great political theorist Hannah Arendt viewed the Balfour Declaration as a disaster by turning Zionism into a vassal of Great Britain, violating the basic tenet of Zionism: independent political self-determination for the Jews.[38]

The circumstances during which the Balfour Declaration was under negotiation by Zionist leaders with European government officials are striking: this was the era of secret treaties, negotiations, and promises, all undertaken by men who gathered in the halls of government, private clubs, and over cigars and whiskey. Britain had carried out secret negotiations with France over the very un-Zionist 1916 Sykes-Picot Treaty that carved the Levant between them, with the land from Jerusalem to the north under Anglo-French control. At the same time, Sir Arthur Henry McMahon, the high commissioner in Egypt, sent letters to Hussein bin Ali, Sharif of Mecca, promising Arab independence from the Persian Gulf to the Mediterranean in exchange for an Arab revolt against the Ottomans. Meanwhile, the once mighty Ottoman empire was disintegrating, toppled by European powers and Russian revolutionaries, who, having arrested the tsar in March 1917, were on the verge of the revolution that brought to power a provisional government ambivalent about the Entente.

When the Balfour Declaration was issued, European countries had reached the zenith of imperialism, with 85 percent of the land mass of earth under colonial rule. The British public had supported entry into the war in 1914, but elsewhere in the British empire, the war intensified nationalist battles for independence and gave rise to new political movements. The Easter Rising in Ireland of April 1916 led to the creation of Sinn Fein in 1917, and in 1917 Edmund Montagu, who had just become Secretary of State for India, announced a commission that would investigate Indian self-determination. Was the Balfour Declaration and the subsequent Zionist claims on its behalf an extension of European imperial power or part of the worldwide rebellions for independent sovereignty? In the hundred years since, Zionist leaders have sought to thread the needle, presenting Jewish nationalist goals both as consonant with Western interests in the Middle East and as a revival of a native, indigenous Jewish presence in the biblical homeland.

Fitting the Balfour Declaration into the Zionist narrative was not always easy, in part because British policies toward Zionism turned sour during the Mandate years, and because some Zionist leaders, such as Jabotinsky, wanted to view the movement as an internal Jewish effort.[39] A gift from the British did not fit the Zionist ideology that called for a negation of the diaspora, including a sharp break with the conventional Jewish politics of *shtadlanut* [intercession], Jewish lobbying at the highest levels of government, precisely the diasporic politics that Zionism claimed it wanted to overcome. Balfour is not a new form of Jewish politics, but a continuation of vertical Jewish politics, argues historian Arie Dubnov, creating an "imperial triangle" of British, Arabs, and Jews, a continuation of *shtadlanut*. Yet precisely because the Balfour Declaration is a prime example of diasporic *shtadlanut*, Zionist historians give the Balfour Declaration a subservient role to Jewish efforts driving the movement for Jewish sovereignty. Other scholars, including Palestinian historians, view the Balfour Declaration as an alignment of Zionism with European imperialist politics and proof of Zionism's culpability in colonialism.

Seen within the larger context of worldwide rebellions against European colonialism that were on the verge of breaking out, the Balfour Declaration is also an extraordinary achievement of Zionist political prowess. Few if any nonstate political actors were able to achieve the attention of high-level European imperial government actors as successfully as the Zionist leaders and turn a small paragraph into an international commitment. How do we understand their success? Not only did Zionist leaders appeal with effective strategy, presenting themselves as representatives of "the Jews" despite representing only a small fraction and regarded with animosity or indifference by a majority of Jews, they calculated how best to present Zionism as supporting the war and expanding—not undermining—the global order of European imperialism. To that end, Zionist leaders of the era, especially Weizmann and Nahum Sokolow, had to present Jewish aspirations for statehood not as rival to European sovereignty but as a tool to bolster British, French, and Italian imperial aims. Although the Zionist leaders had already become a presence within European politics, negotiating with the highest levels of governments, Sokolow presented Zionist efforts as simple, neutral, and naïve. In soothing the French, for example, he assured Francois Georges-Picot of Jewish subservience: "Jews are in the position of a child who cannot tell whether he likes his father or mother best; it is hardly for them to say whether they would prefer England or France as suzerain power, and that therefore the question must be settled between the Governments themselves."[40]

For British, French, and Italian government officials, Zionism seemed to function to their benefit, offering an extension of European interests in the Middle East, led by Jews of Europe. Most remarkably, the French and Italian governments came to regard British claims to Palestine with mild acceptance, despite France's claims as late as April 1917 that Palestine "should be included in the French sphere."[41] For Italy and the Vatican, Britain was key to keeping the French out of Palestine and protecting places of Catholic religious significance, since France, during an anticlerical campaign, had broken relations with the Vatican in 1904.[42]

Once the State of Israel was established, the Balfour Declaration seemed a fleeting moment of British support that the Zionists had turned to their political advantage. The initial Zionist optimism toward the British had eroded almost immediately and was then crushed during the Mandate era. Not surprisingly, Zionist historiography, Yoav Gelber writes, almost immediately began to discount the role of the Balfour Declaration, preferring to emphasize Jewish self-reliance rather than considering Zionism as a pawn in British hands.[43] British behavior combined with the horrors of World War II led Jews in Israel and around the world to believe that they had to "distrust others and rely on themselves alone."[44] Decades later, Israeli prime minister Golda Meir believed, as Pnina Lahav notes in her contribution to this volume, that "Israel came about not because of the good will of the British empire and its Balfour Declaration but rather because of the brave actions and sacrifices of the Yishuv."[45]

That was the propaganda. In reality, even as the disparagement of outside assistance prevailed in Israeli historical and cultural narratives, its politicians were pursuing a politics of "vertical alliances" which, Dubnov argues, allowed them to discourage direct, public negotiation with neighboring governments and with their neighbors on the land, the Palestinian Arabs. A culture of self-reliance and independence, though contrary to the reality, fit the Zionist narrative, and clashes with Arabs confirmed Zionist claims to "manliness" and the negation of the passive, weak, emasculated diasporic male Jew, creating a "phantasm of complete self-reliance."[46]

"It's a boy!" So proclaimed Sir Mark Sykes as he came out of the room where the Balfour Declaration had just been approved to congratulate Chaim Weizmann.[47] "A boy" meant Balfour had won; a girl, one assumes, would convey failure. The politics of gender was not simply an undercurrent in Zionism, it was a forthright tool of propaganda, negotiation, and realpolitik. Zionism was becoming one of the great triumphs of Jewish maleness, and the English knew it. Jews were to be gendered male by Zionism as an essential element of the negation of the diaspora and the putative emasculation of Jewish men brought by piety, study, and lack of sovereignty. In addition, the Zionist movement itself had to be gendered male. Despite that, many Jewish women became devoted to the Zionist cause, sometimes in seeming contradiction to its principles. How did women experience Zionism? The American Jewish activist Jessie Sampter, for example, both supported Zionism and violated its ideological boundaries by advocating pacifism and internationalism alongside nationalism. As Sarah Imhoff relates in this volume, Sampter's very body, disabled and disfigured from polio, was a living repudiation of the strong, healthy male body that Zionism was supposed to produce.[48] As an American who moved to Palestine after the Balfour Declaration, and as a lesbian living with her partner in Jerusalem, Sampter violated conventions and embraced contradictions. In her publications as a Zionist thinker and in her private correspondence, Sampter confronts us with the tensions that marked her life and correspond to the contradictions in the lives of Jewish women who are both Jewish and yet live on the margins of Judaism and Zionism. Sampter was a woman who literally embodied the tensions she wrote about.

In treating the Balfour Declaration as their own mandate over Palestine, Zionists used it to stimulate Jewish political action. "In an era riven by racism, nativism, and inequity on the domestic scene and fraught with social and political tensions," as Raider explains, "rival claims to American Jewish communal authority burst into the open and spawned the American Jewish Congress movement."[49] Those tensions and rival claims were negotiated with a politics of gender, race, Orientalism, and Protestant theology. Against this backdrop, the Balfour Declaration became a white male, Western, Christian affirmation of American Jewish national consciousness.

The United States Congress, which was soon to establish a restrictive quota system for immigration, affirmed the Balfour Declaration in 1922 with its own resolution. The US House of

Representatives invited both Jewish and Arab representatives to provide testimony concerning the situation of their communities. Introducing the hearings, Representative Hamilton Fish, Republican of New York, stated that Zionism would establish "in Palestine a refuge for the persecuted Jews of the world where they can develop their own culture, law, and ideals in the ancient land of their fathers, given by Jehovah to Abraham and consecrated in the hearts of the Jewish people as the birthplace of their traditions."[50]

In April 1922, the US House of Representatives Committee on Foreign Affairs invited an Arab American law student, Selim Totah, who was born and raised in Palestine, to testify about conditions there. He was questioned by Congressman Fish about the rate of illiteracy among Palestinian Arabs: Totah claimed the rate was 35 percent, Fish claimed 60 percent.[51] Congressman William Cockrun, Democrat of New York, then challenged Totah about economic development in Palestine, claiming Arabs had not developed their own economy but depended on help from outside, including from Jews. What the *Congressional Record* makes clear is the combination of firm support for a Jewish home, if not a state, in Palestine; contempt for Arabs and Islam; ignorance of the actual conditions in Palestine; and a conviction that Zionism is not only helpful to Jews, but a fulfillment of Christian values as well. Together with Senator Henry Cabot Lodge, Republican of Massachusetts, Fish sponsored a resolution in support of Balfour that passed both houses of Congress in June of 1922.

The speeches delivered by congressional representatives in support of the Balfour Declaration cited the Bible and the suffering and poverty of Jews in Europe through the centuries, decried quotas on Jewish students at Harvard, and aligned Zionism with the US Bill of Rights. In one speech, Jews were praised as the most extraordinary people that ever inhabited this earth and the chief benefactors of humankind. Arabs were mentioned tangentially and warned that if they objected to Jewish sovereignty, they would leave the area either voluntarily or by force. One congressman declared, simultaneously, his support for Zionism and his contempt for Islam:

> There is no good reason why the Jews and Arabs should not live together in perfect peace and harmony in Palestine. They are all Semitic in blood and language, and all worship the same God and the same Hebrew prophets... the fact remains that the Arabs have more lands than they need, and the Jews have none... Mr. Speaker, I despise and hate race prejudice and religious bigotry worse than I do the devil and all his ways... But I draw the line on Mahomet [*sic*], the military conqueror and robber, the forger of oracles, the polygamist.[52]

Another congressman praised the colonizing nature of the Zionist enterprise:

> The colonist Jew is bringing Western culture and civilization into the country, and it is natural that the Moslem [*sic*] Arabs, steeped in ignorance and extreme poverty, would occasionally clash with the newcomers. This is especially true of the Bedouin Arabs, who have no civilization worth the mention.[53]

Congressional Zionism was a political effort, but also a racial, sexual, and religious project. The statements made by the US Congress representatives display a combination of ignorance and arrogance, firm endorsement of the Balfour Declaration, and disregard for the Arab population in Palestine. Their advocacy of the Balfour Declaration is based on the Bible, Orientalism, and imperialist condescension. Selim Totah, invited to testify, was treated with disdain, while the congressmen used the opportunity to introduce long statements about Judaism and Zionism into the *Congressional Record*. One representative's comments portray Arabs in Palestine as incompetent and female-like in their underdevelopment. While Totah explained that the Ottomans had prevented proper economic development of Palestine, his comments went unrecognized.

Totah was badgered as part of a newly emerging phenomenon, Congressional Zionism, which developed a strong voice endorsing Zionism and, subsequently, unmitigated support for the State of Israel that has continued unabated to the present day. Part of the strategy for Representative Fish and his colleagues was to demonstrate that Arabs in Palestine were illiterate and backward, incapable of economic development, and thus justifying Zionist plans. Here we see the reconfigured Orientalism that had also inspired English support for the Balfour Declaration. Palestinians were effeminized, emasculated Arabs, but under Zionists influenced Europe to view Jews as civilized representatives of Western culture—real men. In the Congressional discourse, Jews were vigorous, youthful male conquerors, ready to bring skills and intelligence to cultivate the female, indolent Arab soil of Palestine. Even as the Jews were being transformed into manly Zionists, the United States framed itself as a kind of "manliness coach," a political version of a Boy Scout leader writ large: the man who turns a boy into a man.[54]

The Congressional rhetoric focuses on the transformative: following the lead of the Zionists, it reconfigures the suffering, diasporic Jews into Zionist men. On the one hand, the congressmen speak of Jewish poverty and suffering, while on the other hand, they are confident Jewish industriousness will bring Western culture and civilization to Palestine, transforming Jews from victims to colonizing heroes. Arabs hold the passive, female role, unable to help themselves, and needing Jewish manpower to bring them basic civilizing tools. One congressman has a vision of cohabitation: Jews and Arabs living together in peace in Palestine, since they "are all Semitic in blood and language." Arabs, he seemed to imagine, would bring a dowry of land, while Jews would fertilize that land with the culture and civilization of the West.

Christianity had provided England with a tool to justify its support for Zionism while rejecting claims from other national groups seeking political independence, especially in Ireland and India. English Protestants viewed Jews as living embodiments of biblical Israelites, so that support for Zionism expressed Protestant devotion to the Bible, allowing the British government to defend Balfour as a Christian commitment, not as a political position of support for national self-rule that would have applied to Ireland and India. In the United States, premillennialist Protestants supported Zionism, while some mainline denominations, with missionaries who had established Arab churches, did not, a distinction that has survived to the present.

The situation was more complicated for Catholics. Whereas Protestants lived by the text of the Bible, the Bible for Catholics was distanced, mediated by church interpretation and doctrine. Protestants sought to live in emulation of the people of the Bible, whereas Catholics focused on saints as their models of faith. Certain Protestants felt an affinity with Jews, while Catholics, having been accused of Pharisaism and other Jewish-like sins, declined such affinity. Within the United States, some Catholic leaders, notably the liberal Cardinal James Gibbons of Baltimore, supported the Balfour Declaration, while most opposed it, viewing Palestine as a Christian region and Zionism as "a threat to the church's security" there.[55]

France, Italy, and the Vatican played limited roles in response to the Balfour Declaration, but the Vatican's concern about retaining Christian sovereignty over holy places in Palestine shaped its ambivalence and even opposition to Zionism until 1993, when it finally established diplomatic relations with the State of Israel. England had felt pressure from French-Catholic Canada and from Catholic Ireland, especially after the 1916 Easter Rising, to demonstrate that it was not motivated by anti-Catholicism in denying self-rule.[56] That was helped by emphasizing Protestant affinities to the Bible and Zionist claims to be reviving biblical history.

Not a generic Christianity or Protestantism, but a particular kind of Protestant theology made the Balfour Declaration possible and protected England and America against other claims to independence. This was a Protestant theology markedly distinct from the far more sophisticated and influential Lutheran Protestant theology that had come to fruition in Germany during the same period. Architects of the Balfour Declaration and its supporters in Britain and the United States presented their Christian support for Zionism as the Jews' restoration of a biblical mandate from God.[57] The line of continuity they drew from the Bible to the present—importantly, a Bible shared by Jews and Christians—would not have been formulated by their Protestant counterparts in Germany. For German Protestants, there was no line of continuity from ancient Israelite religion to that of Judaism. Julius Wellhausen, the most influential Hebrew Bible scholar of the nineteenth century, had argued strongly that ancient Israelite religion was no different from that of the Canaanites, and only gradually began to distinguish itself from "paganism" and "idolatry" to become the religion of law in the biblical books of Leviticus and Deuteronomy, a legal system that abandoned, he argued, the high moral teachings of the prophets and laid the foundations for what he viewed as the legalism of rabbinic Judaism.[58] As a religion founded in exile, Judaism, for Wellhausen and most German Protestants, is as distinct from the Israelite religion of the Bible as it is from Christianity and Islam. Moreover, for Wellhausen, Judaism holds no more legitimate claim to the Hebrew Bible than either of the other two religions. Around the same time, a neo-Marcionism emerged within German Protestant theology, encouraged, in part, by Adolf von Harnack, the most important exponent of liberal Protestantism whose writings were translated and read around the world. Neo-Marcionism was a revival of the claims of a second-century heretic, Marcion, that the God of the Old Testament was not the same as the God of the New Testament; the Old Testament, Marcion demanded, should not be part of the Christian

Bible. With the revival of Marcion's ideas in the early twentieth century, some German pastors called for removing the Old Testament from the Christian Bible. Clearly, a positive connection between Christians and Jews and between Jews and the Hebrew Bible was not forthcoming in German Protestantism. Even as most German Jews were not supportive of Zionism, their Protestant counterparts saw no fulfillment of Christianity in Zionism nor in the presence of Jews in Palestine. Neither German Jews nor Christians found religious gratification in the movement.

Are there positive contributions the Balfour Declaration can offer today to Israelis and Palestinians seeking peace? The possibility of a Palestinian state coexisting with the State of Israel seems increasingly remote at present, as does a binational state. Yet several observers, including Ian Lustick and Bernard Avishai, have proposed a confederation of two national entities, Israel and Palestine, under a joint state structure.[59] The Israeli philosopher Omri Boehm has outlined the idea, which he traces to Menachem Begin, Likud party prime minister of Israel from 1977–83, for a federation of two states, Israeli and Palestinian, in the territory between the Jordan River and the Mediterranean Sea. While independent, they would have "a joint constitution, to which each state's legislative, executive, and judicial branches will be subject," including a joint Supreme Court.[60] Nationality would not be equated with citizenship; each country would indeed be its own national homeland, expanding the promise of the Balfour Declaration to two, one for Arabs and one for Jews. The overarching state apparatus would offer a single economy with joint administration of governmental functions: a home for each nation and a state for both nations. If a federated state can emerge over two national homes, perhaps the homeland promise of the Balfour Declaration will come to be seen as wise advice from a fading imperial power navigating the difficult political demands of independent national self-determination from national, ethnic, and religious groups around the globe.

Such proposals are not entirely new. In the aftermath of the May 1921 Arab riots, a young Sephardi Jew, Yosef Hayyim Castel, born in Hebron in 1899 and living in Palestine, sent a seventeen-page memorandum to Weizmann, by then head of the World Zionist Organization, with a detailed analysis of the social and economic conditions and the diverse political views of Arabs in Palestine. He argued that the Balfour Declaration was "the main barrier to collaboration with the Arabs" because the promise of a Jewish home had generated fear that was not allayed by the declaration's promise to the non-Jews in Palestine: "Yet many [Arabs] would agree to Jewish immigration if this declaration would not have been issued."[61] Castel urged a revision of the Balfour Declaration to give greater recognition to Arabs and to create "a shared homeland that should be governed through a political system like in Switzerland or Belgium."[62] Arab opposition was not to Jewish immigration, but to the failure of recognizing that Palestine was also an Arab country. As Evri and Cohen write, Castel's memorandum was "characteristic of his native Sephardi contemporaries: their understanding for the Arab national movement, its feelings and motives, without abandoning the Zionist perspective or their identification with 'our movement' and the Jewish need for a homeland."[63] Castel was not opposed to Zionism, but he wanted Balfour himself to "declare that Palestine was also the national home of the Palestinian Arabs, and thus recognize their national rights to the land."[64] Whether Weizmann read Castel's proposal or showed it to others in the Zionist leadership, is unknown. The revival of a proposal to create a confederated state for two nations, Arab and Jewish, more than a century later, does not seem at present likely to be implemented.

Contributing to the historiography of World War I and the Balfour Declaration, the essays collected in this book offer a carefully examined assessment of a crucial era in American Jewish history that made a distinct impact on Jewish and international affairs, both through the Zionist movement and the American government. The Jewish enthusiasm for the declaration and the formulation of Zionism as an expression of American values, routed through the politics of race, gender, and religion, spawned a Congressional Zionism with its own peculiar motifs that has remained a powerful political force to the present day. Of all the many political commitments made in the twentieth century by the British government, the brief paragraph of 1917 promising the Zionists a "home" dramatically altered the political landscape of the United States, Europe, and the Arab world, and the politics and demography of the Mashriq. In its aftermath, Zionism transformed Arab and Jewish identity and Protestant theological commitments, though not the conflict on the ground that continues unabated. Whether the ultimate outcome will give cause for celebration or end in tragedy remains unclear, but just as Zionism and Palestinian nationalism are constituted by hope, perhaps our politics should be as well.

Endnotes

1 Benny Morris, *Righteous Victims: A History of the Zionist-Arab Conflict* (New York: Knopf, 1999), 73.

2 Yoav Gelber, "The History of Zionist Historiography," in *Making Israel*, ed. Benny Morris (Ann Arbor: University of Michigan Press, 2007), 47.

3 Rashid Khalidi, *The Hundred Years' War on Palestine: A History of Settler Colonialism and Resistance, 1917–2017* (New York: Metropolitan Books, 2020), 26.

4 Shabtai Teveth, *Ben-Gurion and the Palestinian Arabs: From Peace to War* (Oxford: Oxford University Press, 1985), 43.

5 Ian Lustick, "The Balfour Declaration a Century Later: Accidentally Relevant," *Middle East Policy* 24:4 (Winter 2017): 166.

6 Weizmann, "Notes of Conversation at Mr. Balfour's on 22/7/21," Central Zionist Archives, Z4/16055, cited in Jehuda Reinharz, *Chaim Weizmann: The Making of a Statesman* (New York: Oxford University Press, 1993), 357, fn167.

7 See, e.g., Anita Shapira, *Land and Power: The Zionist Resort to Force, 1881-1948* (New York: Oxford University Press, 1992), 83–85; Jonathan Schneer, *The Balfour Declaration: The Origins of the Arab-Israeli Conflict*, pbk. ed. (New York: Random House, 2012), 344–45.

8 See chap. 5 in this volume.

9 Mark Levene, "The Balfour Declaration: A Case of Mistaken Identity," *The English Historical Review* 107:422 (January 1992): 76.

10 James Renton, *The Zionist Masquerade: The Birth of the Anglo-Zionist Alliance, 1914–1918* (New York: Palgrave Macmillan, 2007); Levene, "The Balfour Declaration," 76–77.

11 Renton, *The Zionist Masquerade*, 81.

12 Danny Gutwein, "The Politics of the Balfour Declaration: Nationalism, Imperialism, and the Limits of Zionist-British Cooperation," *Journal of Israeli History* 35:2 (2006): 117–52.

13 Maryanne A. Rhett, *The Global History of the Balfour Declaration: Declared Nation* (New York: Routledge, 2015), 25.

14 Yuval Evri and Hillel Cohen, "Between Shared Homeland to National Home: The Balfour Declaration from a Native Sephardic Perspective," in *The Arab and Jewish Questions: Geographies of Engagement in Palestine and Beyond*, ed. Bashir Bashir and Leila Farsakh (New York: Columbia University Press, 2020), 153.

15 John Darwin, *The Empire Project: The Rise and Fall of the British World System, 1830–1970* (New York: Cambridge University Press, 2009).

16 Richard Ned Lebow, "Woodrow Wilson and the Balfour Declaration," *Journal of Modern History* 40:4 (December 1968): 501–23.

17 See chap. 1 in this volume.

18 See chap. 5 in this volume.

19 See chap. 9 in this volume.

20 Quoted in *ibid.*

21 Karin Loevy, "The Balfour Declaration's Territorial Landscape: Between-Protection and Self-Determination," *Humanity: An International Journal of Human Rights, Humanitarianism, and Development* 12:2 (Summer 2021): 150. 22 Lustick, "The Balfour Declaration a Century Later," 171.

23 *Ibid.*, 169.

24 Hillel Cohen, *Year Zero of the Arab-Israeli Conflict 1929*, trans. Haim Watzman (Waltham, MA: Brandeis University Press), 229.

25 Loevy, "The Balfour Declaration's Territorial Landscape," 150.

26 Morris, *Righteous Victims*, 76.

27 Evri and Cohen, "Between Shared Homeland to National Home," 155.

28 Cohen, *Year Zero*, 190.

29 George Antonius, *The Arab Awakening*, reprint (New York: Gordon Press, 1981).

30 Morris, *Righteous Victims*, 77.

31 Rashid Khalidi, *Palestinian Identity: The Construction of Modern National Identity*, second ed. (New York: Columbia University Press, 2009), 172.

32 Derek J. Penslar, *Zionism: An Emotional State* (unpublished book manuscript), 10.

33 Michael Bar-Zohar, *Ben Gurion: A Biography* (New York: Delacorte Press, 1978), 37.

34 See chap. 9 in this volume.

35 Morris, *Righteous Victims*, 156.

36 *Ibid.*

37 Arye Naor, "The Purifying Effect of Truth: Jabotinsky's Interpretation of the Balfour Declaration," *Israel Studies* 22:3 (Fall 2017): 31–47.

38 Hannah Arendt, "The Crisis of Zionism" (1943), in *The Jewish Writings*, eds. Jerome Kohn and Ron H. Feldman (New York: Schocken Books, 2007), 97–98.

39 See the discussion in Arie Dubnov, "On Vertical Alliances, 'Perfidious Albion,' and the Security Paradigm: Reflections on the Balfour Declaration Centennial and the Winding Road to Israeli Independence," *European Judaism* 52:1 (Spring 2019): 83–85.

40 Quoted in Edy Kaufman, "The French Pro-Zionist Declarations of 1917–1918," *Middle Eastern Studies* 15:3 (October 1979): 377.

41 *Ibid.*, 381.

42 *Ibid.*, 379, see also fn 115.

43 See Gelber, "The History of Zionist Historiography," 47–51. In reviewing the earliest histories of Zionism, Gelber notes Sokolow's own account, immediately refuted by Adolf Böhm, who presented Zionism as an international Jewish development brought into being by organizational efforts; Yitzhak Gruenbaum's *Hatnuah hazionit behitpathutah* (The Development of the Zionist Movement), *1942–54* forges a link between Zionism and Jewish

messianism; and Benzion (Dinaburg) Dinur's Zionist historiography shifts the movement to the Land of Israel.

44 Dubnov, "On Vertical Alliances, 'Perfidious Albion,' and the Security Paradigm," 75.

45 See chap. 8 in this volume.

46 Dubnov, "On Vertical Alliances, 'Perfidious Albion,' and the Security Paradigm," 96.

47 Quoted in *The Letters and Papers of Chaim Weizmann*, vol. 1, series B: August 1898-July 1931, ed. Barnet Litvinoff (Jerusalem: Israeli Universities Press, 1983), 630.

48 See chap. 7 in this volume.

49 See introduction in this volume.

50 House Resolution 360, "National Home for the Jewish People," *Congressional Record*, 9799–820.

51 *Establishment of a National Home in Palestine: Hearings Before the Committee on Foreign Affairs, House of Representatives... on H. Con. R.* 52, 67th Cong. 166–70 (1922): 166.

52 *Congressional Record*, 67–2 Cong. Rec. 9799–820 (1922).

53 *Ibid.*

54 Ultimately, a joint resolution endorsing the Balfour Declaration, introduced by Representative Hamilton Fish and Senator Henry Cabot Lodge, was passed by Congress in June 1922 and signed in September 1922 by President Warren G. Harding.

55 Egal Feldman, *Catholics and Jews in Twentieth-Century America* (Champaign: University of Illinois Press, 2006), 38–39.

56 Rhett, *Global History of the Balfour Declaration*, 25.

57 Victoria Clark, *Allies for Armageddon: The Rise of Christian Zionism* (New Haven, CT: Yale University Press, 2007); Robert O. Smith, *More Desired than Our Own Salvation: The Roots of Christian Zionism* (New York: Oxford University Press, 2013).

58 Julius Wellhausen, *Prolegomena zur Geschichte Israels*, second ed. (Berlin: Georg Reimer, 1883).

59 Lustick, "The Balfour Declaration a Century Later," 166–76; Bernard Avishai, "Confederation: The One Possible Israel-Palestine Solution," *New York Review Daily* (February 2, 2018), https://www.nybooks.com/daily/2018/02/02/confederation-the-one-possible-israel-palestine-solution/.

60 Omri Boehm, *Haifa Republic: A Democratic Future for Israel* (New York: New York Review Books, 2021), 82.

61 Evri and Cohen, "Between Shared Homeland to National Home," 161.

62 *Ibid.*, 163.

63 *Ibid.*, 161.

64 *Ibid.*, 162.

Timeline of American Jewish History in Global Context

American History	American Jewish History	World History *Developments in Zionism and Palestine appear in italics.*
1880 US population: over 50 million, 26 percent increase since 1870. Election of James A. Garfield as 20th US president	**1880** Union of American Hebrew Congregations publishes the first census of American Jewry, estimate 250,000	**1880** First Boer War.
1881 Assassination of Pres. James A. Garfield; Vice President Chester A. Arthur becomes 21st US president	**1881** Pogroms in tsarist Russia impel mass waves of east European Jewish immigration to the United States in large numbers.	**1881** Assassination of Tsar Alexander II. Wave of pogroms in tsarist Russia. *First Aliyah settlers (1881–1903), mostly from eastern Europe and Yemen, immigrate to Ottoman Palestine and create nucleus of rural Jewish colonies.*
		1882 Death of Charles Darwin. British invasion and occupation of Egypt. *Leon Pinsker publishes* Autoemancipation. *Bilu pioneers arrive in Palestine.*
1883 Brooklyn Bridge opens.		**1883** Death of Karl Marx.
1884 Election of Grover Cleveland as 22nd US president. District of Alaska organized.		**1884** Hiram Maxim invents the modern machine gun. Berlin Conference leads to European "Scramble for Africa."

AMERICAN HISTORY	AMERICAN JEWISH HISTORY	WORLD HISTORY
	1885 Reform rabbis adopt Pittsburgh Platform declaring Jews are "no longer a nation, but a religious community" and rejecting Zionism. Kasriel H. Sarasohn launches *Tageblatt* (Daily News), first Yiddish daily paper in New York City.	**1885** Louis Pasteur creates successful vaccine against rabies. Karl Benz invents the first motor car with an internal combustion engine. Founding of Indian National Congress. *Nathan Birnbaum coins the term "Zionism."*
1886 Haymarket Riot (Chicago, IL). Samuel Gompers founds American Federation of Labor. Dedication of Statue of Liberty, New York Harbor.		
	1887 Founding of Jewish Theological Seminary, seminary of Conservative Judaism.	
1888 Election of Benjamin Harrison as 23nd US president.	**1888** Founding of Jewish Publication Society of America. Jewish socialists in New York City establish United Hebrew Trades.	**1888** Jack the Ripper terrifies Whitechapel, London. Imperial Brazil bans slavery.
1889 Jane Addams opens Hull House (Chicago, IL). US Congress passes Sherman Antitrust Act. North Dakota, South Dakota, Montana, and Washington admitted to the Union as the 39th–42nd states.	**1889** Isaac M. Wise creates Central Conference of American Rabbis, the rabbinic body of Reform Judaism.	**1889** Dedication of Eiffel Tower in Paris. Founding of Brazilian Republic.

AMERICAN HISTORY	AMERICAN JEWISH HISTORY	WORLD HISTORY
1890 US population: over 63 million, 25 percent increase since 1880. Oklahoma Territory is organized. Wounded Knee Massacre. Idaho and Wyoming admitted to the Union as 43th and 44th states. Ellis Island opens as US immigration center.		**1890** Italy annexes Eritrea. *Eliezer Ben Yehuda founds Hebrew Language Committee.*
1891 US Congress passes Forest Reserve Act.	**1891** Creation of Baron de Hirsch Fund to support East European Jewish émigrés.	**1891** Pope Leo XIII announces encyclical Rerum Novarum, a major Catholic document on social justice. *Ahad Haam (Asher Zvi Hirsch Ginsberg) visits Palestine and calls for creation of Jewish cultural center.*
1892 Election of Grover Cleveland as 24th US president. Homestead Strike launched by Amalgamated Association of Iron and Steel Workers.	**1892** Founding of American Jewish Historical Society.	**1892** Premier of Pyotr Ilyich Tchaikovsky's *Nutcracker Suite* in St. Petersburg.
1893 World's Columbian Exposition (Chicago, IL). Founding of Anti-Saloon League. Panic of 1893. US military overthrows native Hawaiian government.	**1893** Educational Alliance settlement house opens in New York City. Founding of Jewish Chautauqua Society and National Council of Jewish Women.	**1893** New Zealand becomes first Western nation to enact women's suffrage.
1894 Coxey's Army of unemployed workers marches on Washington, DC.		**1894** Invention of the gramophone. Dreyfus Affair in France.

American History	American Jewish History	World History
		1895 First Sino-Japanese War. Trial of Oscar Wilde and premier of his farcical comedy, *The Importance of Being Earnest*. First Italo-Ethiopian War.
1896 US Supreme court codifies racial segregation ("separate but equal"). Election of William McKinley as 25th US president. Klondike Gold Rush begins. Utah admitted to the US as 45th state after outlawing polygamy.		**1896** Philippine Revolution ends Spanish rule. Klondike Gold Rush in Canada. Henri Becquerel discovers radioactivity. *Theodor Herzl publishes* The Jews' State.
	1897 Founding of Rabbi Isaac Elchanan Theological Seminary. Socialist Yiddish-language newspaper *Forverts* (Forward) begins publication.	**1897** Greco-Turkish War. *1st Zionist Congress (Basel, Switz.) establishes Zionist Organization; Theodor Herzl elected president of Zionist Organization.*
1898 Spanish-American War; US government gains control of Guam, Puerto Rico, the Philippines, and Cuba. Annexation of Hawaii by the United States.	**1898** Founding of Federation of American Zionists and Union of Orthodox Jewish Congregations of America.	**1898** Assassination of Empress Elisabeth of Austria. Boxer Rebellion in China. Wilhelmina becomes queen of the Netherlands. *2nd Zionist Congress (Basel, Switz.) creates Jewish Colonial Trust. Kaiser Wilhelm II visits Palestine and meets with Theodor Herzl.*
1899 Philippine-American War begins. Florence Kelley founds National Consumers' League.	**1899** Founding of National Conference of Jewish Charities. *American Jewish Year Book* begins publication.	**1899** Second Boer War. Famine in India. Rudyard Kipling publishes "The White Man's Burden." *3rd Zionist Congress (Basel, Switz,) affirms Jewish Colonial Trust funds to be used for land acquisition in Palestine and Syria.*

AMERICAN HISTORY	AMERICAN JEWISH HISTORY	WORLD HISTORY
1900 US population: over 76 million, 21 percent increase since 1890. US Congress passes Gold Standard Act. Reelection of US president McKinley. Founding of International Ladies' Garment Workers' Union. Hawaii Territory organized.	**1900** Estimate of American Jewish population: approx. 1 million (1.25 percent of total US population), concentrated in Northeast and Midwest urban centers. Founding of Jewish socialist Arbeter Ring (Workmen's Circle) organization.	**1900** World population: 1.6 billion. Sigmund Freud publishes *The Interpretation of Dreams*. Exposition Universelle in Paris. *4th Zionist Congress (London, Eng.) focuses on political solution to plight of Rumanian Jewry.*
1901 Cuba becomes US protectorate. Assassination of President William McKinley at Pan-American Exposition in Buffalo, NY; Vice President Theodore Roosevelt becomes 26th US president.	**1901** Founding of Rabbinical Assembly, Conservative Judaism's rabbinic association. Establishment of Industrial Removal Office to relocate Jewish immigrants in New York City across the country.	**1901** Establishment of Federation of Australia. Death of Queen Victoria. Boxer Rebellion ends. Marconi transmits first trans-Atlantic radio signal. First Nobel Prizes awarded. *5th Zionist Congress (Basel, Switz.) creates Jewish National Fund; Herzl meets with Sultan Abdul Hamid of Turkey.*
1902 Cuba gains independence from US.	**1902** Founding of Agudat Harabbanim, Union of Orthodox Rabbis. Solomon Schechter appointed head of the Jewish Theological Seminary.	**1902** Egypt's Aswan Dam opens. Cuba gains independence from the United States. Second Boer War ends.
1903 US assumes control of Panama Canal. Orville and Wilbur Wright make first successful flight of motor-propelled aircraft. US grants Panama independence.	**1903** American Jews react to Kishinev pogrom with countrywide gatherings and protests. Emma Lazarus's poem, "The New Colossus," inscribed at base of Statue of Liberty.	**1903** Kishinev pogrom in tsarist Russia. Panama gains independence. *6th Zionist Congress (Basel, Switz.) rejects Theodor Herzl's proposal of East Africa settlement and affirms Land of Israel as focus of Zionism. Founding in Palestine of Anglo-Palestine Bank and Hebrew Teachers' Association.*

American History	American Jewish History	World History
1904 Theodore Roosevelt elected US president and promises "Square Deal." US Supreme Court upholds Sherman Antitrust Act in *Northern Securities Co. v. United States*.		**1904** Russo-Japanese War. Construction of Panama Canal begins. Completion of Trans-Siberian Railway. Roger Casement publishes report detailing King Leopold II of Belgium's abuses in Congo Free State. Germany commences Herero and Namaqua genocide. *Second Aliyah pioneers (1904–1914), mostly from tsarist Russia, immigrate to Ottoman Palestine and create network of rural settlements. Death of Theodor Herzl.*
	1905 American Jewry celebrates 250th anniversary of Jewish arrival in New Amsterdam.	**1905** First Russian Revolution. Nor- way gains independence. Russo- Japanese War ends. Partition of Bengal. Albert Einstein develops theory of relativity. *7th Zionist Congress (Basel, Switzerland) elects David Wolffsohn president of the Zionist Organization and affirms Jewish settlement in Palestine as Zionism's paramount goal. Israel Zangwill quits Zionist Organization, establishes Jewish Territorial Association.*

AMERICAN HISTORY	AMERICAN JEWISH HISTORY	WORLD HISTORY
1906 San Francisco earthquake. US Congress passes Hepburn Act, Pure Food and Drug Act, Meat Inspection Act, and Antiquities Act (expands National Parks system).	**1906** Publication of *Jewish Encyclopedia*. Founding of American Jewish Committee. Harvard University Jewish students create Menorah Society. President Theodore Roosevelt appoints Oscar Straus as secretary of labor and commerce (first Jew to hold cabinet post).	**1906** Alfred Dreyfus exonerated; Dreyfus Affair ends. Founding of All-India Muslim League. *Founding of Bezalel Academy of the Arts in Jerusalem.*
1907 Financial Panic and Depression of 1907. Oklahoma admitted to the Union as 46th state.	**1907** Stephen S. Wise establishes Free Synagogue in New York City. Dropsie College for Hebrew and Cognate Learning is chartered in Philadelphia.	**1907** Peasants' Revolt in Romania. Finland adopts universal suffrage. Japan-Korea Treaty. Indian National Congress splits into factions. Mohandas K. Gandhi initiates campaign of satyagraha. *8th Zionist Congress (The Hague, Netherlands) affirms need for dual political and practical strategy, namely, international recognition of Zionism and Jewish settlement in Palestine.*
1908 William Howard Taft elected as 27th US president. Henry Ford produces Model T automobile.		**1908** Robert Baden-Powell publishes *Scouting for Boys*. Young Turk Revolution. Austria-Hungary annexes Bosnia-Herzegovina. Bulgaria gains independence. Indian National Congress calls for home rule. *Office of Zionist Organization opens in Jaffa. Eliezer Ben Yehuda publishes* Hazvi *(The Gazelle), Palestine's first Hebrew- language daily newspaper.*

American History	American Jewish History	World History
1909 US troops withdraw from Cuba. Founding of NAACP (National Association for Advancement of Colored People).	**1909** Establishment in New York City of Kehillah Jewish communal organization, headed by Judah L. Magnes. Founding of Hebrew Sheltering and Immigrant Aid Society (HIAS).	**1909** Anglo-Siamese Treaty. Robert E. Peary reaches North Pole. Young Turks depose Sultan Abdulhamid II. *9th Zionist Congress (Hamburg, Germany), buoyed by Young Turk Revolution, includes representatives of Palestine Jewish workers' groups. Establishment of Hashomer (The Watchman) organization to protect rural Jewish settlements. Founding of Tel Aviv and first kibbutz, Degania.*
1910 US population: over 92 million inhabitants, 21 percent increase since 1900.	**1910** Establishment of Yiddish secular school system by socialist Zionist Poalei Zion (Workers of Zion) party.	**1910** Halley's Comet visible. Albanian revolt. Establishment of Union of South Africa. Kingdom of Montenegro created. Imperial Japan annexes Korea. Mexican Revolution begins.

AMERICAN HISTORY	AMERICAN JEWISH HISTORY	WORLD HISTORY
1911 Triangle Shirtwaist Factory Fire in New York City. Antitrust suit triggers break up of Standard Oil into smaller companies.	**1911** US Congress abrogates 1832 treaty with Russia owing to refusal by tsarist regime to honor US passports carried by Jews.	**1911** Roald Amundsen reaches South Pole. Italo-Turkish War; Italy captures Libya. Xinhai Revolution ends China's imperial dynasty. *10th Zionist Congress (Basel, Switz.) elects Otto Warburg president of Zionist Organization, focuses on strategic development of Jewish society in Palestine, including Hebrew language and culture and relations with Palestinian Arabs. World Zionist Organization moves headquarters from Cologne to Berlin.*
1912 Theodore Roosevelt launches Progressive ("Bull Moose") party. Woodrow Wilson elected 28th US president. New Mexico and Arizona admitted to the US as 47th and 48th states, respectively. US militaryth forces occupy Nicaragua.	**1912** Louis Marshall becomes president of American Jewish Committee. Founding of Young Israel. Henrietta Szold founds Hadassah, Women's Zionist Organization of America. Jacob H. Schiff finances creation of Library of Congress's Semitic Division.	**1912** Founding of African National Congress. Morocco designated French protectorate. British passenger liner Titanic sinks in North Atlantic Ocean. Establishment of Republic of China. First Balkan War.
1913 Philippine-American War ends. Ratification of Sixteenth and Seventeenth Amendments to the US Constitution establishing federal income tax and direct election of US senators, respectively. US Congress passes Federal Reserve Act.	**1913** Founding of Anti-Defamation League by Bnai Brith, Labor Zionist Alliance by socialist Zionist groups, Intercollegiate Menorah Association, and United Synagogue of Conservative Judaism. Mary Antin publishes *The Promised Land*.	**1913** Mendel Beilis acquitted in Russian trial following accusation of ritual murder. Second Balkan War. Treaty of Bucharest. Niels Bohr introduces quantum mechanics. *11th Zionist Congress (Vienna, Austria) focuses on Jewish settlement activity in Palestine, opening of World Zionist Organization office in Jaffa, and establishment of a Hebrew University in Jerusalem.*

AMERICAN HISTORY	AMERICAN JEWISH HISTORY	WORLD HISTORY
1914 US military forces occupy Vera Cruz, Mexico. President Wilson declares the United States is a neutral nation in European conflict. Wilson orders segregation of federal workplaces. Panama Canal opens.	**1914** Founding of American Jewish Joint Distribution Committee.	**1914** Assassination in Sarajevo of Archduke Franz Ferdinand of Austria. World War I begins. Sultanate of Egypt established as British protectorate.
1915 D.W. Griffith releases *The Birth of a Nation*. German submarines sink British passenger line, *Lusitania*, provoking public outcry against Germany. US military forces occupy Haiti.	**1915** Antisemitic gang lynches Leo Frank in Marietta, Georgia. Moses Alexander elected governor of Idaho (second elected Jewish governor of a US state).	**1915** Armenian Genocide begins. *NILI Jewish espionage network begins work with British intelligence.*
1916 US government purchases US West Indies and Virgin Islands for $25 million. Great Migration (1916–1940) of African Americans from rural South to urban Northeast, Midwest, and West. Wilson reelected US president.	**1916** Pres. Wilson nominates Louis D. Brandeis to US Supreme Court (first Jew appointed to nation's highest court).	**1916** Easter Rising in Ireland. Great Arab Revolt begins. British and French secretly negotiate Sykes-Picot Agreement.

AMERICAN HISTORY	AMERICAN JEWISH HISTORY	WORLD HISTORY
1917 United States enters World War I as member of Allied Powers. US Congress passes Espionage Act.	**1917** Approx. 225,000 Jews serve in US armed forces during World War I. Creation of Jewish Welfare Board to serve religious needs of Jews in the US military. Establishment of Jewish Telegraphic Agency.	**1917** Bolshevik revolution in Russia signals the end of tsarist empire and rise of Soviet Russia. Vladimir Lenin assumes leadership of Russian revolutionary government. Finland gains independence. *British government issues Balfour Declaration favoring the establishment of a Jewish national home in Palestine. British conquest of Palestine ends 400 years of Ottoman rule.*
1918 US Congress passes Sedition Act (extending Espionage Act of 1917). Imprisonment of American socialist leader Eugene V. Debs. United States joins Allied Powers in signing armistice with Central Powers, ending World War I.	**1918** American Jewish Congress meets in Philadelphia and calls on Paris Peace Conference to recognize Jewish national aspirations in Palestine and protect minority rights of East European Jewry. Maurice Schwartz establishes Yiddish Art Theater. Founding of Women's League for Conservative Judaism.	**1918** World War I ends with surrender of Central Powers. Creation of Weimar Republic. Ukraine declares independence. Beginning of Spanish flu pandemic. Belarus declares independence. Establishment of Azerbaijan Democratic Republic. Assassination of Tsar Nicholas II and royal family. Establishment of Kingdom of Yemen. Poland declares independence. Kingdom of Iceland established. British occupy Palestine. First Pan-African Congress meets in Paris under leadership of W.E.B. Du Bois. *Chaim Weizmann (head of Zionist Commission) meets with Emir Feisal (head of Arab nationalist movement); Weizmann and Feisal subsequently pledge intermovement cooperation.*

American History	American Jewish History	World History
1919 Ratification of Eighteenth Amendment to US Constitution initiates Prohibition era.	**1919** Grossinger's Catskill Resort Hotel opens (Liberty, NY).	**1919** Paris Peace Conference imposes Treaty of Versailles. Turkish War of Independence begins. Afghanistan declares independence. *Third Aliyah pioneers (1919–1923), mostly from Russia, Poland, Romania, and Lithuania, immigrate to Mandatory Palestine and bolster rural Jewish cooperative settlement.*
1920 US population: over 106 million inhabitants, 15 percent increase since 1910. Warren G. Harding elected as 29th US president. Ratification of Nineteenth Amendment to US Constitution grants women right to vote. US Congress repeals Sedition Act of 1918 and votes against joining the League of Nations.	**1920** Estimate of American Jewish population: approx. 3.5 million (3.25 percent of total US population). Henry Ford's *Dearborn Independent* publishes "The International Jew: The World's Problem." American Jewish Congress meets in Philadelphia and elects Commission to Paris Peace Conference headed by Julian W. Mack, Louis Marshall, and Stephen S. Wise.	**1920** Founding of League of Nations. Estonian War of Independence. Mexican Revolution ends. *San Remo Peace Conference designates Mandatory Palestine under British rule; Sir Herbert Samuel appointed British High Commissioner. Palestine's Jewish community creates Elected Assembly and National Council. Founding of Haganah clandestine Jewish defense organization. Chaim Weizmann elected president of World Zionist Organization. Founding of Histadrut (General Federation of Labor). Arab riots in Jerusalem.*

AMERICAN HISTORY	AMERICAN JEWISH HISTORY	WORLD HISTORY
1921 US Congress passes Emergency Quota Act, severely curbing legal immigration. Tulsa Race Riot (Tulsa, OK). Former president William Howard Taft appointed chief justice of US Supreme Court. Margaret Sanger founds America Birth Control League.	**1921** *Hadoar* (The Mail), Hebrew periodical of Histadruth Ivrith begins publication.	**1921** Adolf Hitler becomes head of Nazi party. Benito Mussolini establishes Italian National Fascist party. Mao Zedong helps found Chinese Communist Party. *12th Zionist Congress (Carlsbad, Czechoslovakia) endorses Balfour Declaration and League of Nations plan to grant Mandate for Palestine to Britain. Arab riots in Jaffa. Founding of Nahalal, first moshav.*
1922 Teapot Dome scandal.	**1922** Mordecai M. Kaplan creates Society for the Advancement of Judaism (Reconstructionist Judaism); Kaplan's daughter Judith celebrates first American bat mitzvah. Founding of Agudath Israel of America. Hebrew Theological College opens in Chicago. Stephen S. Wise establishes pluralistic Jewish Institute of Religion in New York City.	**1922** Egypt gains independence; British continue to occupy Suez Canal. Russian Civil War ends. Mussolini comes to power in Italy. Discovery of Tutankhamun's tomb in Egypt. Establishment of Irish Free State. Founding of Union of Soviet Socialist Republics (USSR). *League of Nations confirms British Mandate for Palestine. Pinhas Rutenberg founds Palestine Electric Corporation. Churchill White Paper limits Jewish immigration to Palestine.*

AMERICAN HISTORY	AMERICAN JEWISH HISTORY	WORLD HISTORY
1923 Alice Paul authors Equal Rights Amendment. President Warren G. Harding dies in office; Vice President Calvin Coolidge becomes 30th US President. George Gershwin composes "Rhapsody in Blue."	**1923** Founding of Bnai Brith Hillel Foundation at University of Illinois at Champaign-Urbana.	**1923** Khalil Gibran publishes *The Prophet*. Oil is discovered in Iraq. Transjordan gains independence. Founding of Republic of Turkey under leadership of Kemal Ataturk. Adolf Hitler attempts to overthrow Weimar Republic in Beer Hall Putsch. *13th Zionist Congress (Carlsbad, Czechoslovakia), per League of Nations, creates Jewish Agency for Palestine.*
1924 Johnson-Reed Act severely curtails immigration to US from southern Europe, Asia, and the Middle East. Establishment of Federal Bureau of Investigation under J. Edgar Hoover. US Congress passes Indian Citizenship Act. Calvin Coolidge elected as US president.		**1924** Death of Vladimir Lenin followed by power struggle between Joseph Stalin and Leon Trotsky. *Opening of Technion school of engineering and science in Haifa. Fourth Aliyah settlers (1924–1928), mostly from eastern Europe, Yemen, and Iraq, immigrate to Mandatory Palestine and settle in towns and cities.*
1925 Founding of American Negro Labor Congress. 35,000 Ku Klux Klan members march in Washington, DC. Scopes ("Monkey") Trial.	**1925** Establishment of Synagogue Council of America. Election of Florence Prag Kahn to US House of Representatives (first Jewish woman to serve in Congress).	**1925** Adolf Hitler publishes *Mein Kampf* (My Struggle). *Founding of Hebrew University of Jerusalem on Mount Scopus. Opening of Jewish National and University Library. 14th Zionist Congress (Vienna, Austria) includes participation of Revisionist party led by Zeev Jabotinsky.*

American History	American Jewish History	World History
1926 US Congress passes Air Commerce Act.		**1926** Lebanon becomes a semiautonomous republic.
1927 Great Mississippi Flood. Charles A. Lindbergh's nonstop solo flight from New York to Paris. Warner Brothers releases *The Jazz Singer*, with Al Jolson, first film with sound. *Show Boat*, by Jerome Kern and Oscar Hammerstein II, opens on Broadway.	**1927** *American Jewish Year Book* estimates 4,228,000 Jews in the United States, including 17,500 Jewish organizations and 3,118 synagogues.	**1927** World population reaches two billion. Saudi Arabia gains independence. Chinese Civil War begins. Joseph Stalin becomes official leader of Soviet Union. *Death of Ahad Haam. 15th Zionist Congress (Basel, Switz.) discusses crisis of Jewish emigration from Palestine and reelects Chaim Weizmann as president of World Zionist Organization.*
1928 Amelia Earhart becomes first woman to fly solo over Atlantic Ocean. Herbert Hoover elected as 31st US president.	**1928** Founding of Yeshiva College and National Conference of Christians and Jews. Columbia University opens first chair in Jewish history at a secular institution.	**1928** Alexander Fleming discovers penicillin. Kellogg-Briand Pact (General Treaty for Renunciation of War as an Instrument of National Policy) signed in Paris. Chiang Kai-shek, head of Kuomintang party, becomes ruler of China's nationalist government.

AMERICAN HISTORY	AMERICAN JEWISH HISTORY	WORLD HISTORY
1929 Founding of League of United Latin American Citizens. Crash of US stock market, beginning of Great Depression.	**1929** American Jewry harmed by stock market crash and start of Great Depression. Establishment of Union of Sephardic Congregations. Founding of American Academy for Jewish Research. Expansion of Jewish Agency for Palestine to include non-Zionists.	**1929** Stalin assumes control of Soviet Union; Trotsky exiled. *16th Zionist Congress establishes Expanded Jewish Agency for Palestine, including American Jewish non-Zionist representatives. Arab riots in Hebron. Fifth Aliyah immigrants (1929–1939), mostly from central and western Europe immigrate to Mandatory Palestine and settle in towns and cities. 16th Zionist Congress (Zurich, Switz.) approves plan for enlargement of Jewish Agency for Palestine to include non-Zionist representation.*
1930 US population: over 123 million inhabitants, 16 percent increase since 1920.	**1930** Estimate of American Jewish population: approx. 4.25 million (3.5 percent of total US population), including 17,500 Jewish organizations and 3,118 synagogues.	**1930** Mohandas K. Gandhi leads nonviolent Salt March, protesting British colonial rule of India. Haile Selassie becomes emperor of Ethiopia. *Hope Simpson Report and Passfield White Paper recommend limiting Jewish immigration to Palestine.*

AMERICAN HISTORY	AMERICAN JEWISH HISTORY	WORLD HISTORY
1931 US Congress adopts Francis Scott Key's "Star-Spangled Banner" as national anthem. Scottsboro Boys Trial. Completion of Empire State Building in New York City.		**1931** Second Spanish Republic declared. Japan invades Manchuria. South Africa gains independence. *17th Zionist Congress (Basel, Switzerland) decries Passfield White Paper and controversy erupts concerning Chaim Weizmann's pro-British orientation; Weizmann resigns as World Zionist Organization president and Nahum Sokolow is elected president. Founding of Etzel, rightwing Zionist resistance organization.*
1932 Franklin D. Roosevelt elected as 32nd US president. New Deal era begins.	**1932** Establishment of Council of Jewish Federations, a network of 200 Jewish Federations in the United States and Canada.	**1932** Abd al-Azis proclaims Kingdom of Saudi Arabia. Iraq gains independence. *Habimah Theater Company opens in Tel Aviv. First Maccabiah Games are held.*
1933 US Congress passes New Deal social and economic legislation in special hundred-day session. Federal Emergency Relief Administration creates Civilian Conservation Corps. Ratification of Twenty-first Amendment to US Constitution repeals Eighteenth Amendment (Prohibition). Dust Bowl leads to drought in Great Plains (1934, 1936, and 1939). US military withdraws from Nicaragua.	**1933** American Jewish Congress declares boycott of Germany in protest of Nazi persecution of Jews. Antisemitic groups proliferate in North America.	**1933** Rise of Adolph Hitler and Nazi Germany. Japan and Germany announce plans to quit League of Nations. *Founding of Egged intercity bus cooperative. 18th Zionist Congress (Prague, Czechoslovakia) meets in the shadow of Nazi regime's rise to power and following assassination of Labor Zionist leader Chaim Arlosoroff.*

American History	American Jewish History	World History
1934 Creation of US Securities and Exchange Commission. US military forces withdraw from Haiti. Opening of Mother Mosque of America, first American mosque (Cedar Rapids, IA).	**1934** Founding of Jewish Labor Committee. Mordecai M. Kaplan publishes *Judaism as a Civilization*.	**1934** Women in Turkey granted full voting rights. Austrian Civil War. Night of Long Knives cements Adolf Hitler's rule over Germany; Hitler declares himself Fuehrer following death of Pres. Paul von Hindenburg. *Establishment of Sieff Institute (later renamed Weizmann Institute) in Rehovot.*
1935 Pres. Franklin D. Roosevelt creates Works Progress Administration. US Supreme Courts rules National Industrial Recovery Act unconstitutional. US Congress passes National Labor Relations Act and Social Security Act. Pres. Roosevelt dedicates Boulder (Hoover) Dam.	**1935** Zionist advocates gain control of Central Conference of American Rabbis. Founding of Rabbinical Council of America, an English-language Orthodox rabbinic group.	**1935** Nazi Germany enacts anti-Jewish Nuremburg Laws. Hitler orders military conscription of all men. Persia renamed Iran. Franco-Soviet Treaty of Mutual Assistance signed. Italy invades Ethiopia. Restoration of Greek monarchy by military regime. Mao Zedong issues Wayaobu Manifesto, calling for united Chinese front to confront Japanese invasion of China. *19th Zionist Congress (Lucerne, Switzerland) elects Chaim Weizmann as World Zionist Organization president, and David Ben-Gurion as chairman of Jewish Agency for Palestine; Henrietta Szold leads Youth Aliyah effort. Revisionist party secedes from World Zionist Organization.*

Glossary

aliyah: Hebrew for "ascent," used to denote immigration to the Land of Israel.

American Jewish Committee: Established in 1906, the American Jewish Committee (AJC) aimed "to prevent infringement of the civil and religious rights of Jews, and to alleviate the consequences of [Jewish] persecution" ("Report of the American Jewish Committee," *American Jewish Year Book* 10 [1908]: 238). Led by affluent American Jews of central European ancestry—notably Louis Marshall (1856–1929), Jacob Schiff (1847–1920), Mayer Sulzberger (1843–1923), Julian W. Mack (1866–1943), Julius Rosenwald (1862–1932), Joseph Proskauer (1877–1971), and other successful lawyers, bankers, and entrepreneurs—the AJC sought to act as the voice of American Jewry. Though the AJC swiftly developed into a highly effective organization for the protection of Jewish interests and rights, its authority was challenged in the United States by a broad spectrum of Jewish progressives, including labor, women's, and Zionist groups whose members objected to its conservative and patriarchal approach to American Jewish affairs.

American Jewish Congress: In 1916, a broad coalition of American Jewish groups, organizations, and political factions agreed to mount a national election that resulted in a countrywide plenary (1918, 1920). The congress served as American Jewry's wartime flagship and discharged a delegation to accompany President Woodrow Wilson to the Paris Peace Conference.

Ashkenazi Jews: Yiddish-speaking Jews of eastern European ancestry.

Bnai Brith (or B'nai B'rith): The Independent Order of Bnai Brith (Sons of the Covenant), a Jewish fraternal organization founded in New York in 1843, originally modeled itself on the Jewish communal associations characteristic of European Jewry. It swiftly became a regional and then nationwide network of lodges dedicated to social, philanthropic, and political work among American Jews. In response to the notorious Leo Frank case (1913–15), Bnai Brith created the Anti-Defamation League. Though formally non-Zionist in the late nineteenth and early twentieth centuries, Bnai Brith's support of Jewish communal life in Palestine dated back to the 1860s. After World War I, the organization helped bolster Zionist settlement in the *Yishuv*. In the 1940s, Bnai Brith became openly Zionist in its political orientation.

Federation of American Zionists: Established in 1898, the Federation of American Zionists (FAZ) originated as an umbrella group of the fledgling Zionist movement in the United States. In 1918, the American Jewish jurists Louis D. Brandeis (1856–1941) and Julian W. Mack (1866–1943) assumed leadership of the FAZ. During World War I, a talented group of Brandeis loyalists known as the Brandeis-Mack group renamed the FAZ the Zionist Organization of America (ZOA) and transformed the ZOA into a nationwide political organization with significant political clout. In 1921, at the ZOA's national convention in Cleveland, Ohio, Brandeis and his adherents, who differed from Chaim Weizmann (1874–1952), architect of the British government's Balfour Declaration (1917), and the leadership of European Zionism in favoring a policy of private economic investment in Palestine, withdrew from the ZOA. Thereafter, Louis Lipsky (1876–1963), representing Weizmann's American supporters, became the ZOA president. The Lipsky administration was unable to sustain the ZOA's previous growth, but it successfully negotiated the 1924 merger of the major annual Zionist fundraising efforts that led to the creation of the United Palestine Appeal. In 1929, the Brandeis-Mack group regained control of the ZOA. The ZOA was never a mass organization, but together with the Hadassah Women's Zionist Organization of America, founded in 1912 by the Zionist leader Henrietta Szold (1860–1945), it generally represented the mainstream of American Jewish opinion regarding Zionism and the campaign for Jewish statehood.

Hadassah: Founded in 1912 by the notable American Zionist leader Henrietta Szold (1860–1945), the Hadassah Women's Zionist Organization of America began as the autonomous women's auxiliary of the ZOA but became a fully independent entity in 1933. Expanding its medical and health-related activity in the *Yishuv*—activity that began with the creation of the American Zionist Medical Unit (1918) and the Hadassah Nurses' Training School (1921)—Hadassah grew to provide a wide range of services, including infant welfare stations, school lunch programs, youth villages, and communal health and recreation centers. In 1936, the organization officially opened the Hadassah School of Nursing at the Hebrew University of Jerusalem, and in 1939 it established the Rothschild-Hadassah University Hospital, the *Yishuv*'s first major medical research and care center. In the prestate era, Hadassah, which became the largest American Zionist group and a fundraising powerhouse, boasted a talented array of leaders including Szold, Alice Seligsberg (1873–1940), Irma (Rama) Lindheim (1886–1978), Zipporah "Zip" Szold (1888–1979), Rose G. Jacobs (1888–1975), Rose L. Halperin (1896–1978), Judith G. Epstein (1895–1988), and Tamar de Sola Pool (1890–1981).

Jewish National Fund (JNF): Known in Hebrew as Keren Kayemet Leyisrael, founded at the Fifth Zionist Congress in 1901 to further the acquisition of land and development of Jewish colonies in Palestine.

kibbutz (pl. kibbutzim): Hebrew term for a cooperative rural settlement in Palestine/Israel.

Passover: The Jewish festival of Passover derives from the Hebrew Bible (Lev. 23:5) and is intended to commemorate the liberation of the ancient Israelites from Egyptian slavery as recounted in Exodus. Observed annually, the holiday starts on the fifteenth day of the Hebrew month of Nisan and lasts for seven days (in the Land of Israel) or eight days (in the diaspora). The holiday includes unique ritual customs and dietary restrictions including the consumption of unleavened flatbread known as matzah (pl. matzot) (Exod. 12:8).

Poalei Zion: The socialist Zionist party Poalei Zion (Hebrew for Workers of Zion) originated in tsarist Russia in the late nineteenth century and sought to combine the class interests of the Jewish proletariat with political Zionism and the realization of socialism. The American branch of the party was transplanted to the United States in the early twentieth century with the mass immigration of eastern European Jews to American shores.

pogrom: Russian term for anti-Jewish riot perpetrated by the Christian population against eastern European Jews; widespread in Russia between 1881 and 1921 and generally accompanied by destruction, looting of property, murder, and rape.

Sephardic Jews: The term used to identify Ladino-speaking Jews of Iberian ancestry and/or Jews who trace their ancestry to the Mediterranean basin, north Africa, and the Arab lands.

Shabbat: Hebrew term for Sabbath.

shtetl: Yiddish for a small town or village in eastern Europe.

tallit: Hebrew for prayer shawl.

Talmud: The term refers to either of two works written between 400-500 CE, one compiled in Babylon and the other in Palestine, which contain discussions of Jewish Law. Each of these works contain the Mishnah along with the Gemara, a commentary on and a supplement to the Mishnah. While both books are important documents, the Babylonian Talmud is seen as being more authoritative because of its greater length and historical influence over Jews and Judaism.

Tisha B'Av (ninth of Av): An annual fast day observed according to the Hebrew calendar on the ninth day of the month of Av, commemorates the destruction of the First and Second Temples in Jerusalem, which supposedly occurred on the same date. Over time, *Tisha Beav* also came to be regarded as a day for mourning other tragedies in Jewish history

Torah: The Hebrew Bible or Pentateuch.

World Zionist Organization: The World Zionist Organization (WZO) was created in 1897 by the First Zionist Congress in Basel, Switzerland. The WZO was charged with the responsibility of coordinating and implementing the political, financial, and development strategies of the Zionist movement in the diaspora and Palestine. In time, the composition of the executive of the WZO became nearly identical with that of the Jewish Agency for Palestine. In practical terms, the former reflected the political priorities of the Zionist parties, while the latter (after World War I) served as a public body that managed the relationship between the British Mandatory government and the *Yishuv.*

yeshivah: The Hebrew and Yiddish term for a school for advanced Talmudic study.

Yishuv: Hebrew term for the Jewish community in Palestine before the creation of the State of Israel in 1948; the Old Yishuv refers to the traditional, religiously observant Jewish community established prior to 1881.

Yom Kippur: The Jewish holiday Yom Kippur (Day of Atonement), a solemn day of repentance and fasting lasting twenty-four hours, occurs on the tenth day of the month of Tishrei in the Hebrew calendar. It is a day of abstention from all manner of food, drink, work, and sexual relations. The regulations for observing Yom Kippur derive from Lev. 16:1–34 (where it is called the Sabbath of Sabbaths) and 23:26–32 as well as Num. 29:7–11. According to rabbinic tradition, Yom Kippur marks the day Moses descended from Mount Sinai with the Decalogue and announced the divine pardon of the Israelites for the sin of worshipping the golden calf.

Zionism: Modern Jewish nationalism.

Zionist Organization of America: See Federation of American Zionists above.

CONTRIBUTORS

JESSICA COOPERMAN (Muhlenberg College) is an associate professor in the Department of Religion Studies and director of the Jewish Studies Program at Muhlenberg College in Allentown, Pennsylvania. She teaches courses on modern Jewish history and culture, religion in the United States, and religion and violence. Her research focuses on American Judaism and American conceptions of religious pluralism, and she is particularly interested in the relationship between religion and the modern state. She is the author of *Making Judaism Safe for America: World War I and the Origins of Religious Pluralism* (New York University Press, 2018).

SUSANNAH HESCHEL (Dartmouth College) is the Eli M. Black Distinguished Professor of Jewish Studies at Dartmouth College. Her scholarship focuses on Jewish and Protestant thought during the ninteenth and twentieth centuries, including the history of biblical scholarship, Jewish scholarship on Islam, and the history of antisemitism. Her numerous publications include *Abraham Geiger and the Jewish Jesus* (University of Chicago Press, 1998), which won a National Jewish Book Award; *The Aryan Jesus: Christian Theologians and the Bible in Nazi Germany* (Princeton University Press, 2008); and *Jüdischer Islam: Islam und Jüdische-Deutsch Selbstbestimmung* (Mathes und Seitz, 2018). She has been a visiting professor at the Universities of Frankfurt and Cape Town as well as Princeton University, and she is the recipient of numerous grants, including from the Ford Foundation, Carnegie Foundation, a yearlong Rockefeller Fellowship at the National Humanities Center, and a Guggenheim Fellowship. In 2011–12 she held a fellowship at the Wissenschaftskolleg in Berlin. She has received four honorary doctorates from universities in the United States, Canada, and Germany. In 2015 she was elected a member of the American Society for the Study of Religion. She serves on the academic advisory council of the Center for Jewish Studies in Berlin and on the Board of Trustees of Trinity College.

Philip Hollander (Cornell University) serves as a Hebrew lecturer in Cornell University's Department of Near Eastern Studies. His recent publications include *From Schlemiel to Sabra: Zionist Masculinity and Palestinian Hebrew Literature* (Indiana University Press, 2019); "Pursuing Universalism through the Particular: Zionism and Transnational Modernism in Levi Aryeh Arieli's 'In the Light of Venus,'" *Shofar* 39:2 (2021): 85–122; and "Challenging Contemporary Historiography in Shmu'el Yosef Agnon's *Only Yesterday*," *Israel Studies* 25:3 (Summer 2020): 106–29.

Sarah Imhoff (Indiana University-Bloomington) is a professor in the Department of Religious Studies and the Borns Jewish Studies Program at Indiana University. She writes about religion and the body with a particular interest in gender, sexuality, and American religion. She is author of *Masculinity and the Making of American Judaism* (Indiana University Press, 2017) and *The Lives of Jessie Sampter: Queer, Disabled, Zionist* (Duke University Press, 2022). Her work has appeared in *The Journal of Religion, Religion and American Culture, American Jewish History, Religious Studies Review, Jewish Social Studies*, and other academic journals and edited volumes. She is a founding co-editor of the journal *American Religion*.

Pnina Lahav (Boston University) is Emerita Professor of Law and a member of the Elie Wiesel Center for Jewish Studies at Boston University. Her fields of expertise are constitutional law, first amendment law and legal history. Of late she has focused her research on the status and history of women. She is the recipient of the Association for Israel Studies Lifetime Achievement Award (2017). She is the author of *Judgment in Jerusalem: Chief Justice Simon Agranat and the Zionist Century* (University of California Press, 1997) and *The Only Woman in the Room: Golda Meir and Her Path to Power* (Princeton University Press, 2022).

MARK A. RAIDER (University of Cincinnati) is professor of modern Jewish history in the Department of History and director of the University's Center for Studies in Jewish Education and Culture. His recent publications include *New Perspectives in American Jewish History: A Documentary Tribute to Jonathan D. Sarna,* with Gary Phillip Zola (Brandeis University Press, 2021); *The Essential Hayim Greenberg: Essays and Addresses on Jewish Culture, Socialism, and Zionism* (University of Alabama Press, 2017); "'Girded for the Superhuman Task': American Jews and the Trope of the Zionist Pioneer, 1925-1956," *American Jewish History* 103:3 (2019); and "Moshe Dayan: 'Israel's No. 1 Hero' (in America)," *Journal of Israeli History* 37:1 (2019). He has been a visiting professor at Brandeis University, Clark University, Hebrew Union College-Jewish Institute of Religion, and the University of Haifa.

JEHUDA REINHARZ is director of the Tauber Institute for the Study of European Jewry at Brandeis University, president and CEO of the Jack, Joseph, and Morton Mandel Foundation, and past president of Brandeis University. Born in Haifa, Israel, he immigrated to the United States as a teenager in 1961 and earned concurrent bachelor's degrees from Columbia University and the Jewish Theological Seminary, a master's degree in medieval Jewish history from Harvard University, and a doctorate in modern Jewish history from Brandeis. Dr. Reinharz was a professor at the University of Michigan before becoming the Richard Koret Professor of Modern Jewish History at Brandeis in 1982. Two years later he was named director of the Tauber Institute, and eight years later he founded the Jacob and Libby Goodman Institute for the Study of Zionism and Israel. From 1991 to 1994 he served as provost and senior vice president for academic affairs at Brandeis, and in 1994 he was named its seventh president. Dr. Reinharz is the author of more than one hundred articles and thirty-seven books in various languages. His *The Jew in the Modern World: A Documentary History,* edited with Paul Mendes-Flohr, appeared in two expanded editions and is one of the most widely adopted college texts in modern Jewish history. His two-volume biography of Chaim Weizmann, the first President of Israel, has won many prizes in Israel and the United States. The third and final volume of the biography was written with Motti Golani and appeared in Hebrew in 2021; followed by the English-language translation, *Chaim Weizmann: A Biography* (Brandeis University Press, 2024). He is also the recipient of numerous honorary degrees.

ZOHAR SEGEV (University of Haifa) holds the Reuben Hecht Chair in Zionism and History at the University of Haifa and teaches courses on American Jewish history and Zionist history. Dr. Segev is the author of *From Ethnic Politicians to National Leaders: American Zionist Leadership, the Holocaust, and the Establishment of Israel* (Berghahn Books, 2007), *The World Jewish Congress during the Holocaust: Between Activism and Restraint* (De Gruyter, 2014), and *Immigration, Ideology, and Public Activity from an American Jewish Perspective: A Journey across Three Continents* (Brill, 2022). His articles have appeared in the *American Jewish Archives Journal, American Jewish History, Israel Studies, Jewish Quarterly Review, Journal of Modern Jewish Studies, Studies in Ethnicity and Nationalism*, and elsewhere.

CHRISTOPHER M. STERBA (San Francisco State University) is senior lecturer in American studies at San Francisco State University. He is the author of *Good Americans: Italian and Jewish Immigrants During the First World War* (Oxford University Press, 2003), and has published articles in several journals, including *The New England Quarterly, Journal of American Studies, Western Historical Quarterly*, and the *Journal of American Ethnic History*. He is currently completing a new book titled *Buster, Mae, and Spencer: The Great War Generation and the Remaking of American Popular Culture*. In 2012–13, he was the Fulbright Professor of American Literature and Culture at the Universitetet i Bergen, Norway.

DANIEL J. TICHENOR (University of Oregon) is the Philip H. Knight Chair of Political Science and Director of the Wayne Morse Center Program for Democratic Governance at the University of Oregon. He has published seven books and over seventy scholarly articles and chapters. He is author of *Dividing Lines: The Politics of Immigration Control in America* (Princeton University Press, 2001); *The Oxford Handbook of the Politics of International Migration*, with Marc Rosenblum (Oxford University Press, 2011); *Rivalry and Reform: Presidents, Social Movements, and the Transformation of American Politics*, with Sidney Milkis (University of Chicago Press, 2019); and *Democracy's Child: Young People and the Politics of Control, Leverage, and Agency*, with Alison Gash (Oxford University Press, 2022). His forthcoming book is *Unsettled: Governing Immigration in a Polarized Nation* (Princeton University Press). His research awards include the American Political Science Association's Gladys M. Kammerer Award, Jack Walker Award, Mary Parker Follett

Award, Polity Prize, and Charles Redd Award. He has been a research fellow at the Brookings Institution and the Princeton School of Policy and International Affairs, and he was named to the inaugural class of Andrew Carnegie Fellows in 2015.

GARY PHILLIP ZOLA (Hebrew Union College-Jewish Institute of Religion) is the Edward M. Ackerman Family Distinguished Professor of the American Jewish Experience & Reform Jewish History at Hebrew Union College-Jewish Institute of Religion in Cincinnati, as well as the executive director emeritus of The Jacob Rader Marcus Center of the American Jewish Archives. Dr. Zola serves as editor of The Marcus Center's award-winning biannual publication, *The American Jewish Archives Journal*. President Barack Obama appointed Dr. Zola on three separate occasions (2011, 2014, and 2017) to serve as a member of the US Commission for the Preservation of America's Heritage Abroad, an independent agency of the federal government. Established by public law in 1985, the commission exists to foster the preservation and protection of the cemeteries, monuments, and historic buildings associated with the foreign heritage of United States citizens. Although HUC-JIR presidents have received appointments to US commissions, Prof. Zola is the first regular member of the College-Institute's faculty to receive such a presidential appointment. His books include *New Perspectives in American Jewish History: A Documentary Tribute to Jonathan D. Sarna*, with Mark A. Raider (Brandeis University Press, 2021); *We Called Him Rabbi Abraham: Lincoln and American Jewry, a Documentary History* (Southern Illinois University Press, 2014); *American Jewish History: A Primary Source Reader*, with Marc Dollinger (Brandeis University Press, 2014); *A Place of Our Own: The Rise of Reform Jewish Camping in America*, with Michael M. Lorge (University of Alabama Press, 2006); and *Isaac Harby of Charleston, 1788-1828* (University of Alabama Press, 1994).

INDEX